Yuto Tsukuda

Volume 27, eh? When we first started working on this series, I never dreamed it would have more volumes than a certain famous manga I bought as a kid. We wouldn't have been able to do it without you. Thank you! I hope you continue to follow the series!

Shun Saeki

There's going to be a third season of the anime! It never would have happened without the gracious help of our editing staff and the generous support of you readers. Thank you very much!

About the authors

Yuto Tsukuda won the 34th Jump Juniketsu Newcomers' Manga Award for his one-shot story *Kiba ni Naru*. He made his *Weekly Shonen Jump* debut in 2010 with the series *Shonen Shikku*. His follow-up series, *Food Wars!: Shokugeki no Soma*, is his first English-language release.

Shun Saeki made his *Jump NEXT!* debut in 2011 with the one-shot story *Kimi to Watashi no Renai Soudan*. *Food Wars!: Shokugeki no Soma* is his first *Shonen Jump* series.

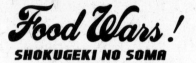

Food Wars!
SHOKUGEKI NO SOMA

Volume 27
Shonen Jump Advanced Manga Edition
Story by Yuto Tsukuda, Art by Shun Saeki
Contributor Yuki Morisaki

Translation: Adrienne Beck
Touch-Up Art & Lettering: James Gaubatz, Mara Coman
Design: Alice Lewis
Editor: Jennifer LeBlanc

Printed in the U.S.A.

Published by VIZ Media, LLC
P.O. Box 77010
San Francisco, CA 94107

10 9 8 7 6 5 4 3 2 1
First printing, December 2018

VIZ MEDIA
viz.com

SHONEN JUMP ADVANCED
shonenjump.com

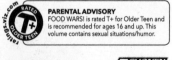

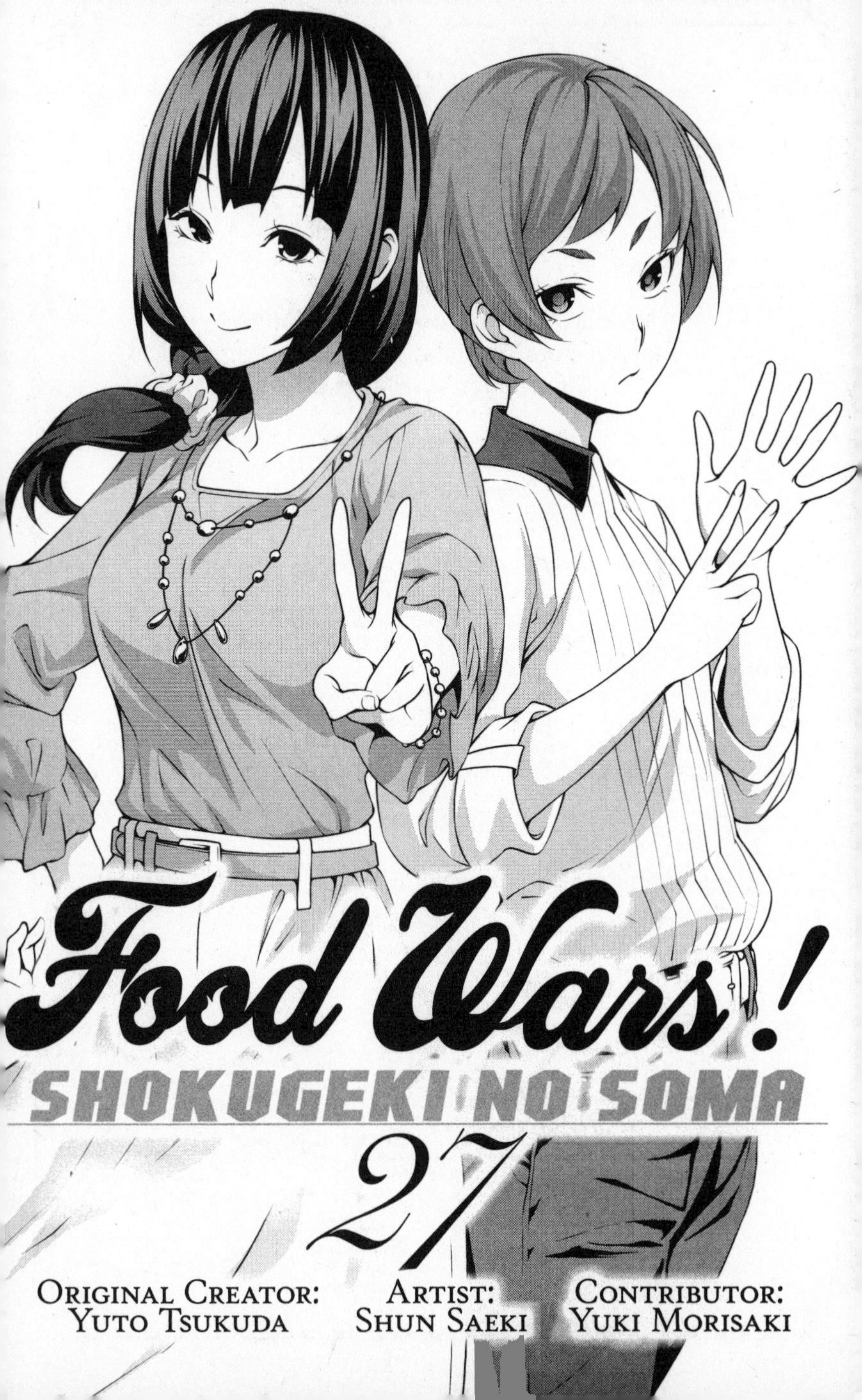

Food Wars!

SHOKUGEKI NO SOMA

27

ORIGINAL CREATOR:
YUTO TSUKUDA

ARTIST:
SHUN SAEKI

CONTRIBUTOR:
YUKI MORISAKI

CHARACTERS

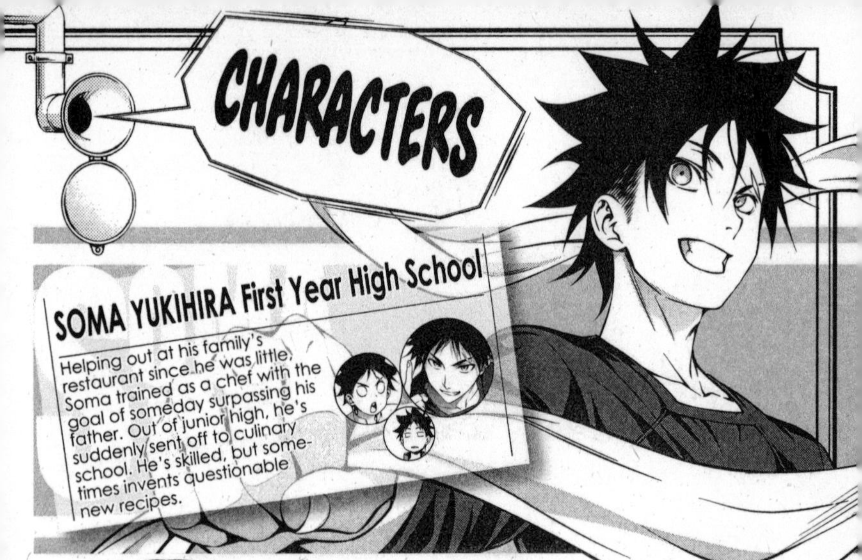

SOMA YUKIHIRA First Year High School

Helping out at his family's restaurant since he was little, Soma trained as a chef with the goal of someday surpassing his father. Out of junior high, he's suddenly sent off to culinary school. He's skilled, but sometimes invents questionable new recipes.

Shokugeki no SOMA

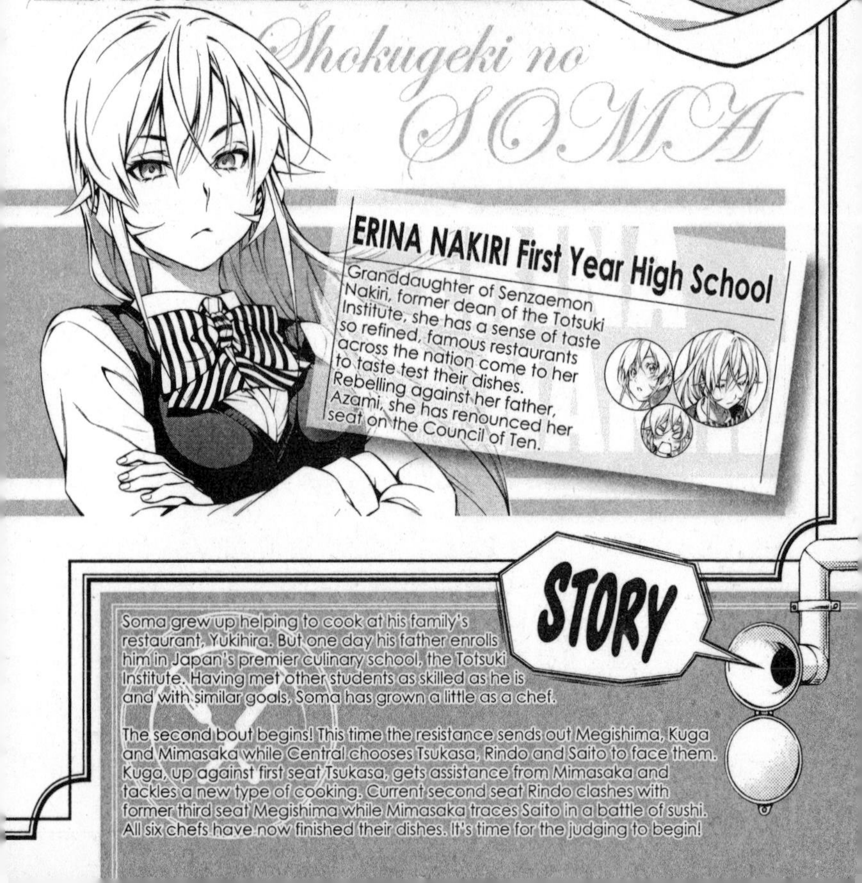

ERINA NAKIRI First Year High School

Granddaughter of Senzaemon Nakiri, former dean of the Totsuki Institute, she has a sense of taste so refined, famous restaurants across the nation come to her to taste test their dishes. Rebelling against her father, Azami, she has renounced her seat on the Council of Ten.

STORY

Soma grew up helping to cook at his family's restaurant, Yukihira. But one day his father enrolls him in Japan's premier culinary school, the Totsuki Institute. Having met other students as skilled as he is and with similar goals, Soma has grown a little as a chef.

The second bout begins! This time the resistance sends out Megishima, Kuga and Mimasaka while Central chooses Tsukasa, Rindo and Saito to face them. Kuga, up against first seat Tsukasa, gets assistance from Mimasaka and tackles a new type of cooking. Current second seat Rindo clashes with former third seat Megishima while Mimasaka traces Saito in a battle of sushi. All six chefs have now finished their dishes. It's time for the judging to begin!

Shokugeki no SOMA

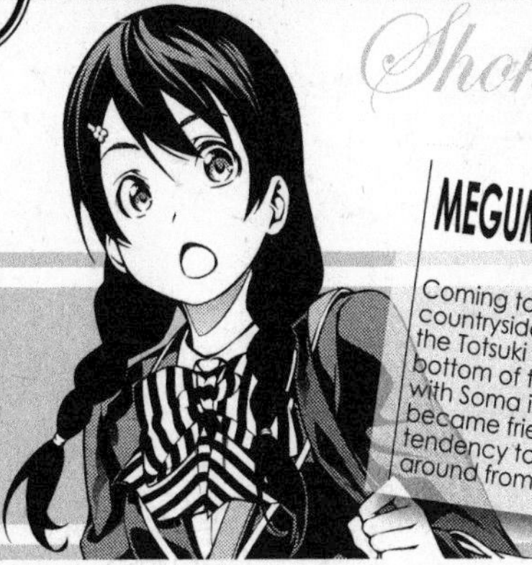

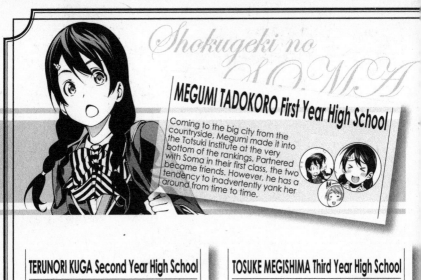

MEGUMI TADOKORO First Year High School

Coming to the big city from the countryside, Megumi made it into the Totsuki Institute at the very bottom of the rankings. Partnered with Soma in their first class, the two became friends. However, he has a tendency to inadvertently yank her around from time to time.

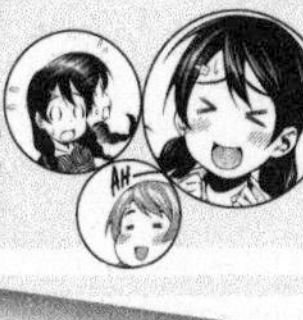
AH

TERUNORI KUGA Second Year High School

The former eighth seat, he lost his spot on the council when he chose to oppose the Azami administration. He's captain of the Chinese-Cooking Research Society.

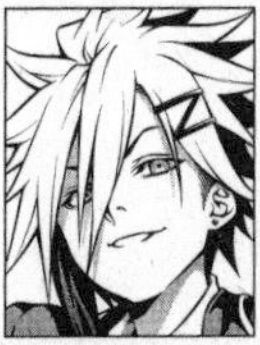

TOSUKE MEGISHIMA Third Year High School

The former council third seat, he lost his position for resisting the Azami administration. He is known to some as the Ramen Master.

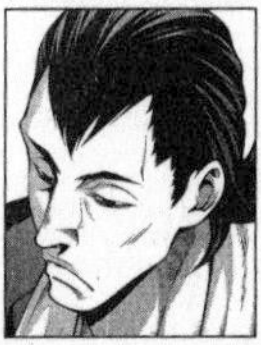

SUBARU MIMASAKA First Year High School

He cooks by tracing the actions of other chefs. After losing to Soma in a shokugeki, he reforms his cheating ways and begins to take his cooking seriously.

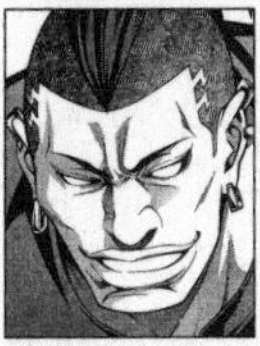

EISHI TSUKASA Third Year High School

The current first seat on Totsuki's Council of Ten. He comes off as meek and weak-willed at first, but he has absolute confidence in his skills as a chef.

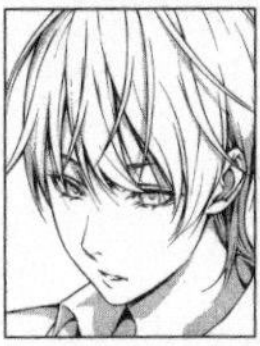

RINDO KOBAYASHI Third Year High School

The current second seat on Totsuki's Council of Ten, Rindo is friendly, sociable and easygoing. Having met Soma during the Moon Festival, she finds him intriguing.

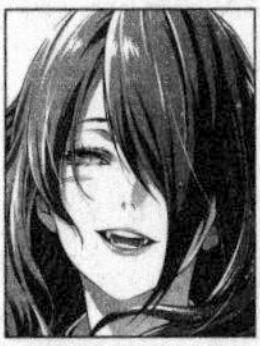

SOMEI SAITO Third Year High School

The current fourth seat on Totsuki's Council of Ten. A gifted sushi chef, he greatly values Bushido. He calls his favorite sword (i.e., butcher knife) Isanakiri.

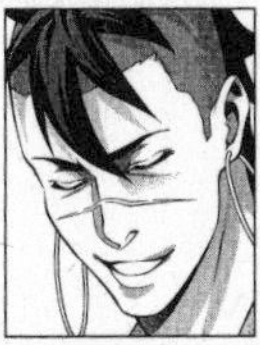

Food Wars! SHOKUGEKI NO SOMA

27

Table of Contents

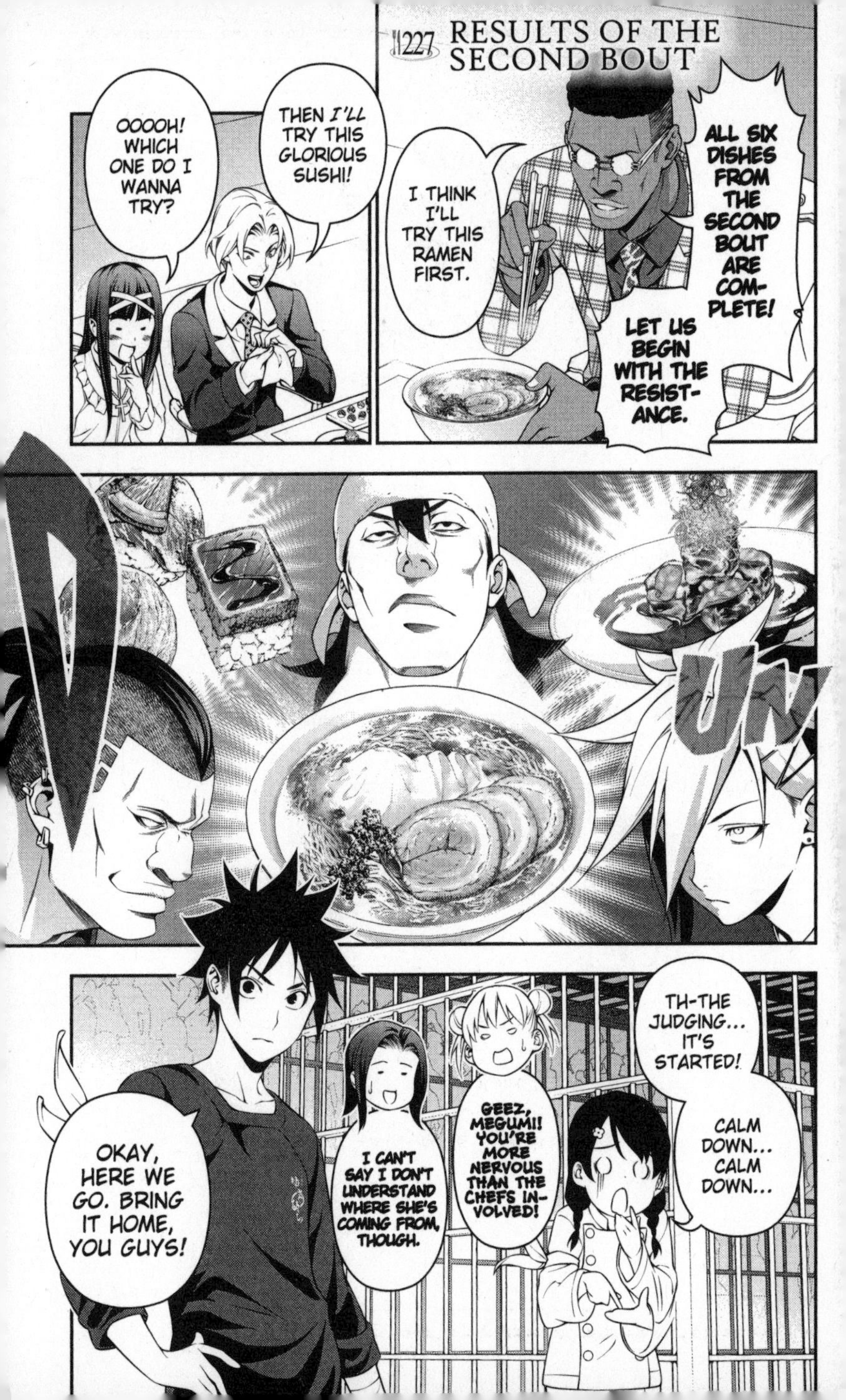
227 RESULTS OF THE SECOND BOUT
ALL SIX DISHES FROM THE SECOND BOUT ARE COMPLETE!
LET US BEGIN WITH THE RESISTANCE.
I THINK I'LL TRY THIS RAMEN FIRST.
THEN I'LL TRY THIS GLORIOUS SUSHI!
OOOOH! WHICH ONE DO I WANNA TRY?
DUN
TH-THE JUDGING... IT'S STARTED!
CALM DOWN... CALM DOWN...
GEEZ, MEGUMI! YOU'RE MORE NERVOUS THAN THE CHEFS INVOLVED!
I CAN'T SAY I DON'T UNDERSTAND WHERE SHE'S COMING FROM, THOUGH.
OKAY, HERE WE GO. BRING IT HOME, YOU GUYS!

227 RESULTS OF THE SECOND BOUT

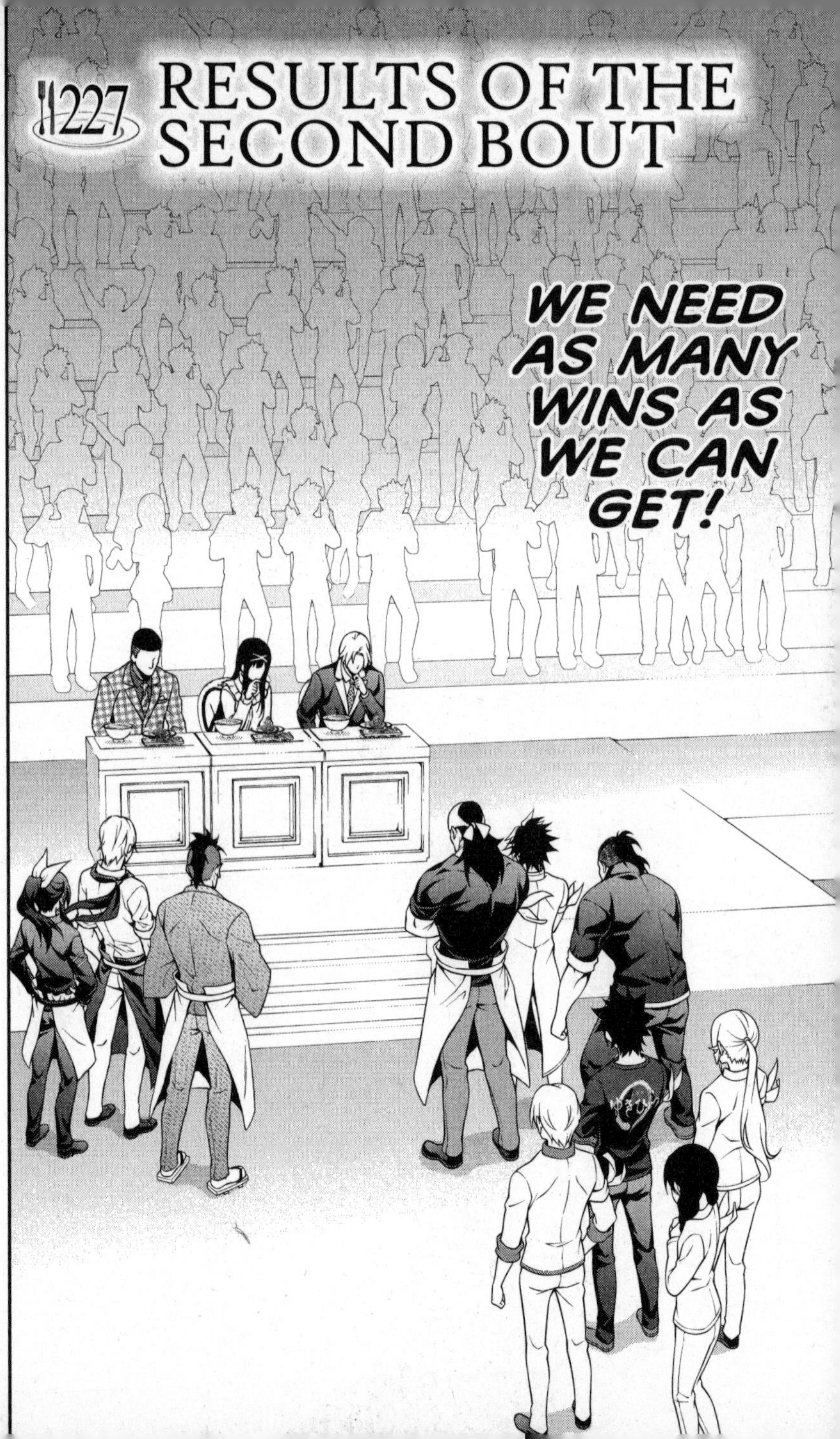
WE NEED AS MANY WINS AS WE CAN GET!

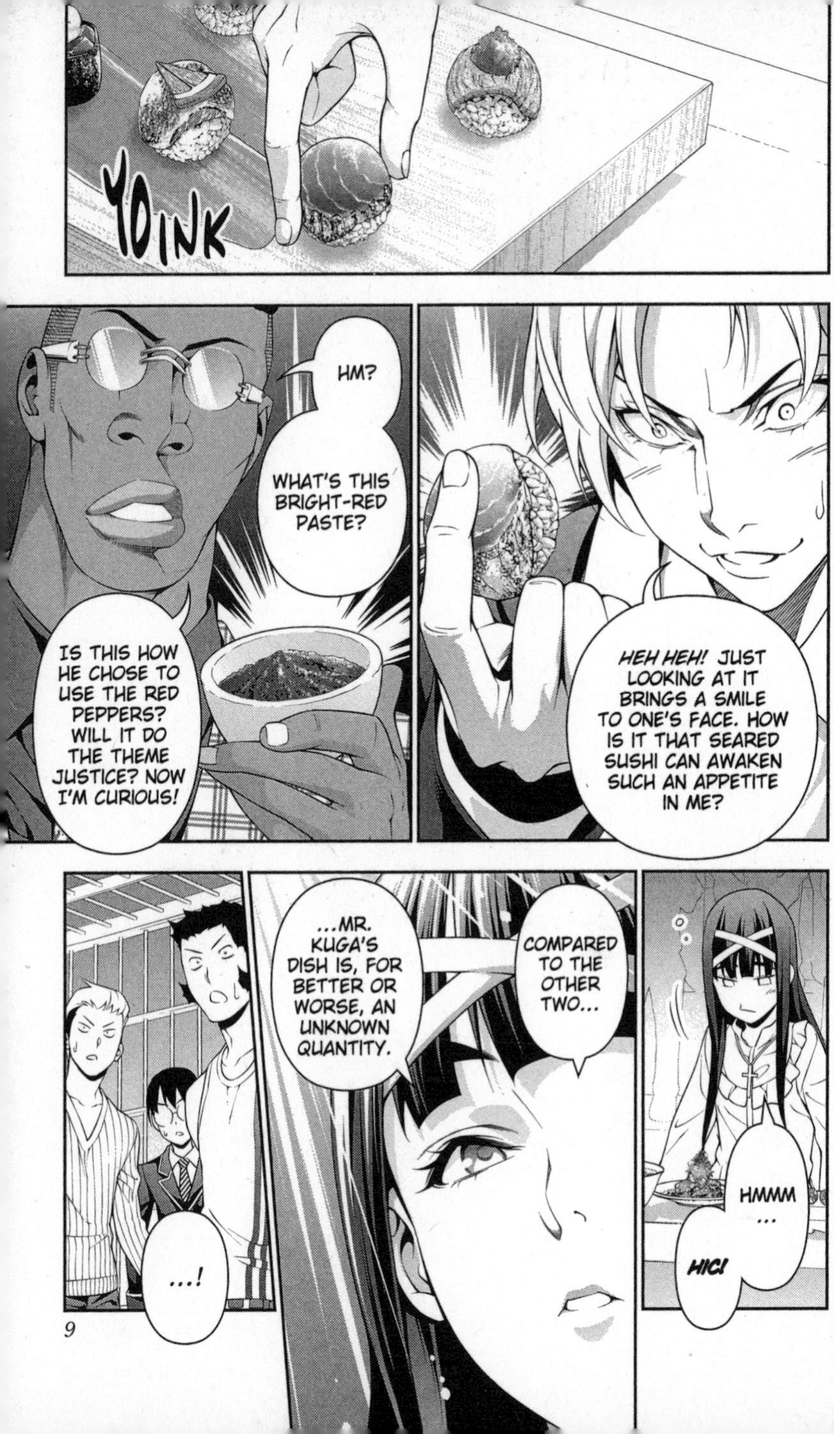
YOINK
HEH HEH! JUST LOOKING AT IT BRINGS A SMILE TO ONE'S FACE. HOW IS IT THAT SEARED SUSHI CAN AWAKEN SUCH AN APPETITE IN ME?
HM?
WHAT'S THIS BRIGHT-RED PASTE?
IS THIS HOW HE CHOSE TO USE THE RED PEPPERS? WILL IT DO THE THEME JUSTICE? NOW I'M CURIOUS!
HMMM...
HIC!
COMPARED TO THE OTHER TWO...
...MR. KUGA'S DISH IS, FOR BETTER OR WORSE, AN UNKNOWN QUANTITY.
...!

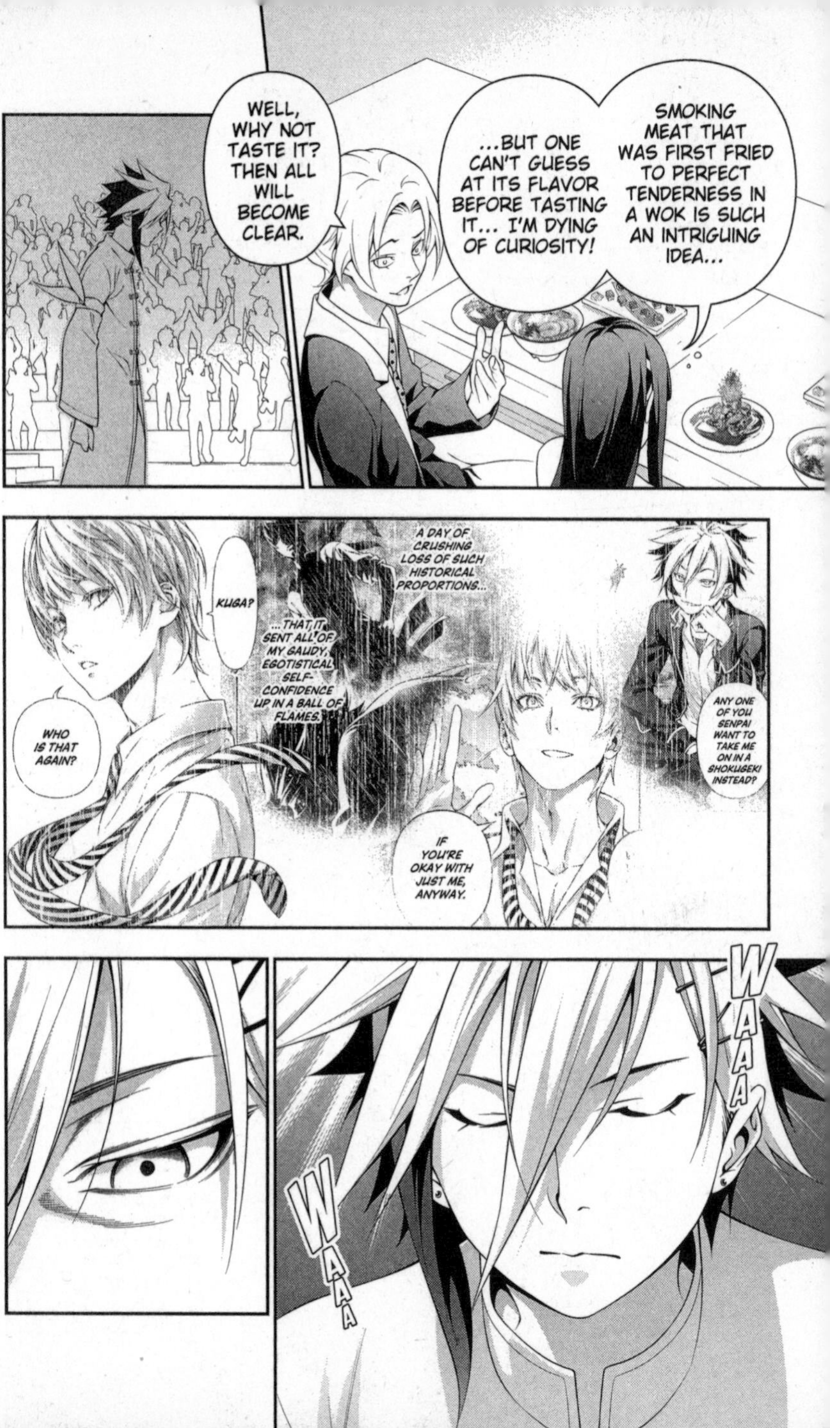
SMOKING MEAT THAT WAS FIRST FRIED TO PERFECT TENDERNESS IN A WOK IS SUCH AN INTRIGUING IDEA...
...BUT ONE CAN'T GUESS AT ITS FLAVOR BEFORE TASTING IT... I'M DYING OF CURIOSITY!
WELL, WHY NOT TASTE IT? THEN ALL WILL BECOME CLEAR.
A DAY OF CRUSHING LOSS OF SUCH HISTORICAL PROPORTIONS...
...THAT IT SENT ALL OF MY GAUDY, EGOTISTICAL SELF-CONFIDENCE UP IN A BALL OF FLAMES.
ANY ONE OF YOU SENPAI WANT TO TAKE ME ON IN A SHOKUGEKI INSTEAD?
IF YOU'RE OKAY WITH JUST ME, ANYWAY.
KUGA?
WHO IS THAT AGAIN?
WAAAA
WAAAA

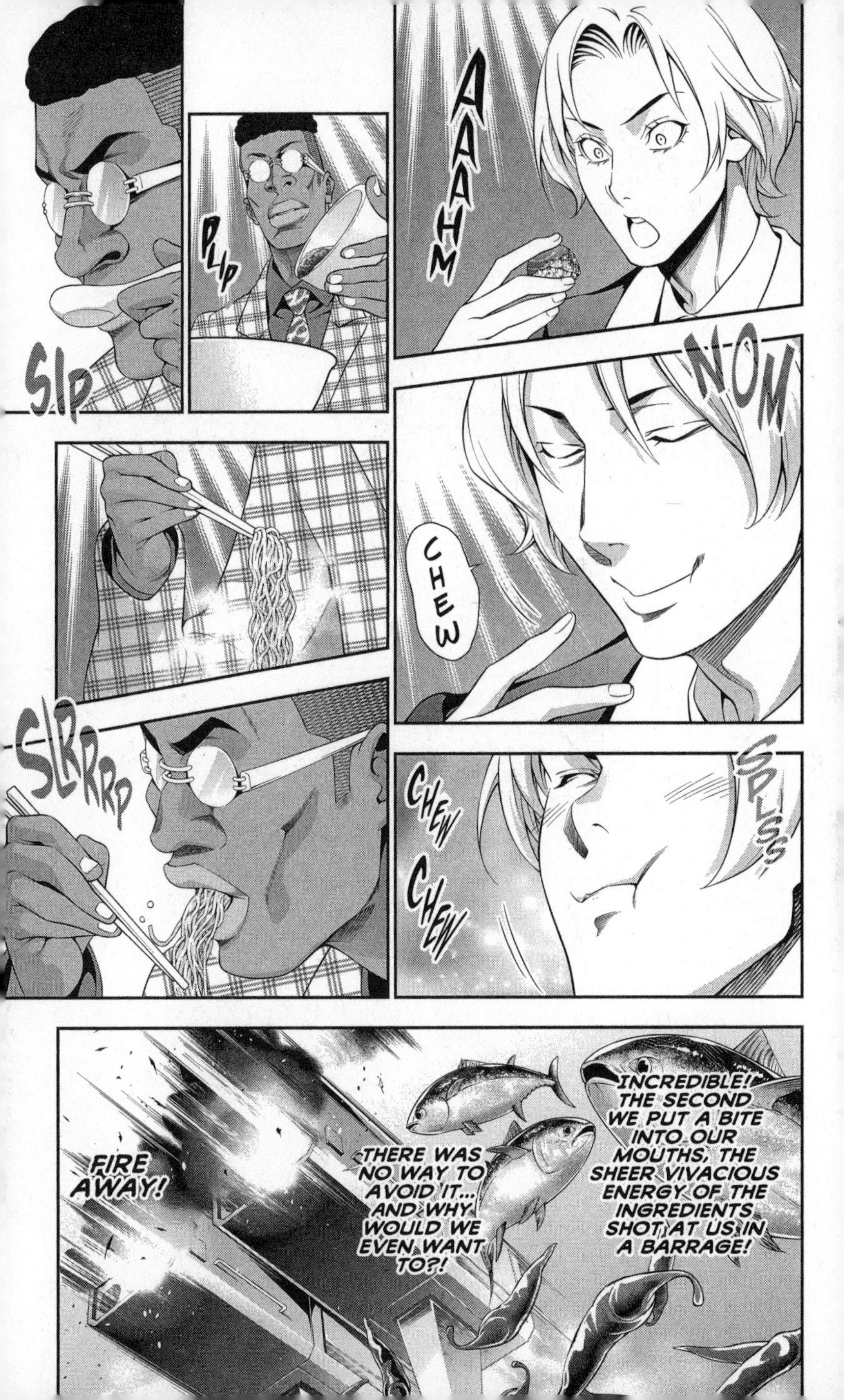
AAAAHM
PLIP
SLIP
NOM
CHEW
CHEW CHEW
SPLSS
SLRRRP
INCREDIBLE! THE SECOND WE PUT A BITE INTO OUR MOUTHS, THE SHEER VIVACIOUS ENERGY OF THE INGREDIENTS SHOT AT US IN A BARRAGE!
THERE WAS NO WAY TO AVOID IT... AND WHY WOULD WE EVEN WANT TO?!
FIRE AWAY!

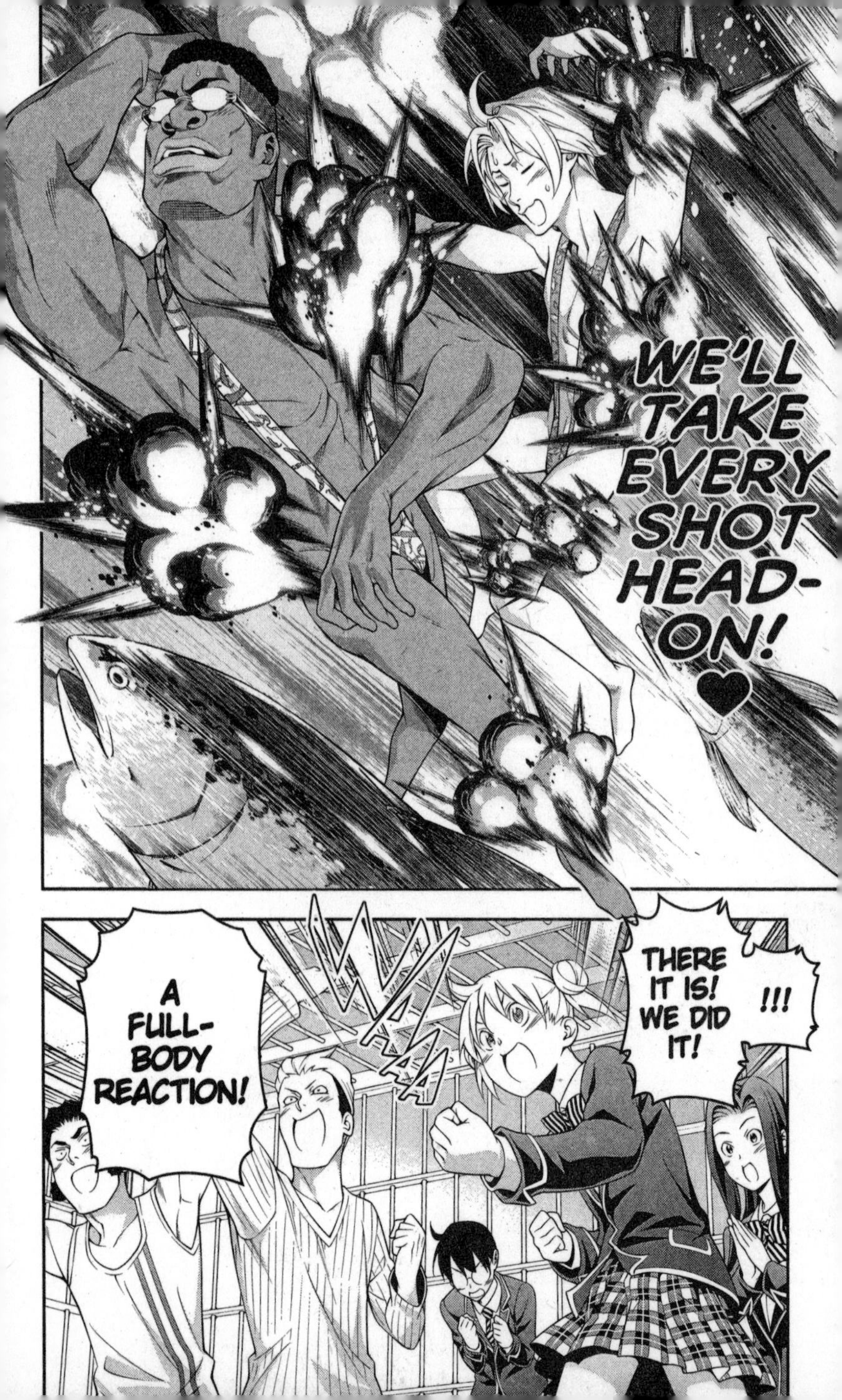
WE'LL TAKE EVERY SHOT HEAD-ON! ♥
THERE IT IS! WE DID IT!
!!!
A FULL-BODY REACTION!

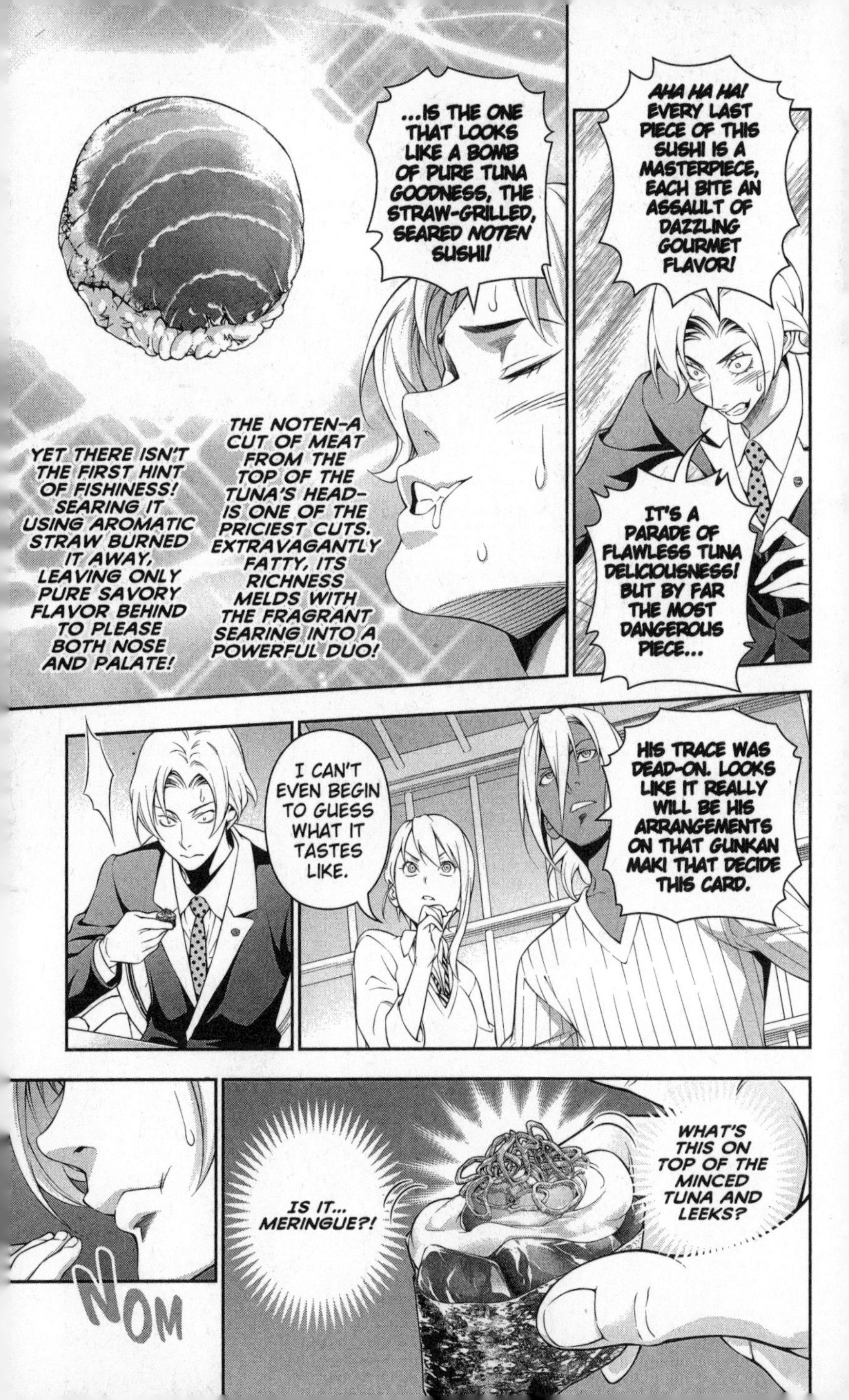
AHA HA HA! EVERY LAST PIECE OF THIS SUSHI IS A MASTERPIECE, EACH BITE AN ASSAULT OF DAZZLING GOURMET FLAVOR!
IT'S A PARADE OF FLAWLESS TUNA DELICIOUSNESS! BUT BY FAR THE MOST DANGEROUS PIECE...
...IS THE ONE THAT LOOKS LIKE A BOMB OF PURE TUNA GOODNESS, THE STRAW-GRILLED, SEARED NOTEN SUSHI!
THE NOTEN—A CUT OF MEAT FROM THE TOP OF THE TUNA'S HEAD—IS ONE OF THE PRICIEST CUTS. EXTRAVAGANTLY FATTY, ITS RICHNESS MELDS WITH THE FRAGRANT SEARING INTO A POWERFUL DUO!
YET THERE ISN'T THE FIRST HINT OF FISHINESS! SEARING IT USING AROMATIC STRAW BURNED IT AWAY, LEAVING ONLY PURE SAVORY FLAVOR BEHIND TO PLEASE BOTH NOSE AND PALATE!
HIS TRACE WAS DEAD-ON. LOOKS LIKE IT REALLY WILL BE HIS ARRANGEMENTS ON THAT GUNKAN MAKI THAT DECIDE THIS CARD.
I CAN'T EVEN BEGIN TO GUESS WHAT IT TASTES LIKE.
WHAT'S THIS ON TOP OF THE MINCED TUNA AND LEEKS?
IS IT... MERINGUE?!
NOM

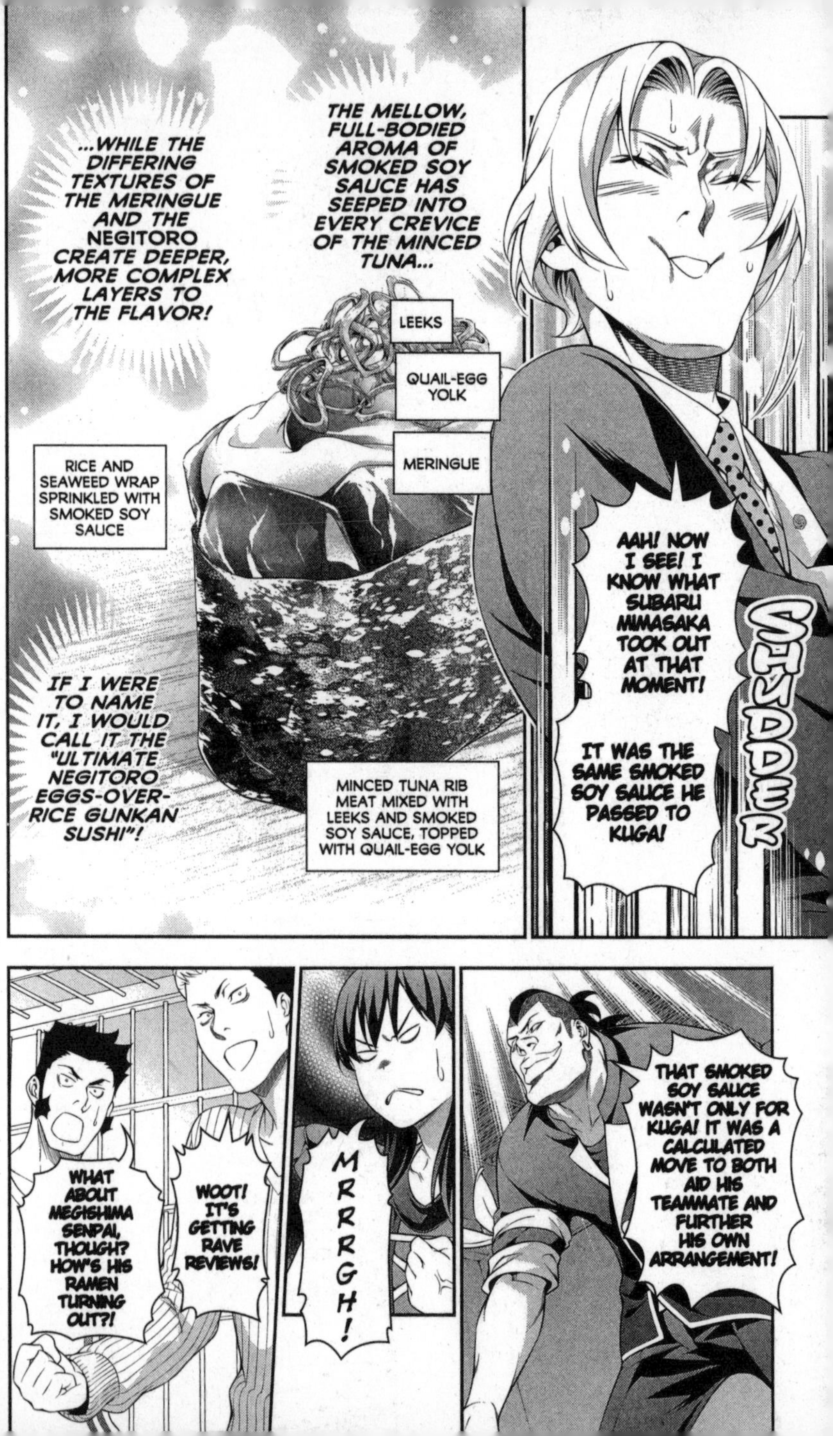
AAH! NOW I SEE! I KNOW WHAT SUBARU MIMASAKA TOOK OUT AT THAT MOMENT!
IT WAS THE SAME SMOKED SOY SAUCE HE PASSED TO KUGA!
SHUDDER
THE MELLOW, FULL-BODIED AROMA OF SMOKED SOY SAUCE HAS SEEPED INTO EVERY CREVICE OF THE MINCED TUNA...
...WHILE THE DIFFERING TEXTURES OF THE MERINGUE AND THE NEGITORO CREATE DEEPER, MORE COMPLEX LAYERS TO THE FLAVOR!
LEEKS
QUAIL-EGG YOLK
MERINGUE
RICE AND SEAWEED WRAP SPRINKLED WITH SMOKED SOY SAUCE
MINCED TUNA RIB MEAT MIXED WITH LEEKS AND SMOKED SOY SAUCE, TOPPED WITH QUAIL-EGG YOLK
IF I WERE TO NAME IT, I WOULD CALL IT THE "ULTIMATE NEGITORO EGGS-OVER-RICE GUNKAN SUSHI"!
THAT SMOKED SOY SAUCE WASN'T ONLY FOR KUGA! IT WAS A CALCULATED MOVE TO BOTH AID HIS TEAMMATE AND FURTHER HIS OWN ARRANGEMENT!
MRRRGH!
WOOT! IT'S GETTING RAVE REVIEWS!
WHAT ABOUT MEGISHIMA SENPAI, THOUGH? HOW'S HIS RAMEN TURNING OUT?!

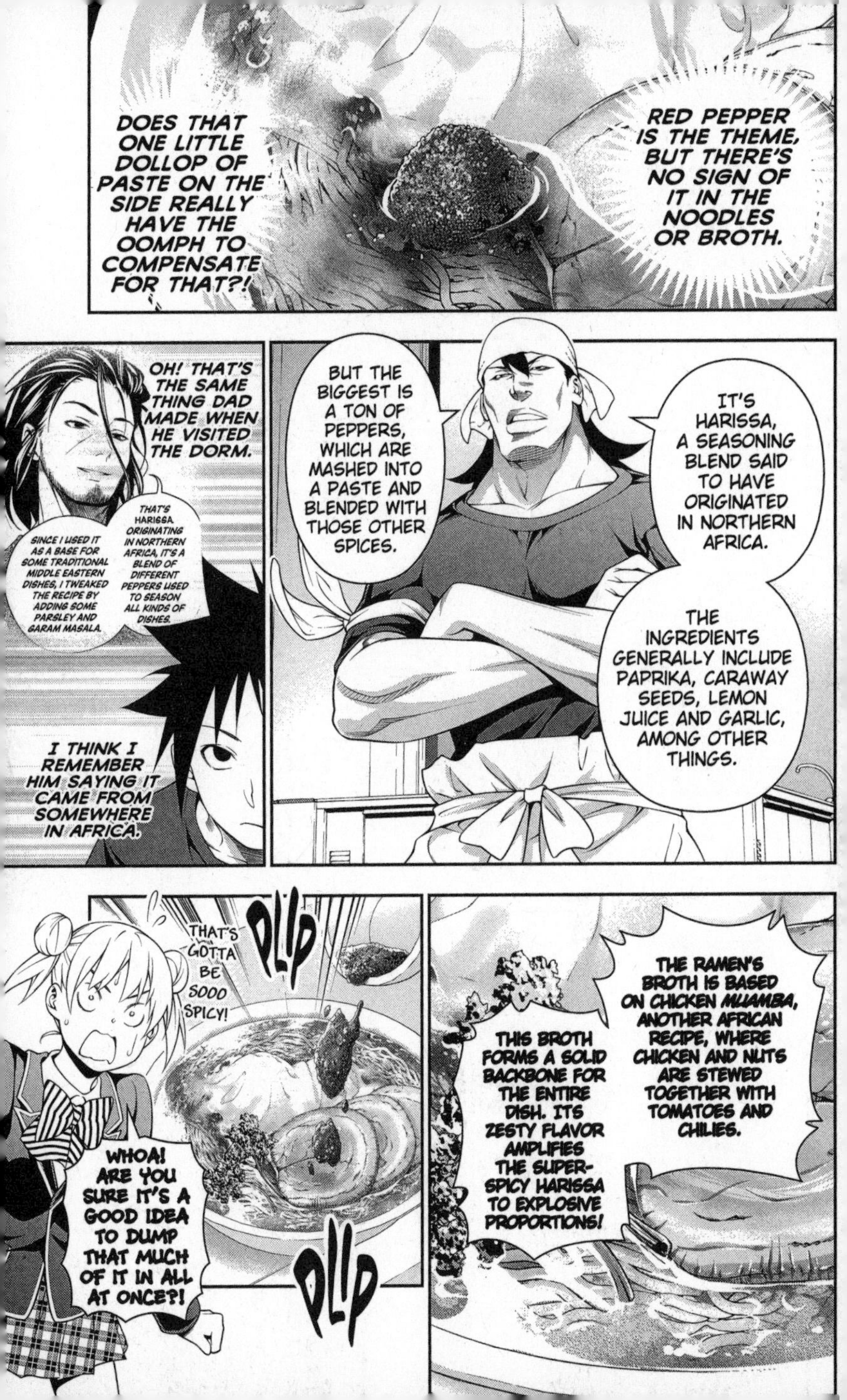
RED PEPPER IS THE THEME, BUT THERE'S NO SIGN OF IT IN THE NOODLES OR BROTH.
DOES THAT ONE LITTLE DOLLOP OF PASTE ON THE SIDE REALLY HAVE THE OOMPH TO COMPENSATE FOR THAT?!
IT'S HARISSA, A SEASONING BLEND SAID TO HAVE ORIGINATED IN NORTHERN AFRICA.
THE INGREDIENTS GENERALLY INCLUDE PAPRIKA, CARAWAY SEEDS, LEMON JUICE AND GARLIC, AMONG OTHER THINGS.
BUT THE BIGGEST IS A TON OF PEPPERS, WHICH ARE MASHED INTO A PASTE AND BLENDED WITH THOSE OTHER SPICES.
OH! THAT'S THE SAME THING DAD MADE WHEN HE VISITED THE DORM.
THAT'S HARISSA ORIGINATING IN NORTHERN AFRICA. IT'S A BLEND OF DIFFERENT PEPPERS USED TO SEASON ALL KINDS OF DISHES.
SINCE I USED IT AS A BASE FOR SOME TRADITIONAL MIDDLE EASTERN DISHES, I TWEAKED THE RECIPE BY ADDING SOME PARSLEY AND GARAM MASALA.
I THINK I REMEMBER HIM SAYING IT CAME FROM SOMEWHERE IN AFRICA.
THE RAMEN'S BROTH IS BASED ON CHICKEN *MUAMBA*, ANOTHER AFRICAN RECIPE, WHERE CHICKEN AND NUTS ARE STEWED TOGETHER WITH TOMATOES AND CHILIES.
THIS BROTH FORMS A SOLID BACKBONE FOR THE ENTIRE DISH. ITS ZESTY FLAVOR AMPLIFIES THE SUPER-SPICY HARISSA TO EXPLOSIVE PROPORTIONS!
PLIP
THAT'S GOTTA BE SOOO SPICY!
WHOA! ARE YOU SURE IT'S A GOOD IDEA TO DUMP THAT MUCH OF IT IN ALL AT ONCE?!
PLIP

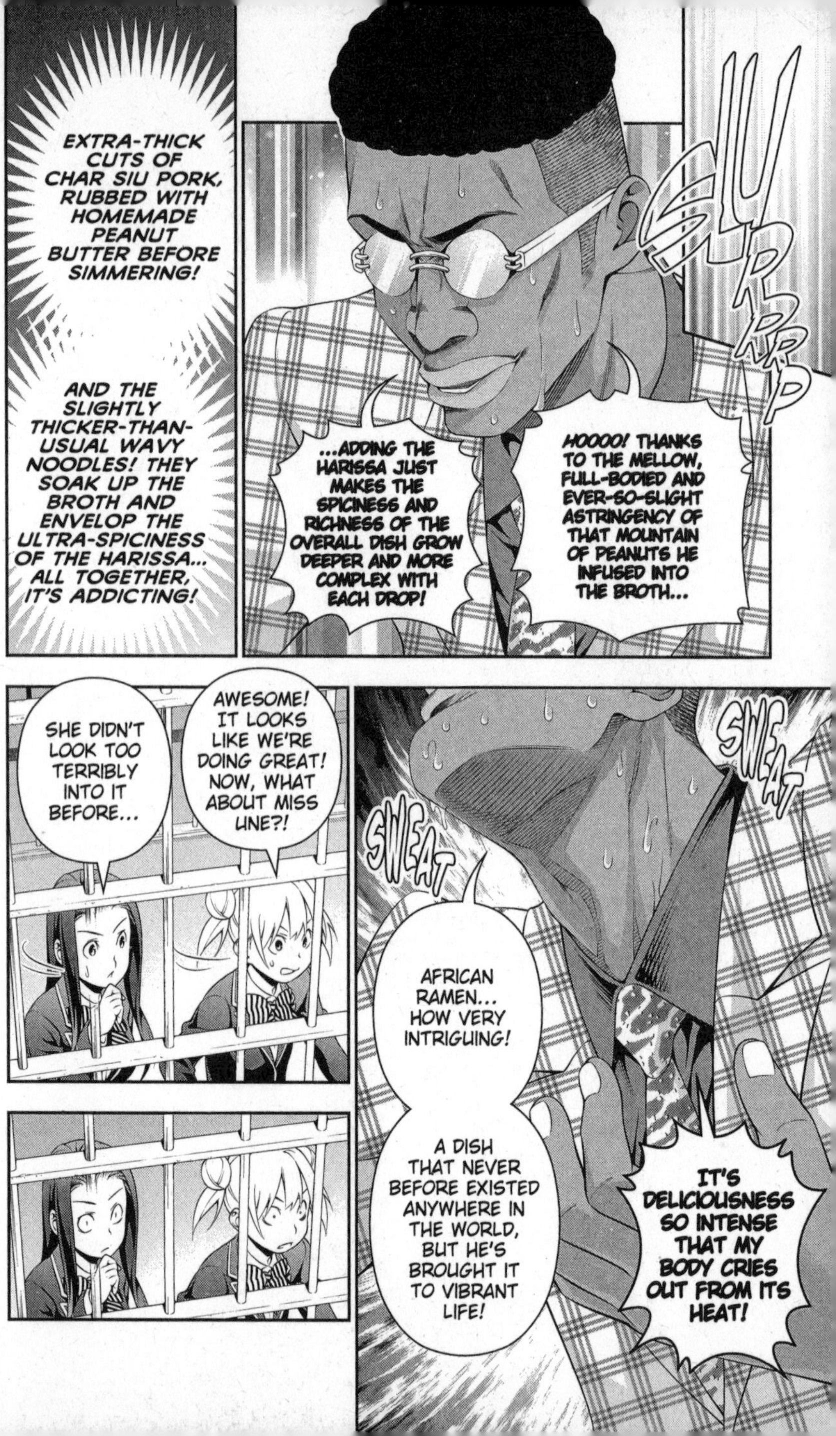
SLURRRP
HOOOO! THANKS TO THE MELLOW, FULL-BODIED AND EVER-SO-SLIGHT ASTRINGENCY OF THAT MOUNTAIN OF PEANUTS HE INFUSED INTO THE BROTH...
...ADDING THE HARISSA JUST MAKES THE SPICINESS AND RICHNESS OF THE OVERALL DISH GROW DEEPER AND MORE COMPLEX WITH EACH DROP!
EXTRA-THICK CUTS OF CHAR SIU PORK, RUBBED WITH HOMEMADE PEANUT BUTTER BEFORE SIMMERING!
AND THE SLIGHTLY THICKER-THAN-USUAL WAVY NOODLES! THEY SOAK UP THE BROTH AND ENVELOP THE ULTRA-SPICINESS OF THE HARISSA... ALL TOGETHER, IT'S ADDICTING!
SWEAT
SWEAT
AFRICAN RAMEN... HOW VERY INTRIGUING!
A DISH THAT NEVER BEFORE EXISTED ANYWHERE IN THE WORLD, BUT HE'S BROUGHT IT TO VIBRANT LIFE!
IT'S DELICIOUSNESS SO INTENSE THAT MY BODY CRIES OUT FROM ITS HEAT!
AWESOME! IT LOOKS LIKE WE'RE DOING GREAT! NOW, WHAT ABOUT MISS UNE?!
SHE DIDN'T LOOK TOO TERRIBLY INTO IT BEFORE...

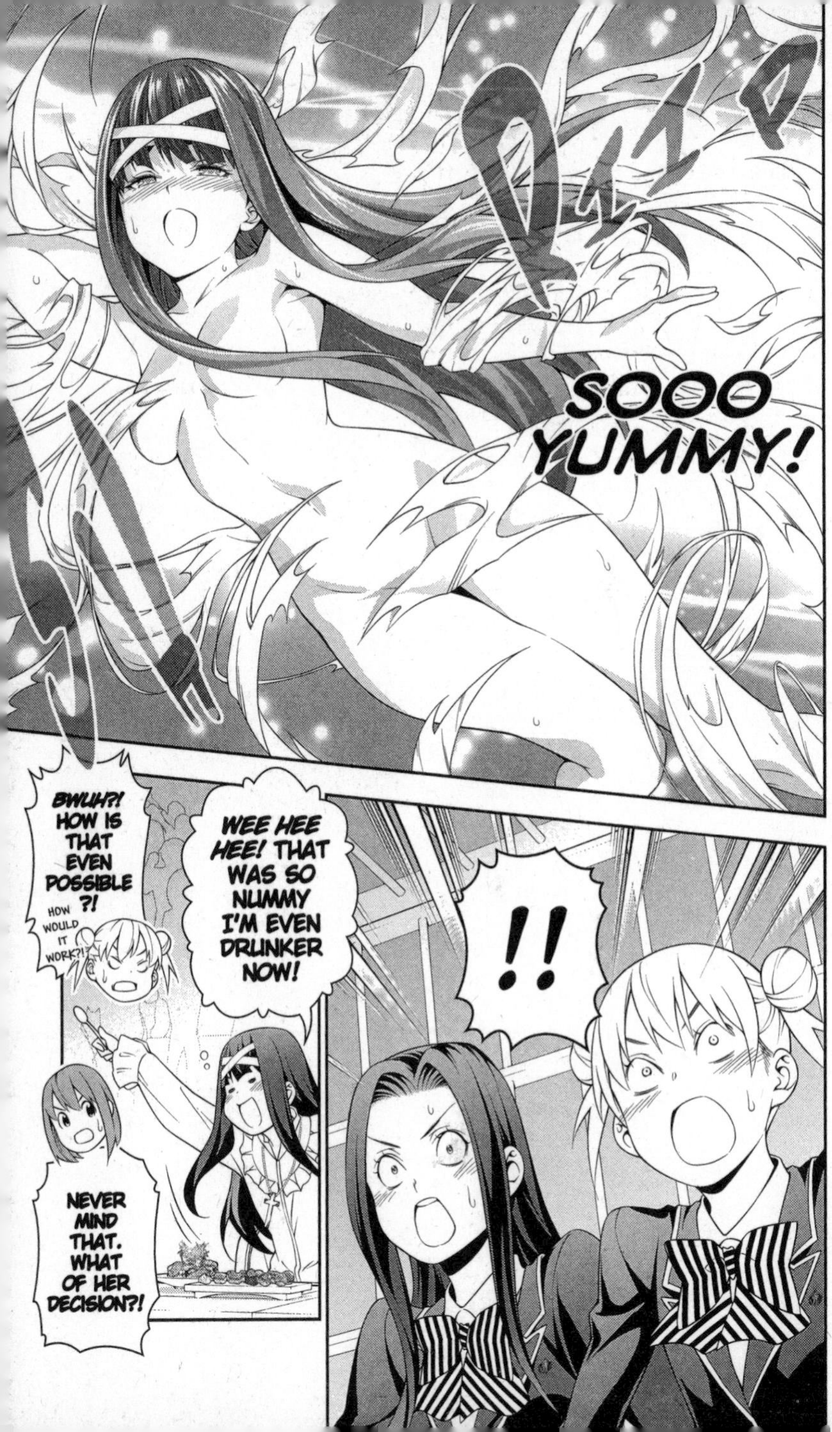
SOOO YUMMY!
!!
WEE HEE HEE! THAT WAS SO NUMMY I'M EVEN DRUNKER NOW!
BWUH?! HOW IS THAT EVEN POSSIBLE?!
HOW WOULD IT WORK?!
NEVER MIND THAT. WHAT OF HER DECISION?!

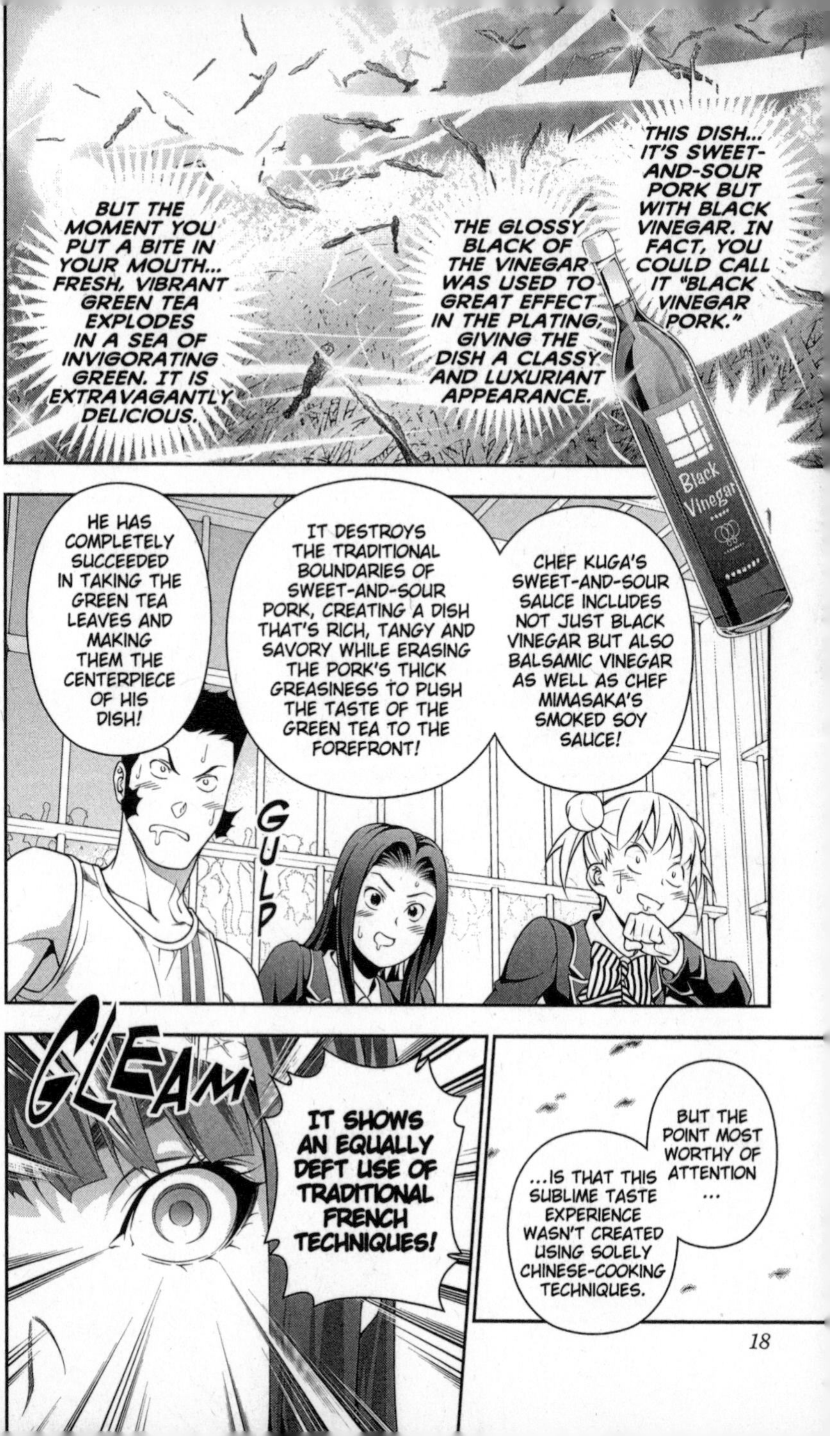
THIS DISH... IT'S SWEET-AND-SOUR PORK BUT WITH BLACK VINEGAR. IN FACT, YOU COULD CALL IT "BLACK VINEGAR PORK."
THE GLOSSY BLACK OF THE VINEGAR WAS USED TO GREAT EFFECT IN THE PLATING, GIVING THE DISH A CLASSY AND LUXURIANT APPEARANCE.
BUT THE MOMENT YOU PUT A BITE IN YOUR MOUTH... FRESH, VIBRANT GREEN TEA EXPLODES IN A SEA OF INVIGORATING GREEN. IT IS EXTRAVAGANTLY DELICIOUS.
Black Vinegar
CHEF KUGA'S SWEET-AND-SOUR SAUCE INCLUDES NOT JUST BLACK VINEGAR BUT ALSO BALSAMIC VINEGAR AS WELL AS CHEF MIMASAKA'S SMOKED SOY SAUCE!
IT DESTROYS THE TRADITIONAL BOUNDARIES OF SWEET-AND-SOUR PORK, CREATING A DISH THAT'S RICH, TANGY AND SAVORY WHILE ERASING THE PORK'S THICK GREASINESS TO PUSH THE TASTE OF THE GREEN TEA TO THE FOREFRONT!
HE HAS COMPLETELY SUCCEEDED IN TAKING THE GREEN TEA LEAVES AND MAKING THEM THE CENTERPIECE OF HIS DISH!
GULP
BUT THE POINT MOST WORTHY OF ATTENTION ...
...IS THAT THIS SUBLIME TASTE EXPERIENCE WASN'T CREATED USING SOLELY CHINESE-COOKING TECHNIQUES.
GLEAM
IT SHOWS AN EQUALLY DEFT USE OF TRADITIONAL FRENCH TECHNIQUES!

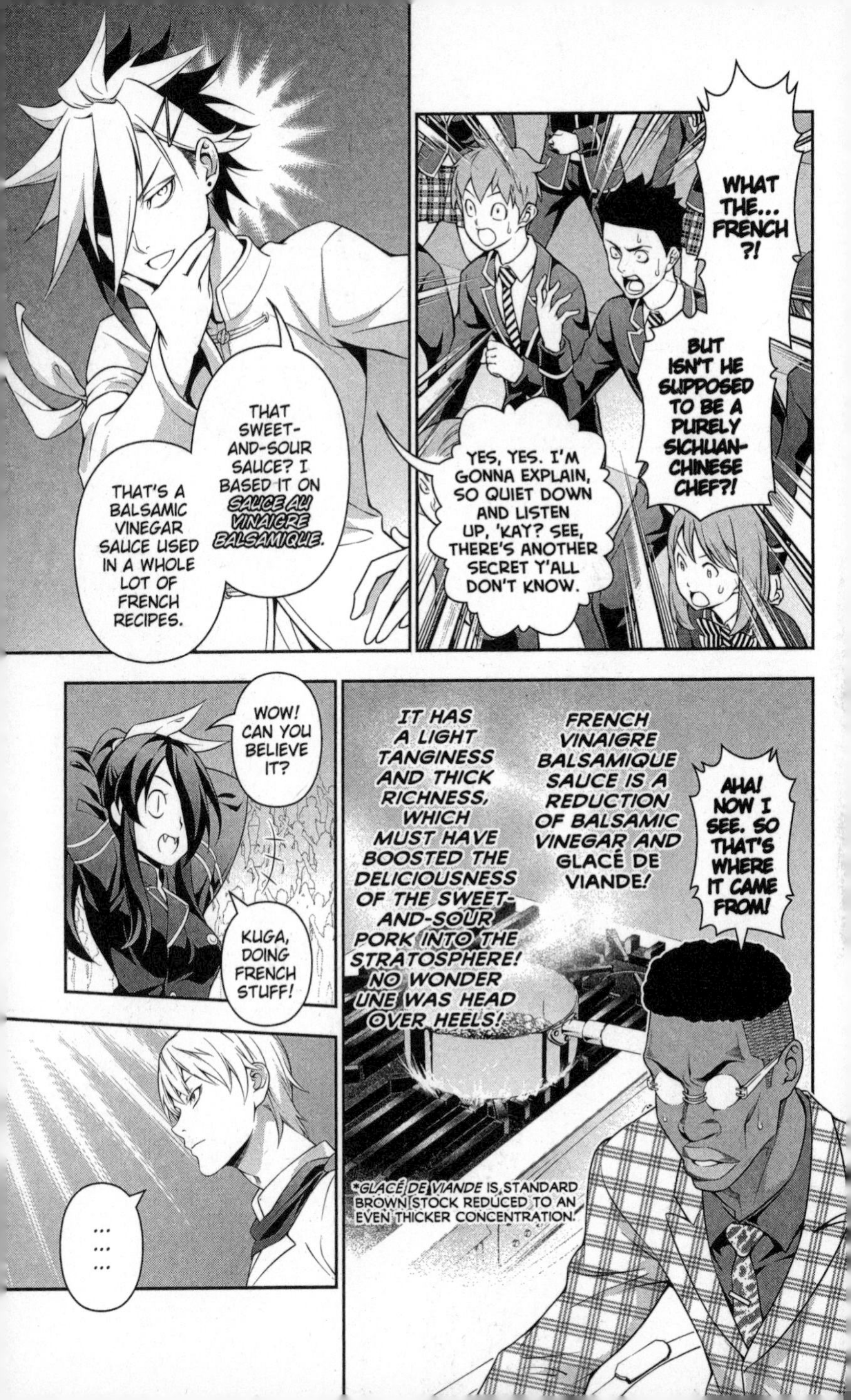
WHAT THE... FRENCH?!
BUT ISN'T HE SUPPOSED TO BE A PURELY SICHUAN-CHINESE CHEF?!
YES, YES. I'M GONNA EXPLAIN, SO QUIET DOWN AND LISTEN UP, 'KAY? SEE, THERE'S ANOTHER SECRET Y'ALL DON'T KNOW.
THAT SWEET-AND-SOUR SAUCE? I BASED IT ON *SAUCE AU VINAIGRE BALSAMIQUE*.
THAT'S A BALSAMIC VINEGAR SAUCE USED IN A WHOLE LOT OF FRENCH RECIPES.
AHA! NOW I SEE. SO THAT'S WHERE IT CAME FROM!
FRENCH VINAIGRE BALSAMIQUE SAUCE IS A REDUCTION OF BALSAMIC VINEGAR AND GLACÉ DE VIANDE!
IT HAS A LIGHT TANGINESS AND THICK RICHNESS, WHICH MUST HAVE BOOSTED THE DELICIOUSNESS OF THE SWEET-AND-SOUR PORK INTO THE STRATOSPHERE! NO WONDER UNE WAS HEAD OVER HEELS!
*GLACÉ DE VIANDE IS STANDARD BROWN STOCK REDUCED TO AN EVEN THICKER CONCENTRATION.
WOW! CAN YOU BELIEVE IT?
KUGA, DOING FRENCH STUFF!
...
...
...

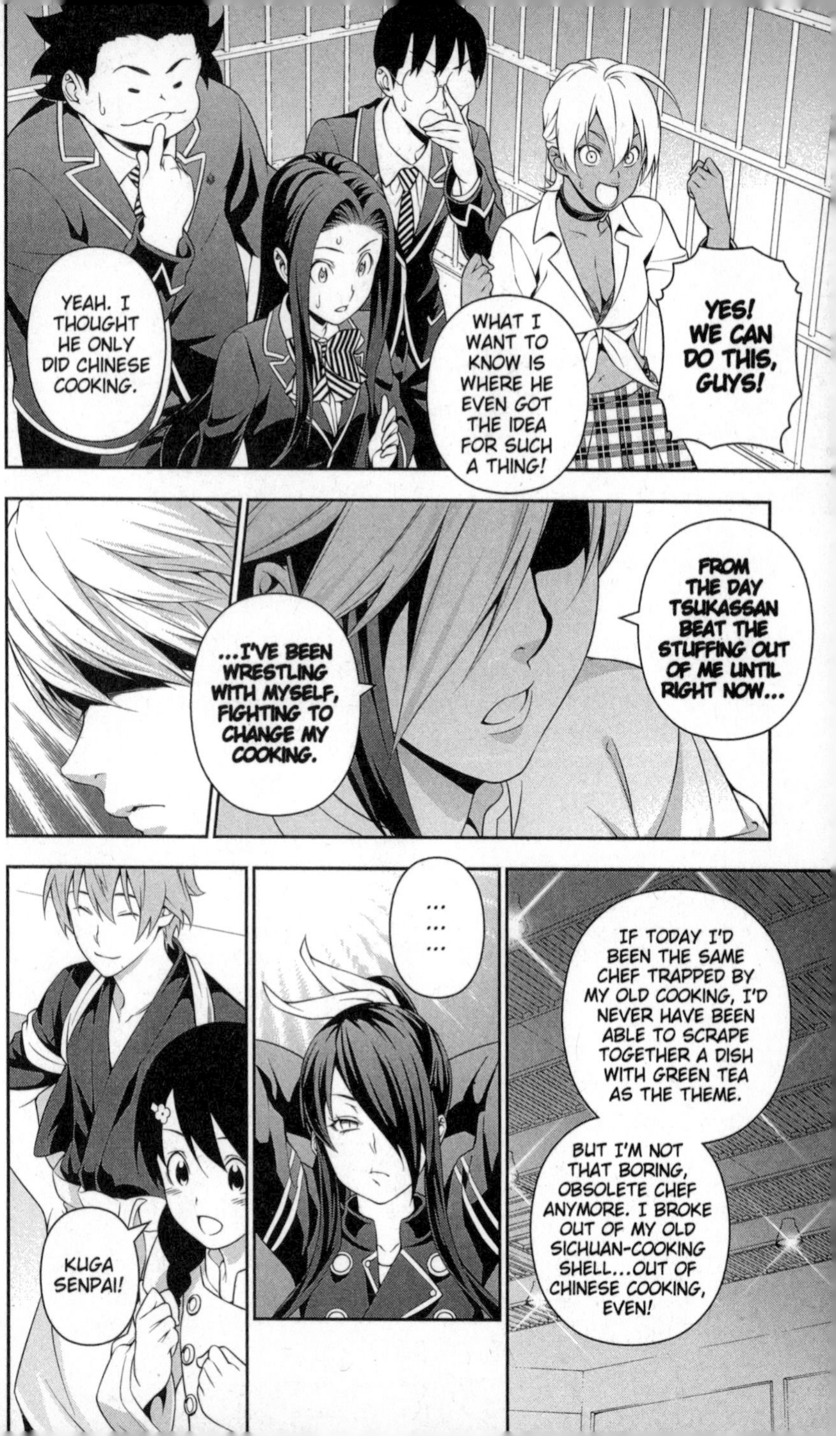
YES! WE CAN DO THIS, GUYS!
WHAT I WANT TO KNOW IS WHERE HE EVEN GOT THE IDEA FOR SUCH A THING!
YEAH. I THOUGHT HE ONLY DID CHINESE COOKING.
FROM THE DAY TSUKASSAN BEAT THE STUFFING OUT OF ME UNTIL RIGHT NOW...
...I'VE BEEN WRESTLING WITH MYSELF, FIGHTING TO CHANGE MY COOKING.
IF TODAY I'D BEEN THE SAME CHEF TRAPPED BY MY OLD COOKING, I'D NEVER HAVE BEEN ABLE TO SCRAPE TOGETHER A DISH WITH GREEN TEA AS THE THEME.
BUT I'M NOT THAT BORING, OBSOLETE CHEF ANYMORE. I BROKE OUT OF MY OLD SICHUAN-COOKING SHELL...OUT OF CHINESE COOKING, EVEN!
... ...
KUGA SENPAI!

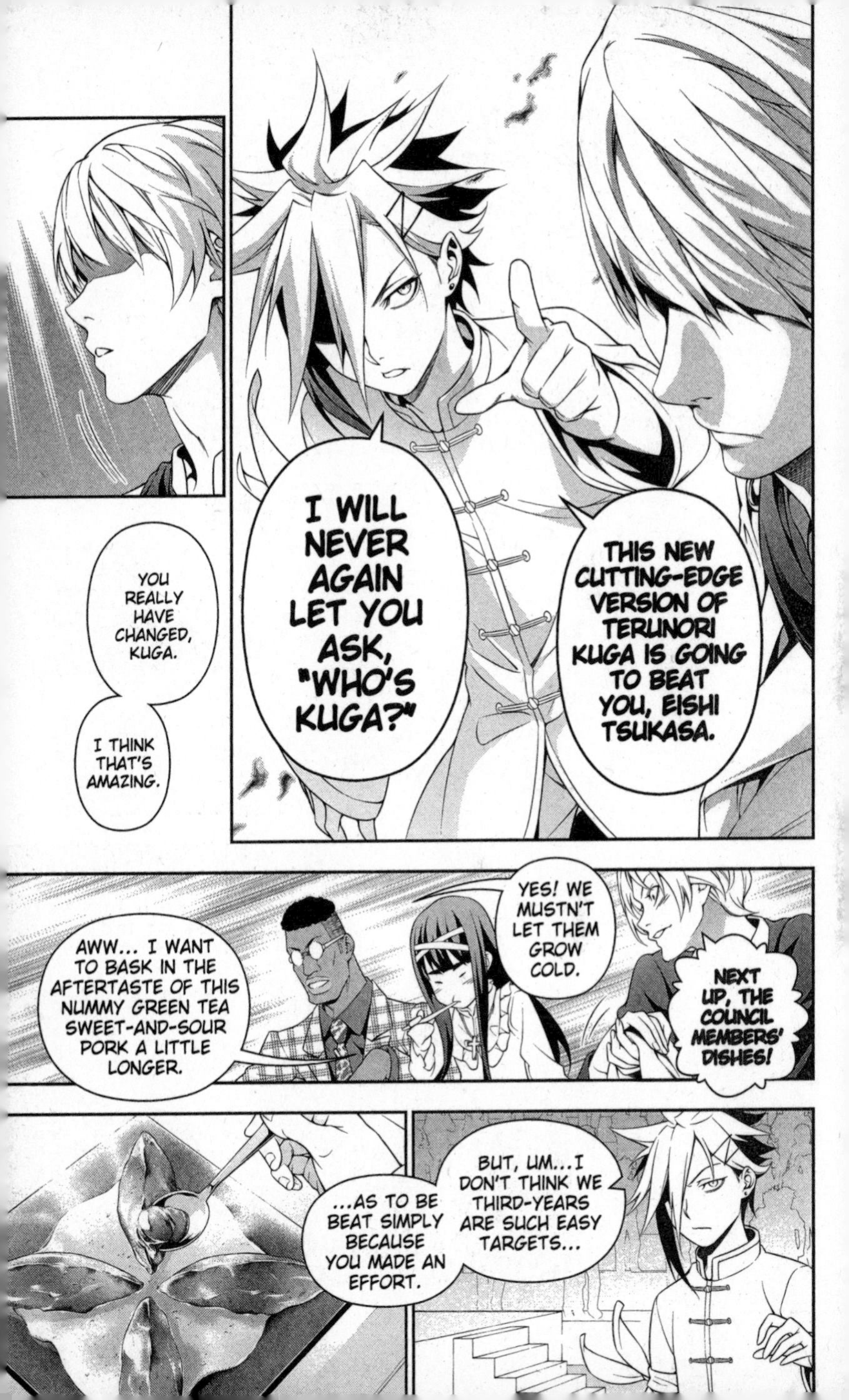
THIS NEW CUTTING-EDGE VERSION OF TERUNORI KUGA IS GOING TO BEAT YOU, EISHI TSUKASA.
I WILL NEVER AGAIN LET YOU ASK, "WHO'S KUGA?"
YOU REALLY HAVE CHANGED, KUGA.
I THINK THAT'S AMAZING.
NEXT UP, THE COUNCIL MEMBERS' DISHES!
YES! WE MUSTN'T LET THEM GROW COLD.
AWW... I WANT TO BASK IN THE AFTERTASTE OF THIS NUMMY GREEN TEA SWEET-AND-SOUR PORK A LITTLE LONGER.
BUT, UM...I DON'T THINK WE THIRD-YEARS ARE SUCH EASY TARGETS...
...AS TO BE BEAT SIMPLY BECAUSE YOU MADE AN EFFORT.

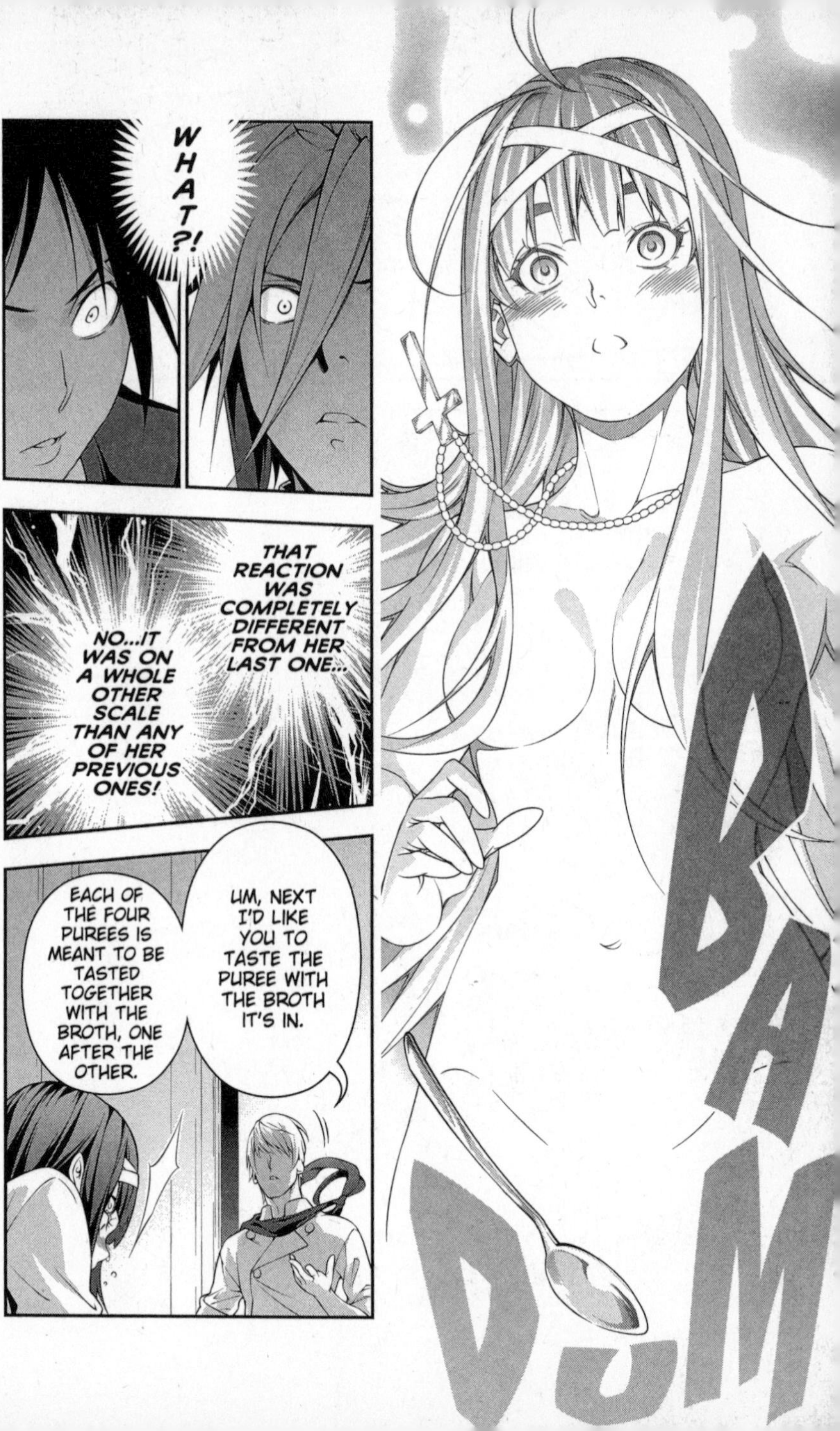
BADUM
WHAT?!
THAT REACTION WAS COMPLETELY DIFFERENT FROM HER LAST ONE...
NO...IT WAS ON A WHOLE OTHER SCALE THAN ANY OF HER PREVIOUS ONES!
UM, NEXT I'D LIKE YOU TO TASTE THE PUREE WITH THE BROTH IT'S IN.
EACH OF THE FOUR PUREES IS MEANT TO BE TASTED TOGETHER WITH THE BROTH, ONE AFTER THE OTHER.

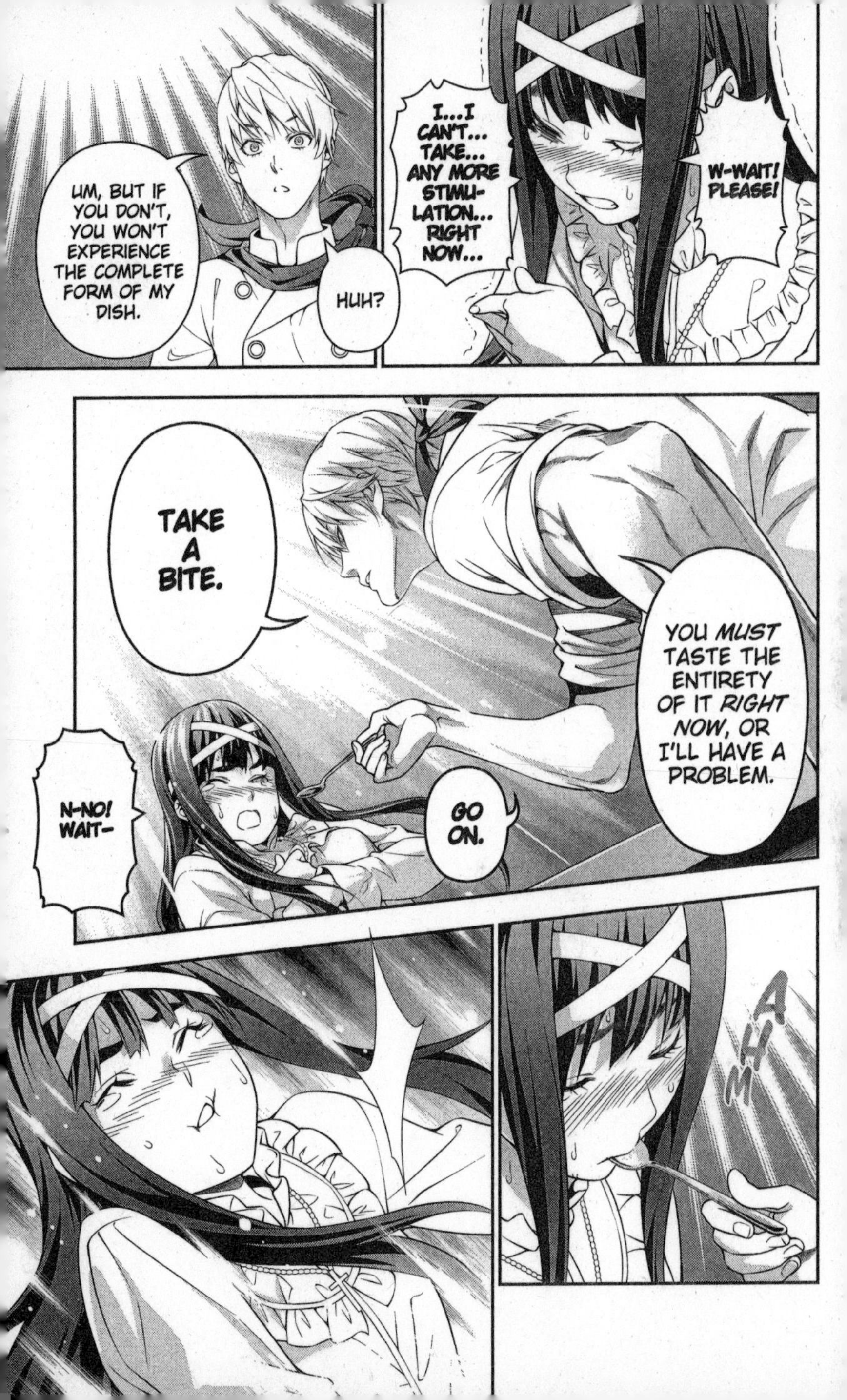
W-WAIT! PLEASE!
I...I CAN'T... TAKE... ANY MORE STIMULATION... RIGHT NOW...
HUH?
UM, BUT IF YOU DON'T, YOU WON'T EXPERIENCE THE COMPLETE FORM OF MY DISH.
TAKE A BITE.
YOU *MUST* TASTE THE ENTIRETY OF IT *RIGHT NOW*, OR I'LL HAVE A PROBLEM.
GO ON.
N-NO! WAIT-
AHM

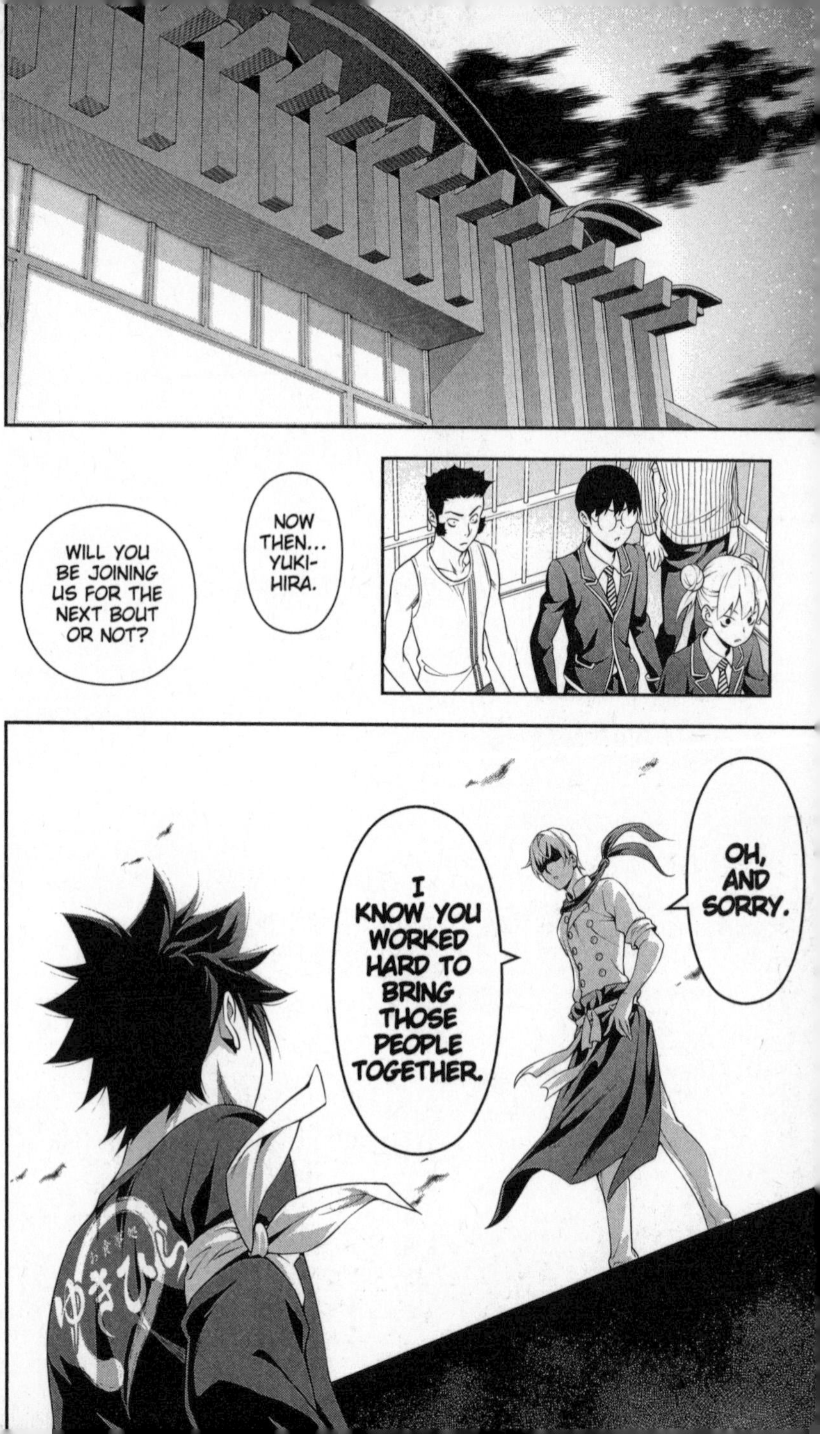
NOW THEN... YUKI-HIRA.
WILL YOU BE JOINING US FOR THE NEXT BOUT OR NOT?
OH, AND SORRY.
I KNOW YOU WORKED HARD TO BRING THOSE PEOPLE TOGETHER.

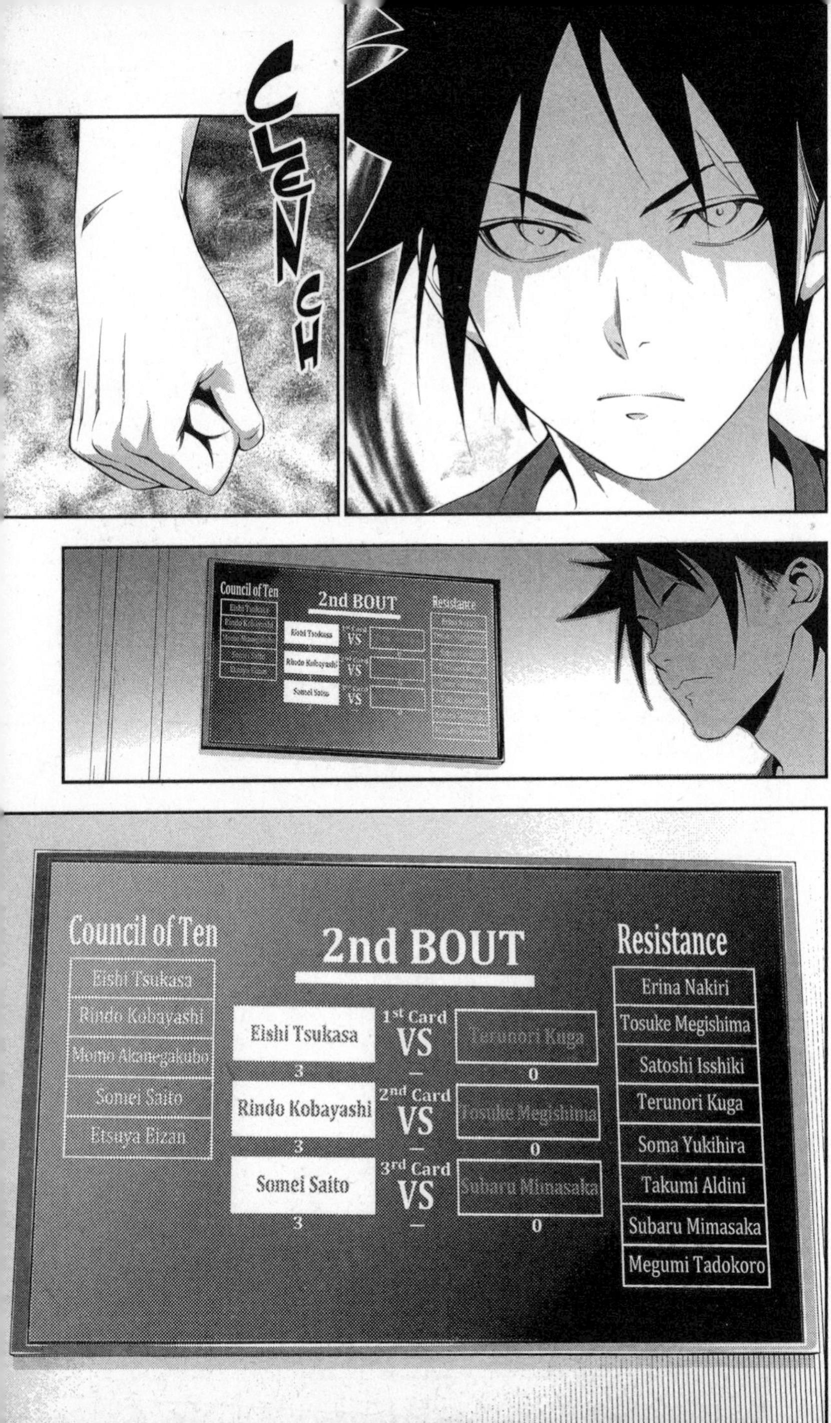
CLENCH
Council of Ten
2nd BOUT
Resistance
Eishi Tsukasa
Rindo Kobayashi
Somei Saito
VS
VS
VS
Council of Ten
Eishi Tsukasa
Rindo Kobayashi
Momo Akanegakubo
Somei Saito
Etsuya Eizan
2nd BOUT
Eishi Tsukasa
3
1st Card
VS
—
Terunori Kuga
0
Rindo Kobayashi
3
2nd Card
VS
—
Tosuke Megishima
0
Somei Saito
3
3rd Card
VS
—
Subaru Mimasaka
0
Resistance
Erina Nakiri
Tosuke Megishima
Satoshi Isshiki
Terunori Kuga
Soma Yukihira
Takumi Aldini
Subaru Mimasaka
Megumi Tadokoro

ARTIST: YUTO TSUKUDA RECIPE BY: YUKI MORISAKI

VOLUME 27 SPECIAL SUPPLEMENT!

PRACTICAL RECIPE #1

KUGA'S GREEN TEA SWEET-AND-SOUR PORK

SIMPLIFIED HOME VERSION

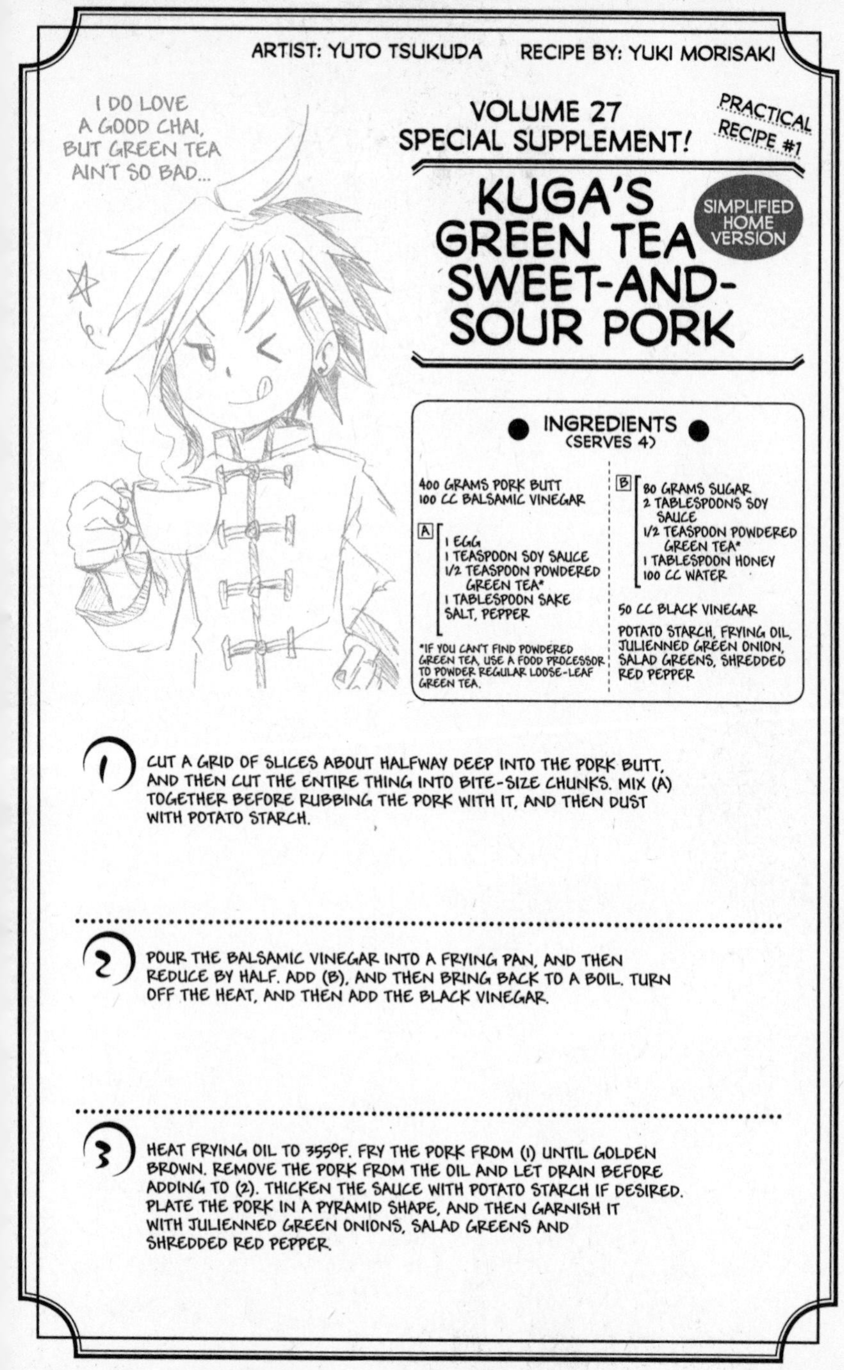
I DO LOVE A GOOD CHAI, BUT GREEN TEA AIN'T SO BAD...

INGREDIENTS
(SERVES 4)

400 GRAMS PORK BUTT
100 CC BALSAMIC VINEGAR

[A]
- 1 EGG
- 1 TEASPOON SOY SAUCE
- 1/2 TEASPOON POWDERED GREEN TEA*
- 1 TABLESPOON SAKE
- SALT, PEPPER

[B]
- 80 GRAMS SUGAR
- 2 TABLESPOONS SOY SAUCE
- 1/2 TEASPOON POWDERED GREEN TEA*
- 1 TABLESPOON HONEY
- 100 CC WATER

50 CC BLACK VINEGAR

POTATO STARCH, FRYING OIL, JULIENNED GREEN ONION, SALAD GREENS, SHREDDED RED PEPPER

*IF YOU CAN'T FIND POWDERED GREEN TEA, USE A FOOD PROCESSOR TO POWDER REGULAR LOOSE-LEAF GREEN TEA.

1. CUT A GRID OF SLICES ABOUT HALFWAY DEEP INTO THE PORK BUTT, AND THEN CUT THE ENTIRE THING INTO BITE-SIZE CHUNKS. MIX (A) TOGETHER BEFORE RUBBING THE PORK WITH IT, AND THEN DUST WITH POTATO STARCH.

2. POUR THE BALSAMIC VINEGAR INTO A FRYING PAN, AND THEN REDUCE BY HALF. ADD (B), AND THEN BRING BACK TO A BOIL. TURN OFF THE HEAT, AND THEN ADD THE BLACK VINEGAR.

3. HEAT FRYING OIL TO 355°F. FRY THE PORK FROM (1) UNTIL GOLDEN BROWN. REMOVE THE PORK FROM THE OIL AND LET DRAIN BEFORE ADDING TO (2). THICKEN THE SAUCE WITH POTATO STARCH IF DESIRED. PLATE THE PORK IN A PYRAMID SHAPE, AND THEN GARNISH IT WITH JULIENNED GREEN ONIONS, SALAD GREENS AND SHREDDED RED PEPPER.

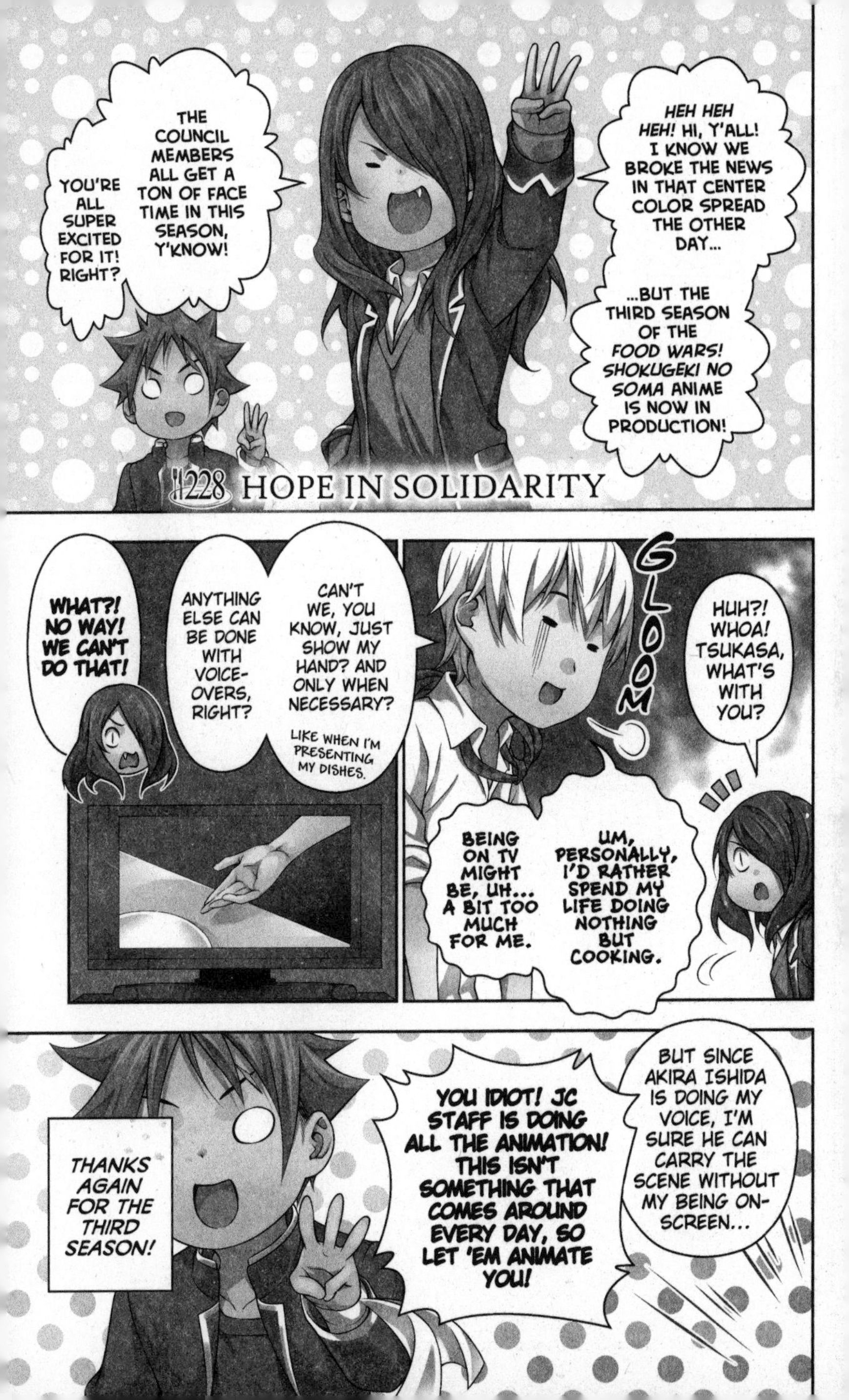
HEH HEH HEH! HI, Y'ALL! I KNOW WE BROKE THE NEWS IN THAT CENTER COLOR SPREAD THE OTHER DAY...
...BUT THE THIRD SEASON OF THE FOOD WARS! SHOKUGEKI NO SOMA ANIME IS NOW IN PRODUCTION!
THE COUNCIL MEMBERS ALL GET A TON OF FACE TIME IN THIS SEASON, Y'KNOW!
YOU'RE ALL SUPER EXCITED FOR IT! RIGHT?
228 HOPE IN SOLIDARITY
GLOOM
HUH?! WHOA! TSUKASA, WHAT'S WITH YOU?
UM, PERSONALLY, I'D RATHER SPEND MY LIFE DOING NOTHING BUT COOKING.
BEING ON TV MIGHT BE, UH... A BIT TOO MUCH FOR ME.
CAN'T WE, YOU KNOW, JUST SHOW MY HAND? AND ONLY WHEN NECESSARY?
LIKE WHEN I'M PRESENTING MY DISHES.
ANYTHING ELSE CAN BE DONE WITH VOICE-OVERS, RIGHT?
WHAT?! NO WAY! WE CAN'T DO THAT!
BUT SINCE AKIRA ISHIDA IS DOING MY VOICE, I'M SURE HE CAN CARRY THE SCENE WITHOUT MY BEING ON-SCREEN...
YOU IDIOT! JC STAFF IS DOING ALL THE ANIMATION! THIS ISN'T SOMETHING THAT COMES AROUND EVERY DAY, SO LET 'EM ANIMATE YOU!
THANKS AGAIN FOR THE THIRD SEASON!

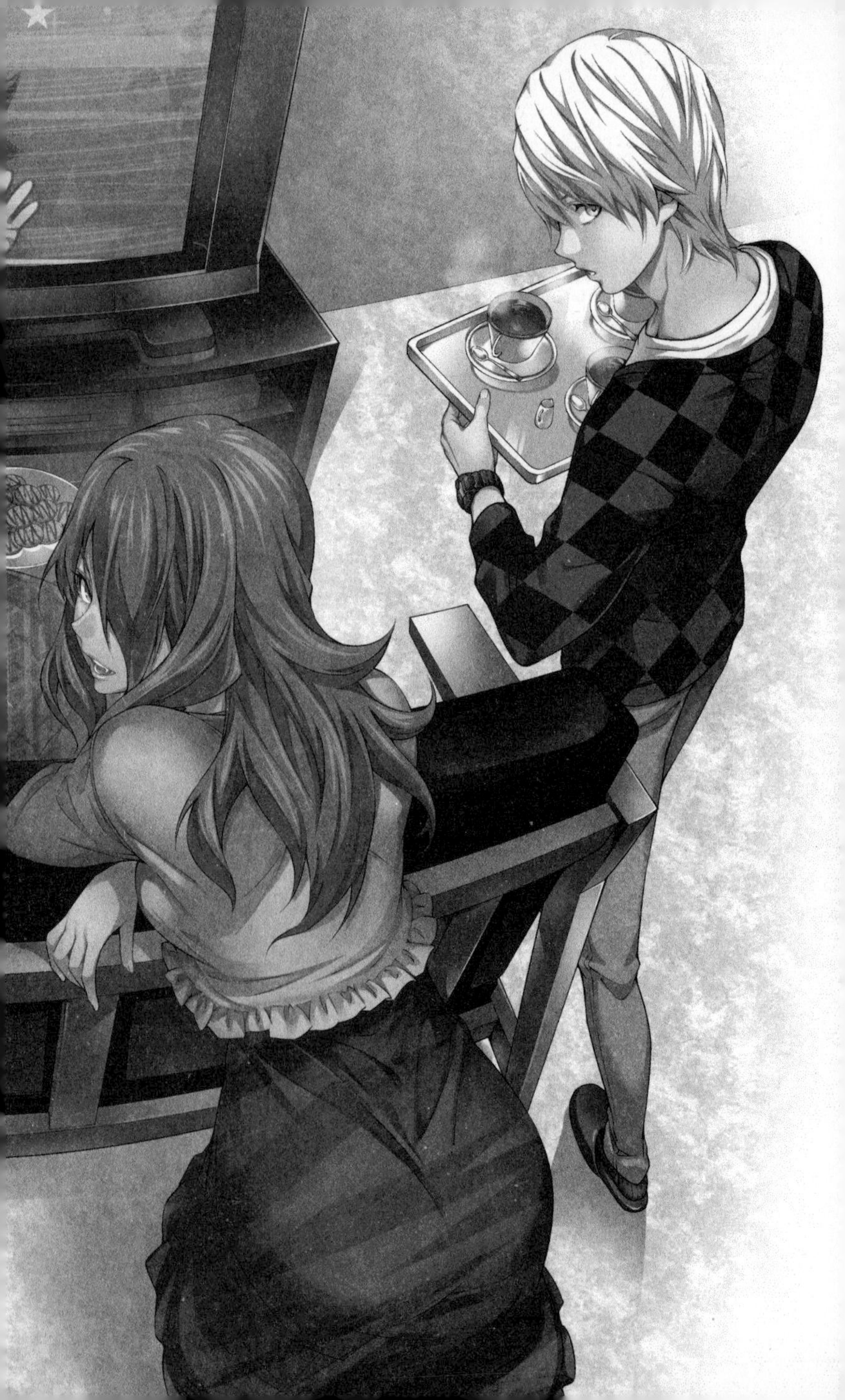

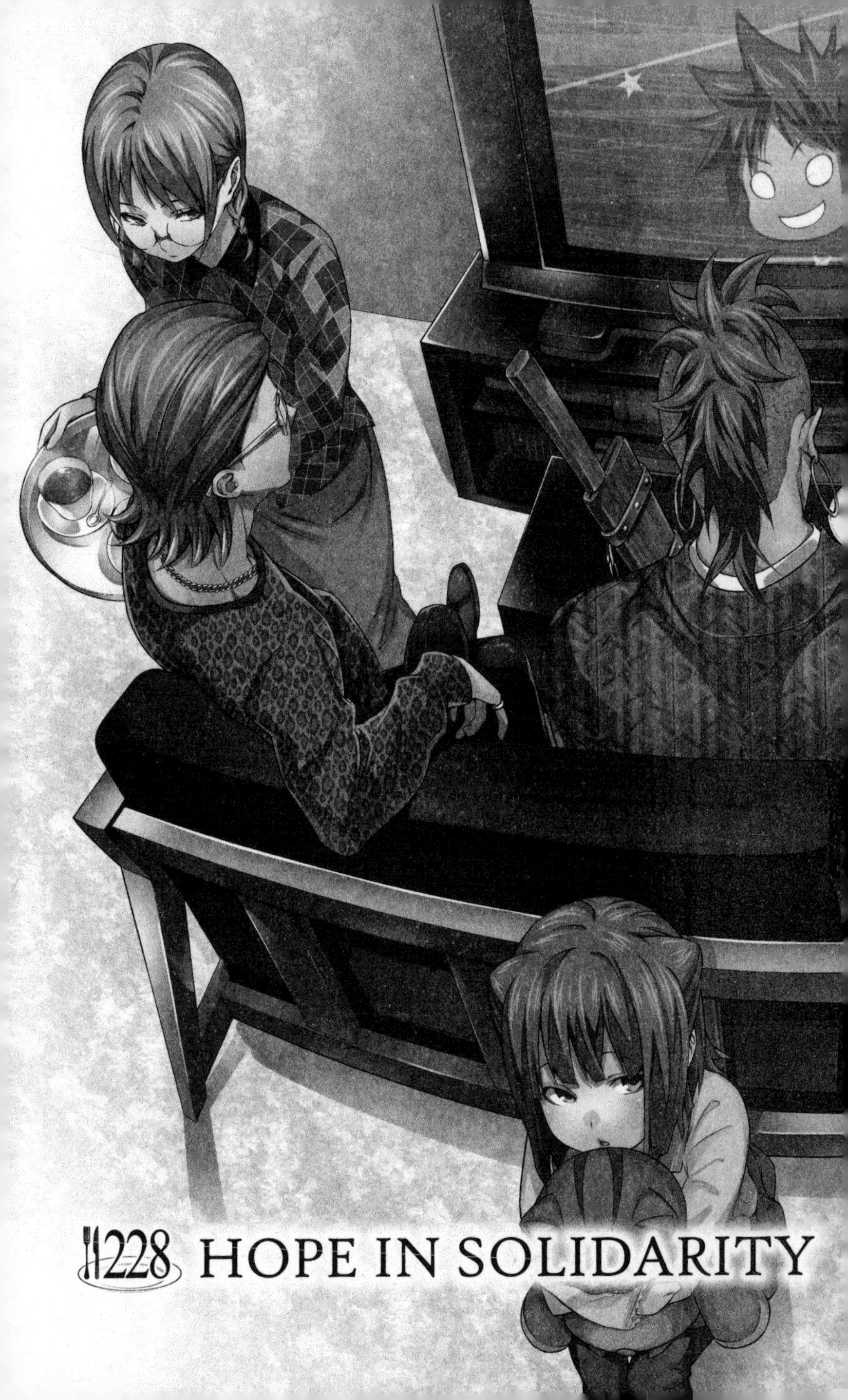
228
HOPE IN SOLIDARITY

ARTIST: YUTO TSUKUDA   RECIPE BY: YUKI MORISAKI

VOLUME 27 SPECIAL SUPPLEMENT!

PRACTICAL RECIPE #2

MEGISHIMA'S AFRICAN RAMEN

SIMPLIFIED HOME VERSION

WARM

MEGISHIMA'S KNIT CAP

HE WEARS IT DURING COLD WEATHER WHEN HE'S PULLING HIS RAMEN CART OUTSIDE.

● INGREDIENTS ●
(SERVES 2)

2 PORTIONS DRY RAMEN NOODLES
500 GRAMS BONE-IN CHICKEN THIGHS
1 ONION
2 MEDIUM POTATOES
1 TABLESPOON EACH GRATED GINGER, CRUSHED GARLIC
1 TABLESPOON OLIVE OIL

Ⓐ 80 GRAMS PEANUT BUTTER (UNSWEETENED)
500 CC BROTH
1 CAN TOMATOES
1 RED PEPPER
2 BAY LEAVES

SALT, PEPPER, SOUR CREAM, PARSLEY, CHAR SIU PORK SLICES

① CUT THE CHICKEN THIGHS INTO BITE-SIZE CHUNKS AND RUB WITH SALT AND PEPPER. MINCE THE ONION, AND THEN DICE THE POTATOES INTO 1/2 INCH CUBES.

② COOK THE CHICKEN FROM (1) IN A FRYING PAN SKIN SIDE DOWN UNTIL GOLDEN BROWN. REMOVE FROM HEAT AND SET TO THE SIDE.

③ IN THE FRYING PAN THAT WAS USED IN (2), HEAT THE OLIVE OIL AND THEN ADD THE ONIONS, GARLIC AND GINGER. SAUTÉ UNTIL THE ONIONS ARE TRANSLUCENT, AND THEN MOVE THEM INTO A HEAVY-BOTTOMED POT.

④ ADD (A) AND THE CHICKEN FROM (2) INTO THE POT FROM (3). BRING TO A BOIL AND SIMMER FOR 20 MINUTES. SEASON TO TASTE WITH SALT AND PEPPER.

⑤ IN A DIFFERENT POT, BOIL PLENTY OF WATER AND COOK THE DRY RAMEN NOODLES ACCORDING TO PACKAGE INSTRUCTIONS. LADLE THE SOUP FROM (4) INTO TWO BOWLS. THOROUGHLY DRAIN THE NOODLES AND ADD TO THE SOUP. TOP WITH SOUR CREAM, PARSLEY AND CHAR SIU PORK SLICES AS DESIRED. PLACE A DIPPING BOWL OF HARISSA ON THE SIDE, AND DONE!

★ HOMEMADE HARISSA

① PLACE ALL INGREDIENTS IN A MORTAR AND GRIND INTO A UNIFORM PASTE. ALTERNATELY, USE A FOOD PROCESSOR TO BLEND THEM INTO A PASTE.

*GREAT FOR PERKING UP SOUPS OR AS A SPREAD ON TOAST! KEEPS FOR ABOUT ONE WEEK IN THE REFRIGERATOR

● INGREDIENTS ●
(SMALL PORTION)

10 RED PEPPERS
2 CLOVES GARLIC
1 TABLESPOON LEMON JUICE
2 TABLESPOONS EXTRA VIRGIN OLIVE OIL
1 TEASPOON EACH CORIANDER POWDER, PAPRIKA, SALT, SUGAR
1/2 TEASPOON EACH CUMIN, CARAWAY SEEDS

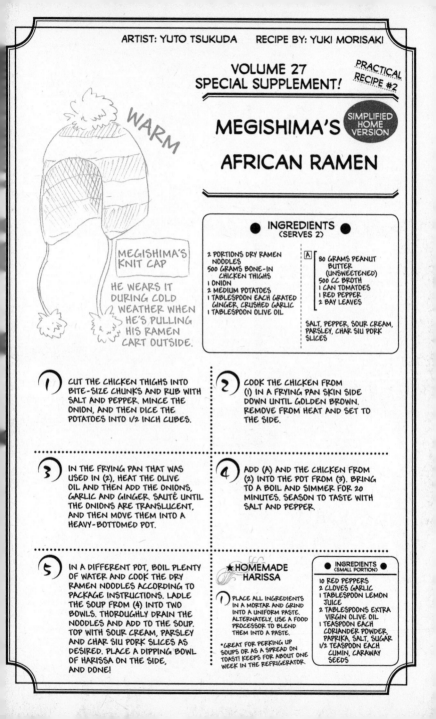

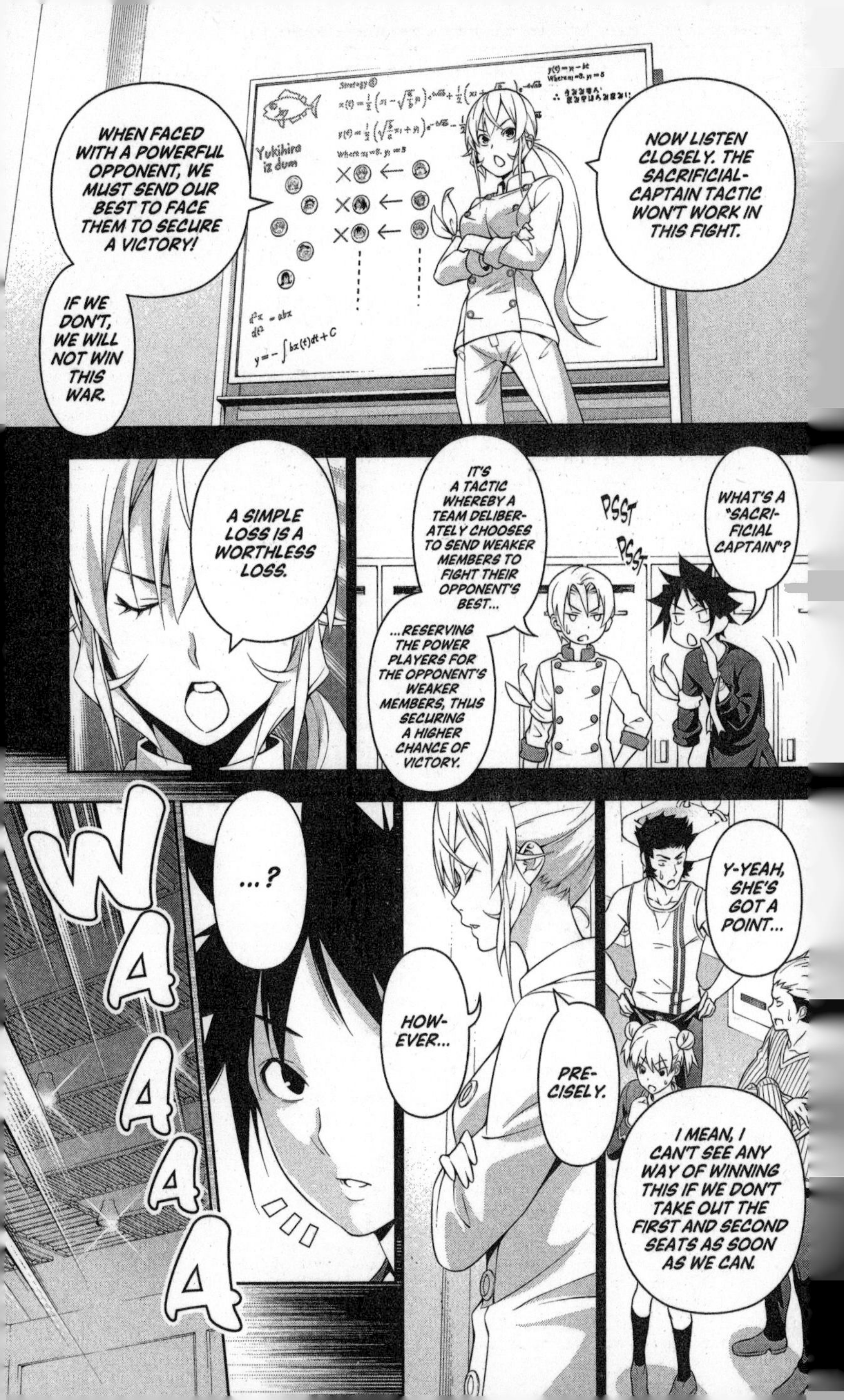
NOW LISTEN CLOSELY. THE SACRIFICIAL-CAPTAIN TACTIC WON'T WORK IN THIS FIGHT.
Yukihira iz dum
WHEN FACED WITH A POWERFUL OPPONENT, WE MUST SEND OUR BEST TO FACE THEM TO SECURE A VICTORY!
IF WE DON'T, WE WILL NOT WIN THIS WAR.
WHAT'S A "SACRIFICIAL CAPTAIN"?
PSST
PSST
IT'S A TACTIC WHEREBY A TEAM DELIBERATELY CHOOSES TO SEND WEAKER MEMBERS TO FIGHT THEIR OPPONENT'S BEST...
...RESERVING THE POWER PLAYERS FOR THE OPPONENT'S WEAKER MEMBERS, THUS SECURING A HIGHER CHANCE OF VICTORY.
A SIMPLE LOSS IS A WORTHLESS LOSS.
Y-YEAH, SHE'S GOT A POINT...
I MEAN, I CAN'T SEE ANY WAY OF WINNING THIS IF WE DON'T TAKE OUT THE FIRST AND SECOND SEATS AS SOON AS WE CAN.
PRECISELY.
HOWEVER...
...?
WAAAAA

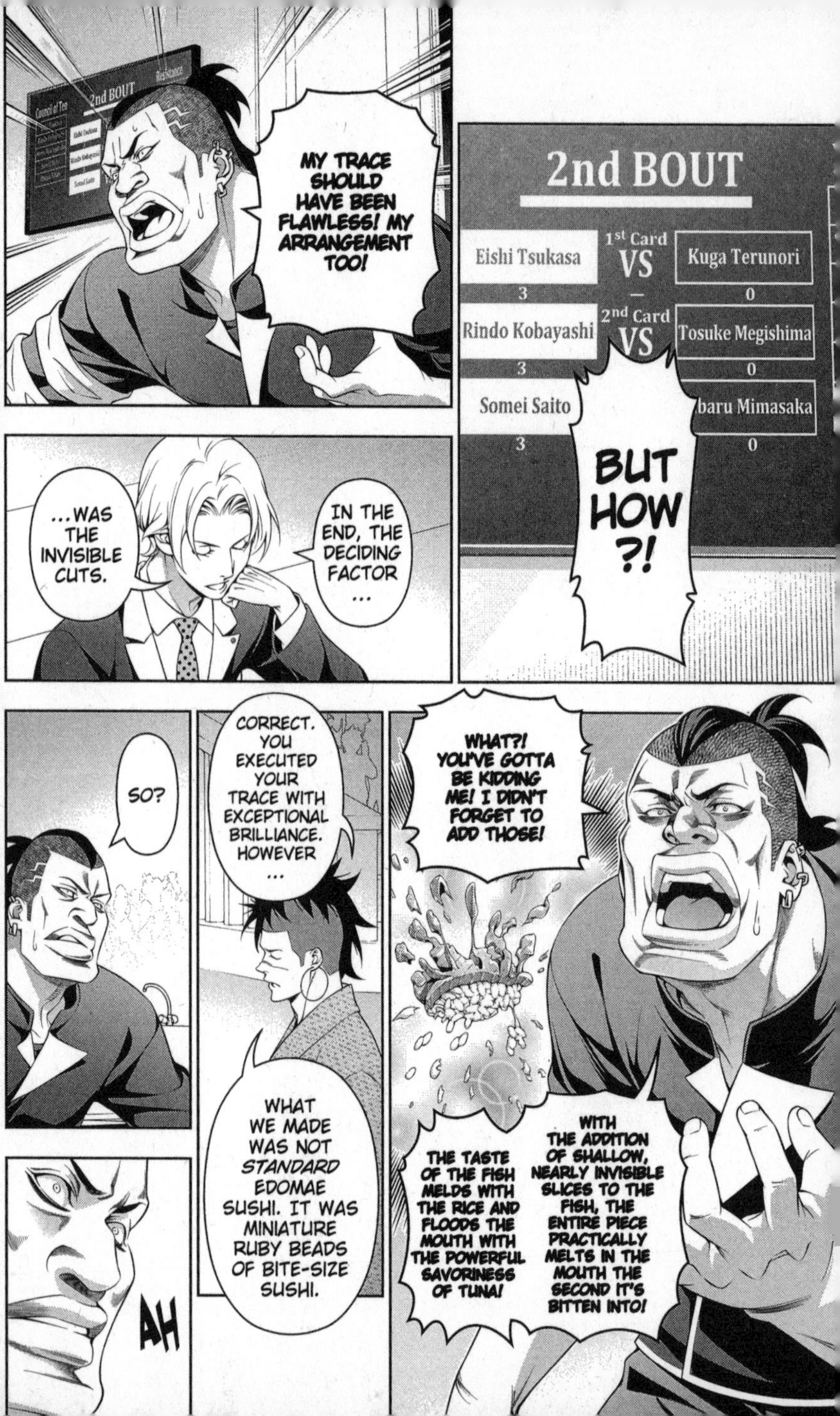
2nd BOUT
Eishi Tsukasa
1st Card VS
Kuga Terunori
3
—
0
Rindo Kobayashi
2nd Card VS
Tosuke Megishima
3
0
Somei Saito
baru Mimasaka
3
0
BUT HOW?!
2nd BOUT
Resistance
Council of Ten
MY TRACE SHOULD HAVE BEEN FLAWLESS! MY ARRANGEMENT TOO!
IN THE END, THE DECIDING FACTOR ...
...WAS THE INVISIBLE CUTS.
WHAT?! YOU'VE GOTTA BE KIDDING ME! I DIDN'T FORGET TO ADD THOSE!
WITH THE ADDITION OF SHALLOW, NEARLY INVISIBLE SLICES TO THE FISH, THE ENTIRE PIECE PRACTICALLY MELTS IN THE MOUTH THE SECOND IT'S BITTEN INTO!
THE TASTE OF THE FISH MELDS WITH THE RICE AND FLOODS THE MOUTH WITH THE POWERFUL SAVORINESS OF TUNA!
CORRECT. YOU EXECUTED YOUR TRACE WITH EXCEPTIONAL BRILLIANCE. HOWEVER ...
WHAT WE MADE WAS NOT *STANDARD* EDOMAE SUSHI. IT WAS MINIATURE RUBY BEADS OF BITE-SIZE SUSHI.
SO?
AH

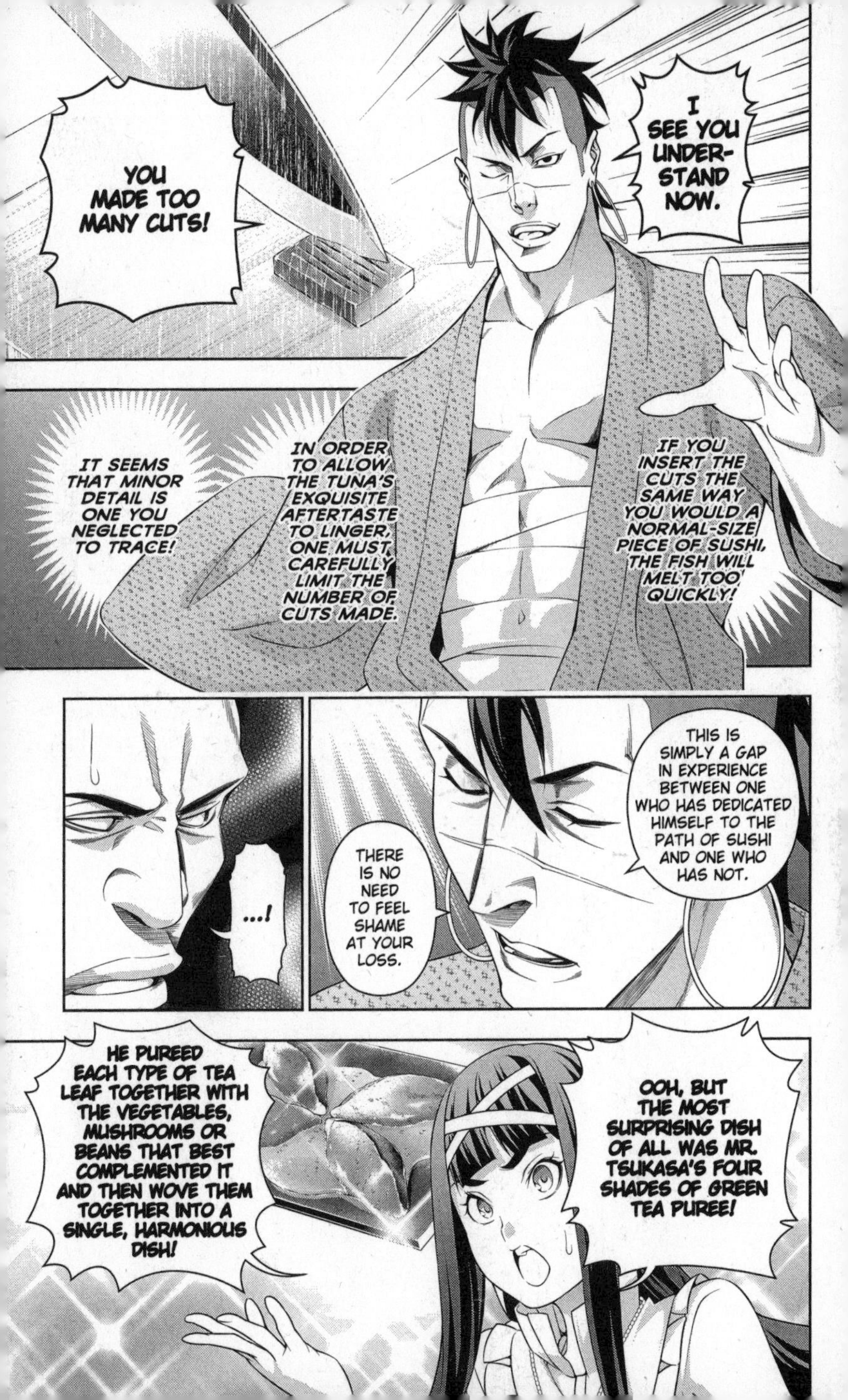

I SEE YOU UNDER-STAND NOW.
YOU MADE TOO MANY CUTS!
IF YOU INSERT THE CUTS THE SAME WAY YOU WOULD A NORMAL-SIZE PIECE OF SUSHI, THE FISH WILL MELT TOO QUICKLY!
IN ORDER TO ALLOW THE TUNA'S EXQUISITE AFTERTASTE TO LINGER, ONE MUST CAREFULLY LIMIT THE NUMBER OF CUTS MADE.
IT SEEMS THAT MINOR DETAIL IS ONE YOU NEGLECTED TO TRACE!
THIS IS SIMPLY A GAP IN EXPERIENCE BETWEEN ONE WHO HAS DEDICATED HIMSELF TO THE PATH OF SUSHI AND ONE WHO HAS NOT.
THERE IS NO NEED TO FEEL SHAME AT YOUR LOSS.
...!
OOH, BUT THE MOST SURPRISING DISH OF ALL WAS MR. TSUKASA'S FOUR SHADES OF GREEN TEA PUREE!
HE PUREED EACH TYPE OF TEA LEAF TOGETHER WITH THE VEGETABLES, MUSHROOMS OR BEANS THAT BEST COMPLEMENTED IT AND THEN WOVE THEM TOGETHER INTO A SINGLE, HARMONIOUS DISH!

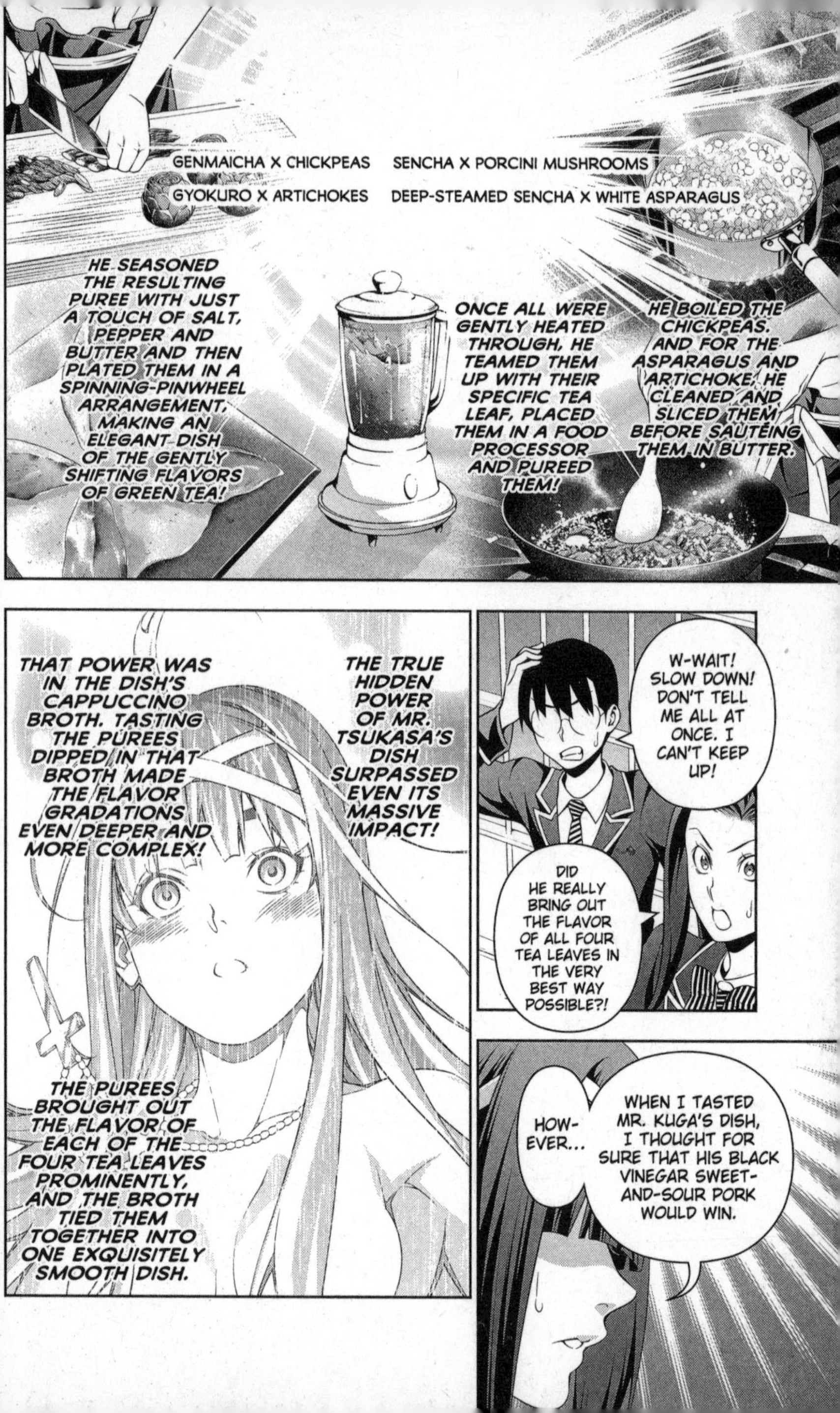
GENMAICHA X CHICKPEAS
SENCHA X PORCINI MUSHROOMS
GYOKURO X ARTICHOKES
DEEP-STEAMED SENCHA X WHITE ASPARAGUS
HE BOILED THE CHICKPEAS. AND FOR THE ASPARAGUS AND ARTICHOKE, HE CLEANED AND SLICED THEM BEFORE SAUTÉING THEM IN BUTTER.
ONCE ALL WERE GENTLY HEATED THROUGH, HE TEAMED THEM UP WITH THEIR SPECIFIC TEA LEAF, PLACED THEM IN A FOOD PROCESSOR AND PUREED THEM!
HE SEASONED THE RESULTING PUREE WITH JUST A TOUCH OF SALT, PEPPER AND BUTTER AND THEN PLATED THEM IN A SPINNING-PINWHEEL ARRANGEMENT, MAKING AN ELEGANT DISH OF THE GENTLY SHIFTING FLAVORS OF GREEN TEA!
W-WAIT! SLOW DOWN! DON'T TELL ME ALL AT ONCE. I CAN'T KEEP UP!
DID HE REALLY BRING OUT THE FLAVOR OF ALL FOUR TEA LEAVES IN THE VERY BEST WAY POSSIBLE?!
WHEN I TASTED MR. KUGA'S DISH, I THOUGHT FOR SURE THAT HIS BLACK VINEGAR SWEET-AND-SOUR PORK WOULD WIN.
HOW-EVER...
THE TRUE HIDDEN POWER OF MR. TSUKASA'S DISH SURPASSED EVEN ITS MASSIVE IMPACT!
THAT POWER WAS IN THE DISH'S CAPPUCCINO BROTH. TASTING THE PUREES DIPPED IN THAT BROTH MADE THE FLAVOR GRADATIONS EVEN DEEPER AND MORE COMPLEX!
THE PUREES BROUGHT OUT THE FLAVOR OF EACH OF THE FOUR TEA LEAVES PROMINENTLY, AND THE BROTH TIED THEM TOGETHER INTO ONE EXQUISITELY SMOOTH DISH.

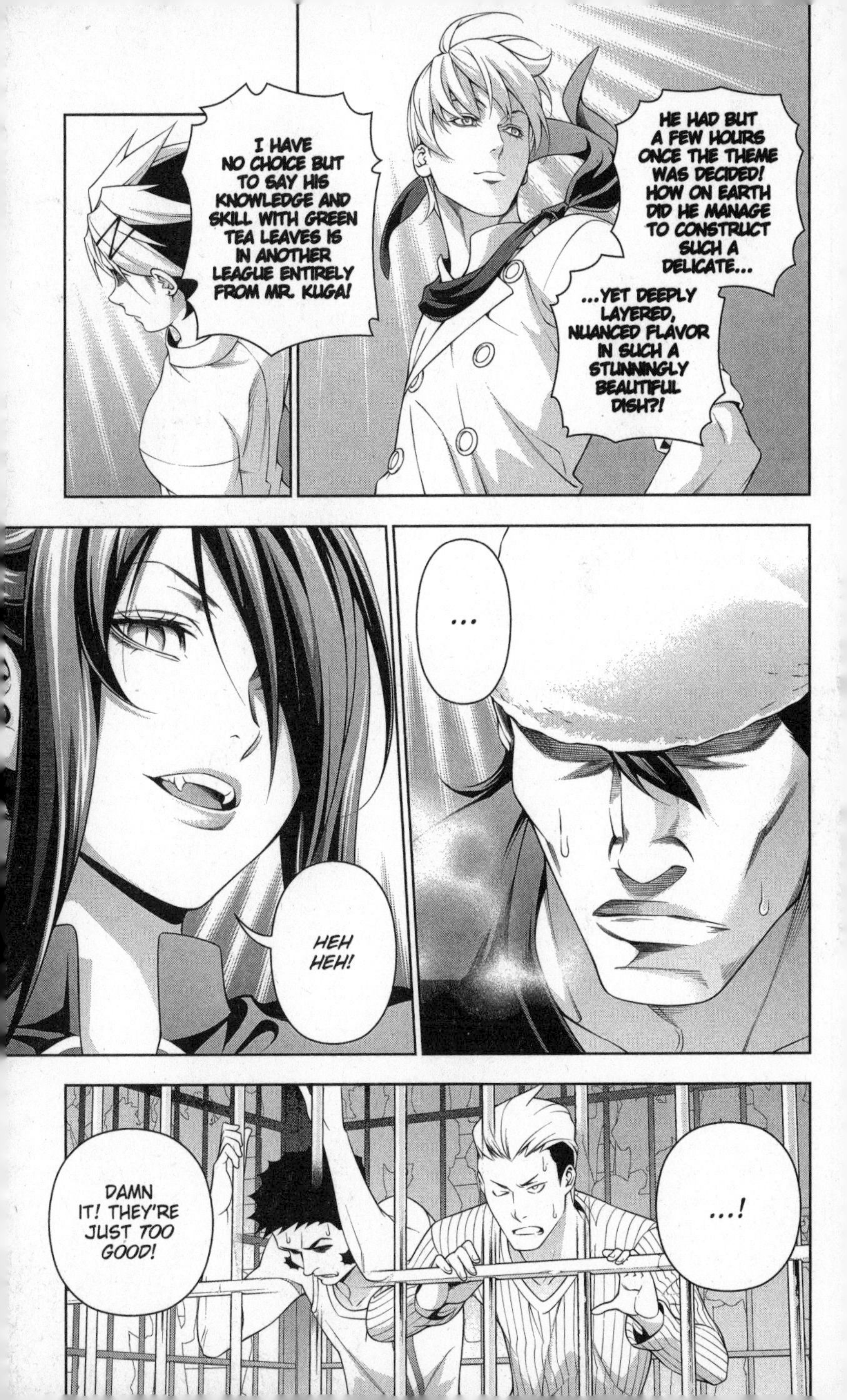
HE HAD BUT A FEW HOURS ONCE THE THEME WAS DECIDED! HOW ON EARTH DID HE MANAGE TO CONSTRUCT SUCH A DELICATE...
...YET DEEPLY LAYERED, NUANCED FLAVOR IN SUCH A STUNNINGLY BEAUTIFUL DISH?!
I HAVE NO CHOICE BUT TO SAY HIS KNOWLEDGE AND SKILL WITH GREEN TEA LEAVES IS IN ANOTHER LEAGUE ENTIRELY FROM MR. KUGA!
...
HEH HEH!
...!
DAMN IT! THEY'RE JUST TOO GOOD!

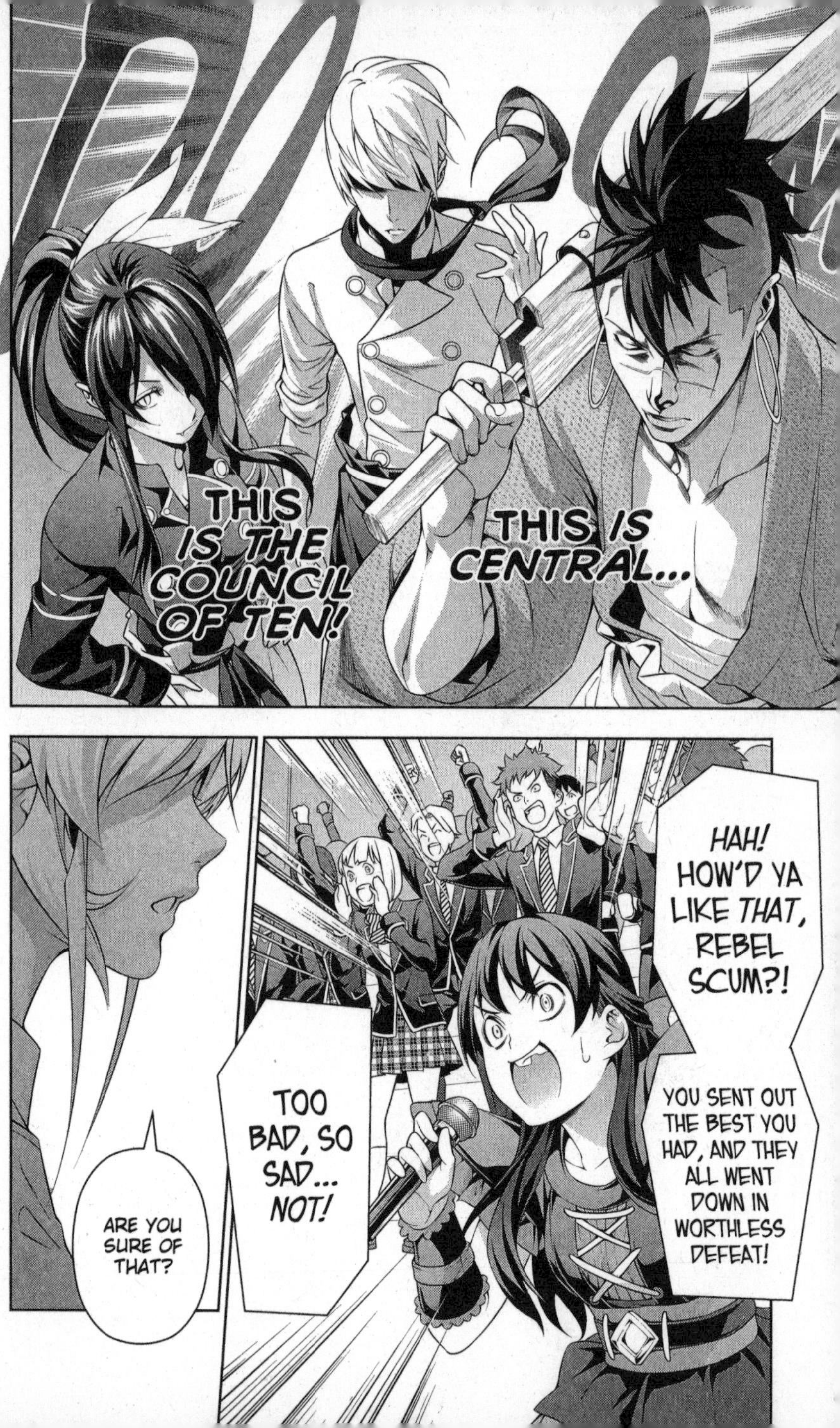
THIS IS CENTRAL...
THIS IS THE COUNCIL OF TEN!
HAH! HOW'D YA LIKE *THAT*, REBEL SCUM?!
YOU SENT OUT THE BEST YOU HAD, AND THEY ALL WENT DOWN IN WORTHLESS DEFEAT!
TOO BAD, SO SAD... *NOT*!
ARE YOU SURE OF THAT?

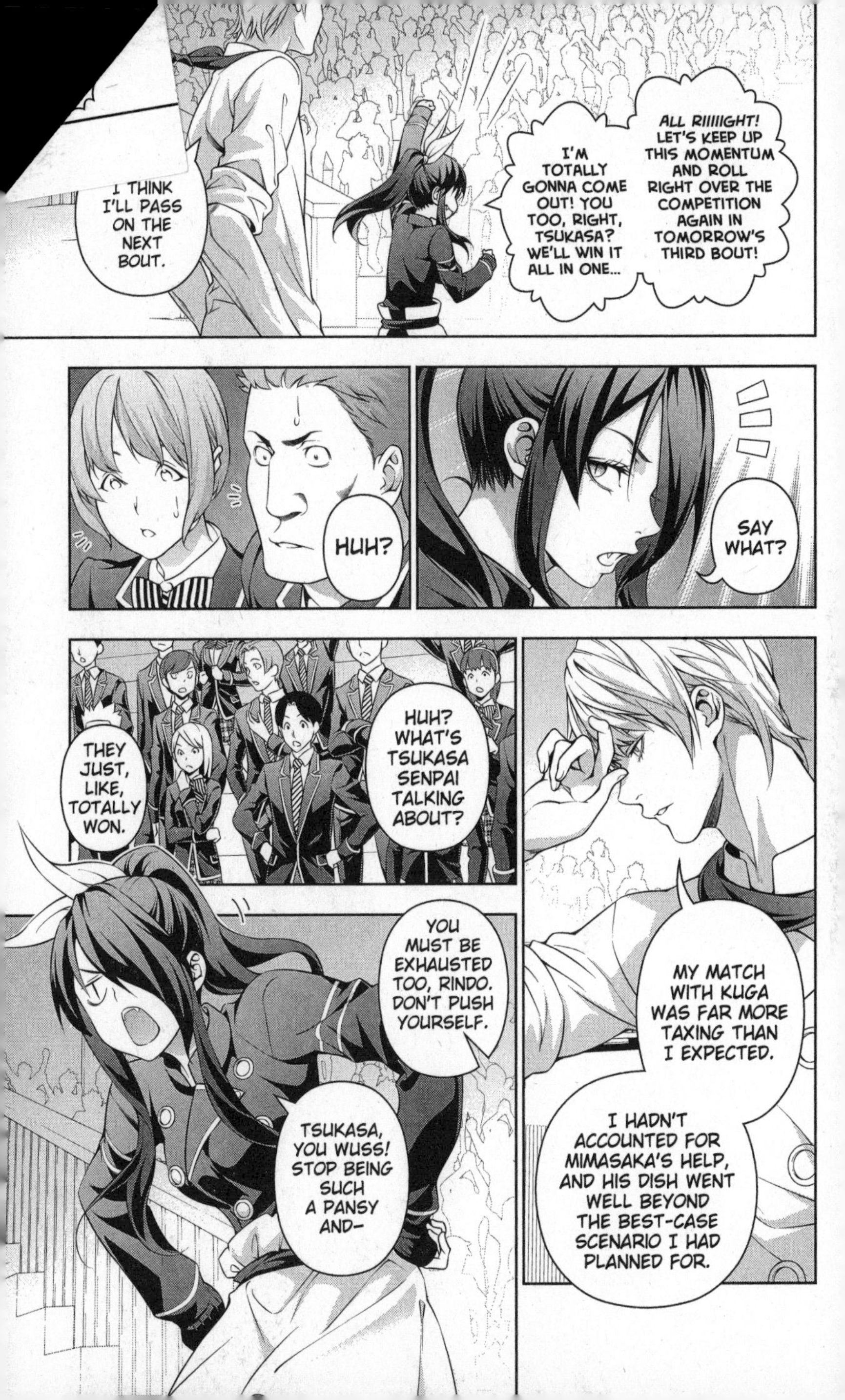
ALL RIIIIGHT! LET'S KEEP UP THIS MOMENTUM AND ROLL RIGHT OVER THE COMPETITION AGAIN IN TOMORROW'S THIRD BOUT!
I'M TOTALLY GONNA COME OUT! YOU TOO, RIGHT, TSUKASA? WE'LL WIN IT ALL IN ONE...
I THINK I'LL PASS ON THE NEXT BOUT.
SAY WHAT?
HUH?
MY MATCH WITH KUGA WAS FAR MORE TAXING THAN I EXPECTED.
I HADN'T ACCOUNTED FOR MIMASAKA'S HELP, AND HIS DISH WENT WELL BEYOND THE BEST-CASE SCENARIO I HAD PLANNED FOR.
HUH? WHAT'S TSUKASA SENPAI TALKING ABOUT?
THEY JUST, LIKE, TOTALLY WON.
YOU MUST BE EXHAUSTED TOO, RINDO. DON'T PUSH YOURSELF.
TSUKASA, YOU WUSS! STOP BEING SUCH A PANSY AND—

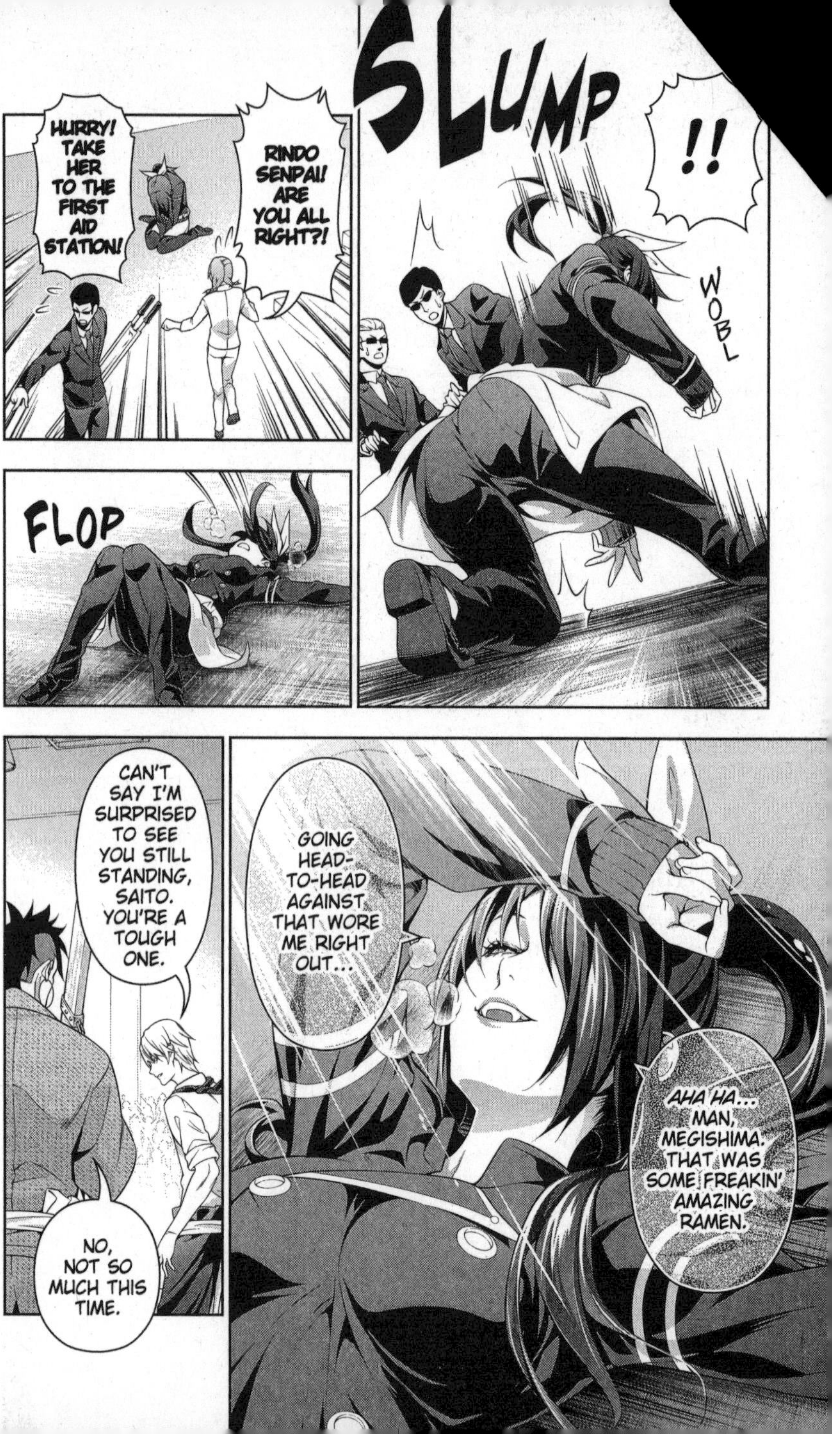
SLUMP
!!
WOBL
RINDO SENPAI! ARE YOU ALL RIGHT?!
HURRY! TAKE HER TO THE FIRST AID STATION!
FLOP
AHA HA... MAN, MEGISHIMA. THAT WAS SOME FREAKIN' AMAZING RAMEN.
GOING HEAD-TO-HEAD AGAINST THAT WORE ME RIGHT OUT...
CAN'T SAY I'M SURPRISED TO SEE YOU STILL STANDING, SAITO. YOU'RE A TOUGH ONE.
NO, NOT SO MUCH THIS TIME.

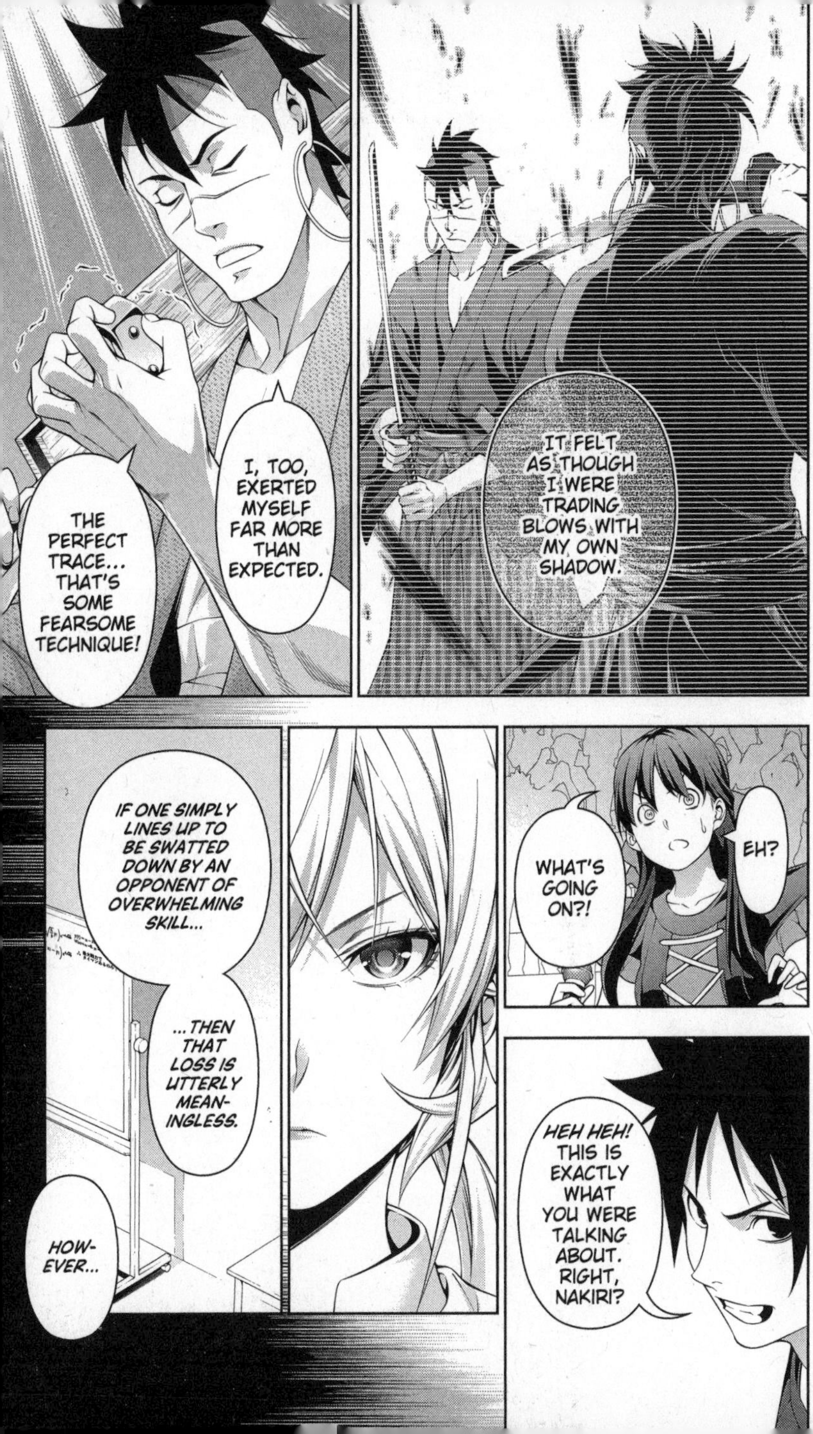
IT FELT AS THOUGH I WERE TRADING BLOWS WITH MY OWN SHADOW.
I, TOO, EXERTED MYSELF FAR MORE THAN EXPECTED.
THE PERFECT TRACE... THAT'S SOME FEARSOME TECHNIQUE!
EH?
WHAT'S GOING ON?!
HEH HEH! THIS IS EXACTLY WHAT YOU WERE TALKING ABOUT. RIGHT, NAKIRI?
IF ONE SIMPLY LINES UP TO BE SWATTED DOWN BY AN OPPONENT OF OVERWHELMING SKILL...
...THEN THAT LOSS IS UTTERLY MEANINGLESS.
HOWEVER...

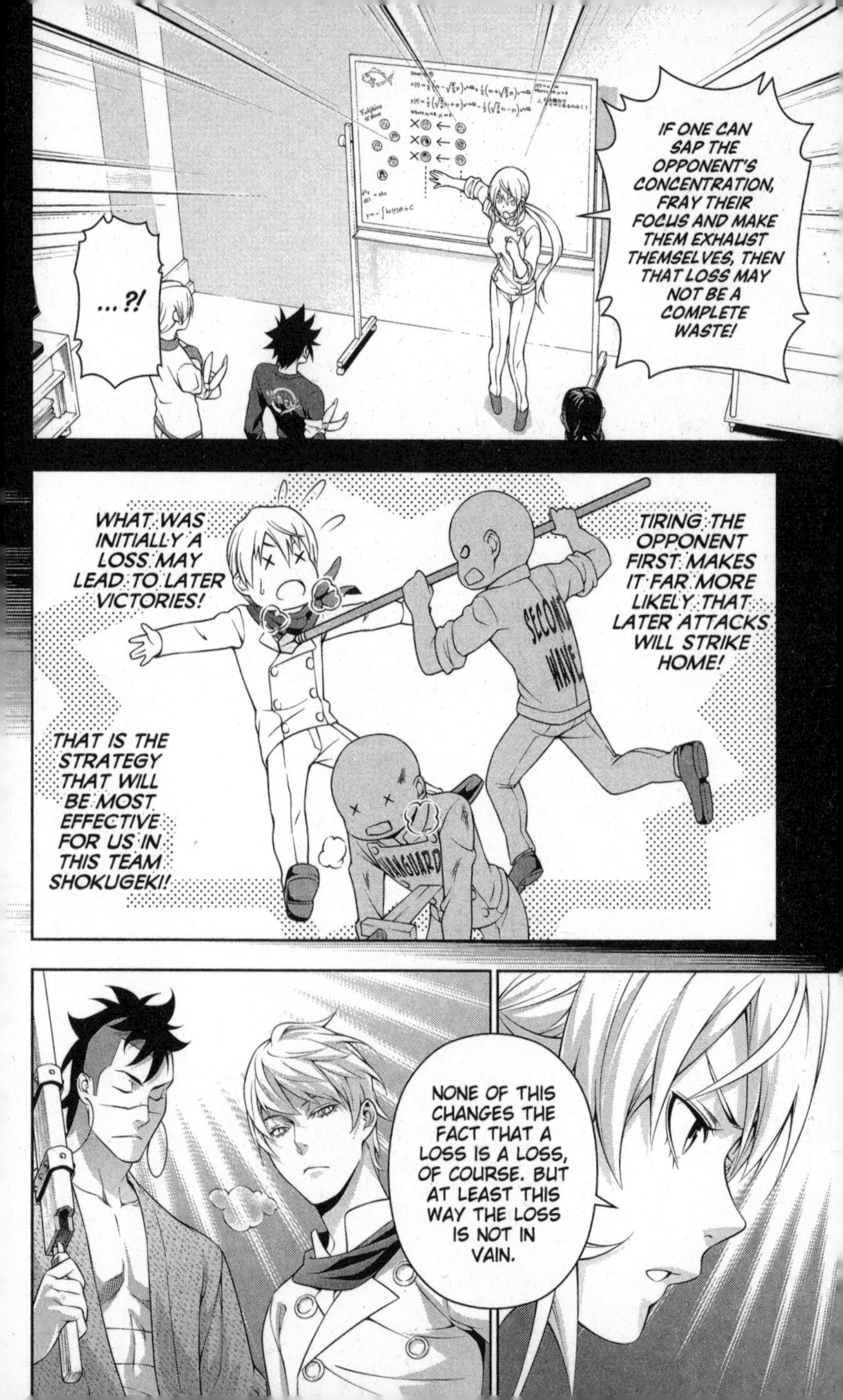
IF ONE CAN SAP THE OPPONENT'S CONCENTRATION, FRAY THEIR FOCUS AND MAKE THEM EXHAUST THEMSELVES, THEN THAT LOSS MAY NOT BE A COMPLETE WASTE!
...?!
TIRING THE OPPONENT FIRST MAKES IT FAR MORE LIKELY THAT LATER ATTACKS WILL STRIKE HOME!
WHAT WAS INITIALLY A LOSS MAY LEAD TO LATER VICTORIES!
THAT IS THE STRATEGY THAT WILL BE MOST EFFECTIVE FOR US IN THIS TEAM SHOKUGEKI!
NONE OF THIS CHANGES THE FACT THAT A LOSS IS A LOSS, OF COURSE. BUT AT LEAST THIS WAY THE LOSS IS NOT IN VAIN.

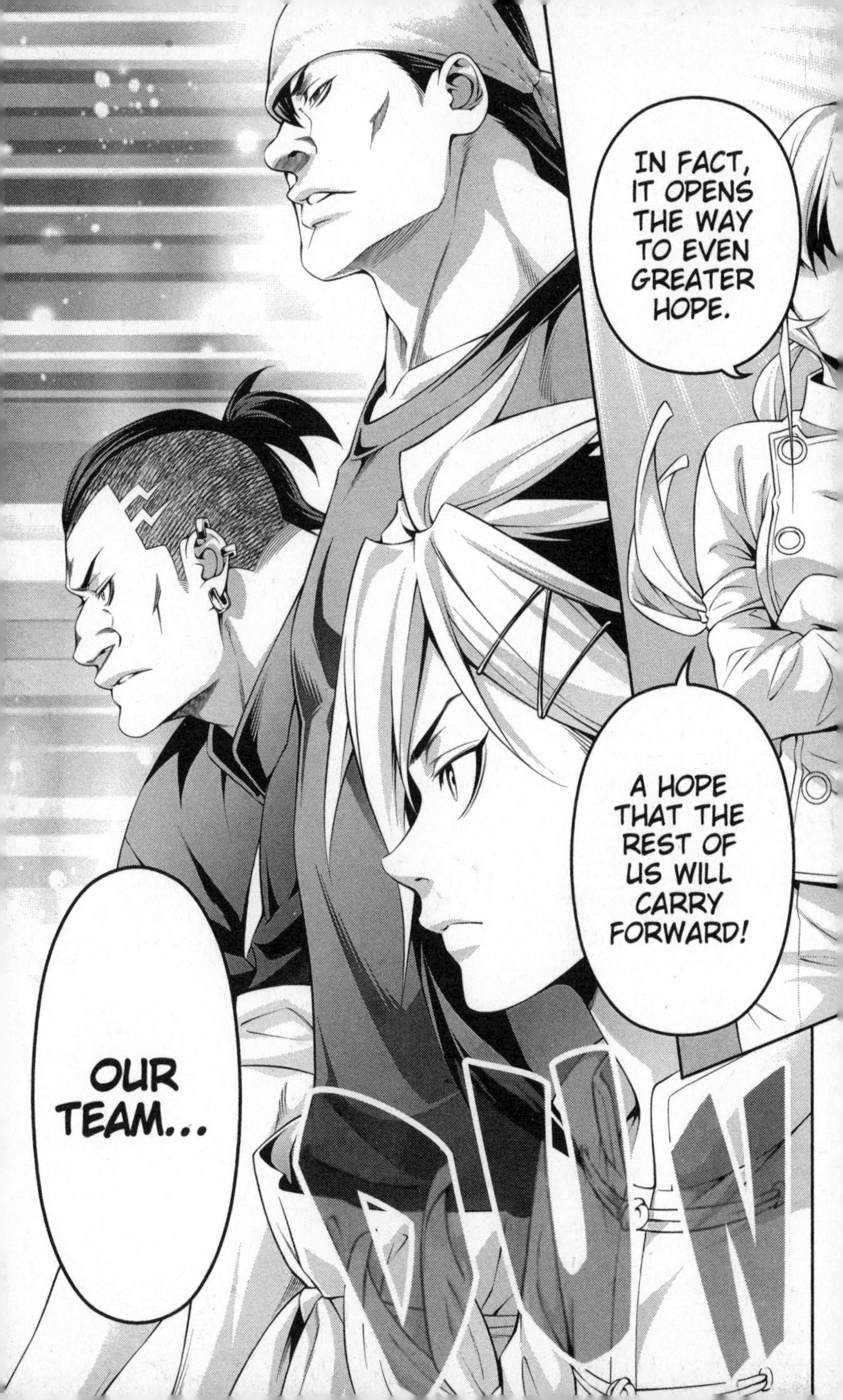
IN FACT, IT OPENS THE WAY TO EVEN GREATER HOPE.
A HOPE THAT THE REST OF US WILL CARRY FORWARD!
OUR TEAM...

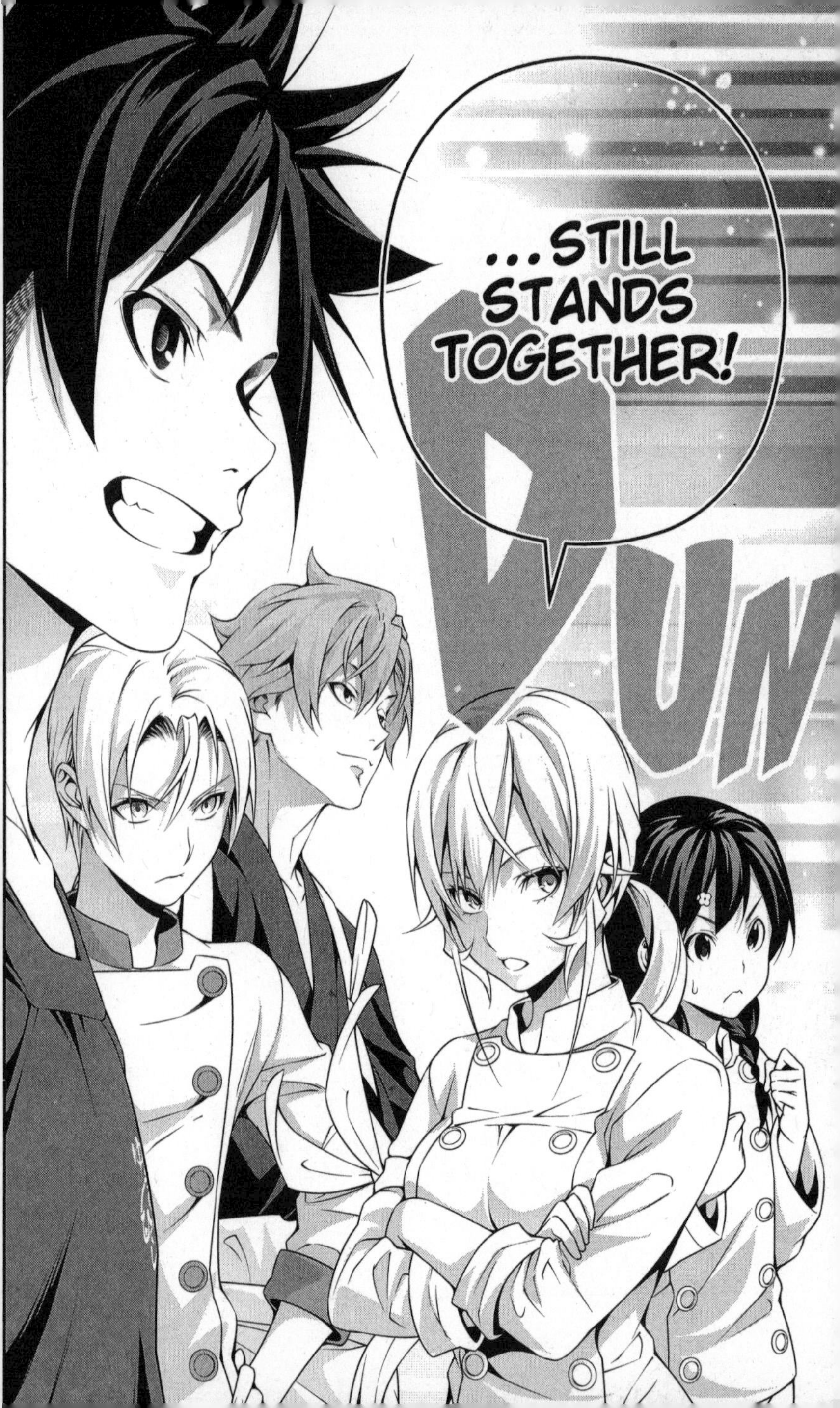
...STILL STANDS TOGETHER!
DUN

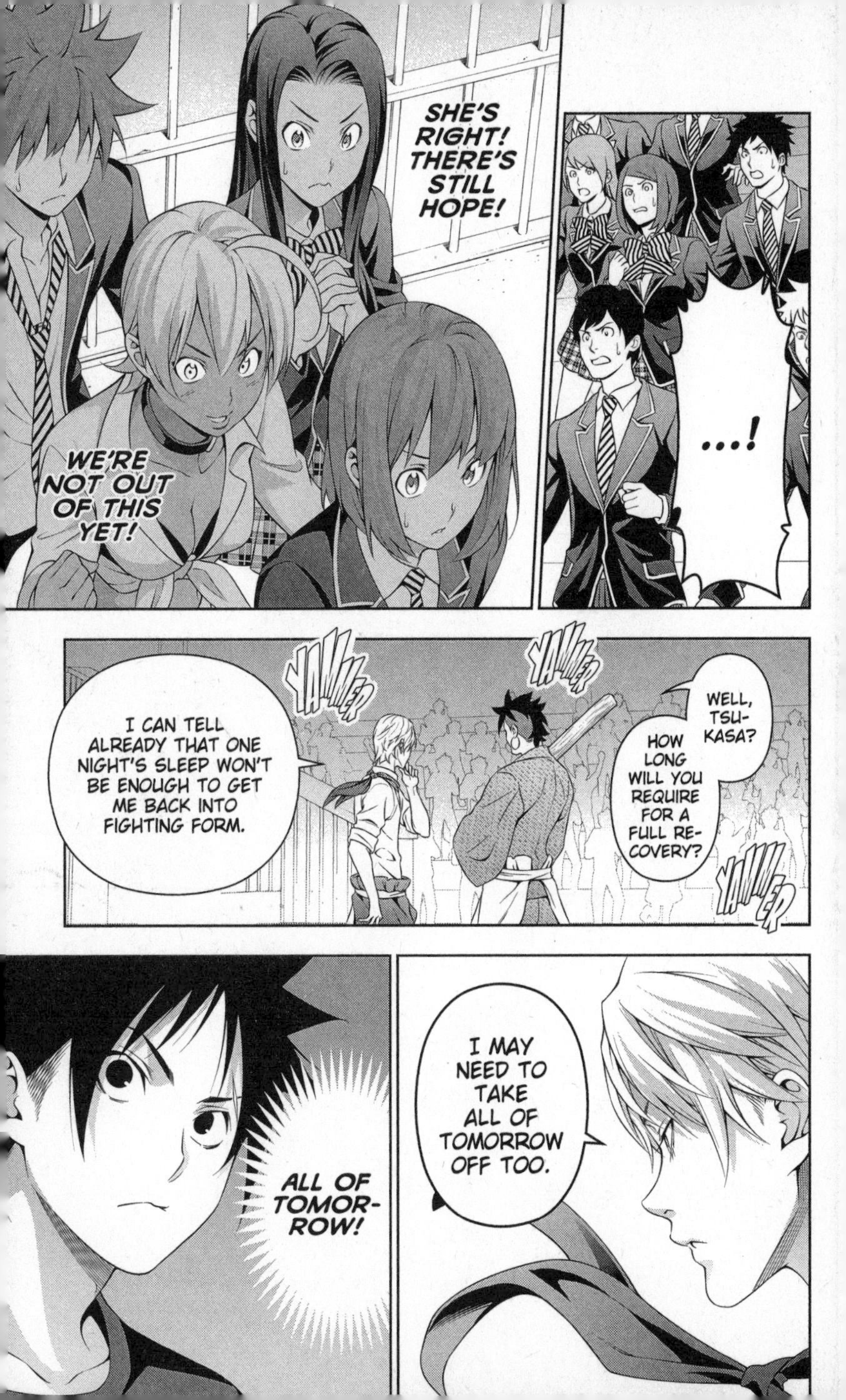
...!
SHE'S RIGHT! THERE'S STILL HOPE!
WE'RE NOT OUT OF THIS YET!
YAMMER
YAMMER
WELL, TSUKASA?
HOW LONG WILL YOU REQUIRE FOR A FULL RECOVERY?
YAMMER
I CAN TELL ALREADY THAT ONE NIGHT'S SLEEP WON'T BE ENOUGH TO GET ME BACK INTO FIGHTING FORM.
I MAY NEED TO TAKE ALL OF TOMORROW OFF TOO.
ALL OF TOMORROW!

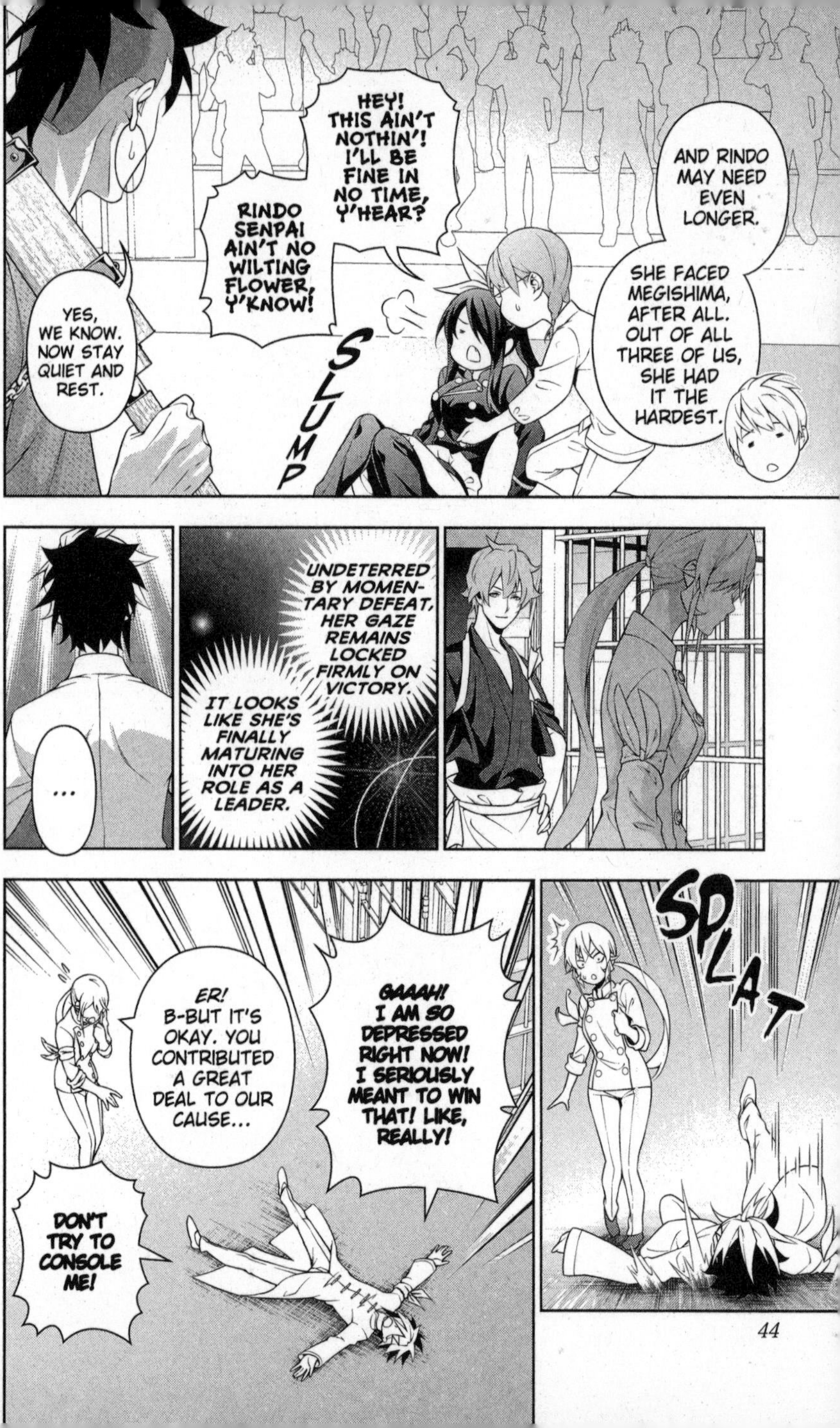
AND RINDO MAY NEED EVEN LONGER.
SHE FACED MEGISHIMA, AFTER ALL. OUT OF ALL THREE OF US, SHE HAD IT THE HARDEST.
HEY! THIS AIN'T NOTHIN'! I'LL BE FINE IN NO TIME, Y'HEAR?
RINDO SENPAI AIN'T NO WILTING FLOWER, Y'KNOW!
SLUMP
YES, WE KNOW. NOW STAY QUIET AND REST.
UNDETERRED BY MOMENTARY DEFEAT, HER GAZE REMAINS LOCKED FIRMLY ON VICTORY.
IT LOOKS LIKE SHE'S FINALLY MATURING INTO HER ROLE AS A LEADER.
...
SPLAT
GAAAH! I AM SO DEPRESSED RIGHT NOW! I SERIOUSLY MEANT TO WIN THAT! LIKE, REALLY!
ER! B-BUT IT'S OKAY. YOU CONTRIBUTED A GREAT DEAL TO OUR CAUSE...
DON'T TRY TO CONSOLE ME!

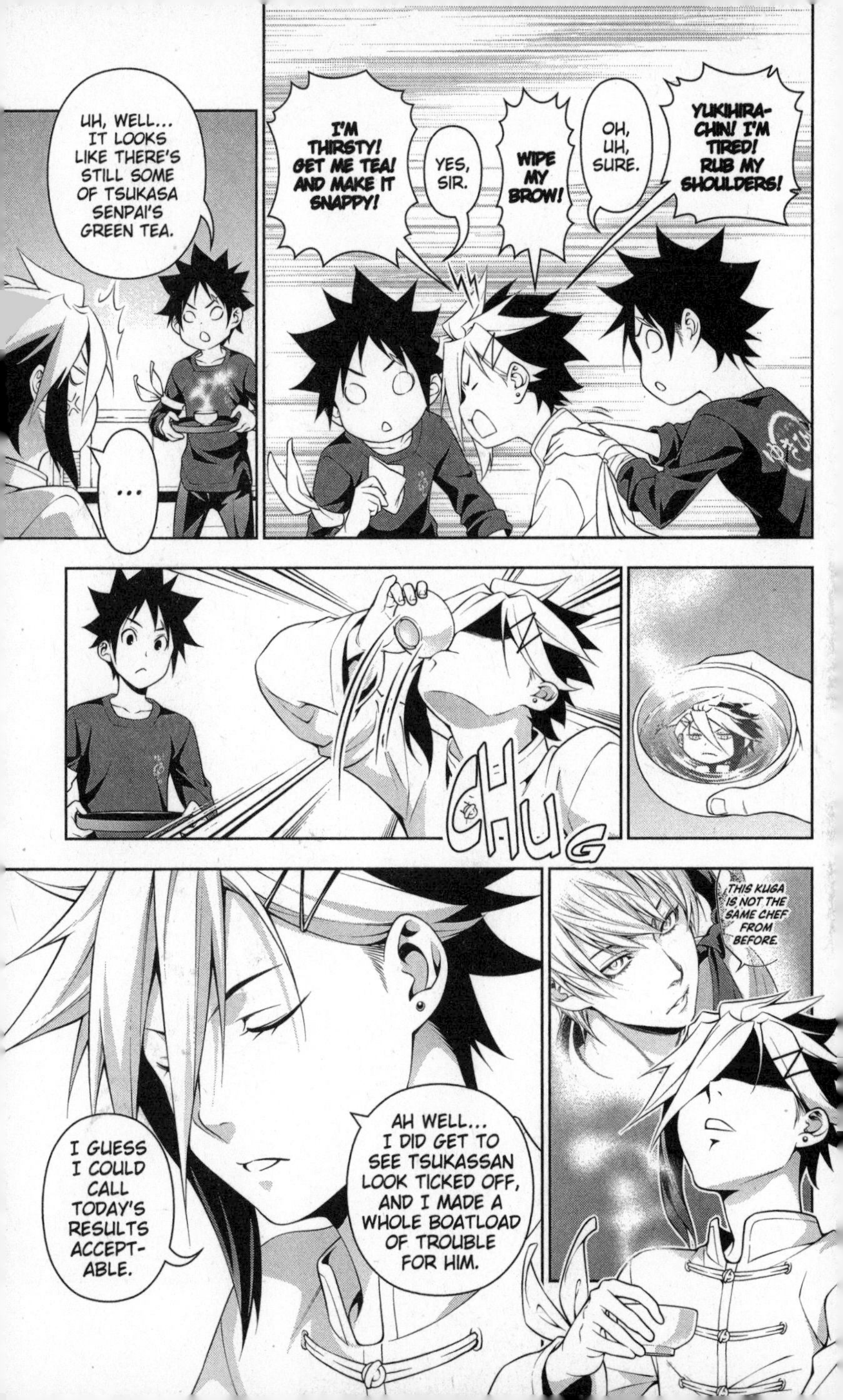
YUKIHIRA-CHIN! I'M TIRED! RUB MY SHOULDERS!
OH, UH, SURE.
WIPE MY BROW!
YES, SIR.
I'M THIRSTY! GET ME TEA! AND MAKE IT SNAPPY!
UH, WELL... IT LOOKS LIKE THERE'S STILL SOME OF TSUKASA SENPAI'S GREEN TEA.
...
CHUG
THIS KUGA IS NOT THE SAME CHEF FROM BEFORE.
AH WELL... I DID GET TO SEE TSUKASSAN LOOK TICKED OFF, AND I MADE A WHOLE BOATLOAD OF TROUBLE FOR HIM.
I GUESS I COULD CALL TODAY'S RESULTS ACCEPT-ABLE.

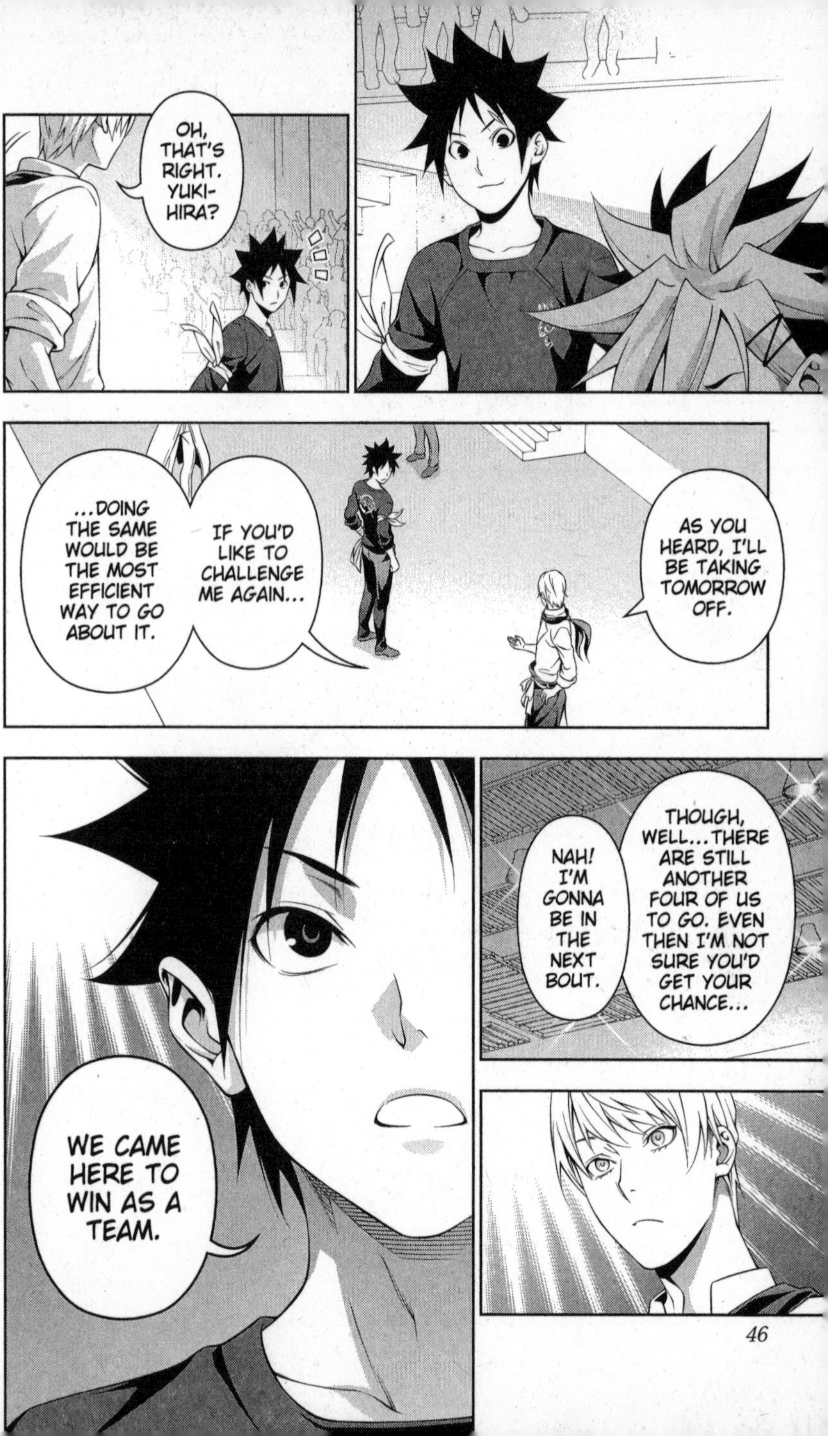
OH, THAT'S RIGHT. YUKI-HIRA?
AS YOU HEARD, I'LL BE TAKING TOMORROW OFF.
IF YOU'D LIKE TO CHALLENGE ME AGAIN...
...DOING THE SAME WOULD BE THE MOST EFFICIENT WAY TO GO ABOUT IT.
THOUGH, WELL... THERE ARE STILL ANOTHER FOUR OF US TO GO. EVEN THEN I'M NOT SURE YOU'D GET YOUR CHANCE...
NAH! I'M GONNA BE IN THE NEXT BOUT.
WE CAME HERE TO WIN AS A TEAM.

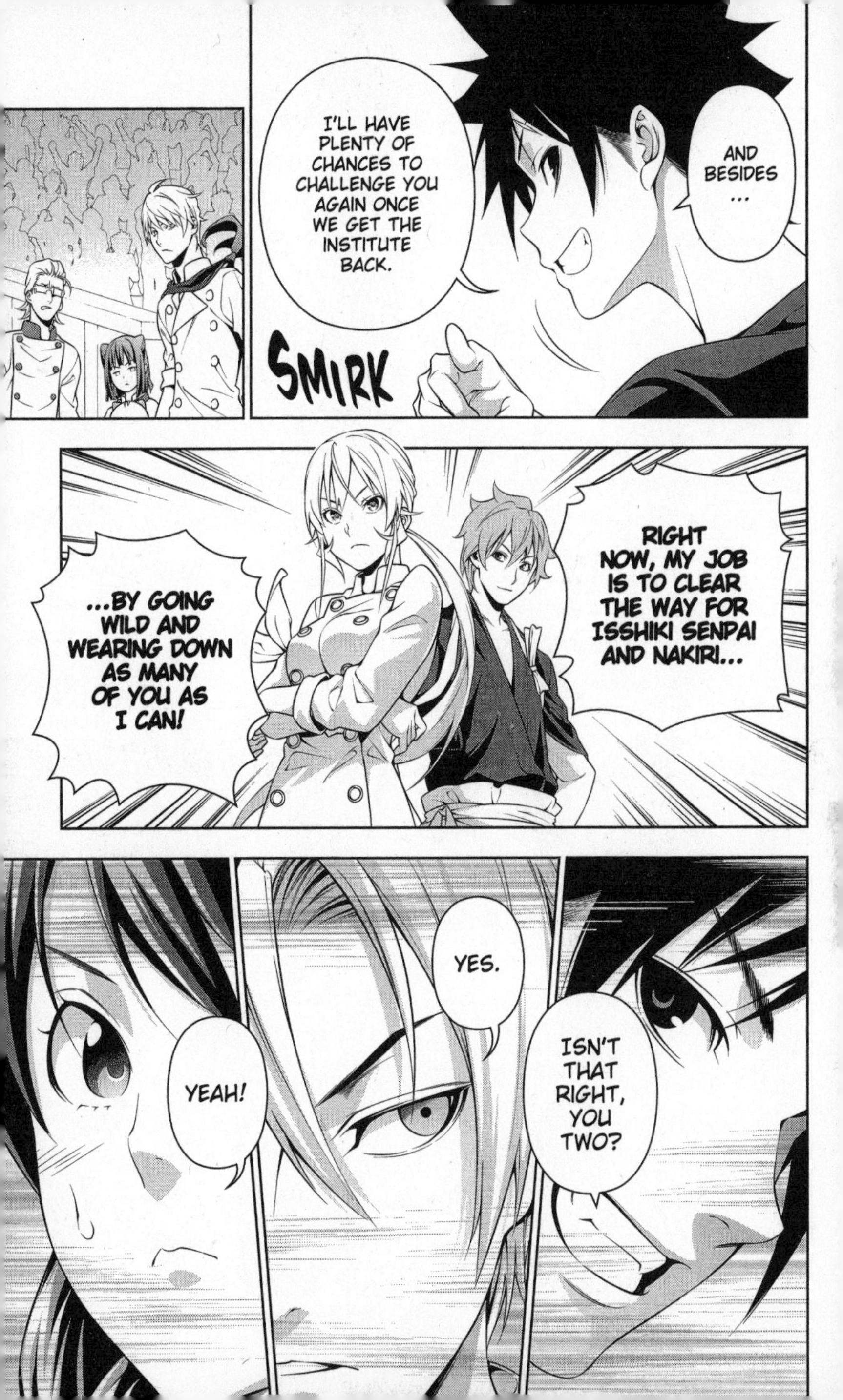
AND BESIDES...
I'LL HAVE PLENTY OF CHANCES TO CHALLENGE YOU AGAIN ONCE WE GET THE INSTITUTE BACK.
SMIRK
RIGHT NOW, MY JOB IS TO CLEAR THE WAY FOR ISSHIKI SENPAI AND NAKIRI...
...BY GOING WILD AND WEARING DOWN AS MANY OF YOU AS I CAN!
ISN'T THAT RIGHT, YOU TWO?
YES.
YEAH!

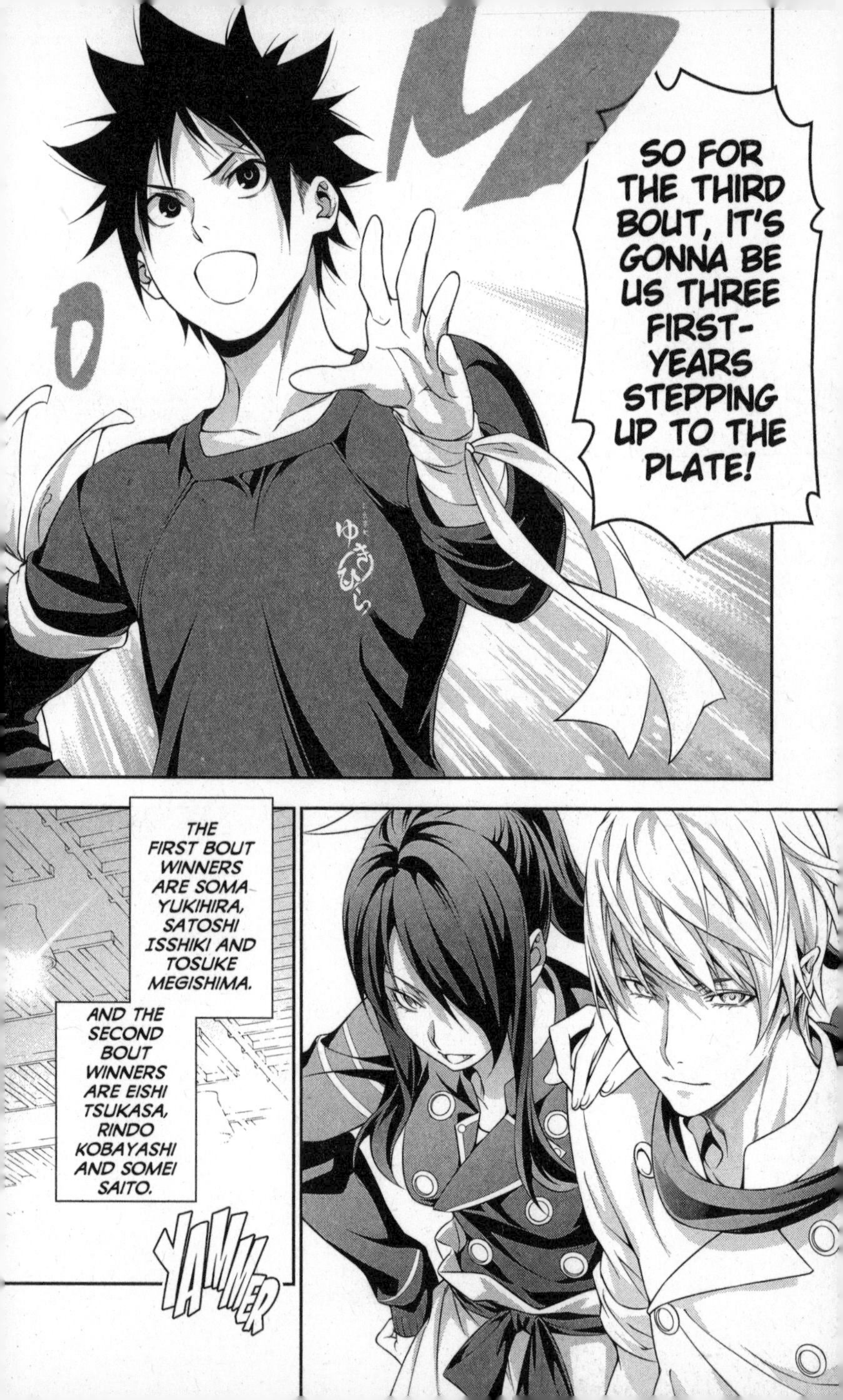
SO FOR THE THIRD BOUT, IT'S GONNA BE US THREE FIRST-YEARS STEPPING UP TO THE PLATE!
ゆきひら
THE FIRST BOUT WINNERS ARE SOMA YUKIHIRA, SATOSHI ISSHIKI AND TOSUKE MEGISHIMA.
AND THE SECOND BOUT WINNERS ARE EISHI TSUKASA, RINDO KOBAYASHI AND SOMEI SAITO.
YAMMER

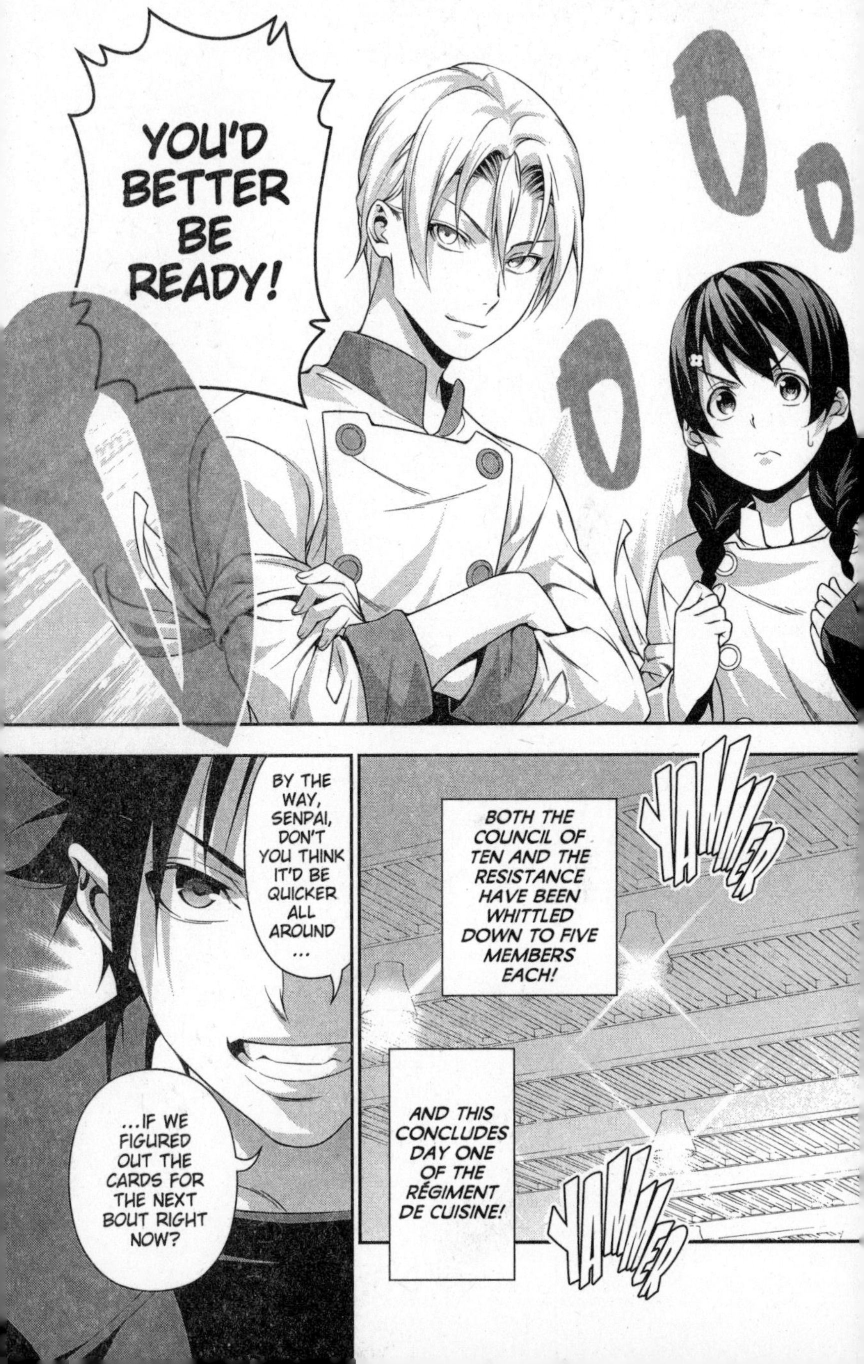

YOU'D BETTER BE READY!
BOTH THE COUNCIL OF TEN AND THE RESISTANCE HAVE BEEN WHITTLED DOWN TO FIVE MEMBERS EACH!
YAMMER
AND THIS CONCLUDES DAY ONE OF THE RÉGIMENT DE CUISINE!
YAMMER
BY THE WAY, SENPAI, DON'T YOU THINK IT'D BE QUICKER ALL AROUND...
...IF WE FIGURED OUT THE CARDS FOR THE NEXT BOUT RIGHT NOW?

ARTIST: YUTO TSUKUDA RECIPE BY: YUKI MORISAKI

VOLUME 27 SPECIAL SUPPLEMENT!

PRACTICAL RECIPE #3

SIMPLIFIED HOME VERSION

SAITO'S MINI SUSHI (2 TYPES)

PLASTIC WRAP IS GREAT FOR GIVING THEM THE PROPER SHAPE.
wrap

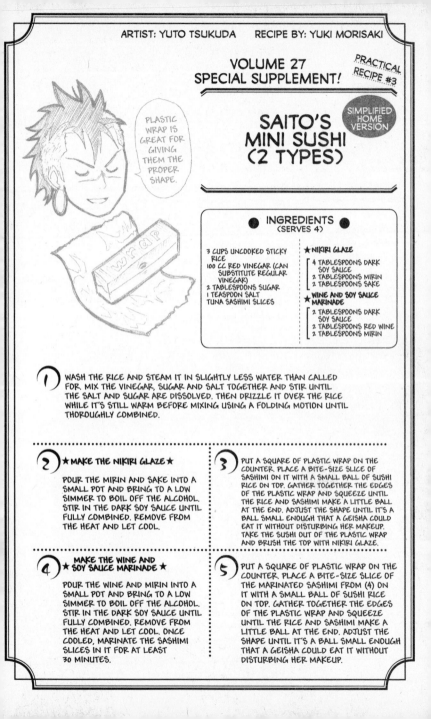

INGREDIENTS
(SERVES 4)

3 CUPS UNCOOKED STICKY RICE
100 CC RED VINEGAR (CAN SUBSTITUTE REGULAR VINEGAR)
2 TABLESPOONS SUGAR
1 TEASPOON SALT
TUNA SASHIMI SLICES

★NIKIRI GLAZE
- 4 TABLESPOONS DARK SOY SAUCE
- 2 TABLESPOONS MIRIN
- 2 TABLESPOONS SAKE

★WINE AND SOY SAUCE MARINADE
- 2 TABLESPOONS DARK SOY SAUCE
- 2 TABLESPOONS RED WINE
- 2 TABLESPOONS MIRIN

1. WASH THE RICE AND STEAM IT IN SLIGHTLY LESS WATER THAN CALLED FOR. MIX THE VINEGAR, SUGAR AND SALT TOGETHER AND STIR UNTIL THE SALT AND SUGAR ARE DISSOLVED. THEN DRIZZLE IT OVER THE RICE WHILE IT'S STILL WARM BEFORE MIXING USING A FOLDING MOTION UNTIL THOROUGHLY COMBINED.

2. ★MAKE THE NIKIRI GLAZE★

POUR THE MIRIN AND SAKE INTO A SMALL POT AND BRING TO A LOW SIMMER TO BOIL OFF THE ALCOHOL. STIR IN THE DARK SOY SAUCE UNTIL FULLY COMBINED. REMOVE FROM THE HEAT AND LET COOL.

3. PUT A SQUARE OF PLASTIC WRAP ON THE COUNTER. PLACE A BITE-SIZE SLICE OF SASHIMI ON IT WITH A SMALL BALL OF SUSHI RICE ON TOP. GATHER TOGETHER THE EDGES OF THE PLASTIC WRAP AND SQUEEZE UNTIL THE RICE AND SASHIMI MAKE A LITTLE BALL AT THE END. ADJUST THE SHAPE UNTIL IT'S A BALL SMALL ENOUGH THAT A GEISHA COULD EAT IT WITHOUT DISTURBING HER MAKEUP. TAKE THE SUSHI OUT OF THE PLASTIC WRAP AND BRUSH THE TOP WITH NIKIRI GLAZE.

4. ★MAKE THE WINE AND SOY SAUCE MARINADE★

POUR THE WINE AND MIRIN INTO A SMALL POT AND BRING TO A LOW SIMMER TO BOIL OFF THE ALCOHOL. STIR IN THE DARK SOY SAUCE UNTIL FULLY COMBINED. REMOVE FROM THE HEAT AND LET COOL. ONCE COOLED, MARINATE THE SASHIMI SLICES IN IT FOR AT LEAST 30 MINUTES.

5. PUT A SQUARE OF PLASTIC WRAP ON THE COUNTER. PLACE A BITE-SIZE SLICE OF THE MARINATED SASHIMI FROM (4) ON IT WITH A SMALL BALL OF SUSHI RICE ON TOP. GATHER TOGETHER THE EDGES OF THE PLASTIC WRAP AND SQUEEZE UNTIL THE RICE AND SASHIMI MAKE A LITTLE BALL AT THE END. ADJUST THE SHAPE UNTIL IT'S A BALL SMALL ENOUGH THAT A GEISHA COULD EAT IT WITHOUT DISTURBING HER MAKEUP.

229 THE THIRD BOUT

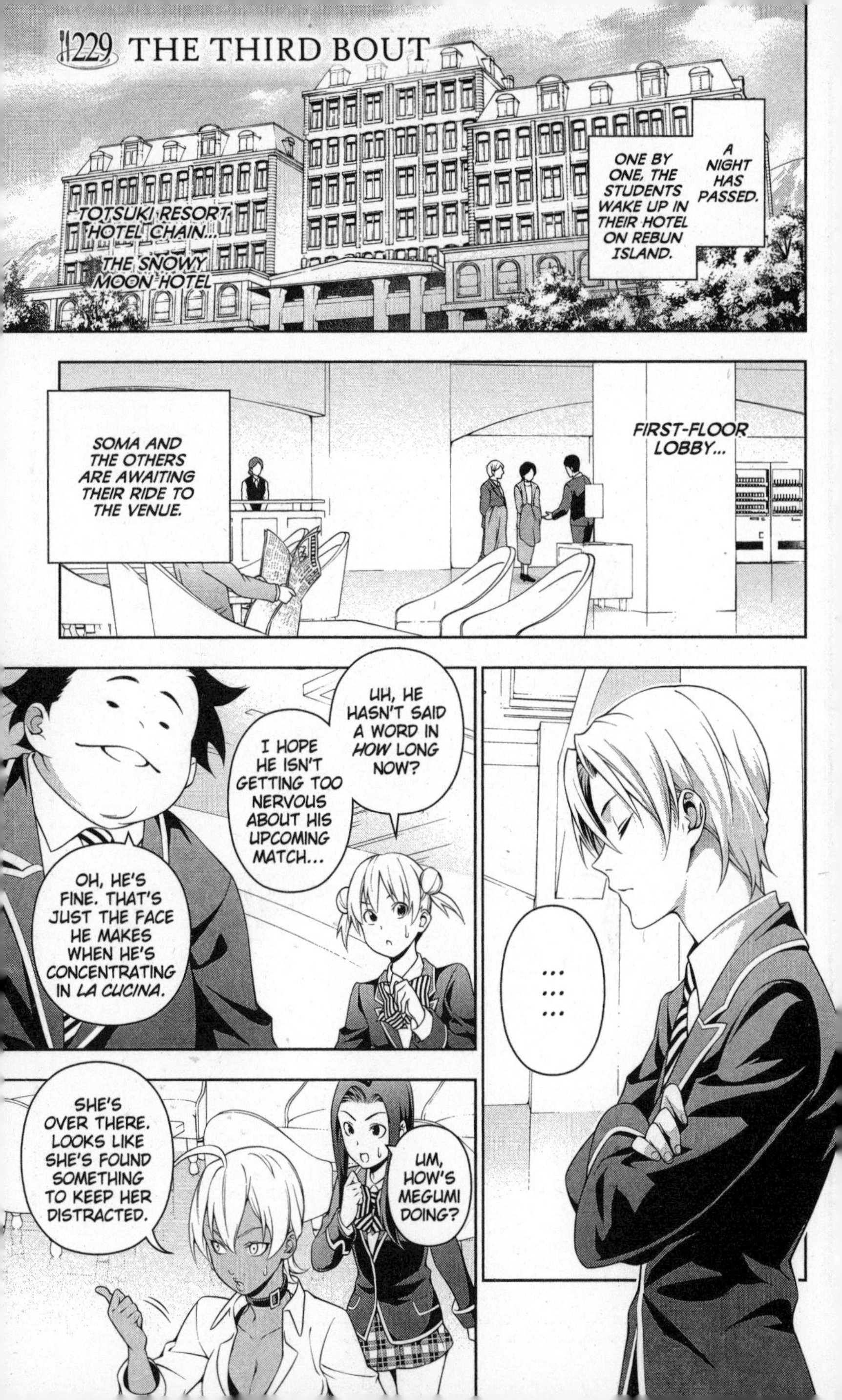
A NIGHT HAS PASSED.
ONE BY ONE, THE STUDENTS WAKE UP IN THEIR HOTEL ON REBUN ISLAND.
TOTSUKI RESORT HOTEL CHAIN...
THE SNOWY MOON HOTEL
FIRST-FLOOR LOBBY...
SOMA AND THE OTHERS ARE AWAITING THEIR RIDE TO THE VENUE.
...
...
...
UH, HE HASN'T SAID A WORD IN *HOW* LONG NOW?
I HOPE HE ISN'T GETTING TOO NERVOUS ABOUT HIS UPCOMING MATCH...
OH, HE'S FINE. THAT'S JUST THE FACE HE MAKES WHEN HE'S CONCENTRATING IN *LA CUCINA*.
UM, HOW'S MEGUMI DOING?
SHE'S OVER THERE. LOOKS LIKE SHE'S FOUND SOMETHING TO KEEP HER DISTRACTED.

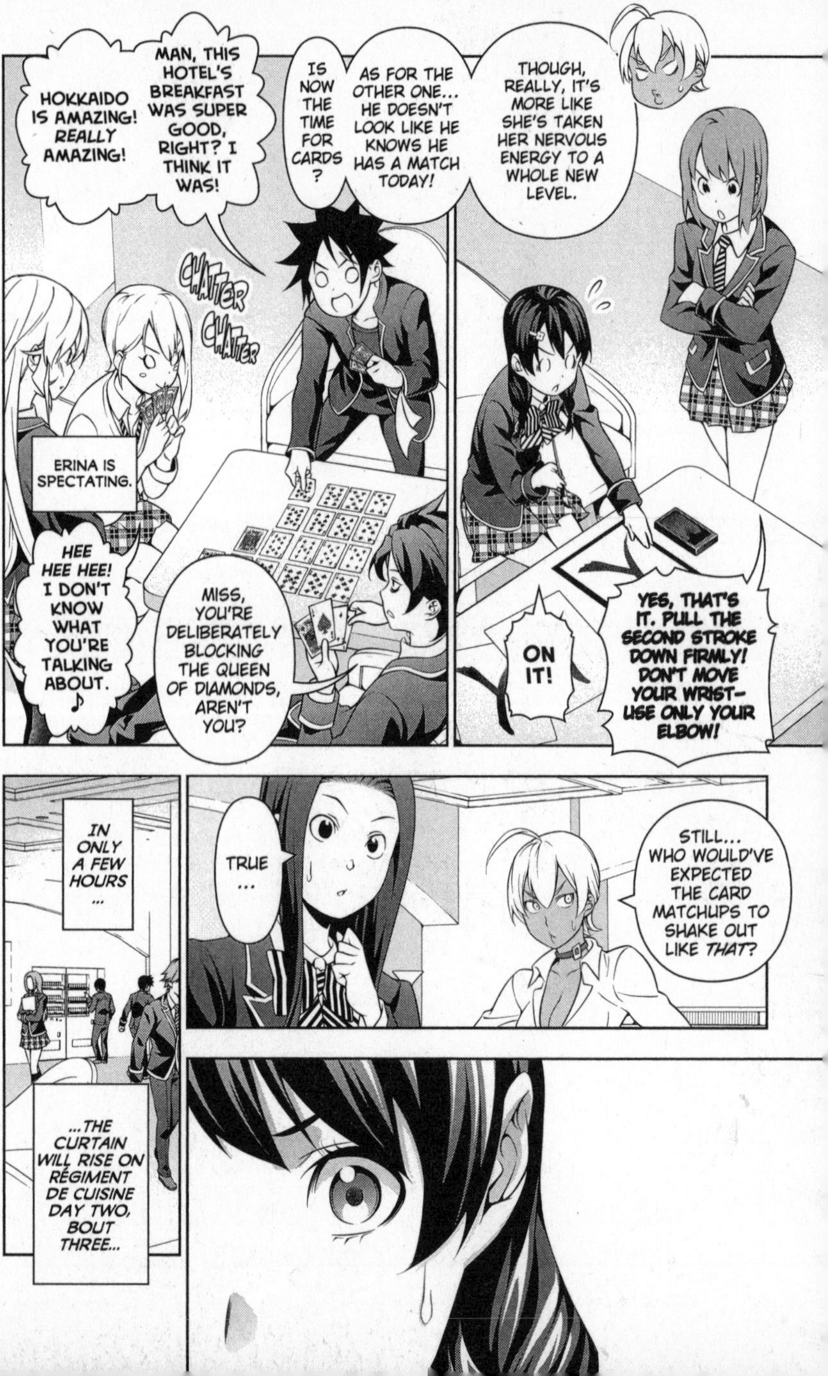
THOUGH, REALLY, IT'S MORE LIKE SHE'S TAKEN HER NERVOUS ENERGY TO A WHOLE NEW LEVEL.
YES, THAT'S IT. PULL THE SECOND STROKE DOWN FIRMLY! DON'T MOVE YOUR WRIST–USE ONLY YOUR ELBOW!
ON IT!
AS FOR THE OTHER ONE... HE DOESN'T LOOK LIKE HE KNOWS HE HAS A MATCH TODAY!
IS NOW THE TIME FOR CARDS?
MAN, THIS HOTEL'S BREAKFAST WAS SUPER GOOD, RIGHT? I THINK IT WAS!
HOKKAIDO IS AMAZING! *REALLY* AMAZING!
CHATTER CHATTER
ERINA IS SPECTATING.
MISS, YOU'RE DELIBERATELY BLOCKING THE QUEEN OF DIAMONDS, AREN'T YOU?
HEE HEE HEE! I DON'T KNOW WHAT YOU'RE TALKING ABOUT. ♪
STILL... WHO WOULD'VE EXPECTED THE CARD MATCHUPS TO SHAKE OUT LIKE *THAT*?
TRUE...
IN ONLY A FEW HOURS...
...THE CURTAIN WILL RISE ON RÉGIMENT DE CUISINE DAY TWO, BOUT THREE...

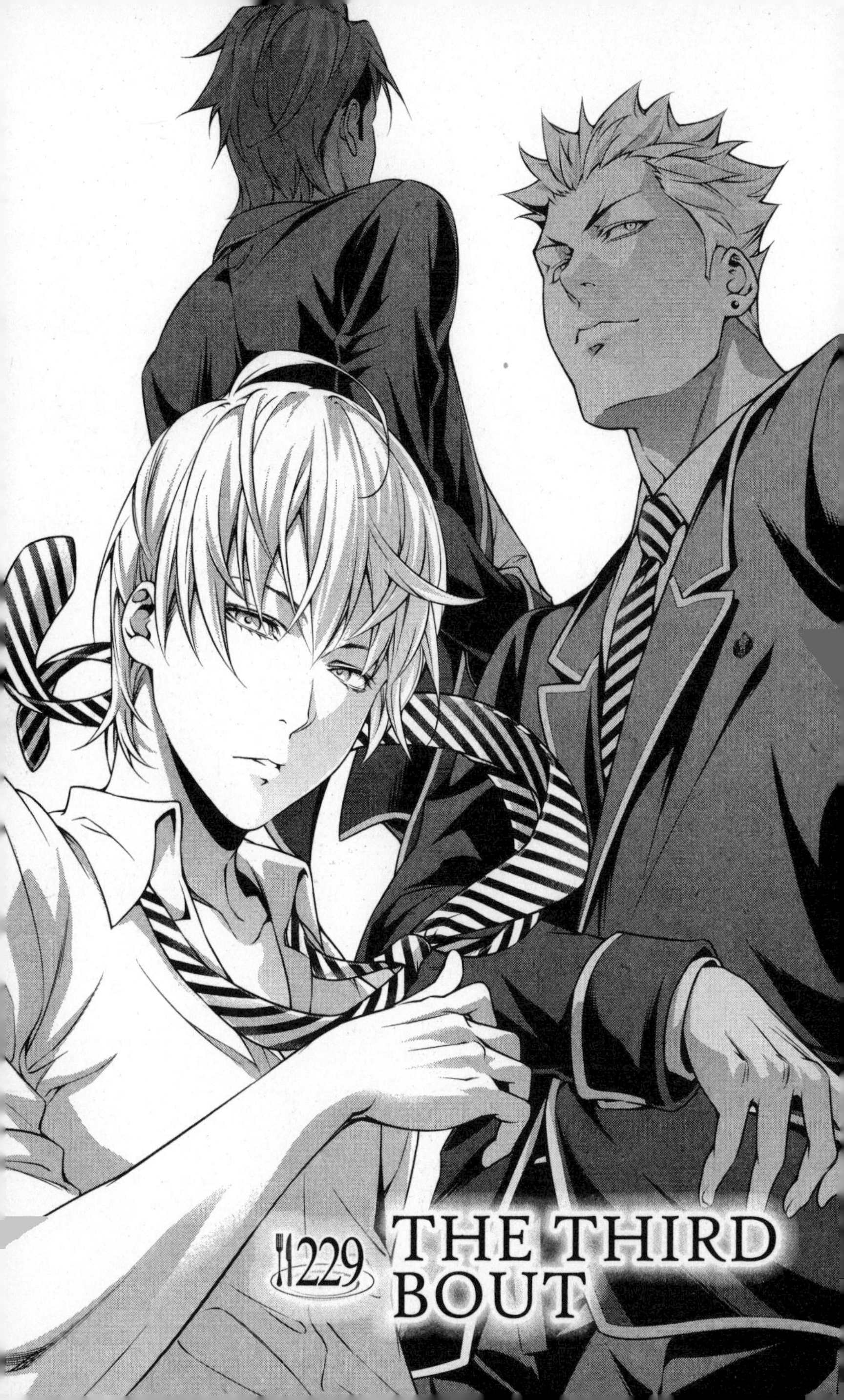
229
THE THIRD BOUT

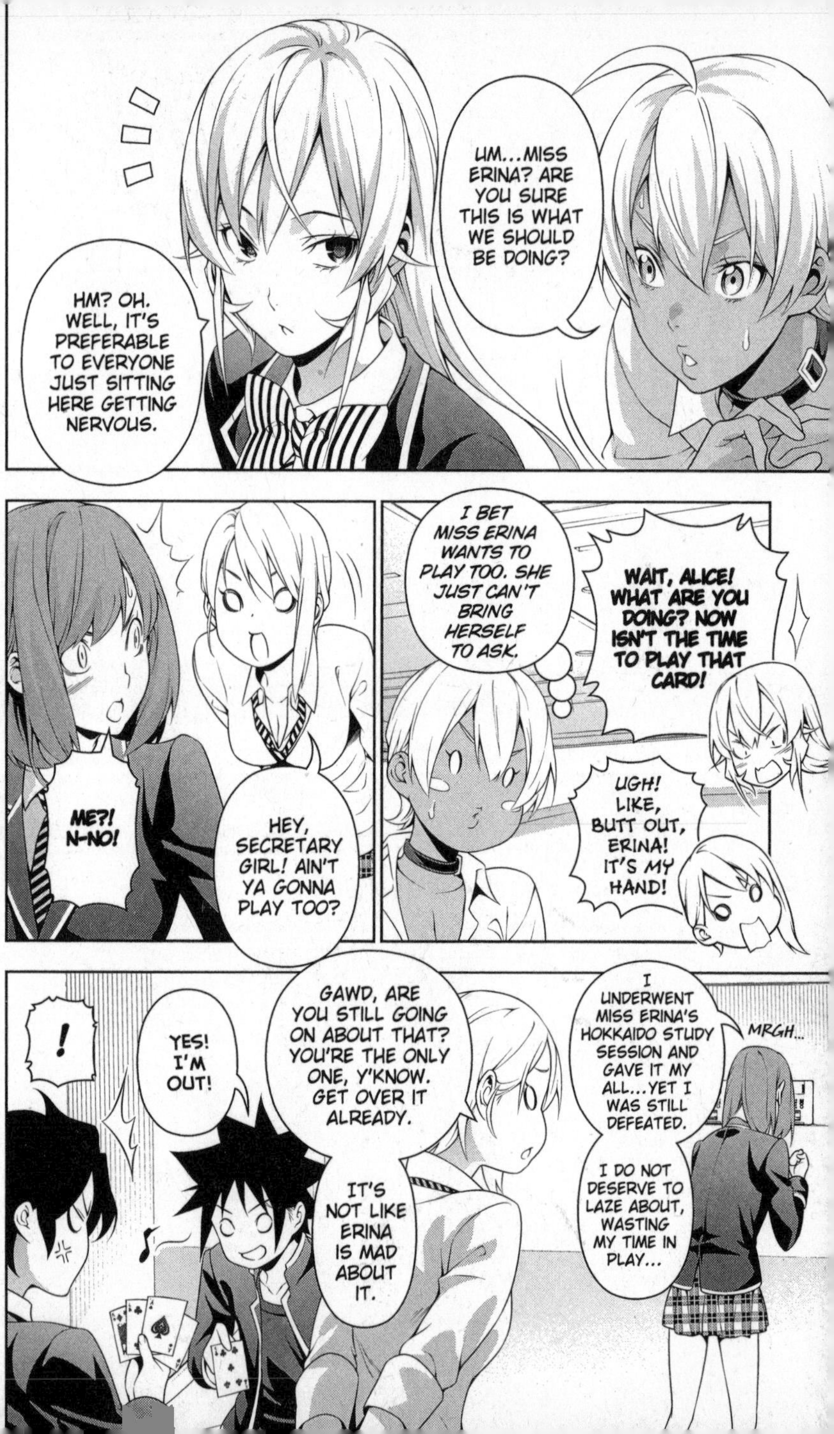
UM...MISS ERINA? ARE YOU SURE THIS IS WHAT WE SHOULD BE DOING?
HM? OH. WELL, IT'S PREFERABLE TO EVERYONE JUST SITTING HERE GETTING NERVOUS.
I BET MISS ERINA WANTS TO PLAY TOO. SHE JUST CAN'T BRING HERSELF TO ASK.
WAIT, ALICE! WHAT ARE YOU DOING? NOW ISN'T THE TIME TO PLAY THAT CARD!
UGH! LIKE, BUTT OUT, ERINA! IT'S MY HAND!
HEY, SECRETARY GIRL! AIN'T YA GONNA PLAY TOO?
ME?! N-NO!
MRGH...
I UNDERWENT MISS ERINA'S HOKKAIDO STUDY SESSION AND GAVE IT MY ALL...YET I WAS STILL DEFEATED.
I DO NOT DESERVE TO LAZE ABOUT, WASTING MY TIME IN PLAY...
GAWD, ARE YOU STILL GOING ON ABOUT THAT? YOU'RE THE ONLY ONE, Y'KNOW. GET OVER IT ALREADY.
IT'S NOT LIKE ERINA IS MAD ABOUT IT.
YES! I'M OUT!
!

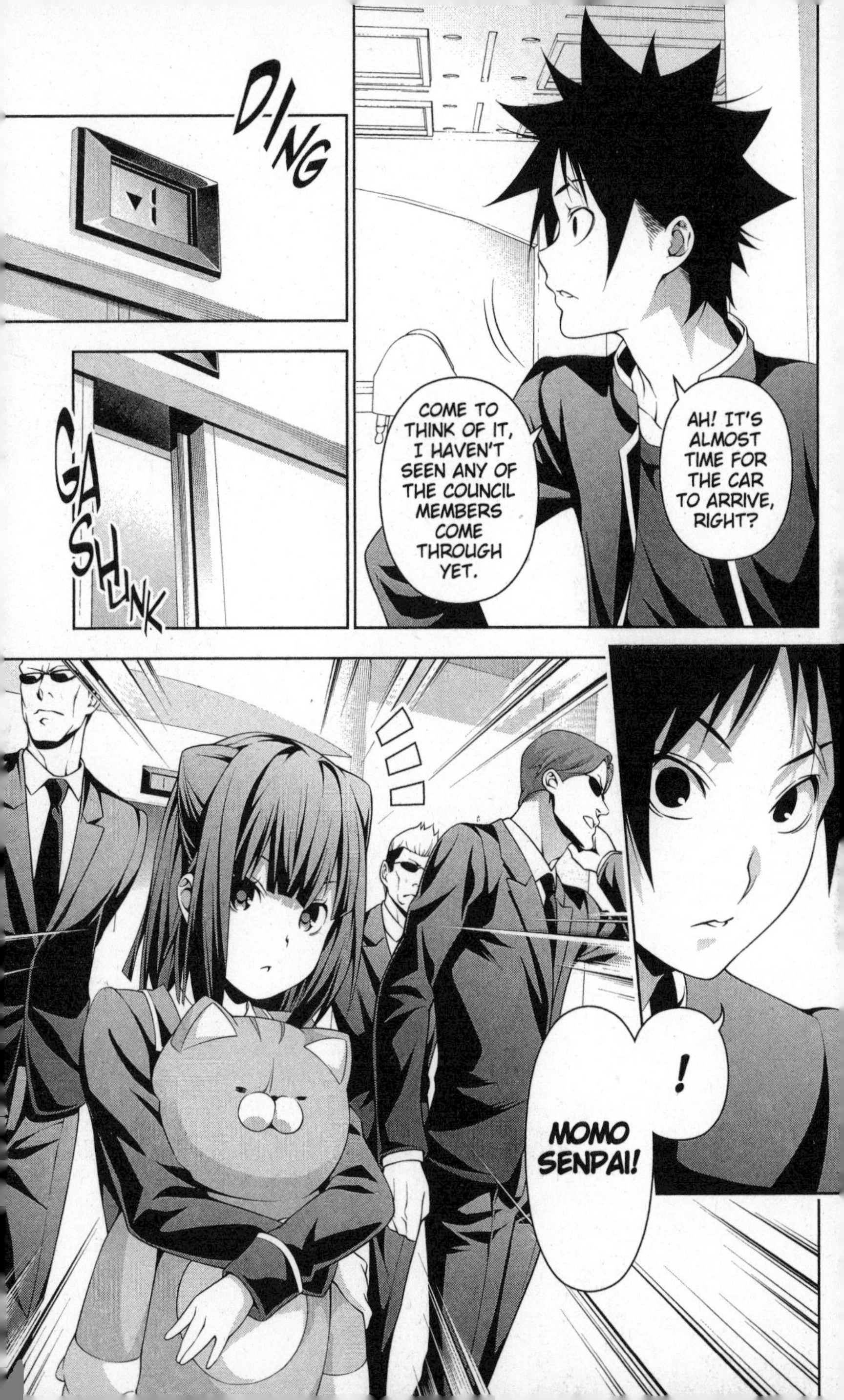
AH! IT'S ALMOST TIME FOR THE CAR TO ARRIVE, RIGHT?
COME TO THINK OF IT, I HAVEN'T SEEN ANY OF THE COUNCIL MEMBERS COME THROUGH YET.
DING
GASHUNK
!
MOMO SENPAI!

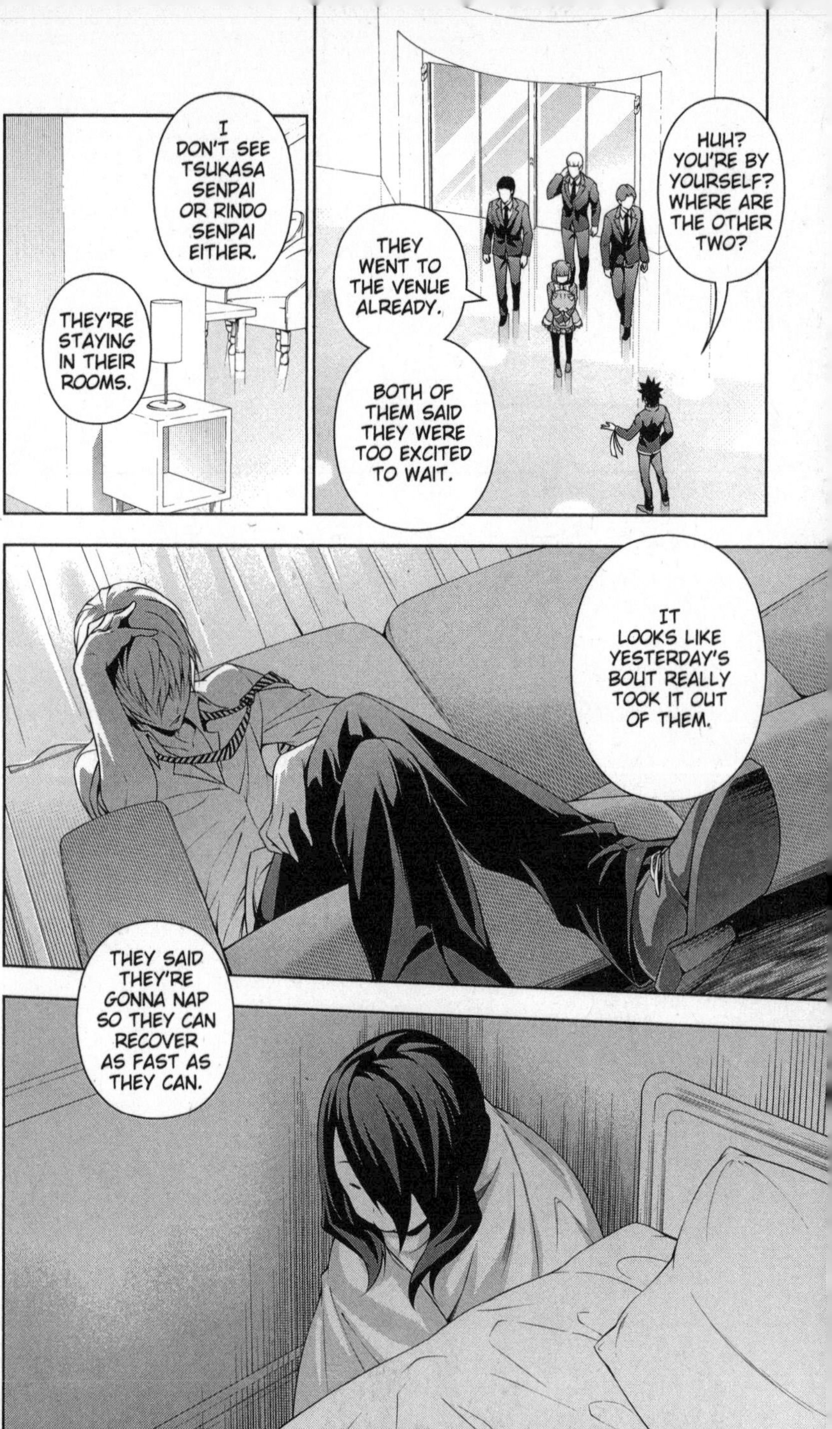
HUH? YOU'RE BY YOURSELF? WHERE ARE THE OTHER TWO?
THEY WENT TO THE VENUE ALREADY.
BOTH OF THEM SAID THEY WERE TOO EXCITED TO WAIT.
I DON'T SEE TSUKASA SENPAI OR RINDO SENPAI EITHER.
THEY'RE STAYING IN THEIR ROOMS.
IT LOOKS LIKE YESTERDAY'S BOUT REALLY TOOK IT OUT OF THEM.
THEY SAID THEY'RE GONNA NAP SO THEY CAN RECOVER AS FAST AS THEY CAN.

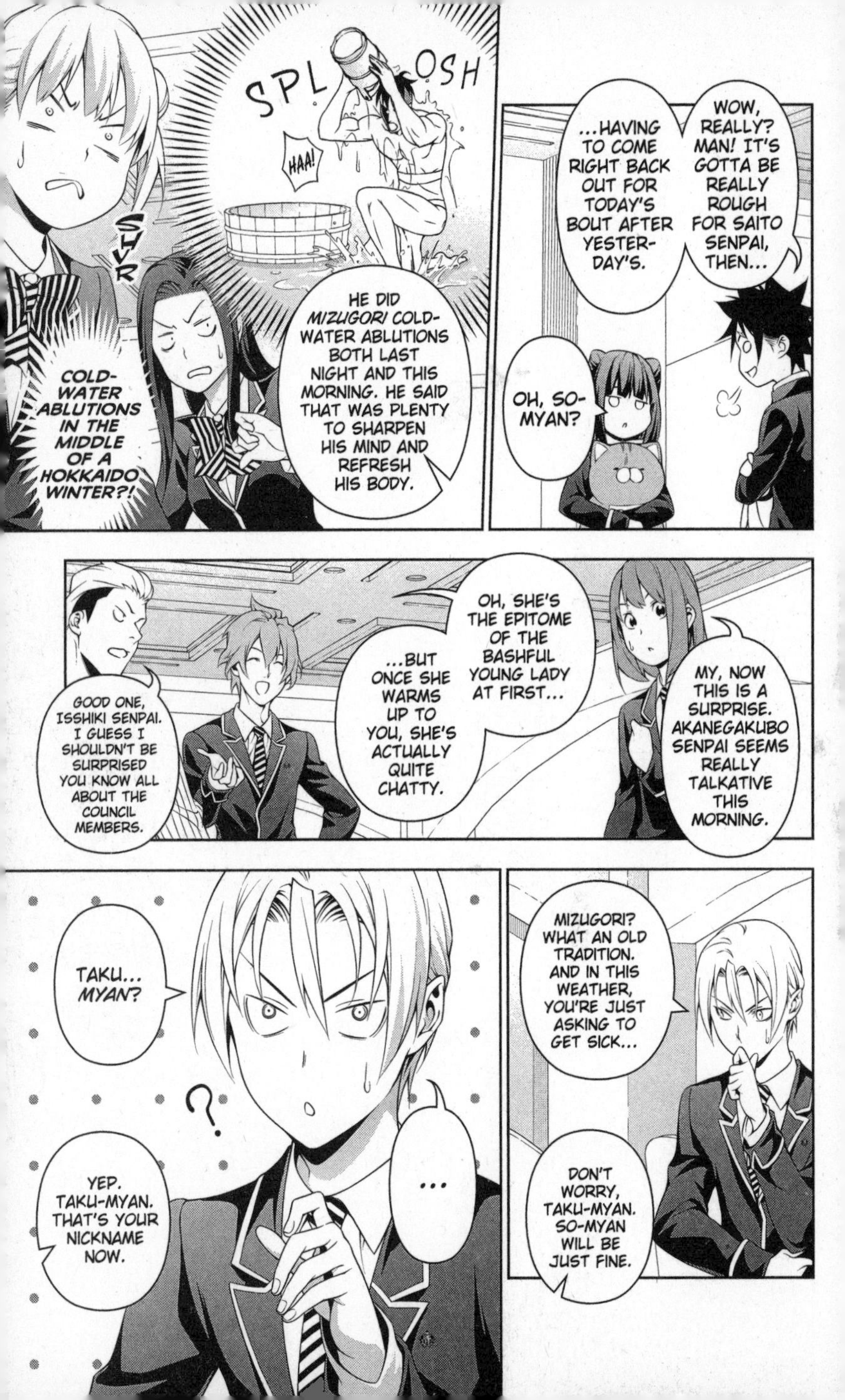
WOW, REALLY? MAN! IT'S GOTTA BE REALLY ROUGH FOR SAITO SENPAI, THEN...
...HAVING TO COME RIGHT BACK OUT FOR TODAY'S BOUT AFTER YESTER-DAY'S.
OH, SO-MYAN?
SPLOSH
HAA!
HE DID *MIZUGORI* COLD-WATER ABLUTIONS BOTH LAST NIGHT AND THIS MORNING. HE SAID THAT WAS PLENTY TO SHARPEN HIS MIND AND REFRESH HIS BODY.
SHVR
COLD-WATER ABLUTIONS IN THE MIDDLE OF A HOKKAIDO WINTER?!
MY, NOW THIS IS A SURPRISE. AKANEGAKUBO SENPAI SEEMS REALLY TALKATIVE THIS MORNING.
OH, SHE'S THE EPITOME OF THE BASHFUL YOUNG LADY AT FIRST...
...BUT ONCE SHE WARMS UP TO YOU, SHE'S ACTUALLY QUITE CHATTY.
GOOD ONE, ISSHIKI SENPAI. I GUESS I SHOULDN'T BE SURPRISED YOU KNOW ALL ABOUT THE COUNCIL MEMBERS.
MIZUGORI? WHAT AN OLD TRADITION. AND IN THIS WEATHER, YOU'RE JUST ASKING TO GET SICK...
DON'T WORRY, TAKU-MYAN. SO-MYAN WILL BE JUST FINE.
TAKU... *MYAN*?
...
?
YEP. TAKU-MYAN. THAT'S YOUR NICKNAME NOW.

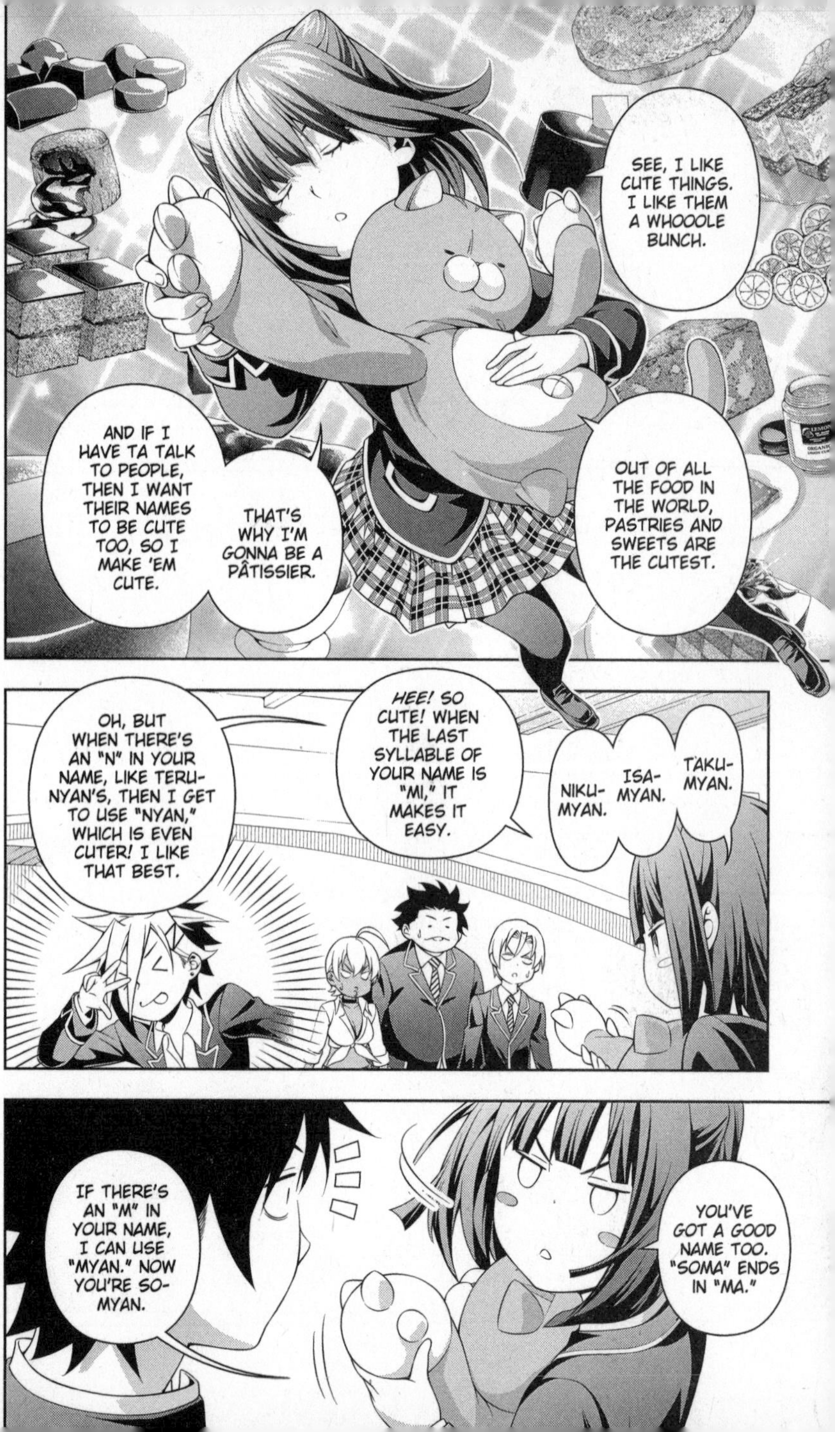
SEE, I LIKE CUTE THINGS. I LIKE THEM A WHOOOLE BUNCH.
OUT OF ALL THE FOOD IN THE WORLD, PASTRIES AND SWEETS ARE THE CUTEST.
THAT'S WHY I'M GONNA BE A PÂTISSIER.
AND IF I HAVE TA TALK TO PEOPLE, THEN I WANT THEIR NAMES TO BE CUTE TOO, SO I MAKE 'EM CUTE.
TAKU-MYAN.
ISA-MYAN.
NIKU-MYAN.
HEE! SO CUTE! WHEN THE LAST SYLLABLE OF YOUR NAME IS "MI," IT MAKES IT EASY.
OH, BUT WHEN THERE'S AN "N" IN YOUR NAME, LIKE TERU-NYAN'S, THEN I GET TO USE "NYAN," WHICH IS EVEN CUTER! I LIKE THAT BEST.
YOU'VE GOT A GOOD NAME TOO. "SOMA" ENDS IN "MA."
IF THERE'S AN "M" IN YOUR NAME, I CAN USE "MYAN." NOW YOU'RE SO-MYAN.

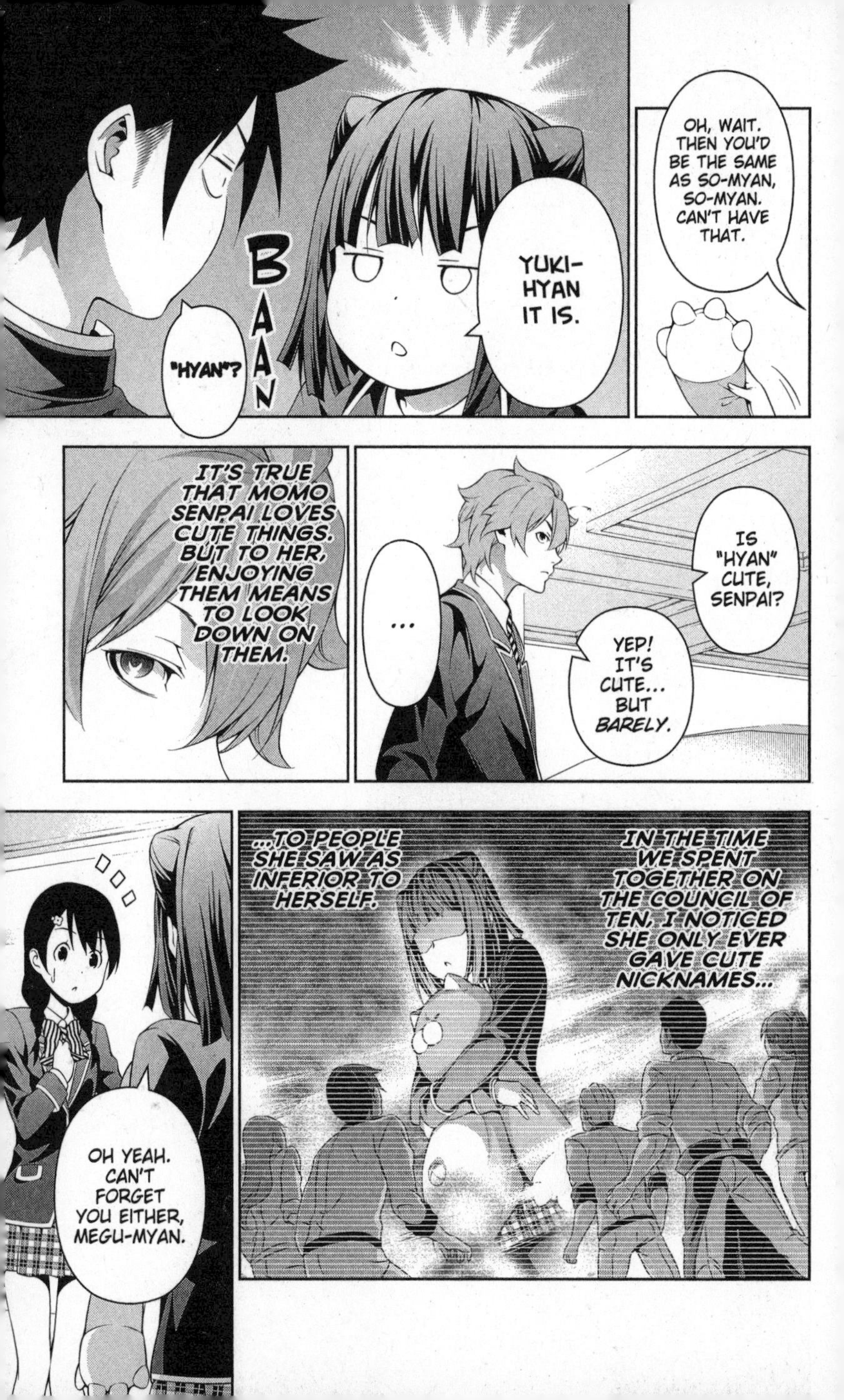

OH, WAIT. THEN YOU'D BE THE SAME AS SO-MYAN, SO-MYAN. CAN'T HAVE THAT.
YUKI-HYAN IT IS.
BAAN
"HYAN"?
IS "HYAN" CUTE, SENPAI?
YEP! IT'S CUTE... BUT BARELY.
...
IT'S TRUE THAT MOMO SENPAI LOVES CUTE THINGS. BUT TO HER, ENJOYING THEM MEANS TO LOOK DOWN ON THEM.
IN THE TIME WE SPENT TOGETHER ON THE COUNCIL OF TEN, I NOTICED SHE ONLY EVER GAVE CUTE NICKNAMES...
...TO PEOPLE SHE SAW AS INFERIOR TO HERSELF.
OH YEAH. CAN'T FORGET YOU EITHER, MEGU-MYAN.

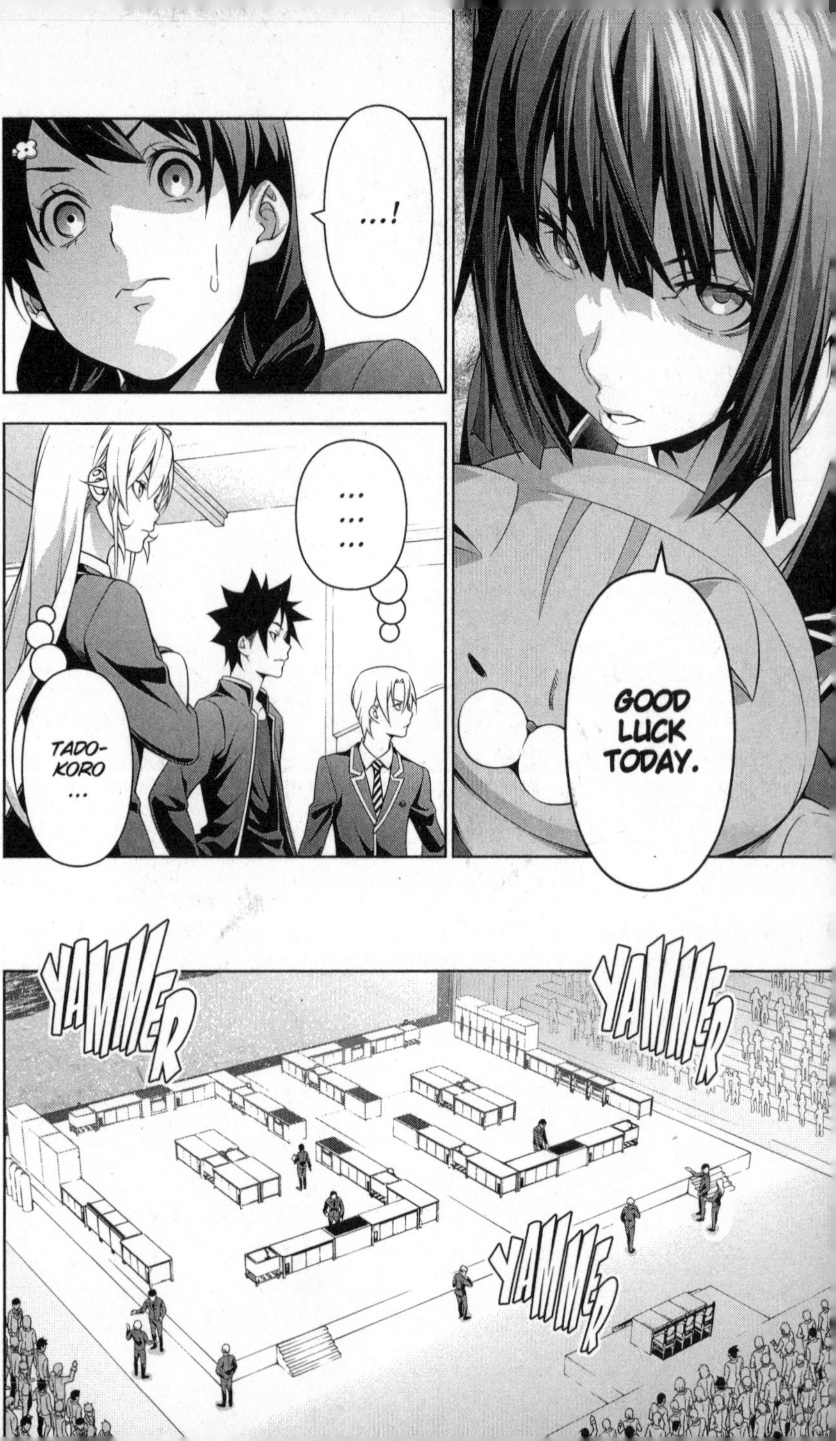
GOOD LUCK TODAY.
...!
... ...
TADO-KORO ...
YAMMER
YAMMER
YAMMER

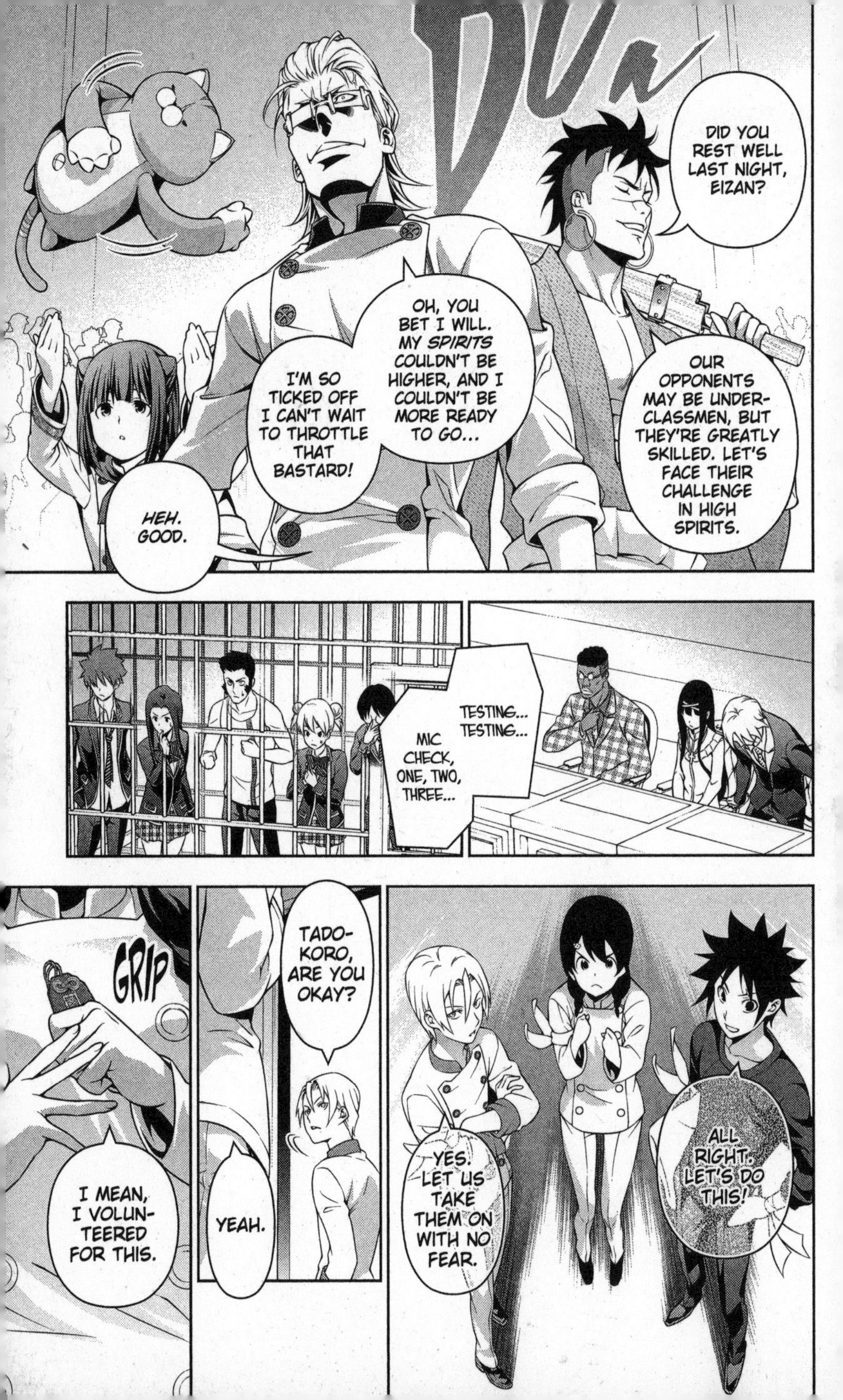
DID YOU REST WELL LAST NIGHT, EIZAN?
OUR OPPONENTS MAY BE UNDER-CLASSMEN, BUT THEY'RE GREATLY SKILLED. LET'S FACE THEIR CHALLENGE IN HIGH SPIRITS.
OH, YOU BET I WILL. MY *SPIRITS* COULDN'T BE HIGHER, AND I COULDN'T BE MORE READY TO GO...
I'M SO TICKED OFF I CAN'T WAIT TO THROTTLE THAT BASTARD!
HEH. GOOD.
TESTING... TESTING...
MIC CHECK, ONE, TWO, THREE...
ALL RIGHT. LET'S DO THIS!
YES. LET US TAKE THEM ON WITH NO FEAR.
TADO-KORO, ARE YOU OKAY?
YEAH.
GRIP
I MEAN, I VOLUN-TEERED FOR THIS.

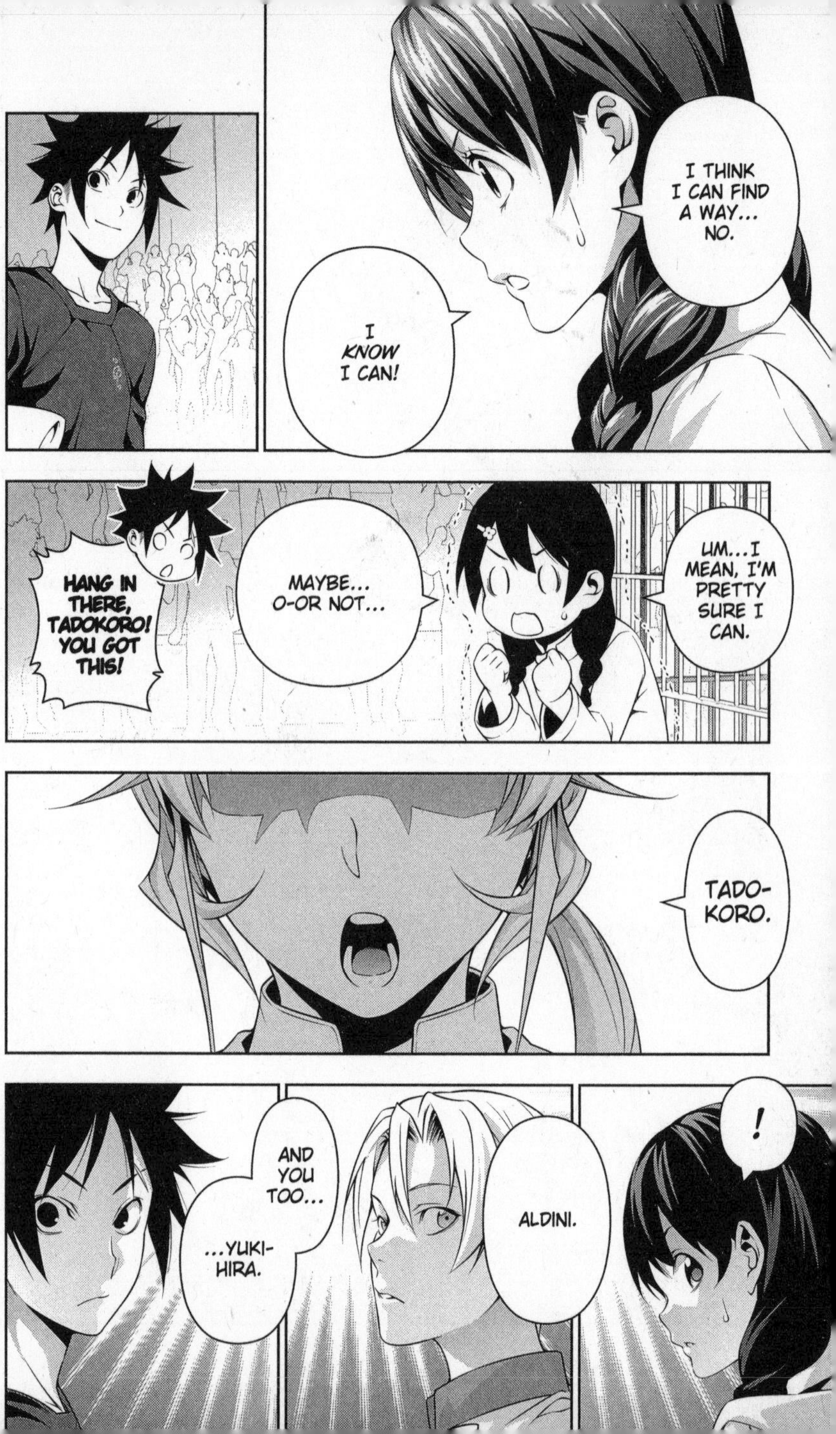
I THINK I CAN FIND A WAY... NO.
I *KNOW* I CAN!
UM...I MEAN, I'M PRETTY SURE I CAN.
MAYBE... O-OR NOT...
HANG IN THERE, TADOKORO! YOU GOT THIS!
TADO-KORO.
!
ALDINI.
AND YOU TOO...
...YUKI-HIRA.

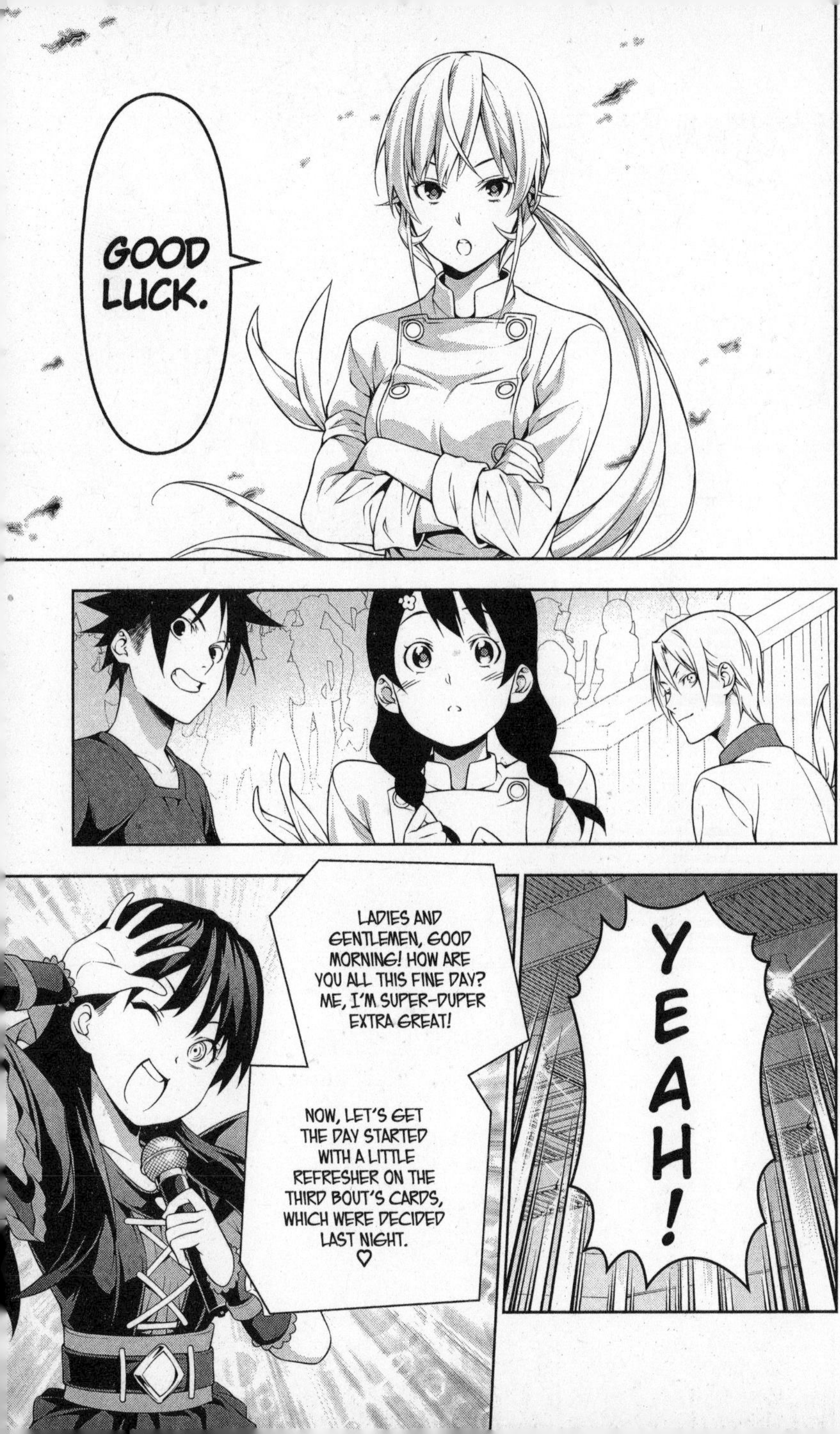
GOOD LUCK.
YEAH!
LADIES AND GENTLEMEN, GOOD MORNING! HOW ARE YOU ALL THIS FINE DAY? ME, I'M SUPER-DUPER EXTRA GREAT!
NOW, LET'S GET THE DAY STARTED WITH A LITTLE REFRESHER ON THE THIRD BOUT'S CARDS, WHICH WERE DECIDED LAST NIGHT. ♡

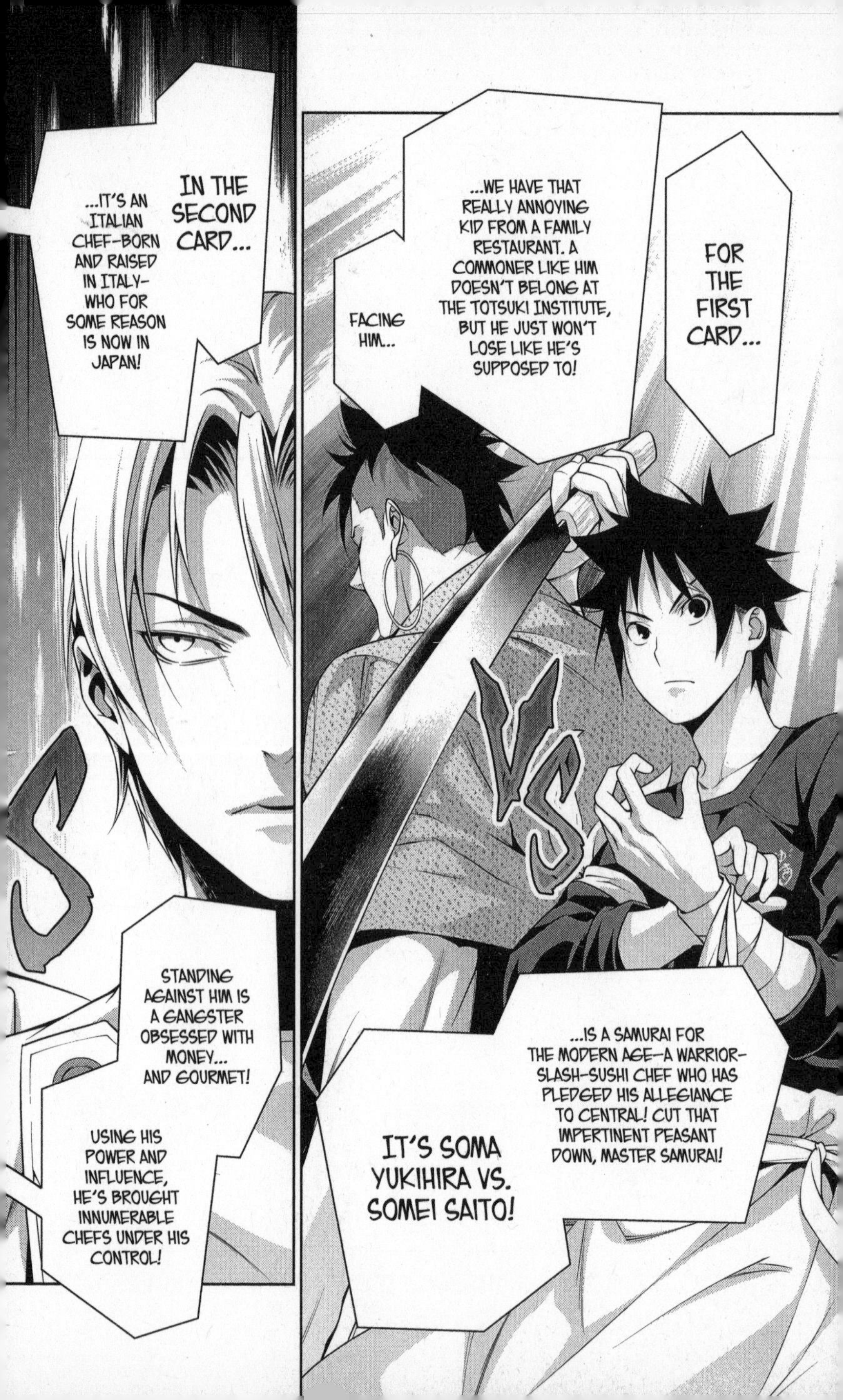
FOR THE FIRST CARD...
...WE HAVE THAT REALLY ANNOYING KID FROM A FAMILY RESTAURANT. A COMMONER LIKE HIM DOESN'T BELONG AT THE TOTSUKI INSTITUTE, BUT HE JUST WON'T LOSE LIKE HE'S SUPPOSED TO!
FACING HIM...
VS
...IS A SAMURAI FOR THE MODERN AGE—A WARRIOR-SLASH-SUSHI CHEF WHO HAS PLEDGED HIS ALLEGIANCE TO CENTRAL! CUT THAT IMPERTINENT PEASANT DOWN, MASTER SAMURAI!
IT'S SOMA YUKIHIRA VS. SOMEI SAITO!
IN THE SECOND CARD...
...IT'S AN ITALIAN CHEF—BORN AND RAISED IN ITALY—WHO FOR SOME REASON IS NOW IN JAPAN!
STANDING AGAINST HIM IS A GANGSTER OBSESSED WITH MONEY... AND GOURMET!
USING HIS POWER AND INFLUENCE, HE'S BROUGHT INNUMERABLE CHEFS UNDER HIS CONTROL!

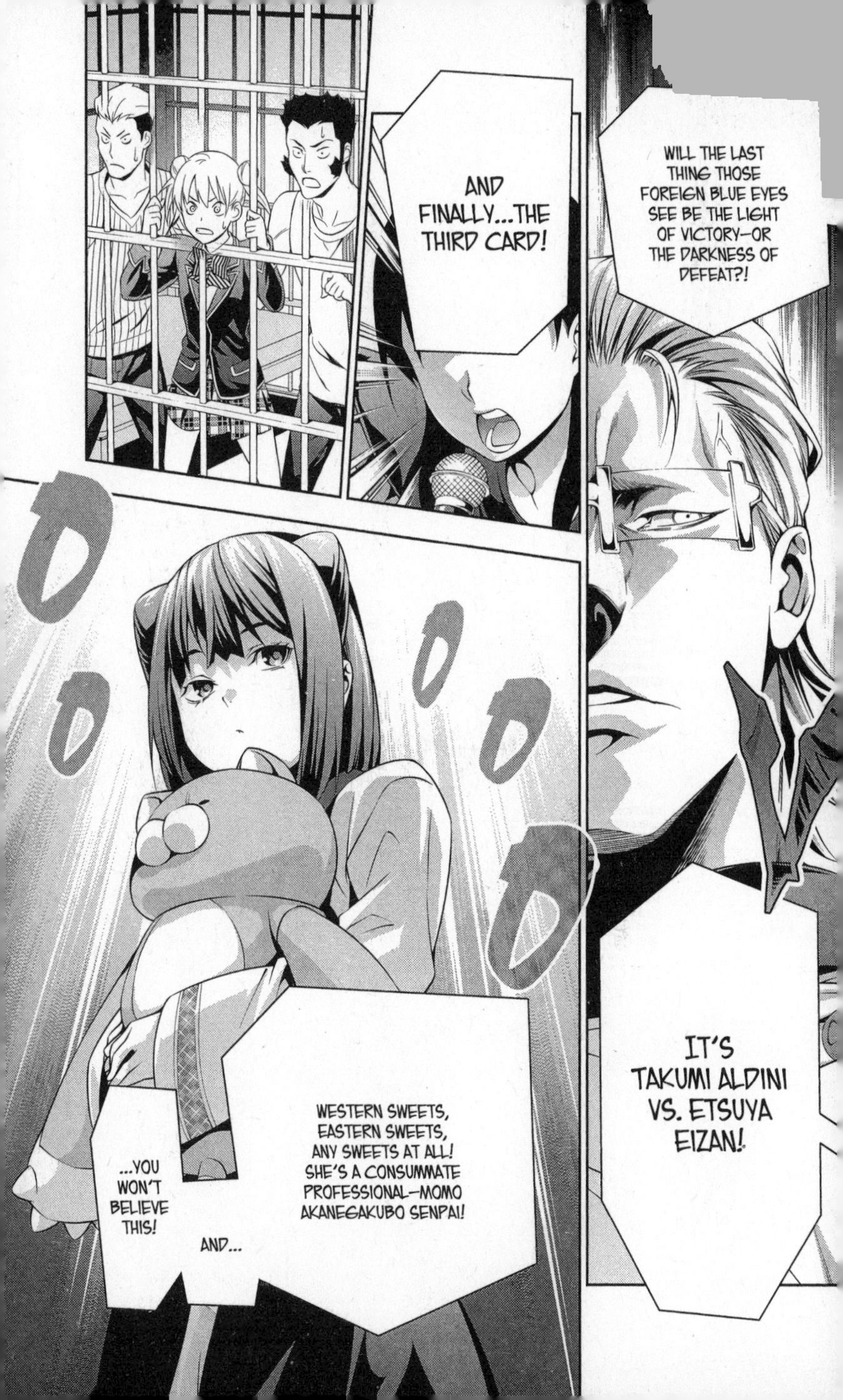
WILL THE LAST THING THOSE FOREIGN BLUE EYES SEE BE THE LIGHT OF VICTORY—OR THE DARKNESS OF DEFEAT?!
IT'S TAKUMI ALDINI VS. ETSUYA EIZAN!
AND FINALLY...THE THIRD CARD!
WESTERN SWEETS, EASTERN SWEETS, ANY SWEETS AT ALL! SHE'S A CONSUMMATE PROFESSIONAL—MOMO AKANEGAKUBO SENPAI!
...YOU WON'T BELIEVE THIS!
AND...

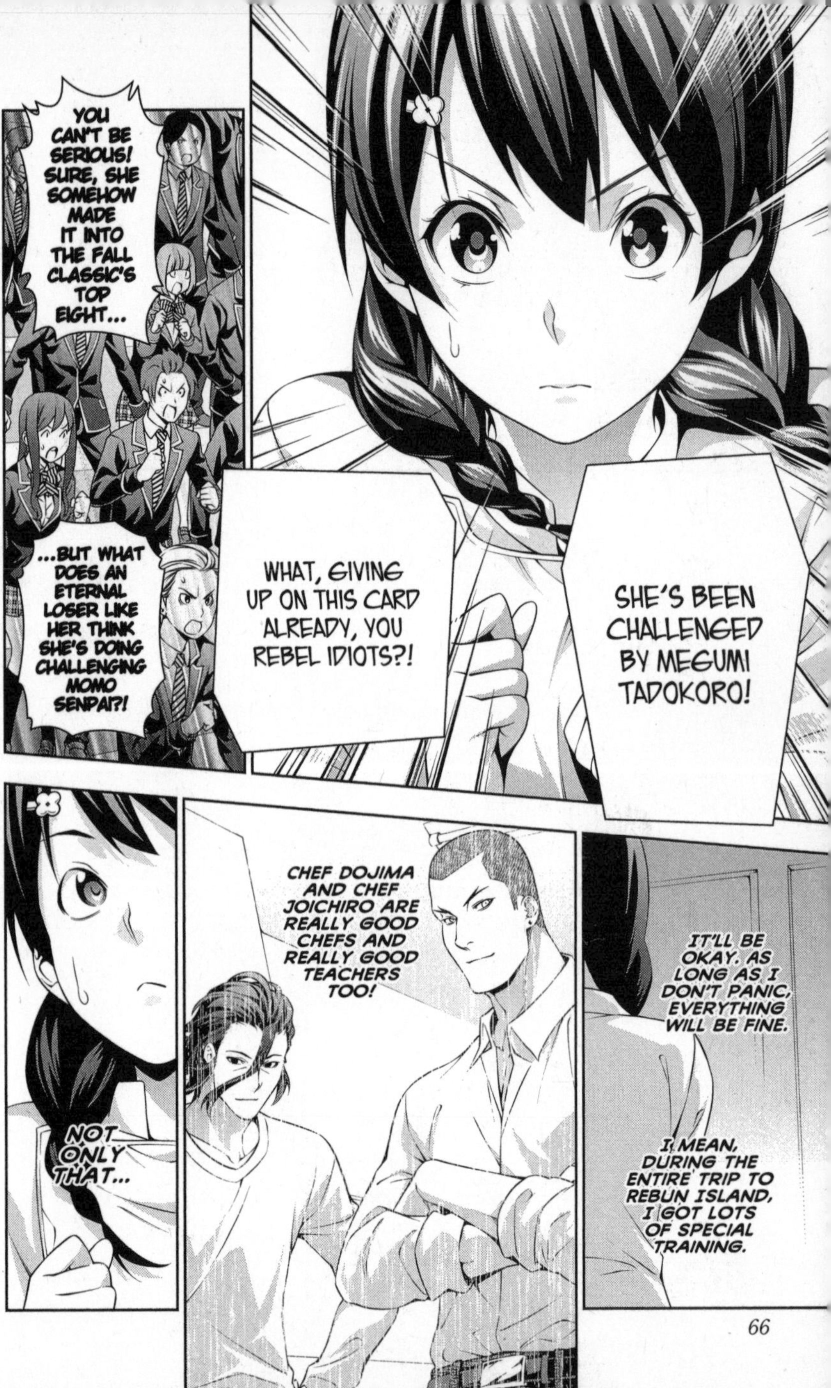
SHE'S BEEN CHALLENGED BY MEGUMI TADOKORO!
WHAT, GIVING UP ON THIS CARD ALREADY, YOU REBEL IDIOTS?!
YOU CAN'T BE SERIOUS! SURE, SHE SOMEHOW MADE IT INTO THE FALL CLASSIC'S TOP EIGHT...
...BUT WHAT DOES AN ETERNAL LOSER LIKE HER THINK SHE'S DOING CHALLENGING MOMO SENPAI?!
IT'LL BE OKAY. AS LONG AS I DON'T PANIC, EVERYTHING WILL BE FINE.
I MEAN, DURING THE ENTIRE TRIP TO REBUN ISLAND, I GOT LOTS OF SPECIAL TRAINING.
CHEF DOJIMA AND CHEF JOICHIRO ARE REALLY GOOD CHEFS AND REALLY GOOD TEACHERS TOO!
NOT ONLY THAT...

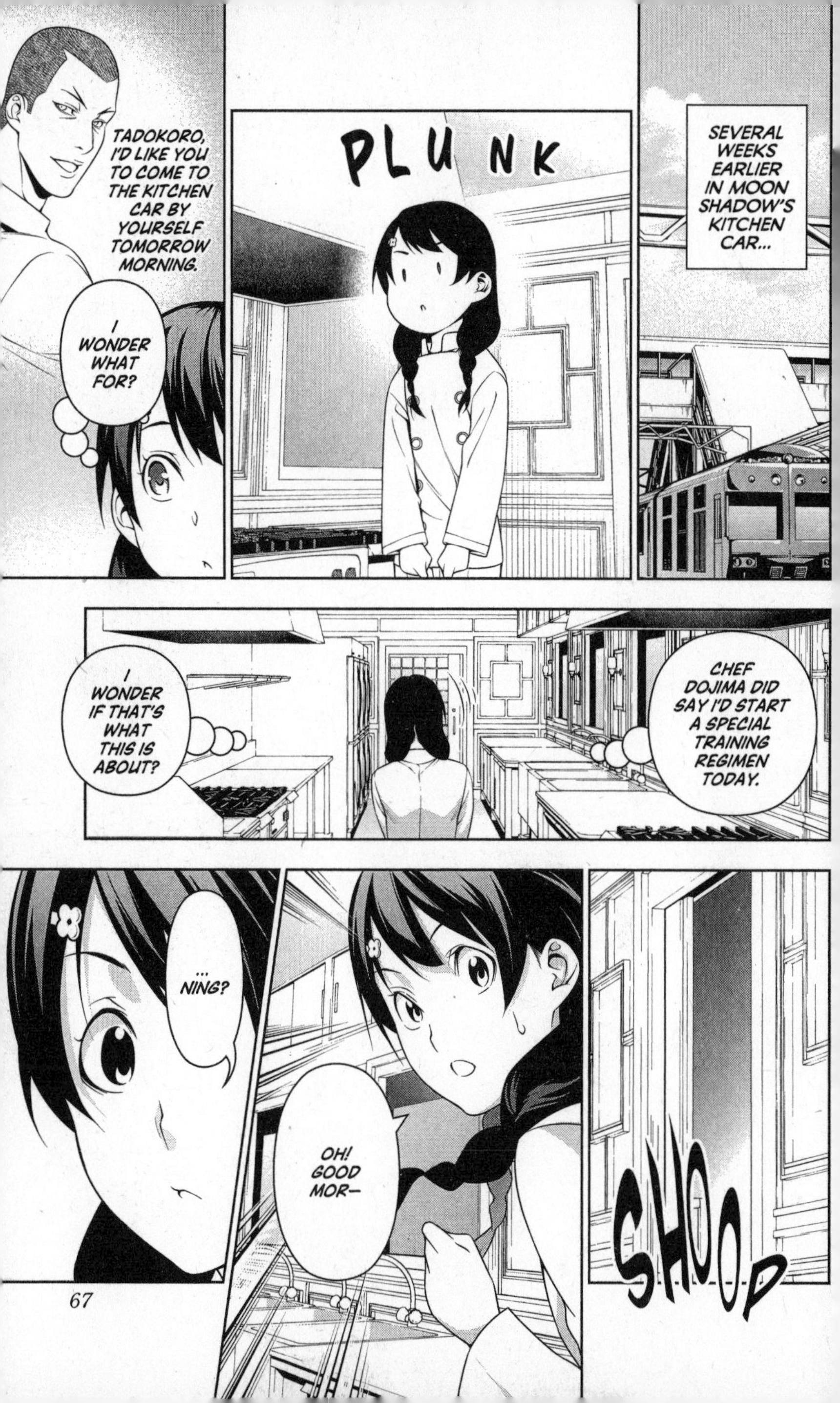
SEVERAL WEEKS EARLIER IN MOON SHADOW'S KITCHEN CAR...
PLUNK
TADOKORO, I'D LIKE YOU TO COME TO THE KITCHEN CAR BY YOURSELF TOMORROW MORNING.
I WONDER WHAT FOR?
CHEF DOJIMA DID SAY I'D START A SPECIAL TRAINING REGIMEN TODAY.
I WONDER IF THAT'S WHAT THIS IS ABOUT?
SHOOP
OH! GOOD MOR—
...NING?

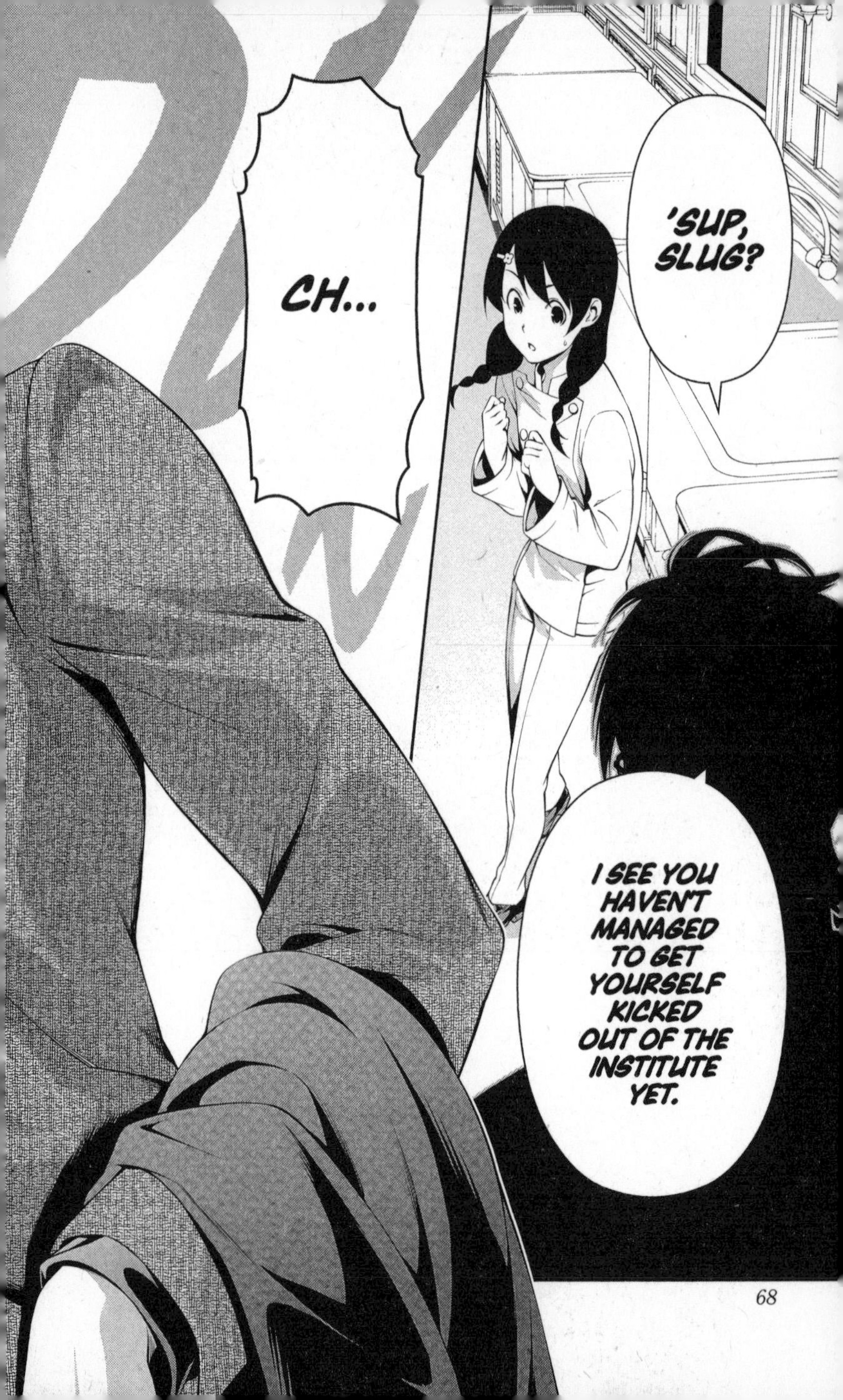
'SUP, SLUG?
I SEE YOU HAVEN'T MANAGED TO GET YOURSELF KICKED OUT OF THE INSTITUTE YET.
CH...

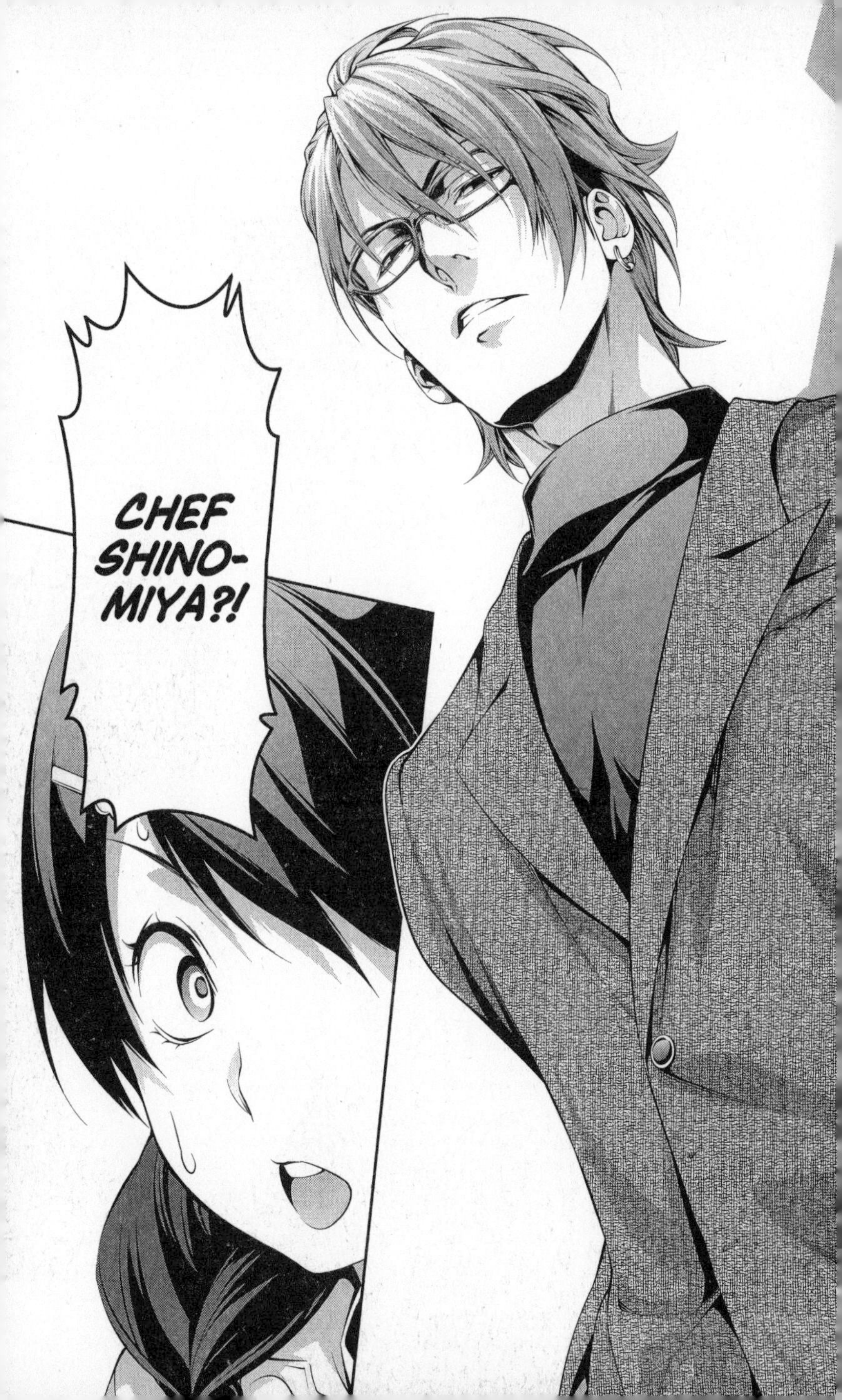
CHEF SHINO-MIYA?!

ARTIST: YUTO TSUKUDA RECIPE BY: YUKI MORISAKI

VOLUME 27
SPECIAL SUPPLEMENT!

PRACTICAL RECIPE #4

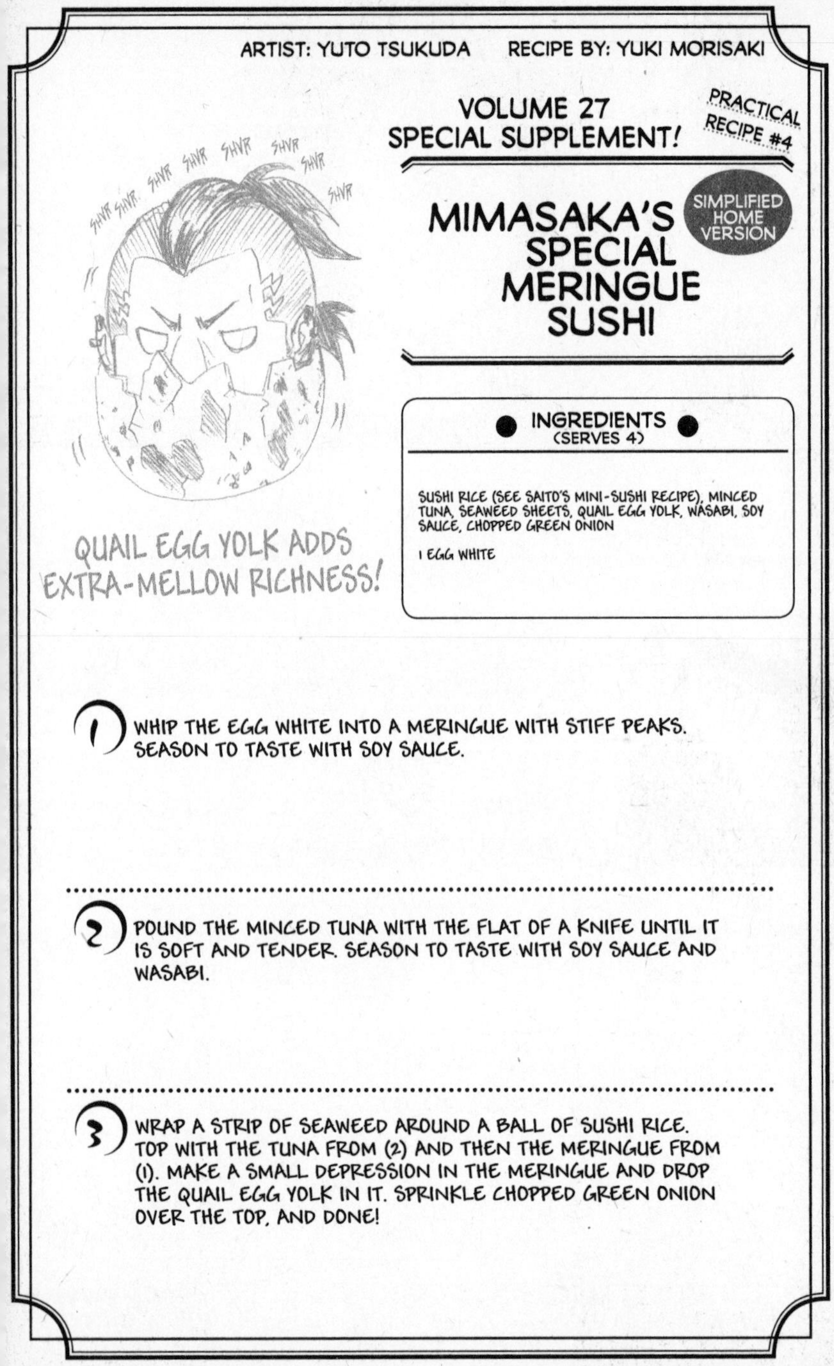
SHVR SHVR SHVR SHVR SHVR SHVR SHVR SHVR SHVR

QUAIL EGG YOLK ADDS EXTRA-MELLOW RICHNESS!

SIMPLIFIED HOME VERSION

MIMASAKA'S SPECIAL MERINGUE SUSHI

INGREDIENTS
(SERVES 4)

SUSHI RICE (SEE SAITO'S MINI-SUSHI RECIPE), MINCED TUNA, SEAWEED SHEETS, QUAIL EGG YOLK, WASABI, SOY SAUCE, CHOPPED GREEN ONION

1 EGG WHITE

1. WHIP THE EGG WHITE INTO A MERINGUE WITH STIFF PEAKS. SEASON TO TASTE WITH SOY SAUCE.

2. POUND THE MINCED TUNA WITH THE FLAT OF A KNIFE UNTIL IT IS SOFT AND TENDER. SEASON TO TASTE WITH SOY SAUCE AND WASABI.

3. WRAP A STRIP OF SEAWEED AROUND A BALL OF SUSHI RICE. TOP WITH THE TUNA FROM (2) AND THEN THE MERINGUE FROM (1). MAKE A SMALL DEPRESSION IN THE MERINGUE AND DROP THE QUAIL EGG YOLK IN IT. SPRINKLE CHOPPED GREEN ONION OVER THE TOP, AND DONE!

230 AIM FOR VICTORY!

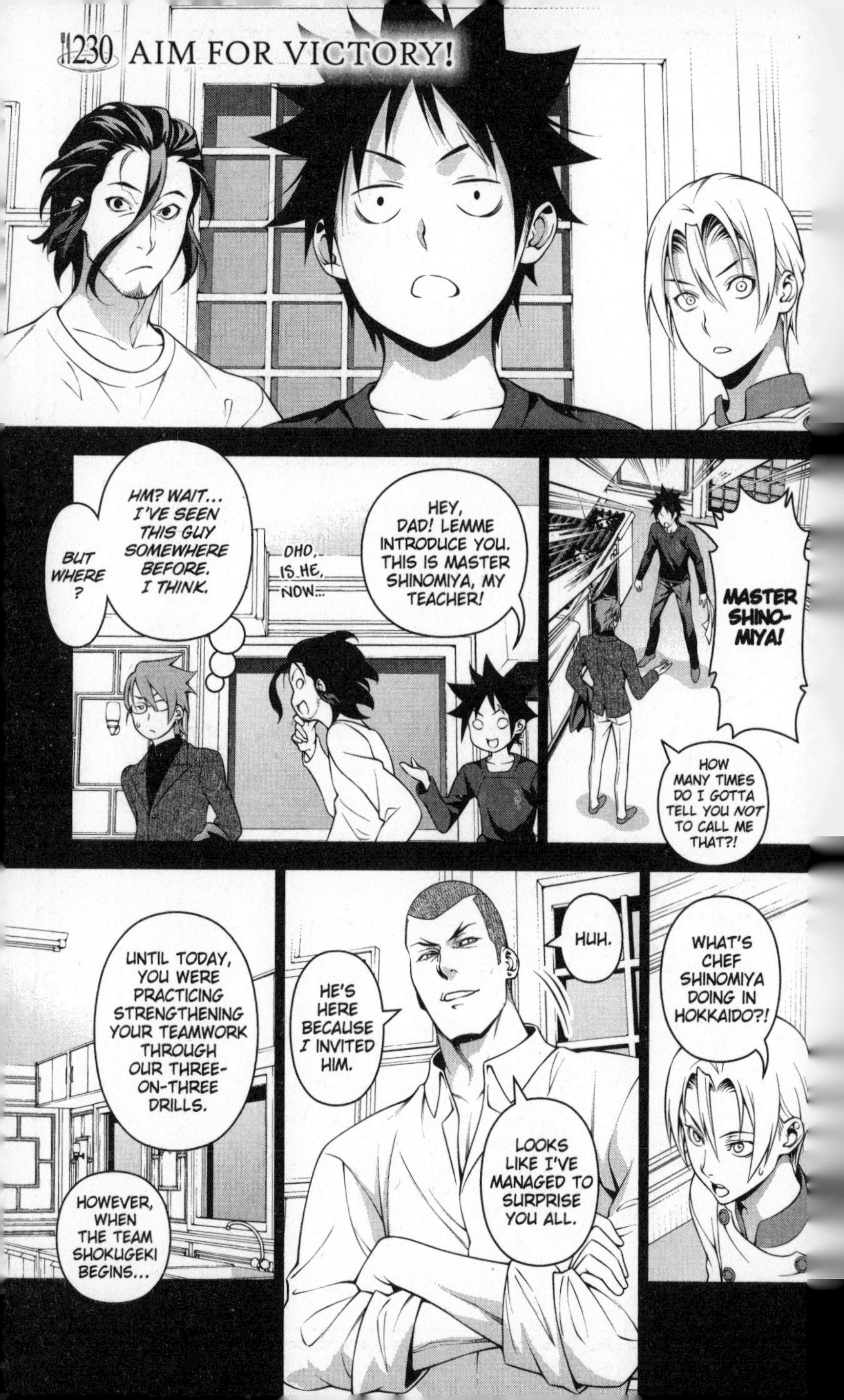
MASTER SHINO-MIYA!
HOW MANY TIMES DO I GOTTA TELL YOU NOT TO CALL ME THAT?!
HEY, DAD! LEMME INTRODUCE YOU. THIS IS MASTER SHINOMIYA, MY TEACHER!
OHO, IS HE, NOW...
HM? WAIT... I'VE SEEN THIS GUY SOMEWHERE BEFORE. I THINK.
BUT WHERE?
WHAT'S CHEF SHINOMIYA DOING IN HOKKAIDO?!
HUH.
HE'S HERE BECAUSE I INVITED HIM.
LOOKS LIKE I'VE MANAGED TO SURPRISE YOU ALL.
UNTIL TODAY, YOU WERE PRACTICING STRENGTHENING YOUR TEAMWORK THROUGH OUR THREE-ON-THREE DRILLS.
HOWEVER, WHEN THE TEAM SHOKUGEKI BEGINS...

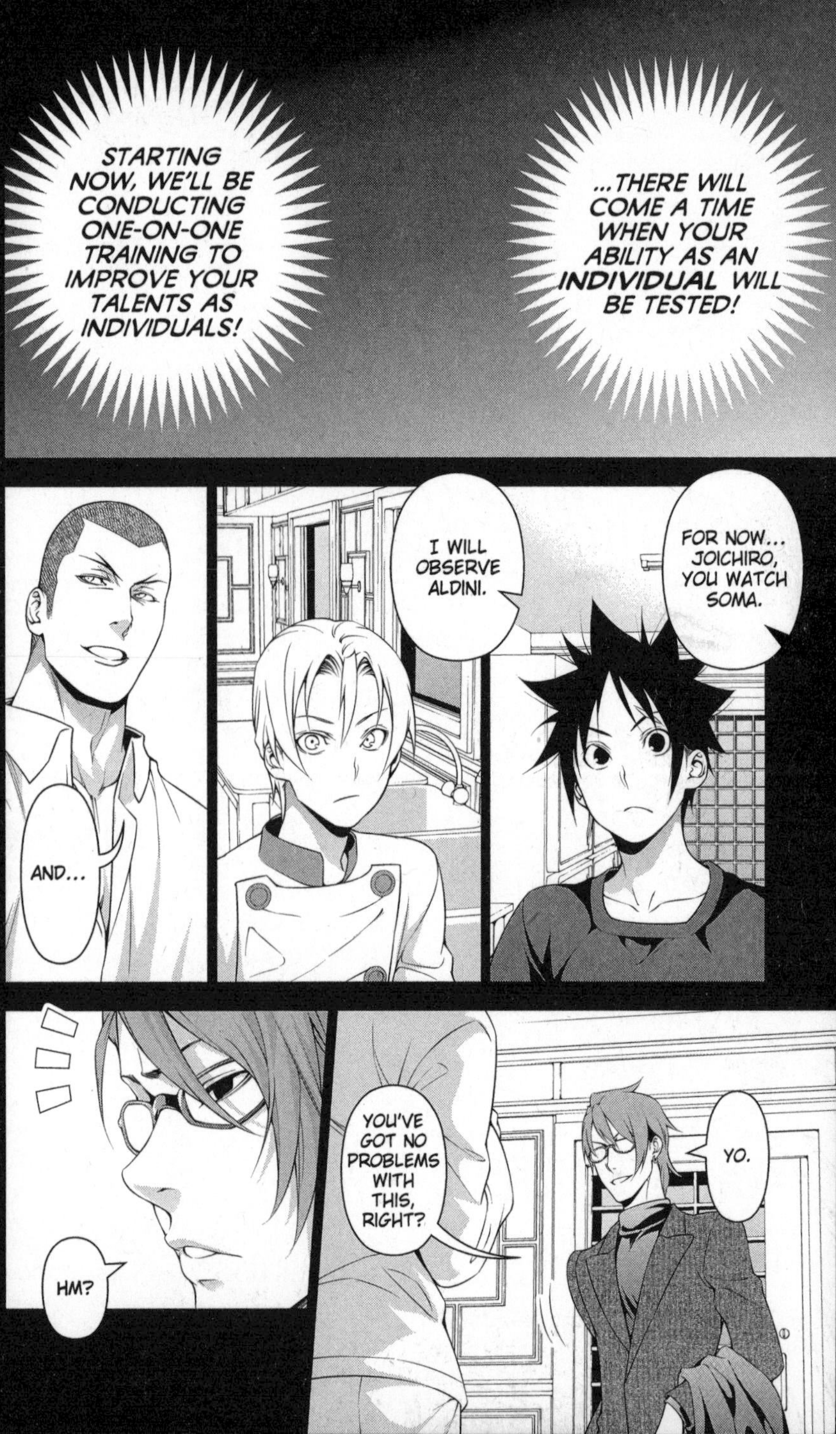
...THERE WILL COME A TIME WHEN YOUR ABILITY AS AN INDIVIDUAL WILL BE TESTED!
STARTING NOW, WE'LL BE CONDUCTING ONE-ON-ONE TRAINING TO IMPROVE YOUR TALENTS AS INDIVIDUALS!
FOR NOW... JOICHIRO, YOU WATCH SOMA.
I WILL OBSERVE ALDINI.
AND...
YO.
YOU'VE GOT NO PROBLEMS WITH THIS, RIGHT?
HM?

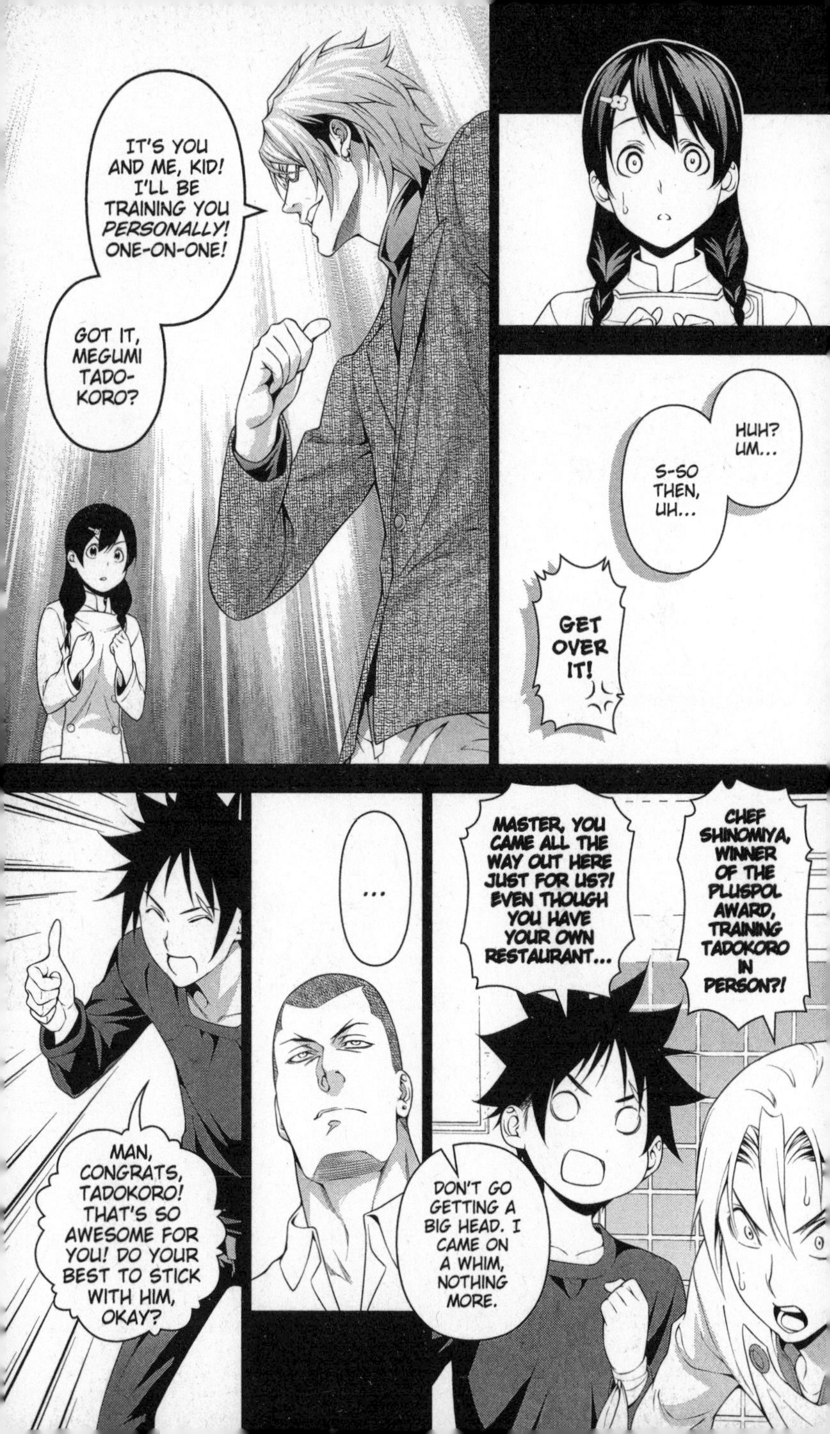
HUH? UM...
S-SO THEN, UH...
GET OVER IT!
IT'S YOU AND ME, KID! I'LL BE TRAINING YOU *PERSONALLY*! ONE-ON-ONE!
GOT IT, MEGUMI TADO-KORO?
CHEF SHINOMIYA, WINNER OF THE PLUSPOL AWARD, TRAINING TADOKORO IN PERSON?!
MASTER, YOU CAME ALL THE WAY OUT HERE JUST FOR US?! EVEN THOUGH YOU HAVE YOUR OWN RESTAURANT...
DON'T GO GETTING A BIG HEAD. I CAME ON A WHIM, NOTHING MORE.
...
MAN, CONGRATS, TADOKORO! THAT'S SO AWESOME FOR YOU! DO YOUR BEST TO STICK WITH HIM, OKAY?

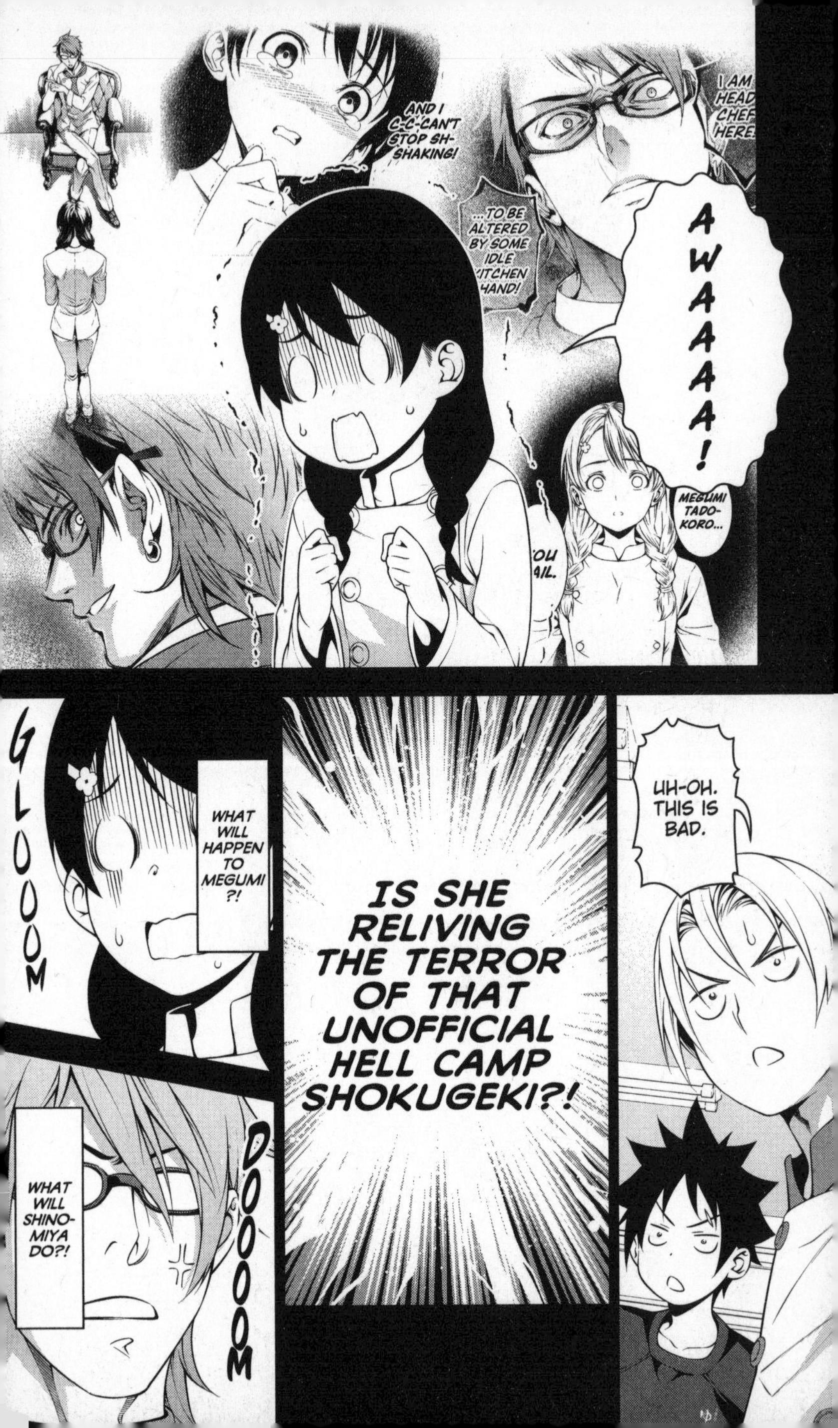
I AM HEAD CHEF HERE!
...TO BE ALTERED BY SOME IDLE KITCHEN HAND!
AND I C-C-CAN'T STOP SH-SHAKING!
AWAAAAAA!
MEGUMI TADOKORO...
OU AIL.
UH-OH. THIS IS BAD.
IS SHE RELIVING THE TERROR OF THAT UNOFFICIAL HELL CAMP SHOKUGEKI?!
GLOOOOM
WHAT WILL HAPPEN TO MEGUMI?!
WHAT WILL SHINOMIYA DO?!
DOOOOOOM

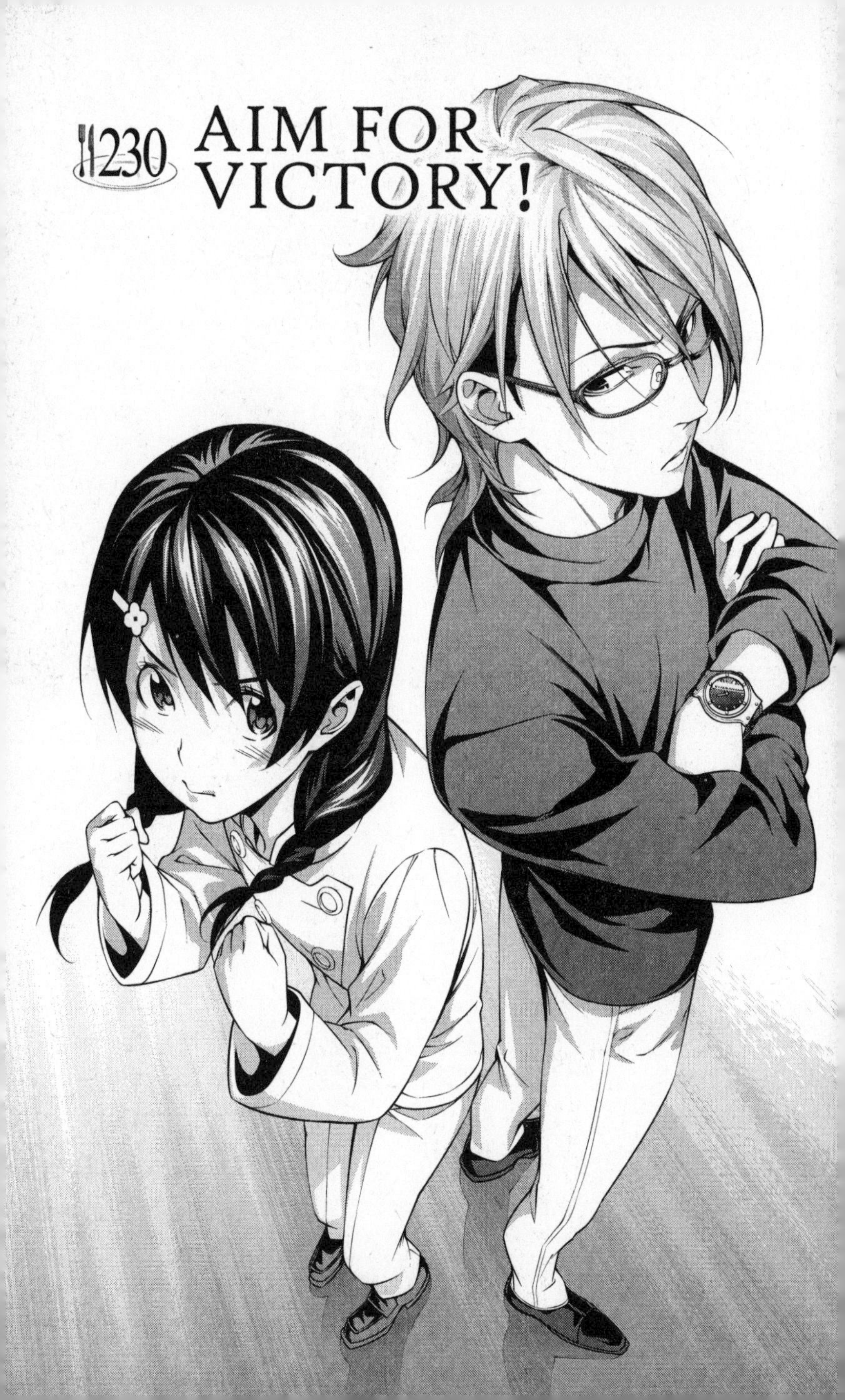
230
AIM FOR VICTORY!

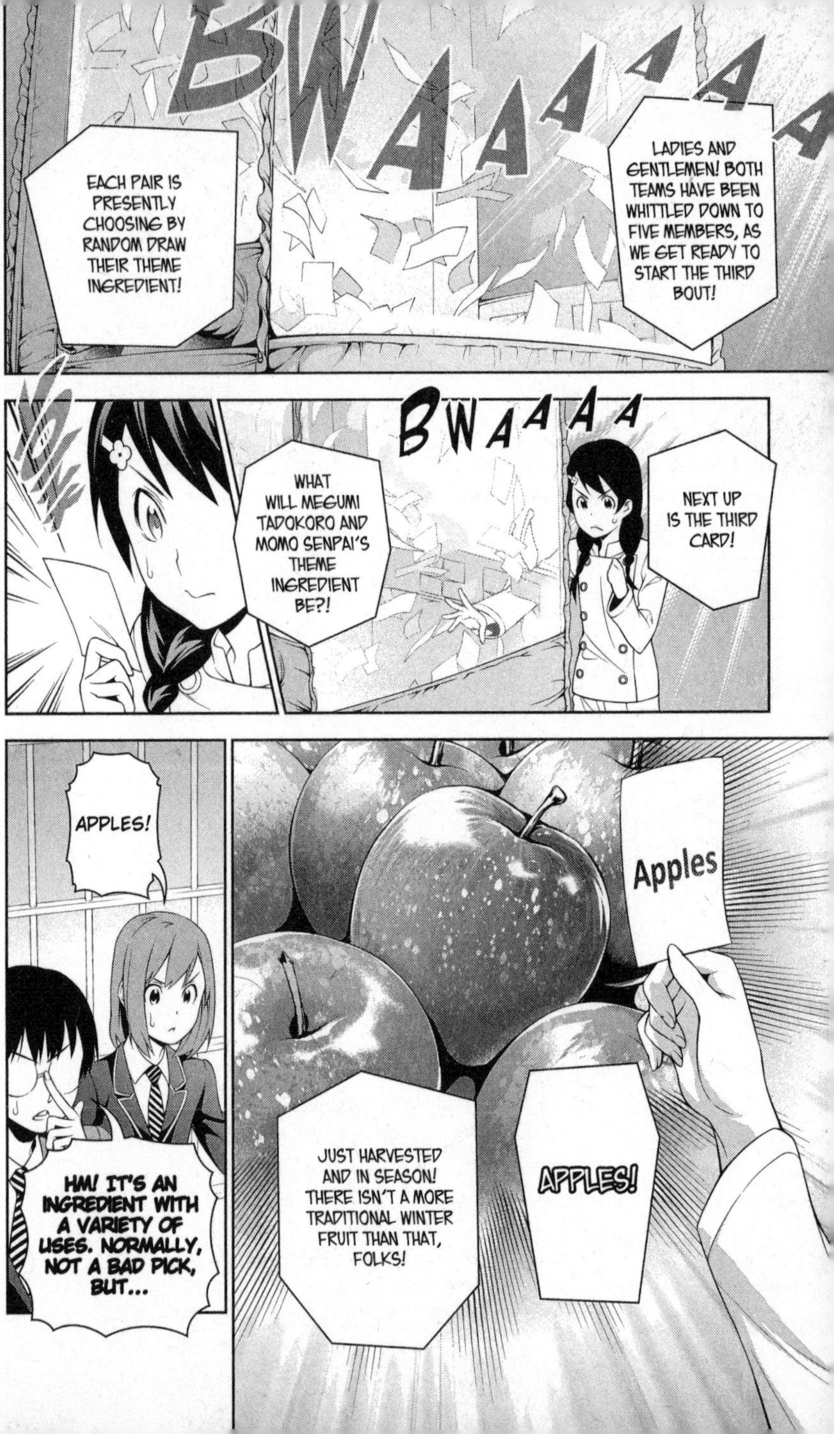
BWAAAAAA
LADIES AND GENTLEMEN! BOTH TEAMS HAVE BEEN WHITTLED DOWN TO FIVE MEMBERS, AS WE GET READY TO START THE THIRD BOUT!
EACH PAIR IS PRESENTLY CHOOSING BY RANDOM DRAW THEIR THEME INGREDIENT!
BWAAAA
NEXT UP IS THE THIRD CARD!
WHAT WILL MEGUMI TADOKORO AND MOMO SENPAI'S THEME INGREDIENT BE?!
Apples
APPLES!
JUST HARVESTED AND IN SEASON! THERE ISN'T A MORE TRADITIONAL WINTER FRUIT THAN THAT, FOLKS!
APPLES!
HM! IT'S AN INGREDIENT WITH A VARIETY OF USES. NORMALLY, NOT A BAD PICK, BUT...

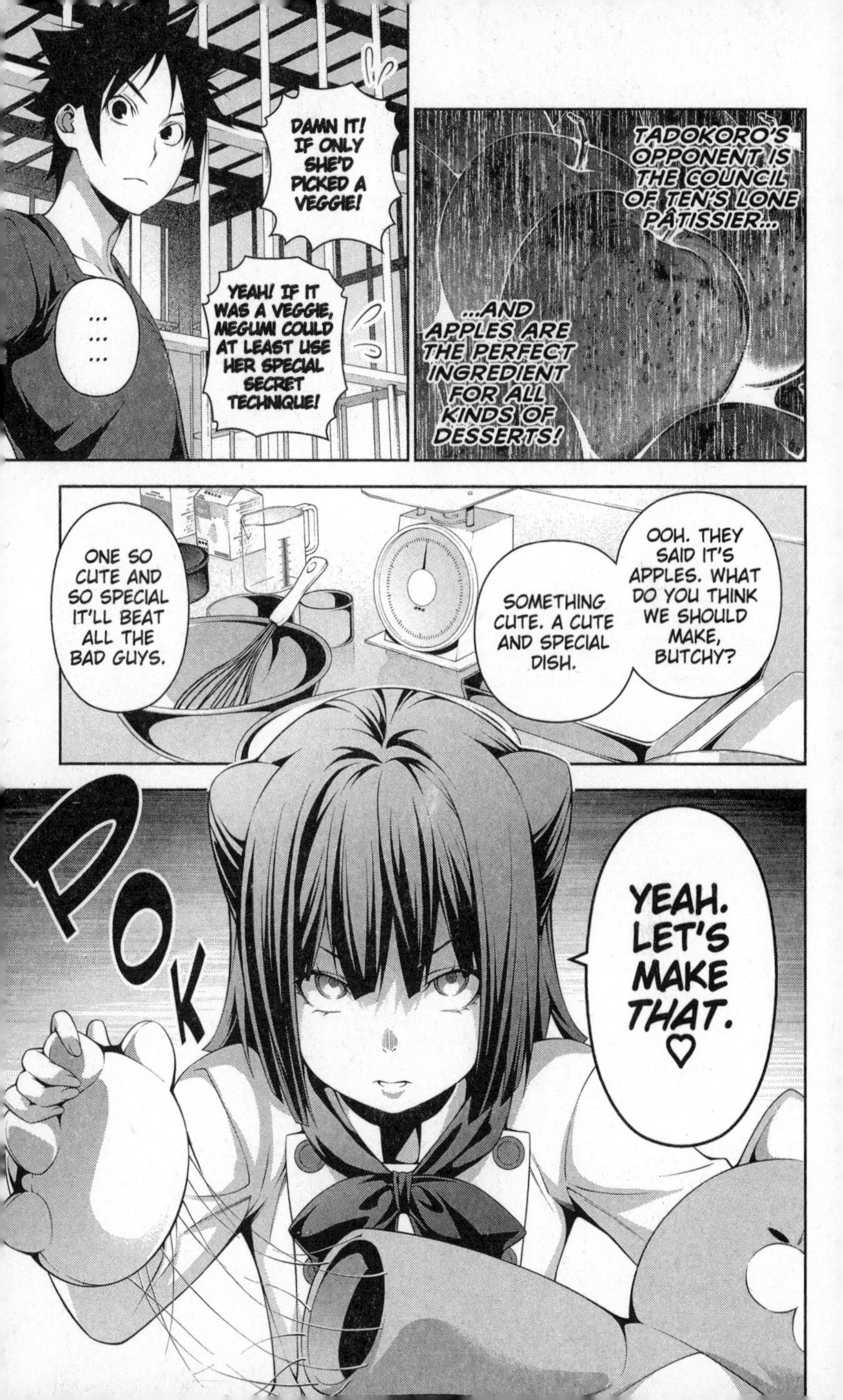
TADOKORO'S OPPONENT IS THE COUNCIL OF TEN'S LONE PÂTISSIER...
...AND APPLES ARE THE PERFECT INGREDIENT FOR ALL KINDS OF DESSERTS!
DAMN IT! IF ONLY SHE'D PICKED A VEGGIE!
YEAH! IF IT WAS A VEGGIE, MEGUMI COULD AT LEAST USE HER SPECIAL SECRET TECHNIQUE!
... ...
OOH. THEY SAID IT'S APPLES. WHAT DO YOU THINK WE SHOULD MAKE, BUTCHY?
SOMETHING CUTE. A CUTE AND SPECIAL DISH.
ONE SO CUTE AND SO SPECIAL IT'LL BEAT ALL THE BAD GUYS.
YEAH. LET'S MAKE *THAT.* ♡
POK

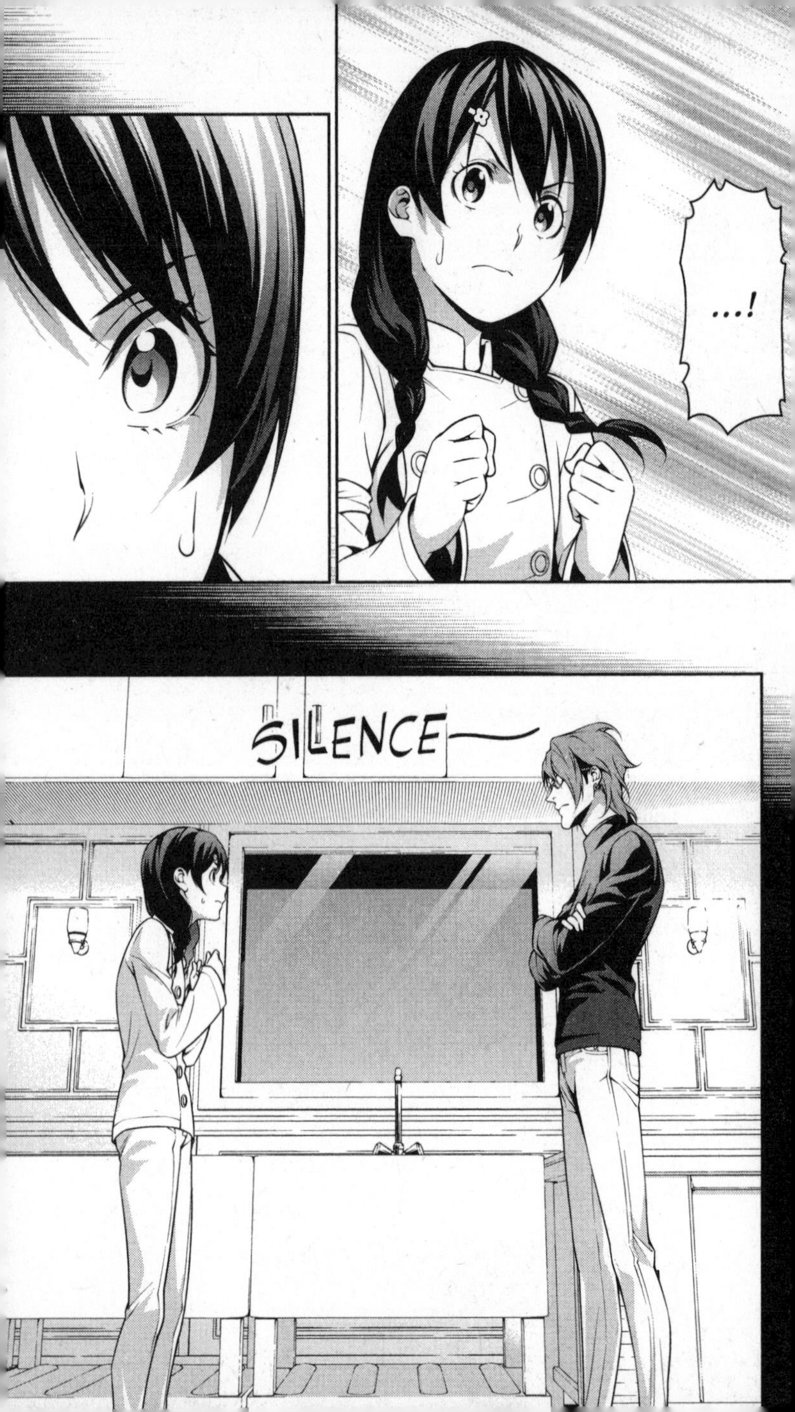
...!
SILLENCE—

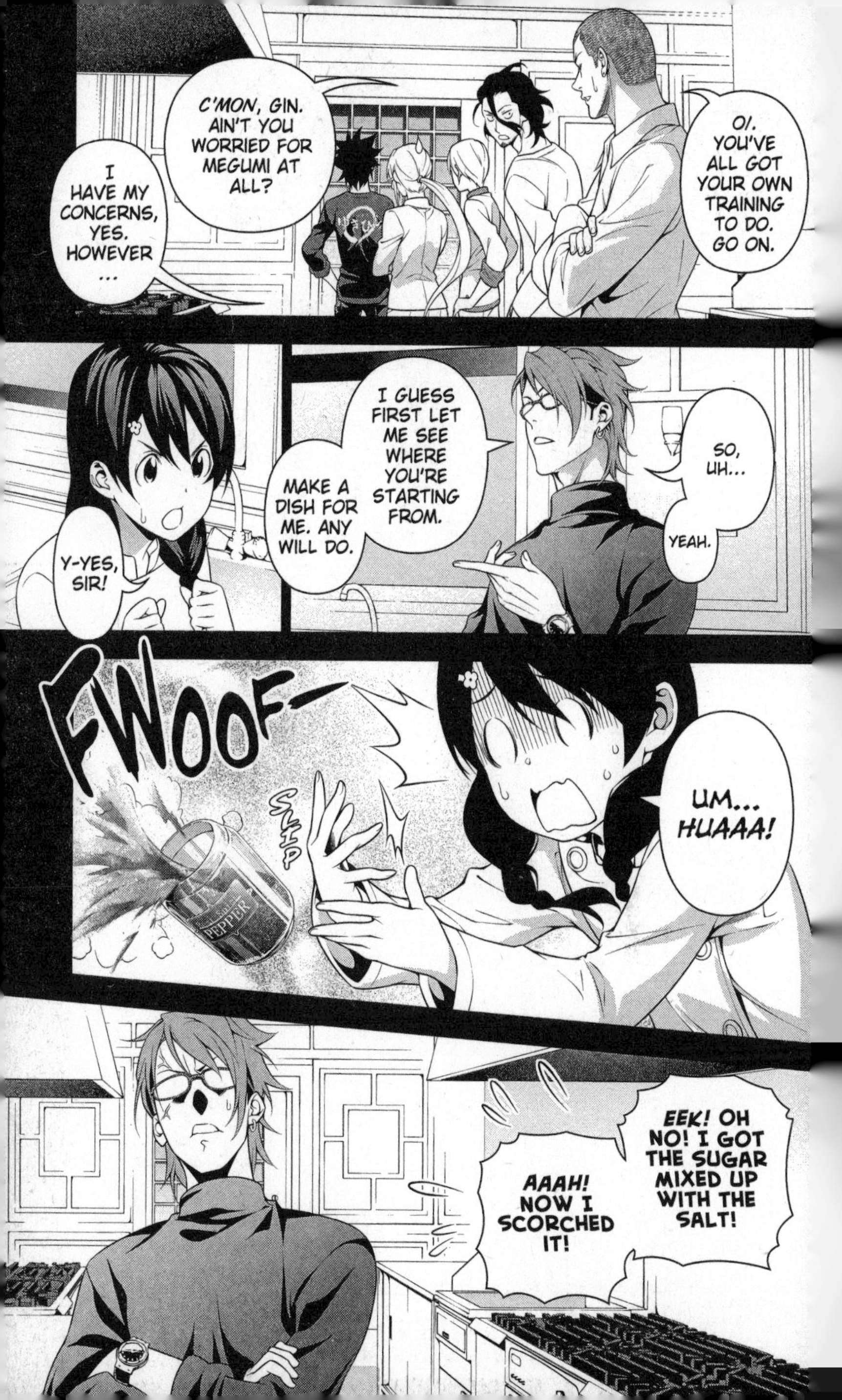
OI. YOU'VE ALL GOT YOUR OWN TRAINING TO DO. GO ON.
C'MON, GIN. AIN'T YOU WORRIED FOR MEGUMI AT ALL?
I HAVE MY CONCERNS, YES. HOWEVER ...
SO, UH...
YEAH.
I GUESS FIRST LET ME SEE WHERE YOU'RE STARTING FROM.
MAKE A DISH FOR ME. ANY WILL DO.
Y-YES, SIR!
UM... HUAAA!
FWOOF-
SLIP
PEPPER
EEK! OH NO! I GOT THE SUGAR MIXED UP WITH THE SALT!
AAAH! NOW I SCORCHED IT!

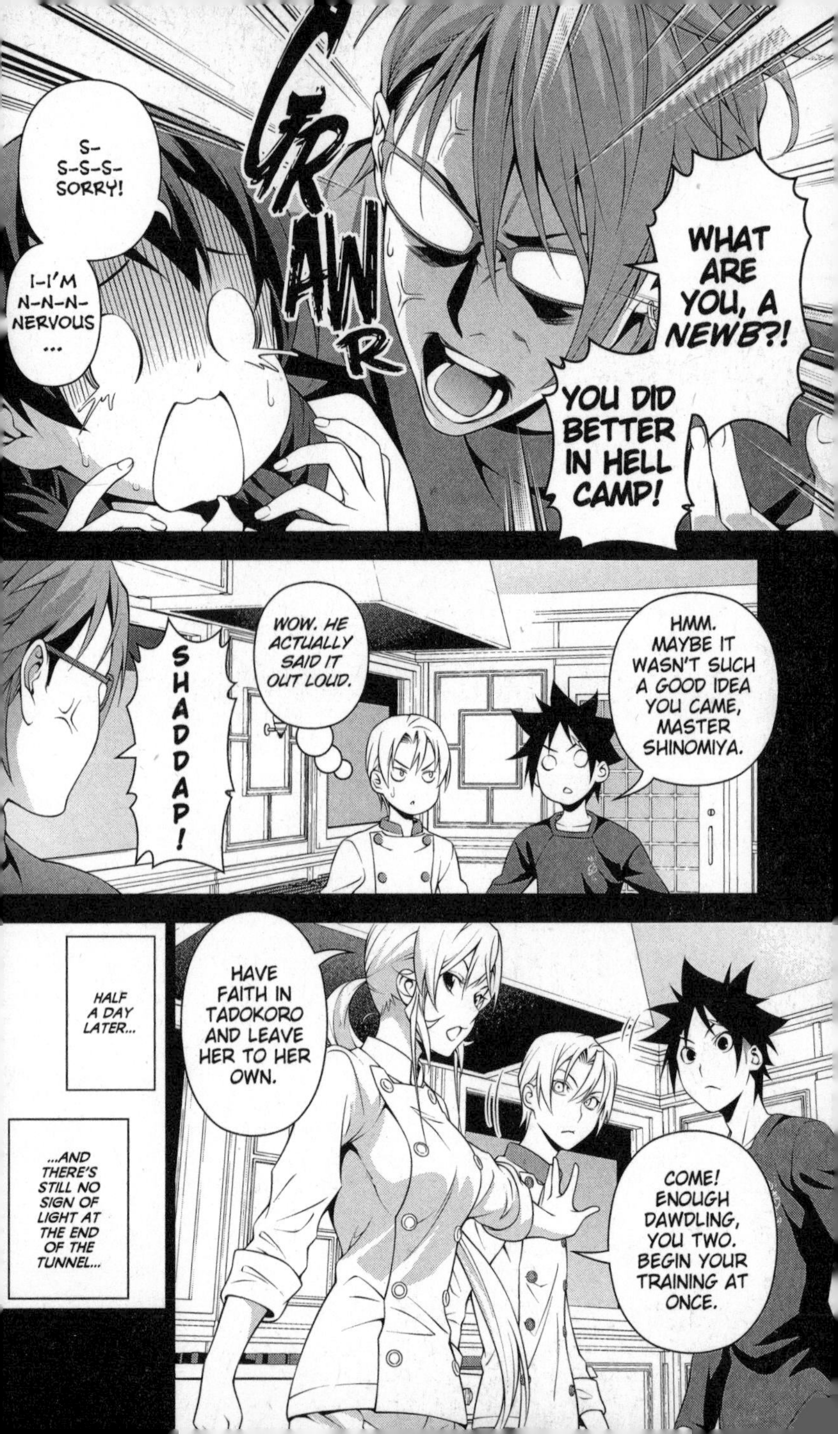
WHAT ARE YOU, A NEWB?!
YOU DID BETTER IN HELL CAMP!
GRAWR
S- S-S-S-SORRY!
I-I'M N-N-N-NERVOUS...
HMM. MAYBE IT WASN'T SUCH A GOOD IDEA YOU CAME, MASTER SHINOMIYA.
WOW. HE ACTUALLY SAID IT OUT LOUD.
SHADDAP!
COME! ENOUGH DAWDLING, YOU TWO. BEGIN YOUR TRAINING AT ONCE.
HAVE FAITH IN TADOKORO AND LEAVE HER TO HER OWN.
HALF A DAY LATER...
...AND THERE'S STILL NO SIGN OF LIGHT AT THE END OF THE TUNNEL...

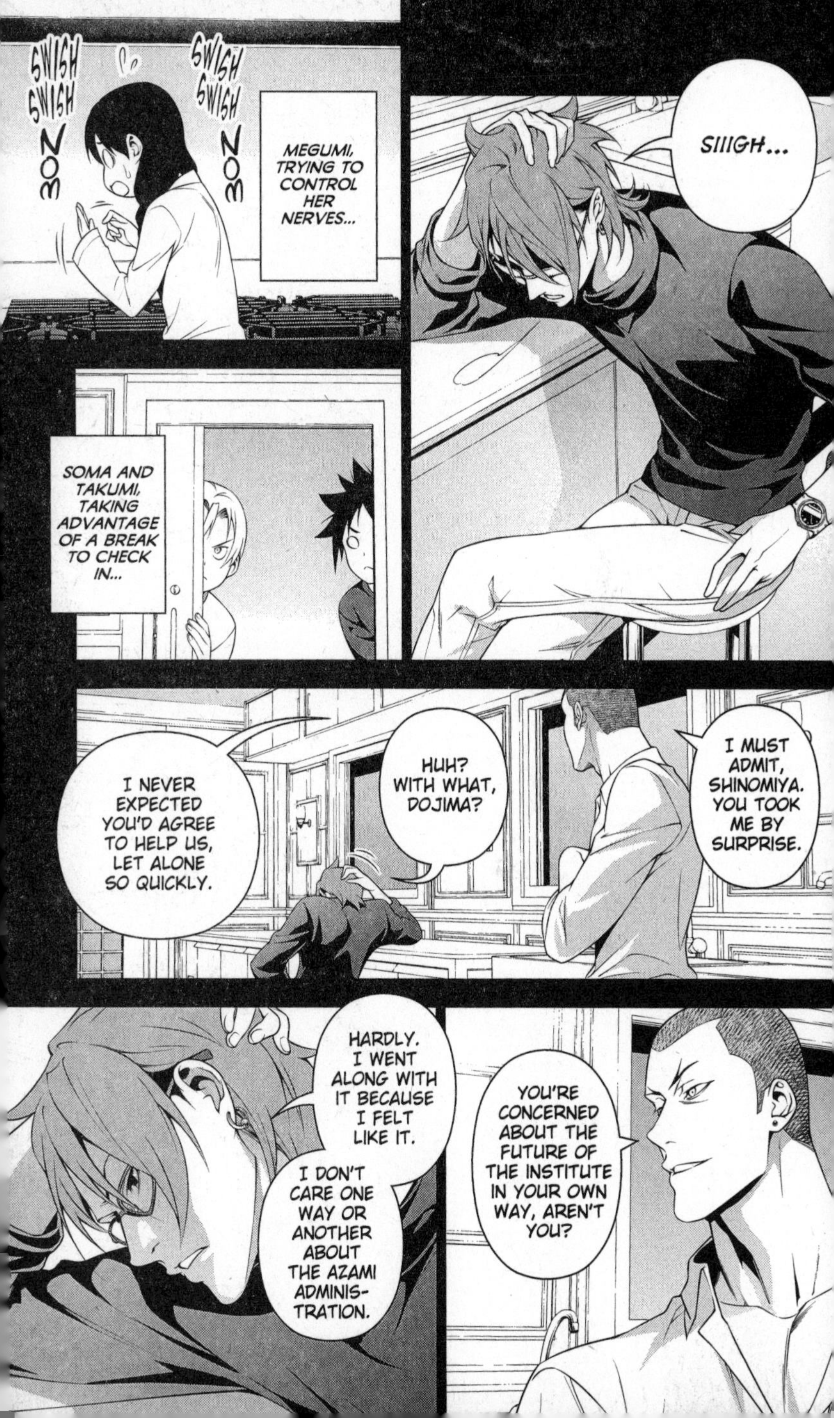
SIIGH...
MEGUMI, TRYING TO CONTROL HER NERVES...
SWISH SWISH NOM
SWISH SWISH NOM
SOMA AND TAKUMI, TAKING ADVANTAGE OF A BREAK TO CHECK IN...
I MUST ADMIT, SHINOMIYA. YOU TOOK ME BY SURPRISE.
HUH? WITH WHAT, DOJIMA?
I NEVER EXPECTED YOU'D AGREE TO HELP US, LET ALONE SO QUICKLY.
YOU'RE CONCERNED ABOUT THE FUTURE OF THE INSTITUTE IN YOUR OWN WAY, AREN'T YOU?
HARDLY. I WENT ALONG WITH IT BECAUSE I FELT LIKE IT.
I DON'T CARE ONE WAY OR ANOTHER ABOUT THE AZAMI ADMINIS-TRATION.

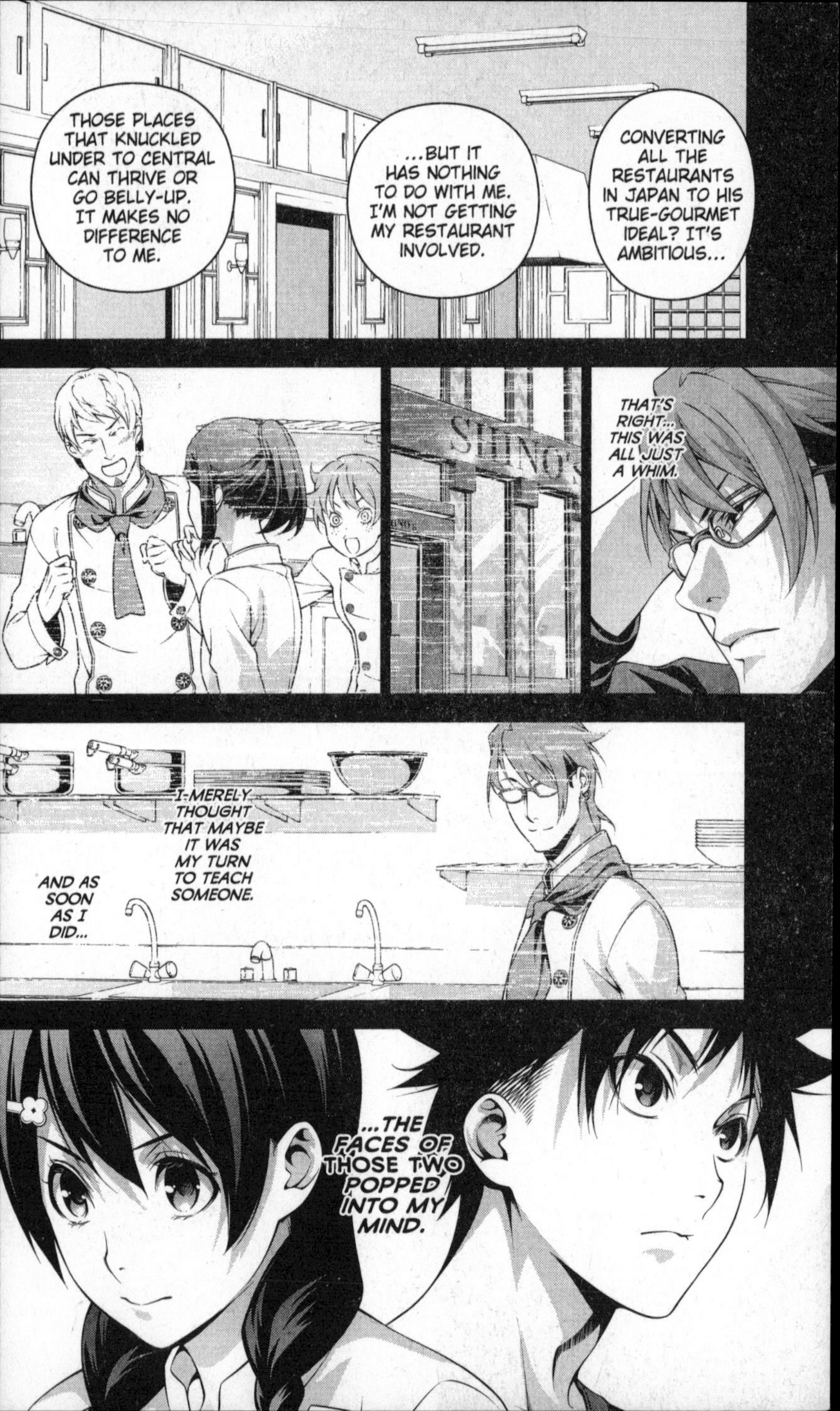
CONVERTING ALL THE RESTAURANTS IN JAPAN TO HIS TRUE-GOURMET IDEAL? IT'S AMBITIOUS...
...BUT IT HAS NOTHING TO DO WITH ME. I'M NOT GETTING MY RESTAURANT INVOLVED.
THOSE PLACES THAT KNUCKLED UNDER TO CENTRAL CAN THRIVE OR GO BELLY-UP. IT MAKES NO DIFFERENCE TO ME.
THAT'S RIGHT... THIS WAS ALL JUST A WHIM.
I MERELY THOUGHT THAT MAYBE IT WAS MY TURN TO TEACH SOMEONE.
AND AS SOON AS I DID...
...THE FACES OF THOSE TWO POPPED INTO MY MIND.

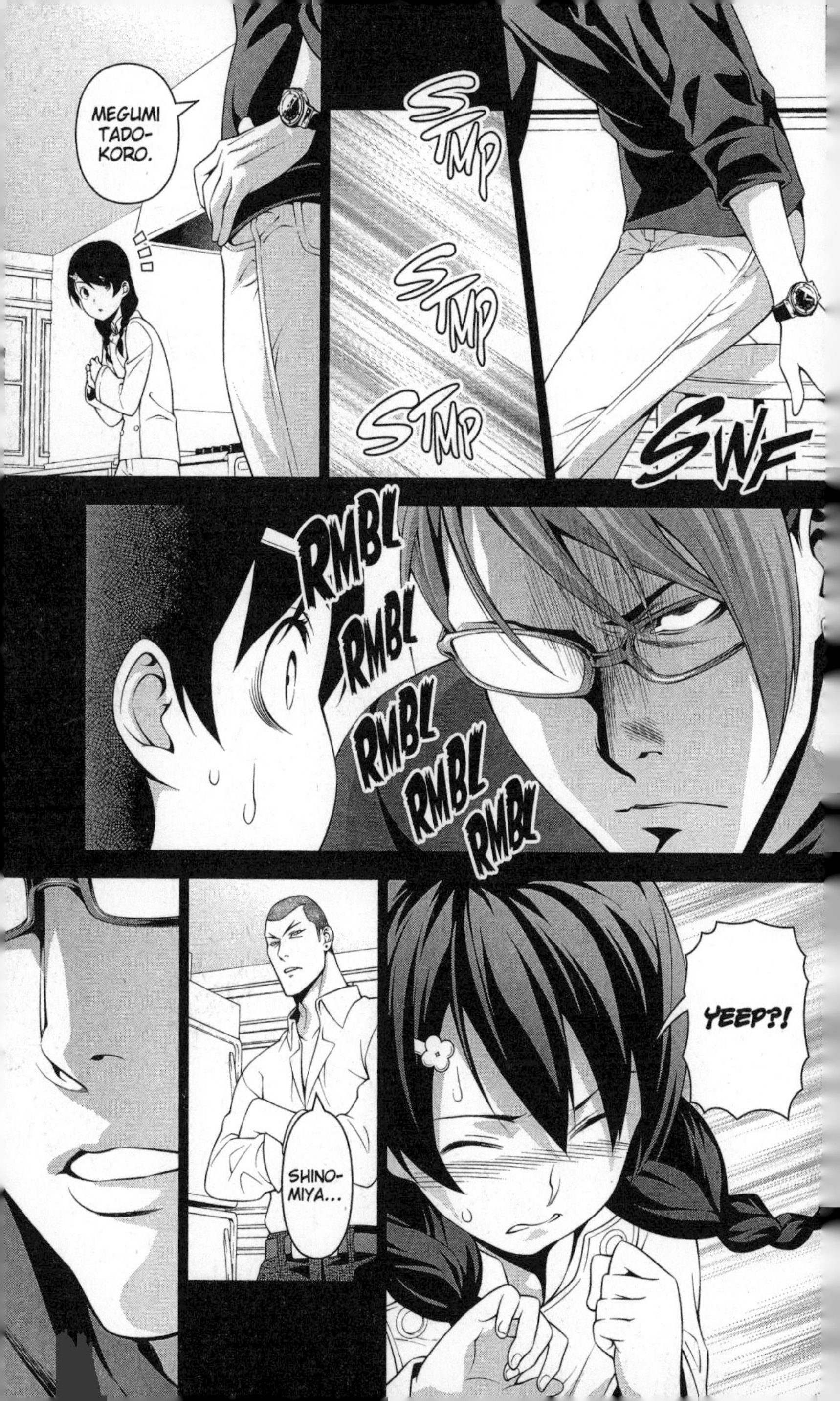
SWF
STMP
STMP
STMP
MEGUMI TADOKORO.
RMBL RMBL RMBL RMBL RMBL RMBL
YEEP?!
SHINOMIYA...

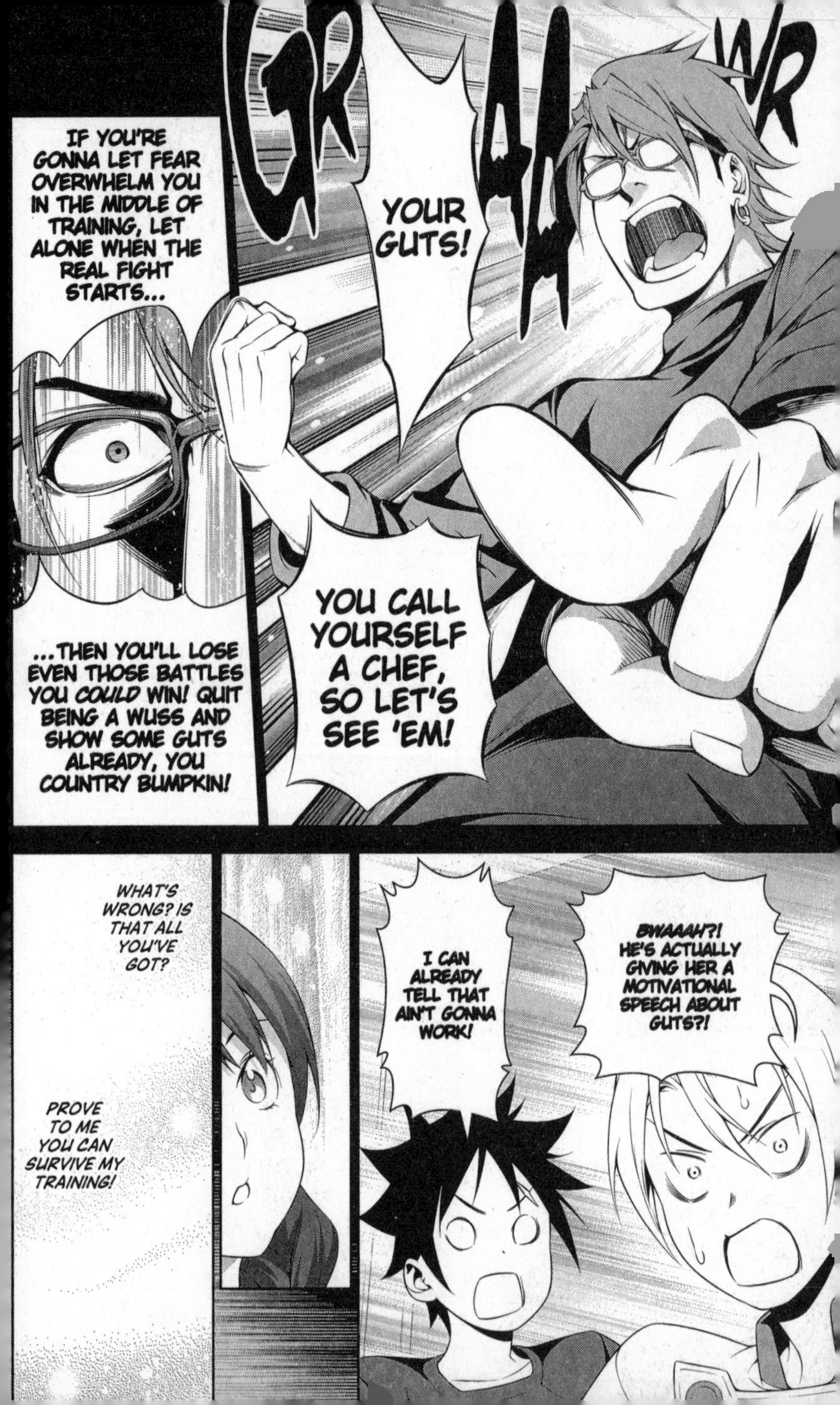
GRAAWR
YOUR GUTS!
YOU CALL YOURSELF A CHEF, SO LET'S SEE 'EM!
IF YOU'RE GONNA LET FEAR OVERWHELM YOU IN THE MIDDLE OF TRAINING, LET ALONE WHEN THE REAL FIGHT STARTS...
...THEN YOU'LL LOSE EVEN THOSE BATTLES YOU COULD WIN! QUIT BEING A WUSS AND SHOW SOME GUTS ALREADY, YOU COUNTRY BUMPKIN!
BWAAAH?! HE'S ACTUALLY GIVING HER A MOTIVATIONAL SPEECH ABOUT GUTS?!
I CAN ALREADY TELL THAT AIN'T GONNA WORK!
WHAT'S WRONG? IS THAT ALL YOU'VE GOT?
PROVE TO ME YOU CAN SURVIVE MY TRAINING!

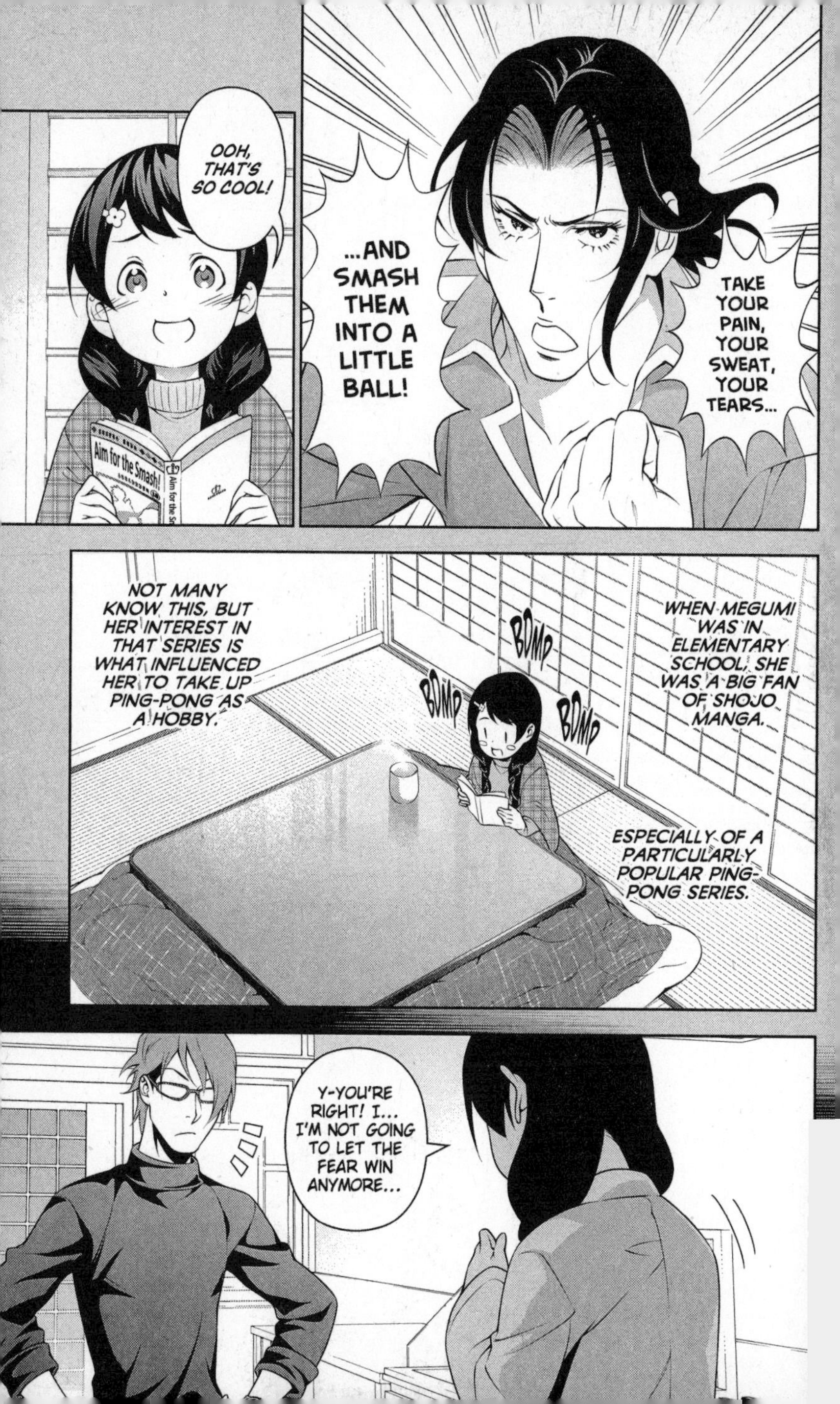
TAKE YOUR PAIN, YOUR SWEAT, YOUR TEARS...
...AND SMASH THEM INTO A LITTLE BALL!
OOH, THAT'S SO COOL!
Aim for the Smash!
WHEN MEGUMI WAS IN ELEMENTARY SCHOOL, SHE WAS A BIG FAN OF SHOJO MANGA.
ESPECIALLY OF A PARTICULARLY POPULAR PING-PONG SERIES.
BOMP
BOMP
BOMP
NOT MANY KNOW THIS, BUT HER INTEREST IN THAT SERIES IS WHAT INFLUENCED HER TO TAKE UP PING-PONG AS A HOBBY.
Y-YOU'RE RIGHT! I... I'M NOT GOING TO LET THE FEAR WIN ANYMORE...

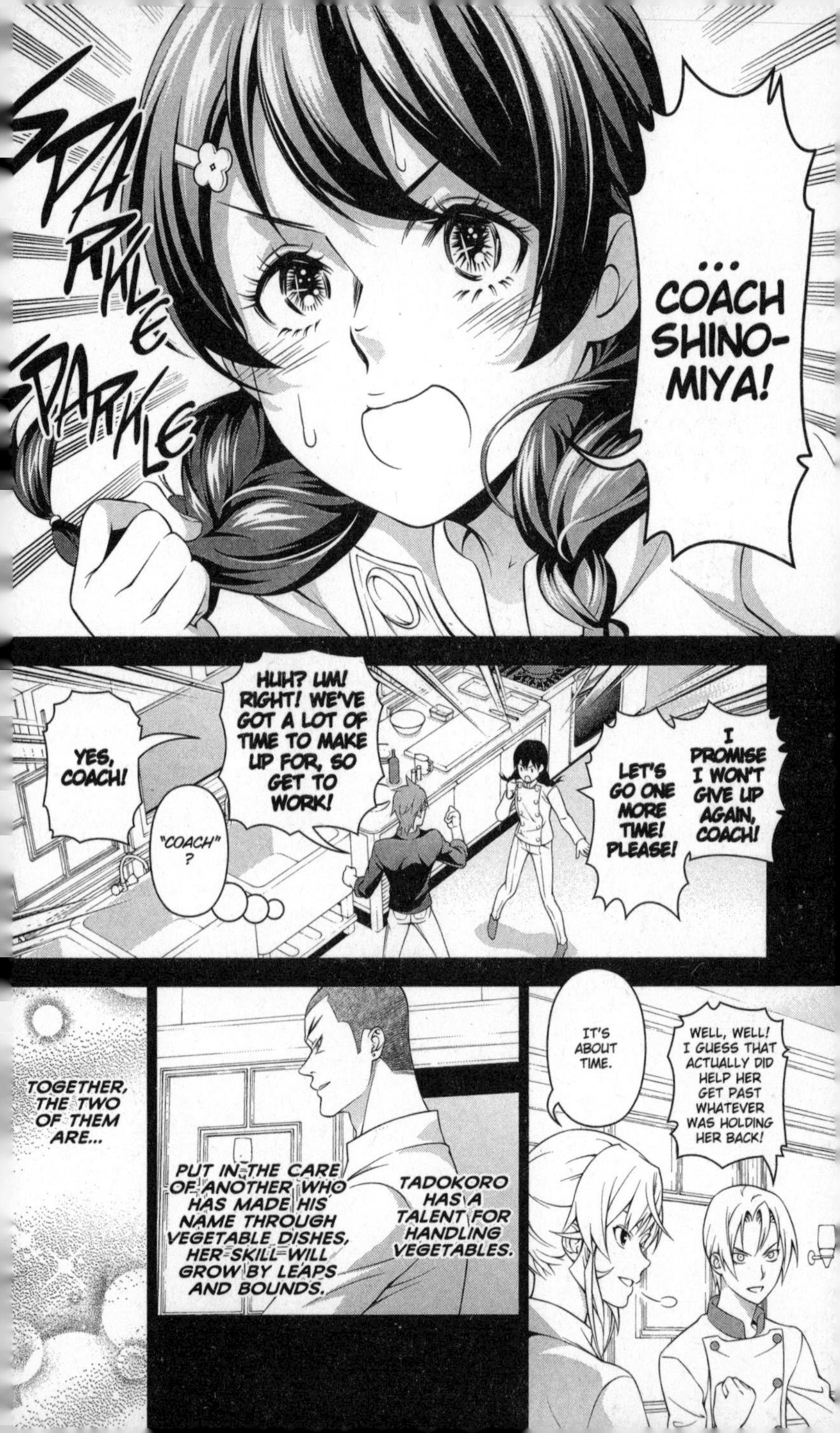
...COACH SHINO-MIYA!
SPARKLE SPARKLE
I PROMISE I WON'T GIVE UP AGAIN, COACH!
LET'S GO ONE MORE TIME! PLEASE!
HUH? UM! RIGHT! WE'VE GOT A LOT OF TIME TO MAKE UP FOR, SO GET TO WORK!
"COACH"?
YES, COACH!
WELL, WELL! I GUESS THAT ACTUALLY DID HELP HER GET PAST WHATEVER WAS HOLDING HER BACK!
IT'S ABOUT TIME.
TADOKORO HAS A TALENT FOR HANDLING VEGETABLES.
PUT IN THE CARE OF ANOTHER WHO HAS MADE HIS NAME THROUGH VEGETABLE DISHES, HER SKILL WILL GROW BY LEAPS AND BOUNDS.
TOGETHER, THE TWO OF THEM ARE...

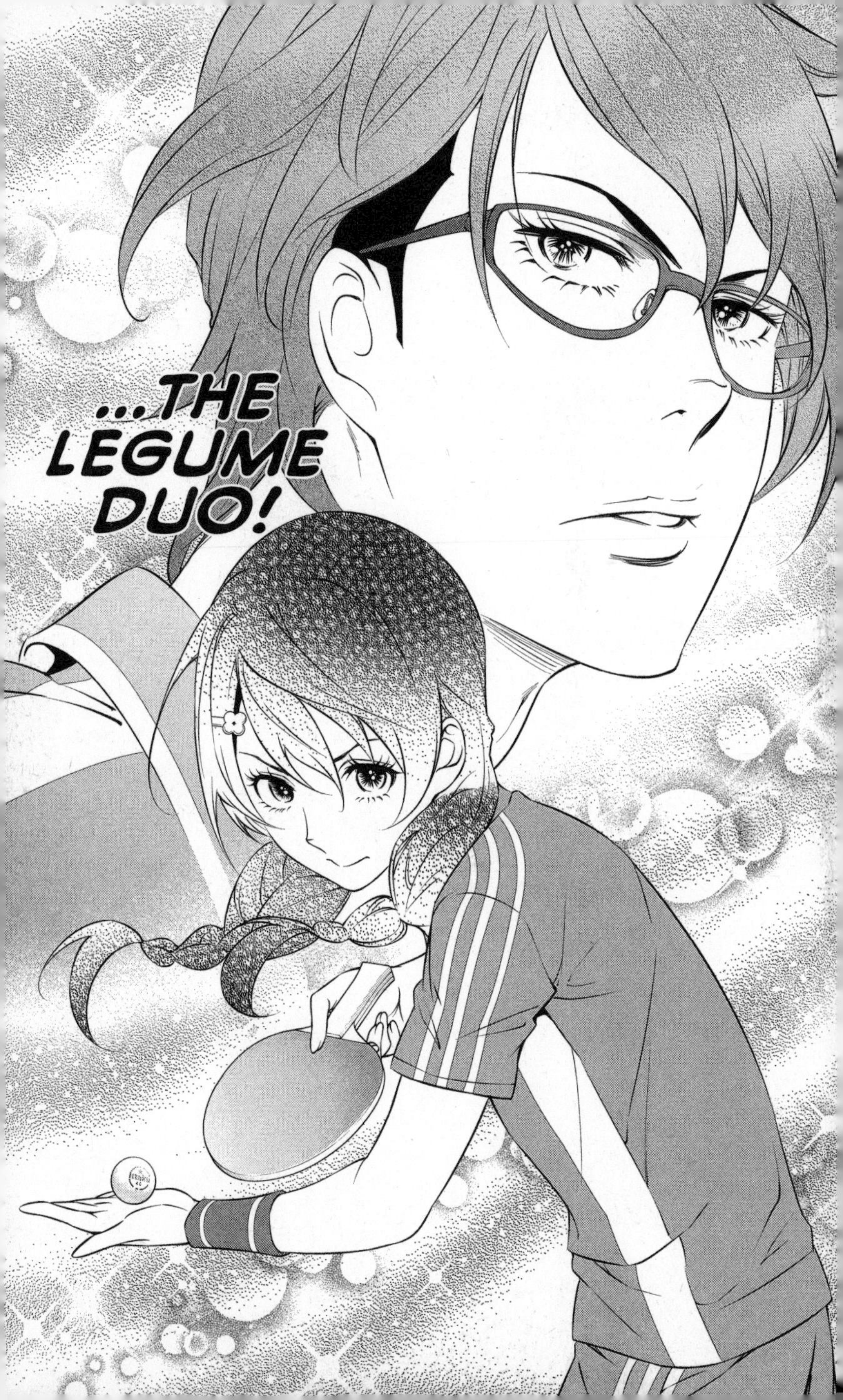
...THE LEGUME DUO!

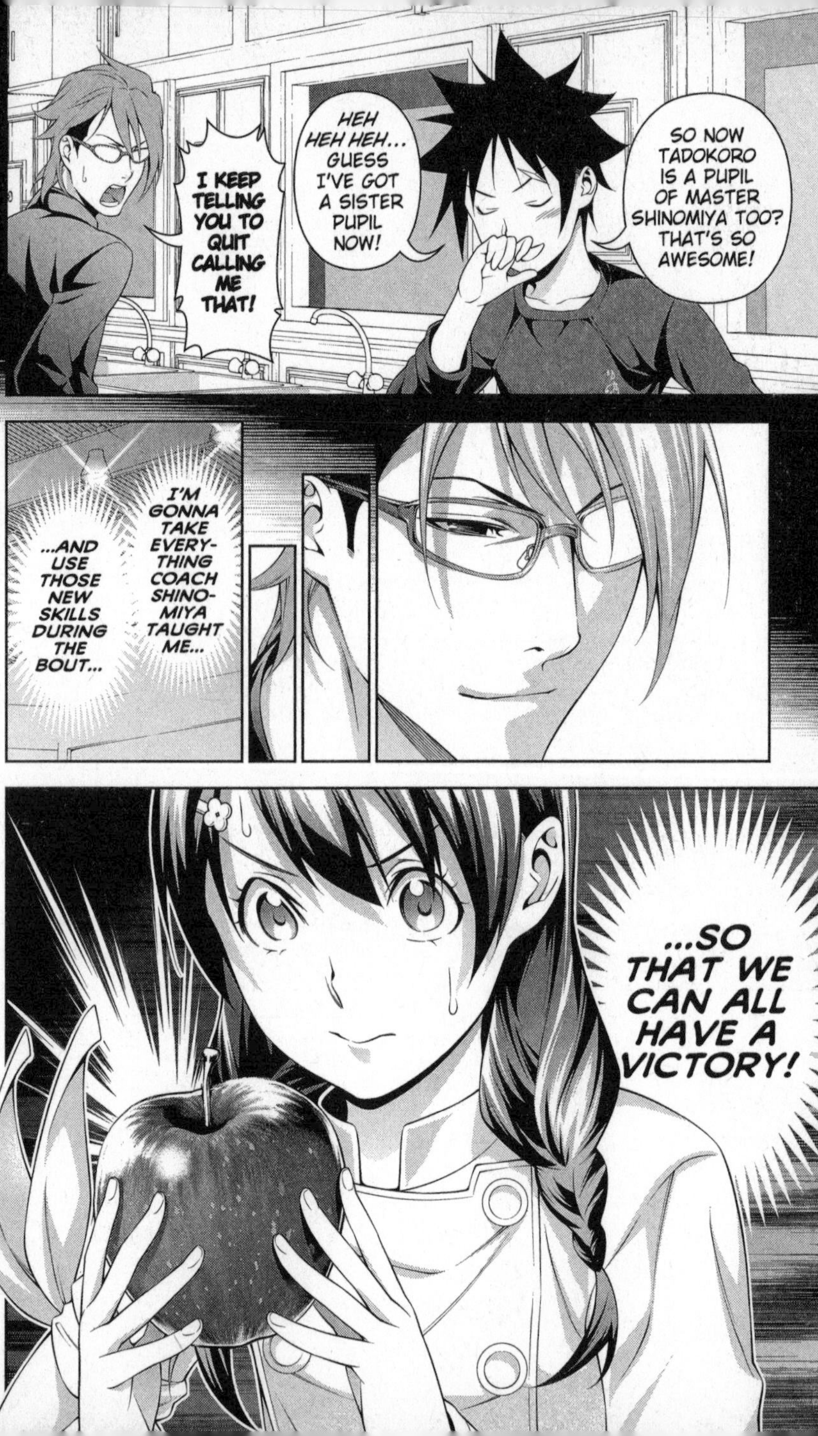
SO NOW TADOKORO IS A PUPIL OF MASTER SHINOMIYA TOO? THAT'S SO AWESOME!
HEH HEH HEH... GUESS I'VE GOT A SISTER PUPIL NOW!
I KEEP TELLING YOU TO QUIT CALLING ME THAT!
I'M GONNA TAKE EVERY-THING COACH SHINO-MIYA TAUGHT ME...
...AND USE THOSE NEW SKILLS DURING THE BOUT...
...SO THAT WE CAN ALL HAVE A VICTORY!

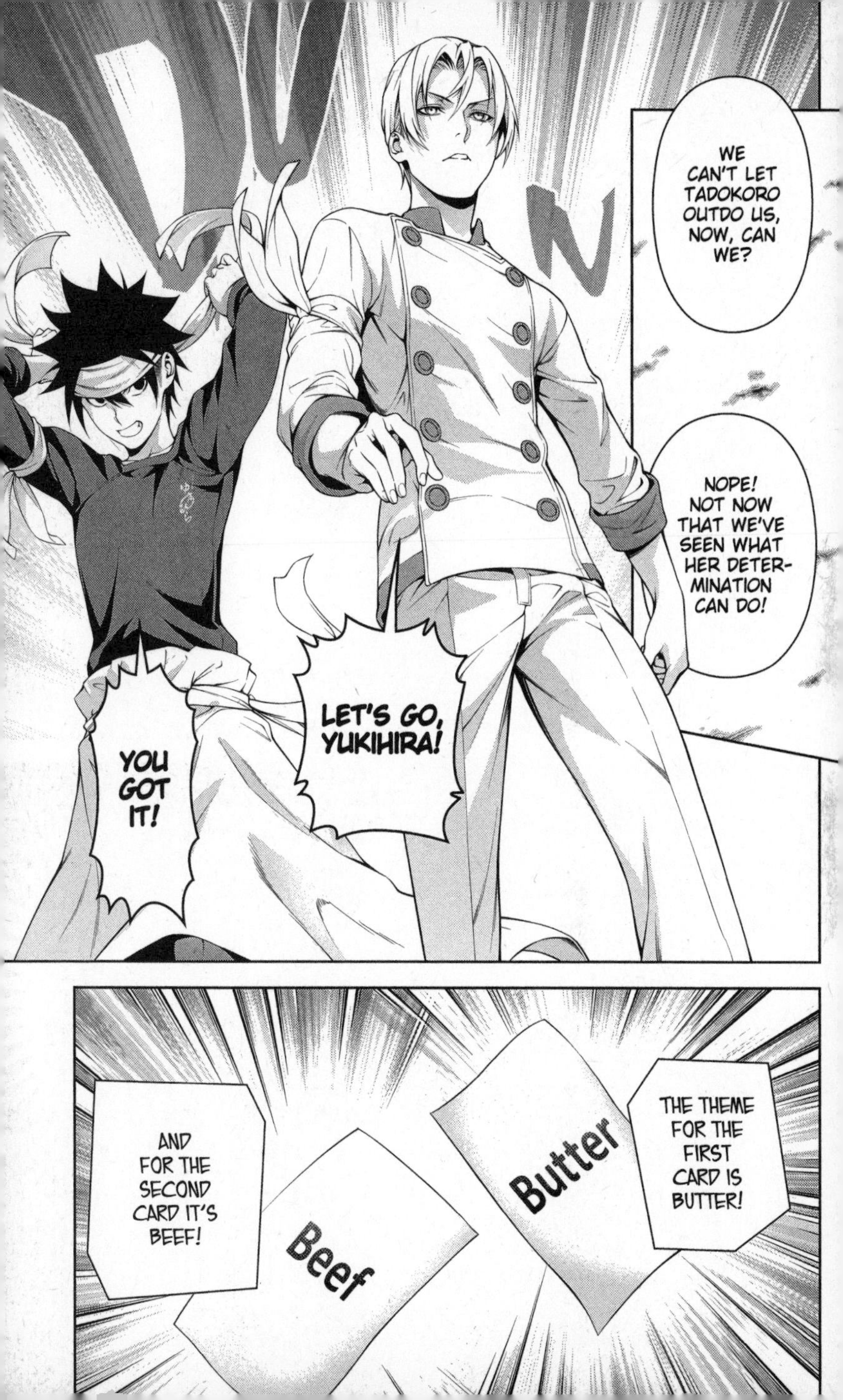
WE CAN'T LET TADOKORO OUTDO US, NOW, CAN WE?
NOPE! NOT NOW THAT WE'VE SEEN WHAT HER DETERMINATION CAN DO!
LET'S GO, YUKIHIRA!
YOU GOT IT!
THE THEME FOR THE FIRST CARD IS BUTTER!
Butter
Beef
AND FOR THE SECOND CARD IT'S BEEF!

ARTIST: YUTO TSUKUDA RECIPE BY: YUKI MORISAKI

VOLUME 27 SPECIAL SUPPLEMENT!

PRACTICAL RECIPE #5

TSUKASA'S GREEN TEA PUREE

SIMPLIFIED HOME VERSION

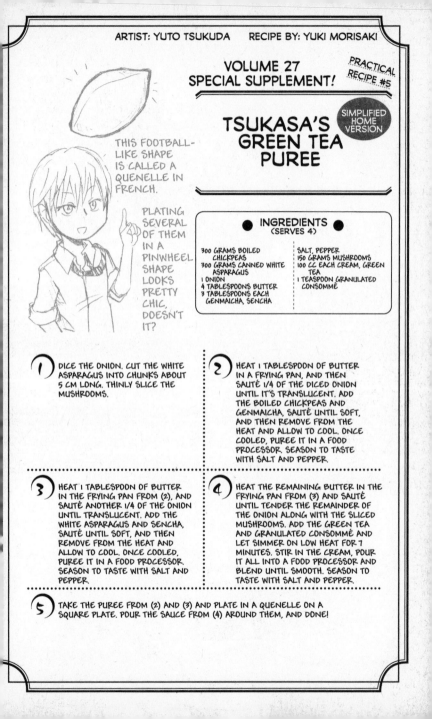

THIS FOOTBALL-LIKE SHAPE IS CALLED A QUENELLE IN FRENCH.

PLATING SEVERAL OF THEM IN A PINWHEEL SHAPE LOOKS PRETTY CHIC, DOESN'T IT?

INGREDIENTS
(SERVES 4)

- 300 GRAMS BOILED CHICKPEAS
- 300 GRAMS CANNED WHITE ASPARAGUS
- 1 ONION
- 4 TABLESPOONS BUTTER
- 3 TABLESPOONS EACH GENMAICHA, SENCHA
- SALT, PEPPER
- 150 GRAMS MUSHROOMS
- 100 CC EACH CREAM, GREEN TEA
- 1 TEASPOON GRANULATED CONSOMMÉ

1. DICE THE ONION. CUT THE WHITE ASPARAGUS INTO CHUNKS ABOUT 5 CM LONG. THINLY SLICE THE MUSHROOMS.

2. HEAT 1 TABLESPOON OF BUTTER IN A FRYING PAN, AND THEN SAUTÉ 1/4 OF THE DICED ONION UNTIL IT'S TRANSLUCENT. ADD THE BOILED CHICKPEAS AND GENMAICHA, SAUTÉ UNTIL SOFT, AND THEN REMOVE FROM THE HEAT AND ALLOW TO COOL. ONCE COOLED, PUREE IT IN A FOOD PROCESSOR. SEASON TO TASTE WITH SALT AND PEPPER.

3. HEAT 1 TABLESPOON OF BUTTER IN THE FRYING PAN FROM (2), AND SAUTÉ ANOTHER 1/4 OF THE ONION UNTIL TRANSLUCENT. ADD THE WHITE ASPARAGUS AND SENCHA, SAUTÉ UNTIL SOFT, AND THEN REMOVE FROM THE HEAT AND ALLOW TO COOL. ONCE COOLED, PUREE IT IN A FOOD PROCESSOR. SEASON TO TASTE WITH SALT AND PEPPER.

4. HEAT THE REMAINING BUTTER IN THE FRYING PAN FROM (3) AND SAUTÉ UNTIL TENDER THE REMAINDER OF THE ONION ALONG WITH THE SLICED MUSHROOMS. ADD THE GREEN TEA AND GRANULATED CONSOMMÉ AND LET SIMMER ON LOW HEAT FOR 7 MINUTES. STIR IN THE CREAM, POUR IT ALL INTO A FOOD PROCESSOR AND BLEND UNTIL SMOOTH. SEASON TO TASTE WITH SALT AND PEPPER.

5. TAKE THE PUREE FROM (2) AND (3) AND PLATE IN A QUENELLE ON A SQUARE PLATE. POUR THE SAUCE FROM (4) AROUND THEM, AND DONE!

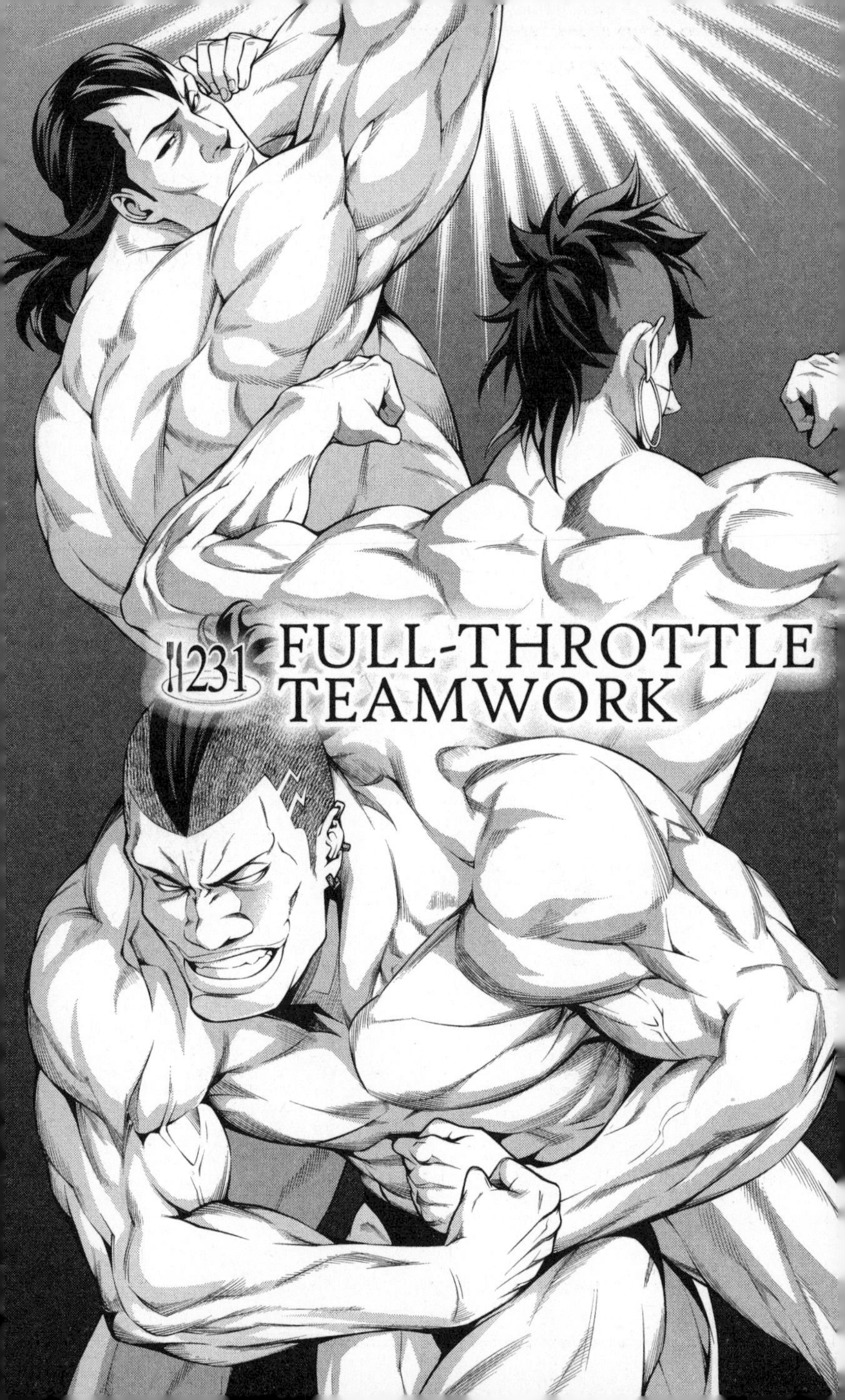
231
FULL-THROTTLE
TEAMWORK

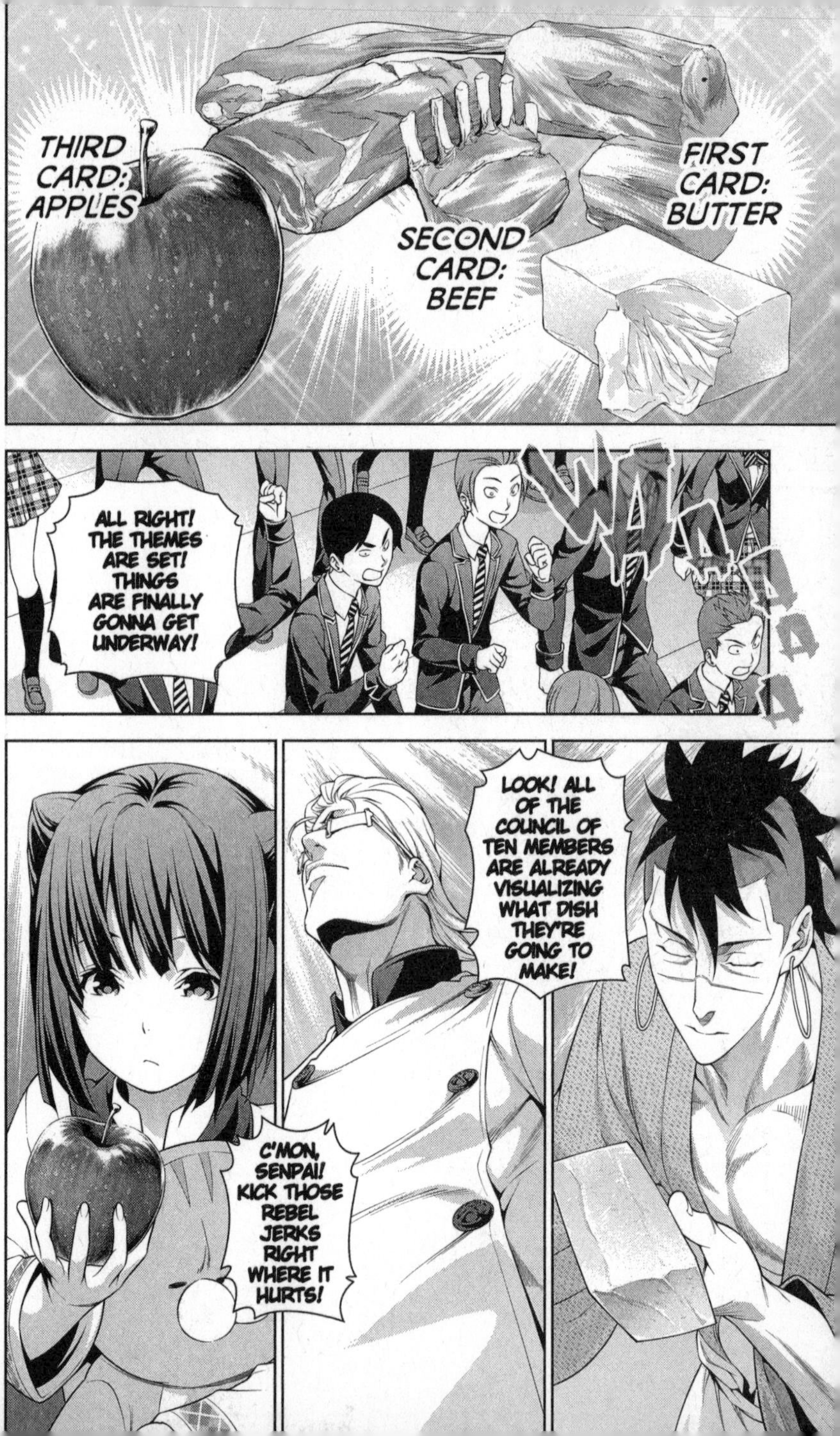
FIRST CARD: BUTTER
SECOND CARD: BEEF
THIRD CARD: APPLES
ALL RIGHT! THE THEMES ARE SET! THINGS ARE FINALLY GONNA GET UNDERWAY!
LOOK! ALL OF THE COUNCIL OF TEN MEMBERS ARE ALREADY VISUALIZING WHAT DISH THEY'RE GOING TO MAKE!
C'MON, SENPAI! KICK THOSE REBEL JERKS RIGHT WHERE IT HURTS!

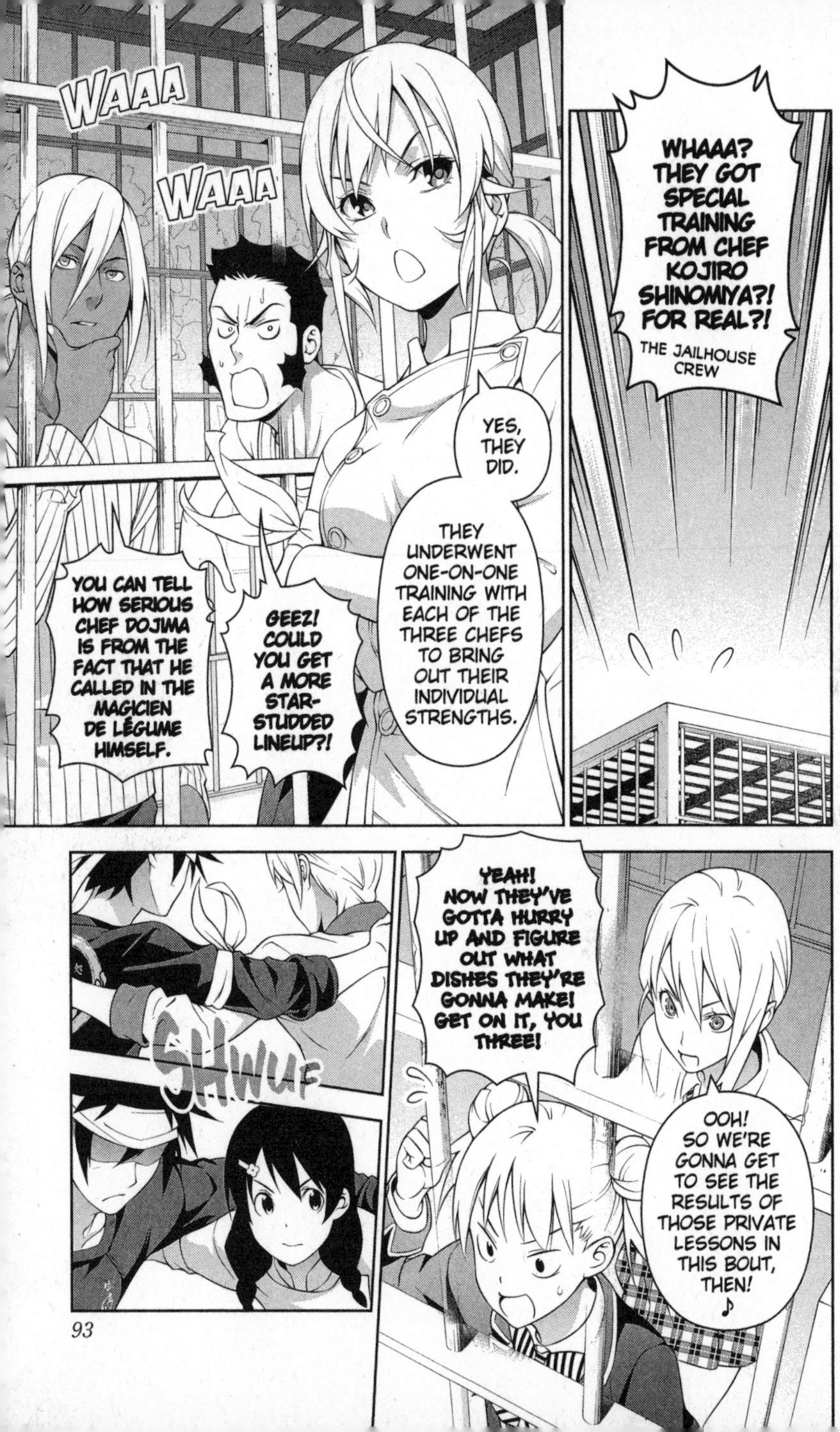
WHAAA? THEY GOT SPECIAL TRAINING FROM CHEF KOJIRO SHINOMIYA?! FOR REAL?!
THE JAILHOUSE CREW
WAAA
WAAA
YES, THEY DID.
THEY UNDERWENT ONE-ON-ONE TRAINING WITH EACH OF THE THREE CHEFS TO BRING OUT THEIR INDIVIDUAL STRENGTHS.
GEEZ! COULD YOU GET A MORE STAR-STUDDED LINEUP?!
YOU CAN TELL HOW SERIOUS CHEF DOJIMA IS FROM THE FACT THAT HE CALLED IN THE MAGICIEN DE LÉGUME HIMSELF.
YEAH! NOW THEY'VE GOTTA HURRY UP AND FIGURE OUT WHAT DISHES THEY'RE GONNA MAKE! GET ON IT, YOU THREE!
OOH! SO WE'RE GONNA GET TO SEE THE RESULTS OF THOSE PRIVATE LESSONS IN THIS BOUT, THEN! ♪
SHWUF

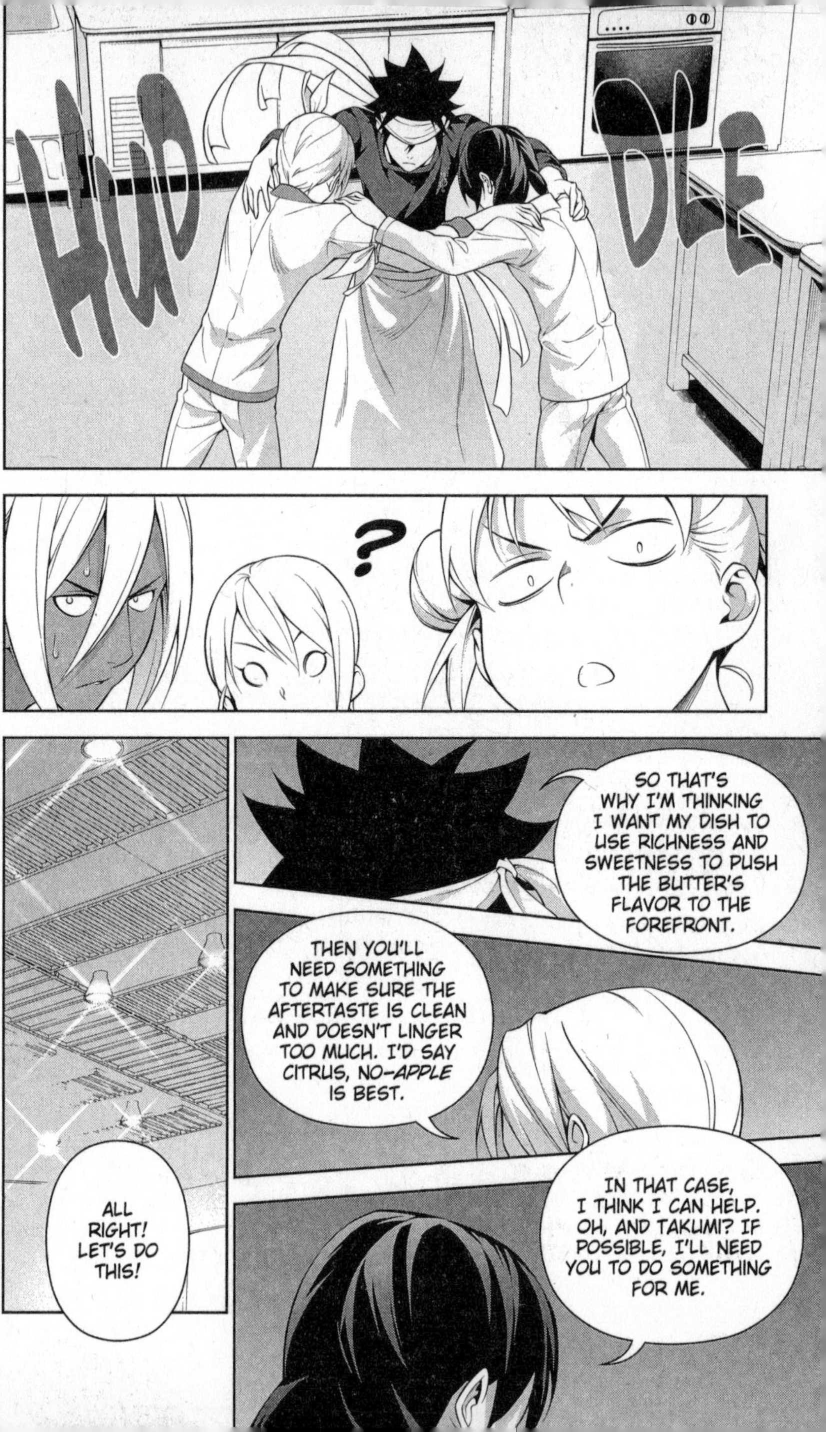
HUDDLE
SO THAT'S WHY I'M THINKING I WANT MY DISH TO USE RICHNESS AND SWEETNESS TO PUSH THE BUTTER'S FLAVOR TO THE FOREFRONT.
THEN YOU'LL NEED SOMETHING TO MAKE SURE THE AFTERTASTE IS CLEAN AND DOESN'T LINGER TOO MUCH. I'D SAY CITRUS, NO–*APPLE* IS BEST.
IN THAT CASE, I THINK I CAN HELP. OH, AND TAKUMI? IF POSSIBLE, I'LL NEED YOU TO DO SOMETHING FOR ME.
ALL RIGHT! LET'S DO THIS!

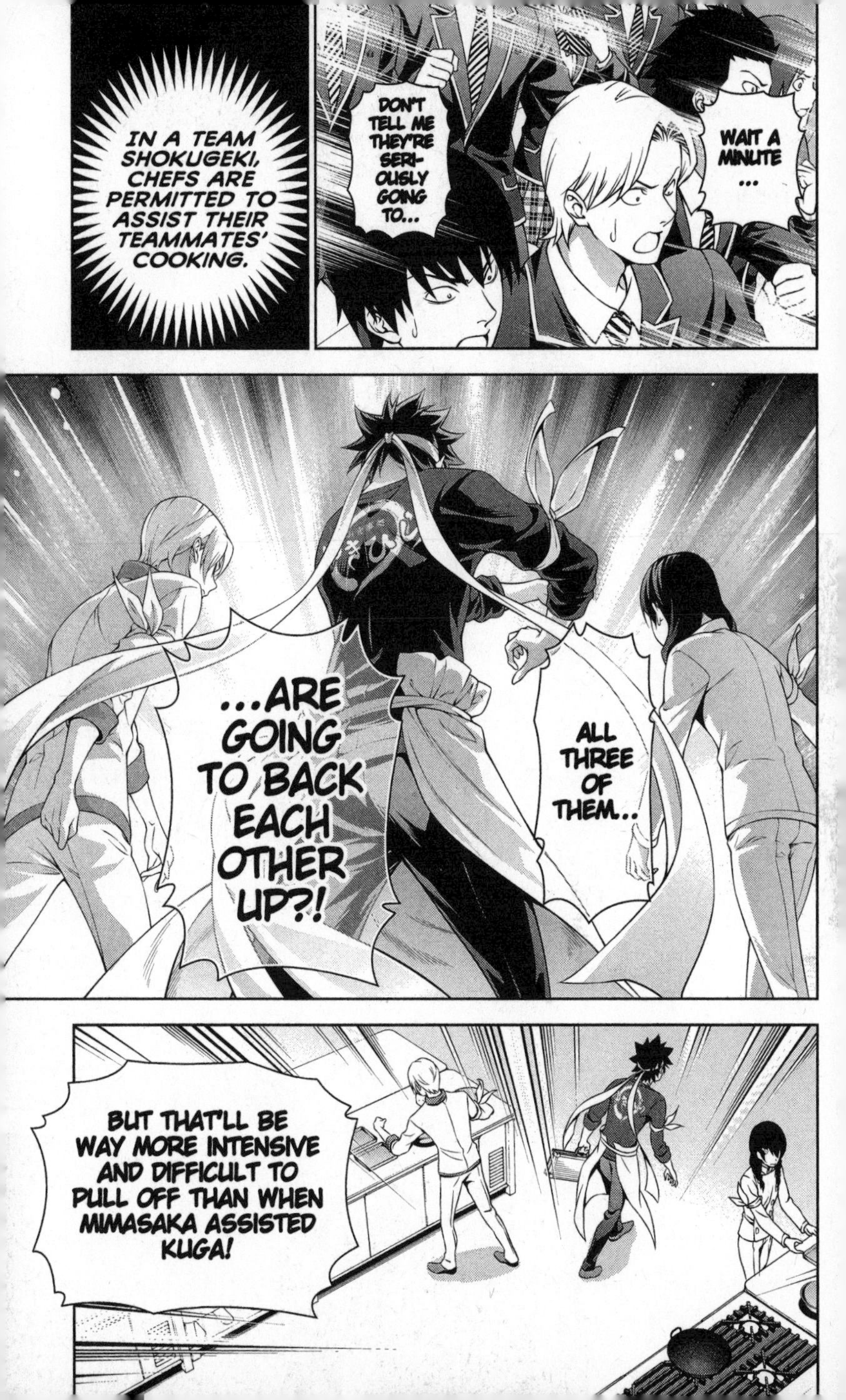
WAIT A MINUTE ...
DON'T TELL ME THEY'RE SERIOUSLY GOING TO...
IN A TEAM SHOKUGEKI, CHEFS ARE PERMITTED TO ASSIST THEIR TEAMMATES' COOKING.
ALL THREE OF THEM...
...ARE GOING TO BACK EACH OTHER UP?!
BUT THAT'LL BE WAY MORE INTENSIVE AND DIFFICULT TO PULL OFF THAN WHEN MIMASAKA ASSISTED KUGA!

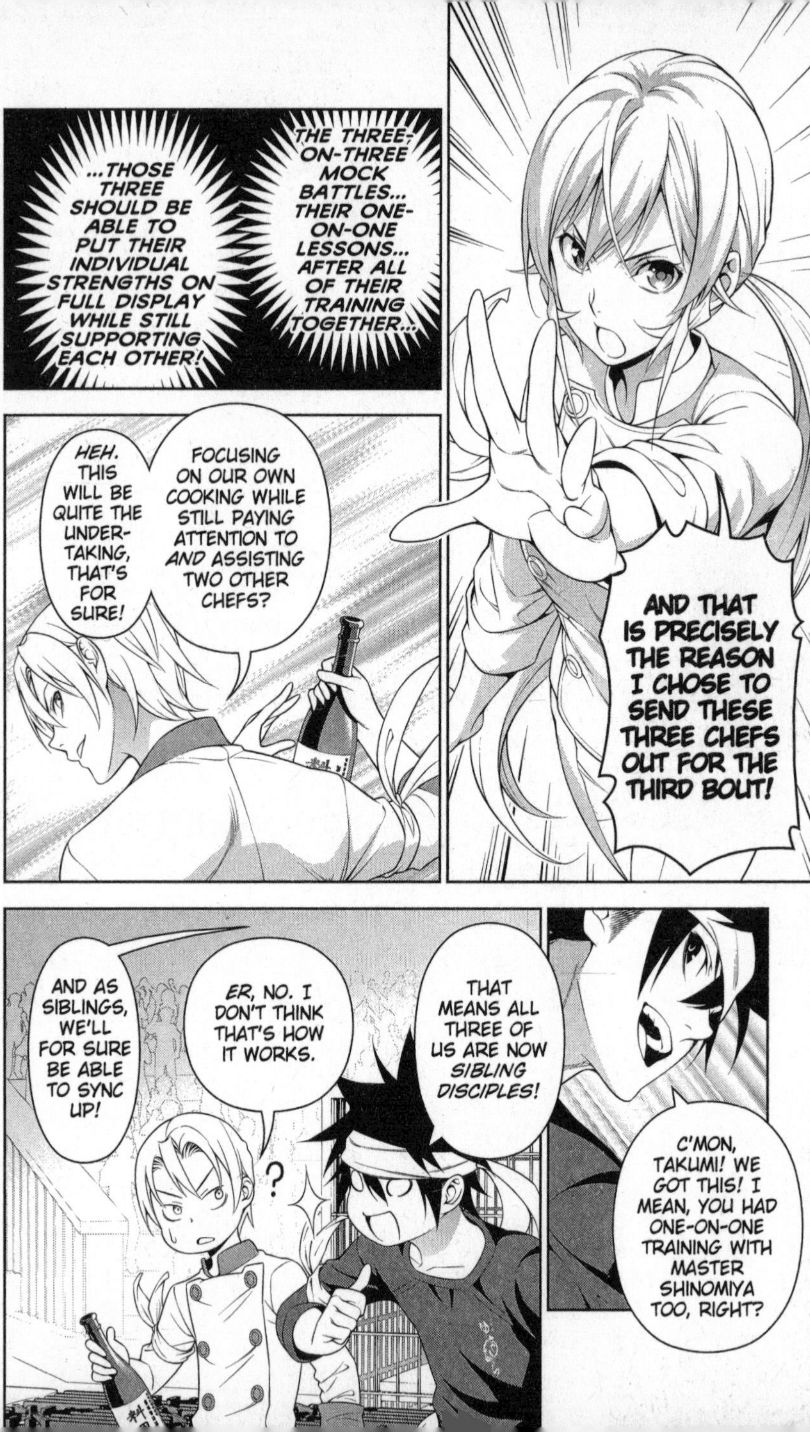
AND THAT IS PRECISELY THE REASON I CHOSE TO SEND THESE THREE CHEFS OUT FOR THE THIRD BOUT!
THE THREE-ON-THREE MOCK BATTLES... THEIR ONE-ON-ONE LESSONS... AFTER ALL OF THEIR TRAINING TOGETHER...
...THOSE THREE SHOULD BE ABLE TO PUT THEIR INDIVIDUAL STRENGTHS ON FULL DISPLAY WHILE STILL SUPPORTING EACH OTHER!
FOCUSING ON OUR OWN COOKING WHILE STILL PAYING ATTENTION TO *AND* ASSISTING TWO OTHER CHEFS?
HEH. THIS WILL BE QUITE THE UNDERTAKING, THAT'S FOR SURE!
C'MON, TAKUMI! WE GOT THIS! I MEAN, YOU HAD ONE-ON-ONE TRAINING WITH MASTER SHINOMIYA TOO, RIGHT?
THAT MEANS ALL THREE OF US ARE NOW *SIBLING DISCIPLES!*
ER, NO. I DON'T THINK THAT'S HOW IT WORKS.
AND AS SIBLINGS, WE'LL FOR SURE BE ABLE TO SYNC UP!
?

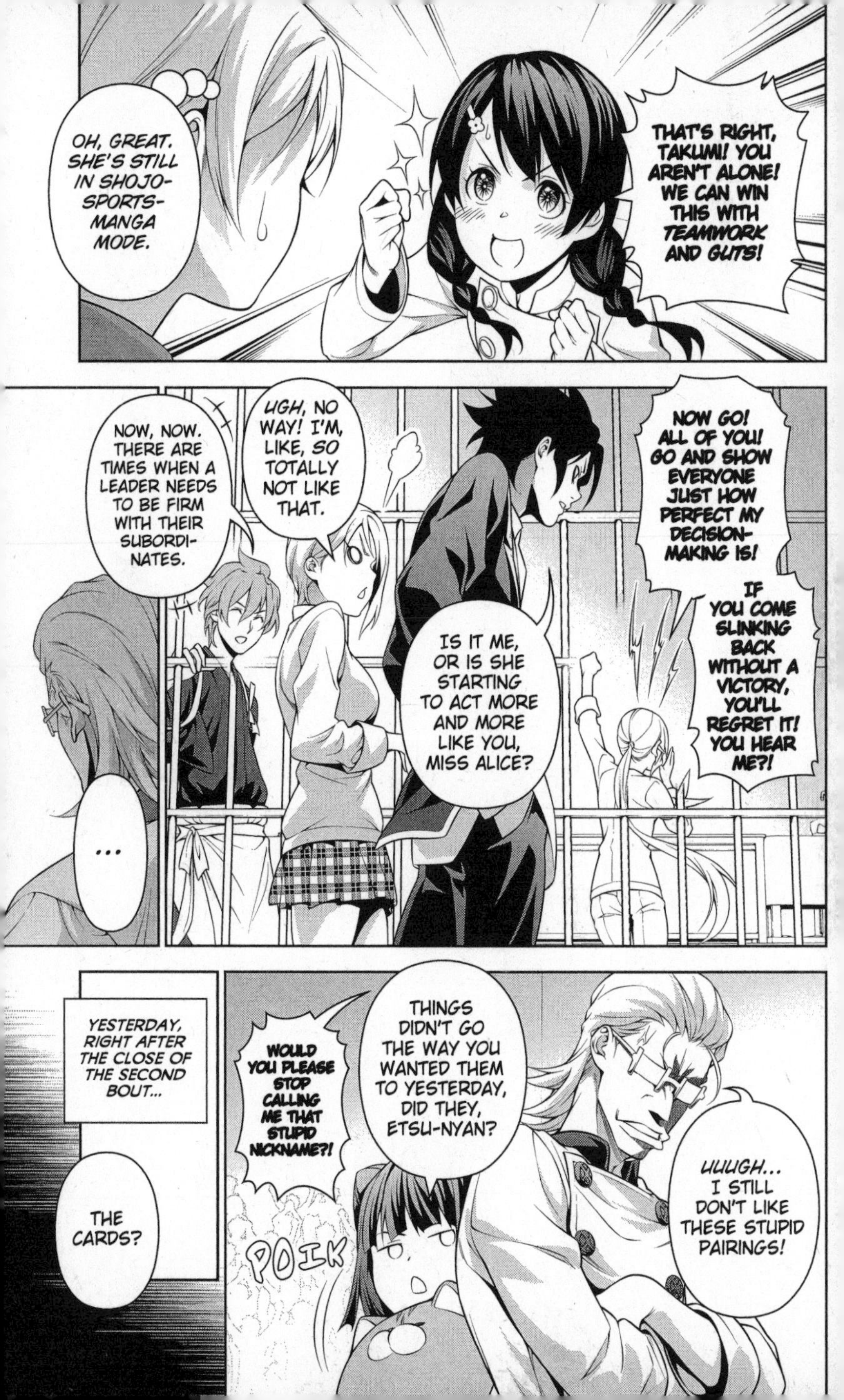
THAT'S RIGHT, TAKUMI! YOU AREN'T ALONE! WE CAN WIN THIS WITH TEAMWORK AND GUTS!
OH, GREAT. SHE'S STILL IN SHOJO-SPORTS-MANGA MODE.
NOW GO! ALL OF YOU! GO AND SHOW EVERYONE JUST HOW PERFECT MY DECISION-MAKING IS!
IF YOU COME SLINKING BACK WITHOUT A VICTORY, YOU'LL REGRET IT! YOU HEAR ME?!
IS IT ME, OR IS SHE STARTING TO ACT MORE AND MORE LIKE YOU, MISS ALICE?
UGH, NO WAY! I'M, LIKE, SO TOTALLY NOT LIKE THAT.
NOW, NOW. THERE ARE TIMES WHEN A LEADER NEEDS TO BE FIRM WITH THEIR SUBORDINATES.
...
THINGS DIDN'T GO THE WAY YOU WANTED THEM TO YESTERDAY, DID THEY, ETSU-NYAN?
WOULD YOU PLEASE STOP CALLING ME THAT STUPID NICKNAME?!
UUUGH... I STILL DON'T LIKE THESE STUPID PAIRINGS!
POIK
YESTERDAY, RIGHT AFTER THE CLOSE OF THE SECOND BOUT...
THE CARDS?

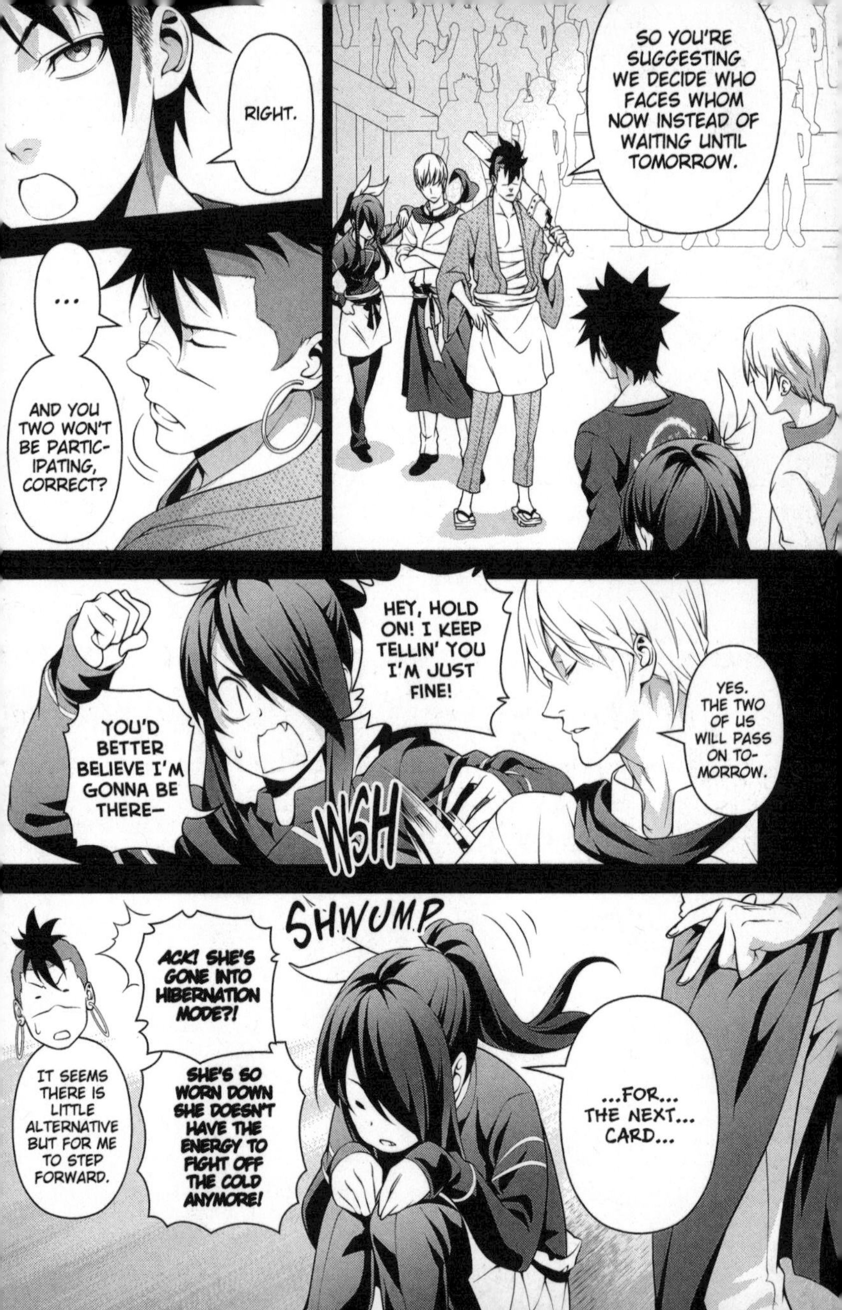

SO YOU'RE SUGGESTING WE DECIDE WHO FACES WHOM NOW INSTEAD OF WAITING UNTIL TOMORROW.
RIGHT.
...
AND YOU TWO WON'T BE PARTIC-IPATING, CORRECT?
YES. THE TWO OF US WILL PASS ON TO-MORROW.
HEY, HOLD ON! I KEEP TELLIN' YOU I'M JUST FINE!
YOU'D BETTER BELIEVE I'M GONNA BE THERE—
WSH
SHWUMP
...FOR... THE NEXT... CARD...
ACK! SHE'S GONE INTO HIBERNATION MODE?!
SHE'S SO WORN DOWN SHE DOESN'T HAVE THE ENERGY TO FIGHT OFF THE COLD ANYMORE!
IT SEEMS THERE IS LITTLE ALTERNATIVE BUT FOR ME TO STEP FORWARD.

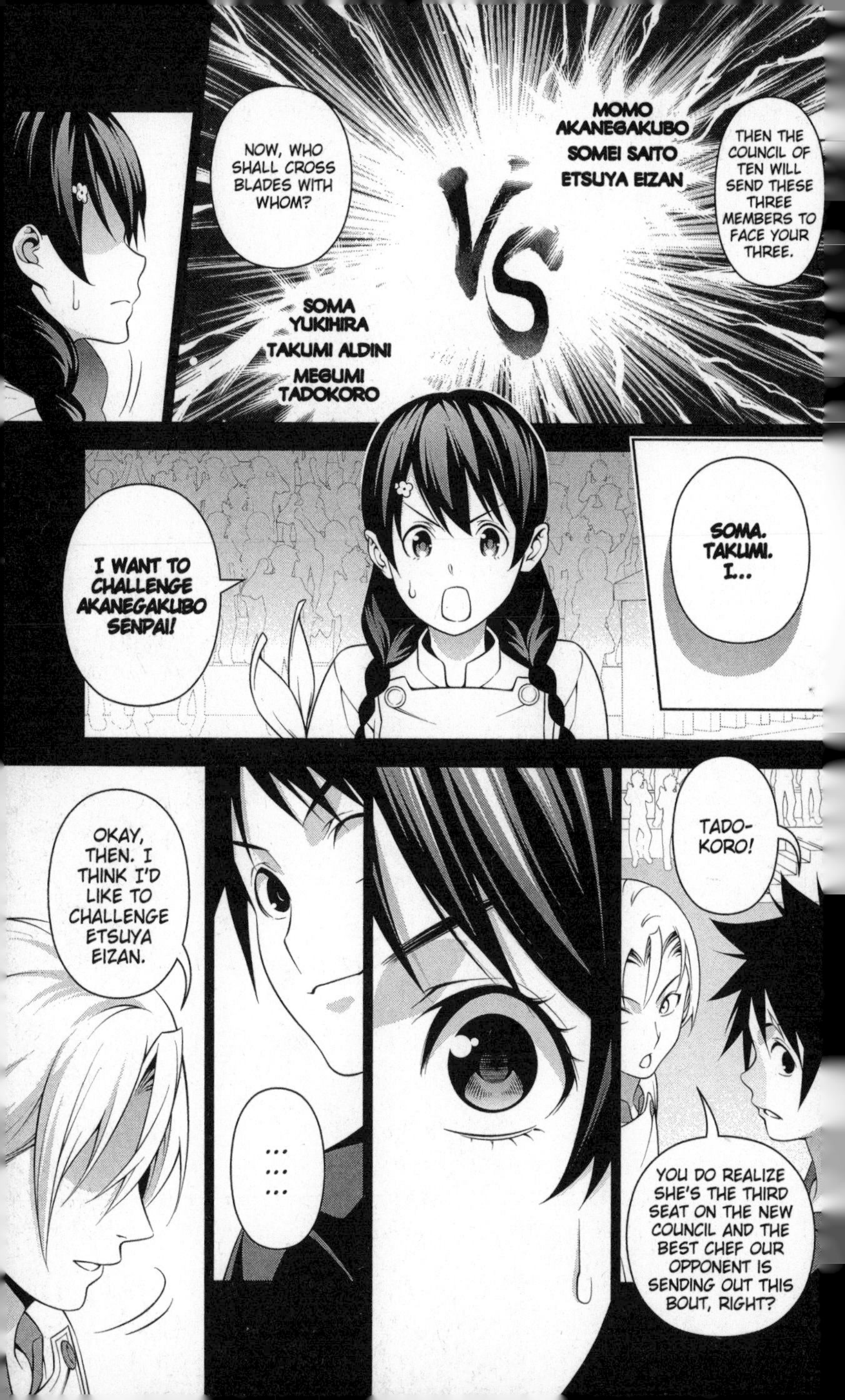
THEN THE COUNCIL OF TEN WILL SEND THESE THREE MEMBERS TO FACE YOUR THREE.
MOMO AKANEGAKUBO
SOMEI SAITO
ETSUYA EIZAN
VS
SOMA YUKIHIRA
TAKUMI ALDINI
MEGUMI TADOKORO
NOW, WHO SHALL CROSS BLADES WITH WHOM?
SOMA. TAKUMI. I...
I WANT TO CHALLENGE AKANEGAKUBO SENPAI!
TADO-KORO!
YOU DO REALIZE SHE'S THE THIRD SEAT ON THE NEW COUNCIL AND THE BEST CHEF OUR OPPONENT IS SENDING OUT THIS BOUT, RIGHT?
... ...
OKAY, THEN. I THINK I'D LIKE TO CHALLENGE ETSUYA EIZAN.

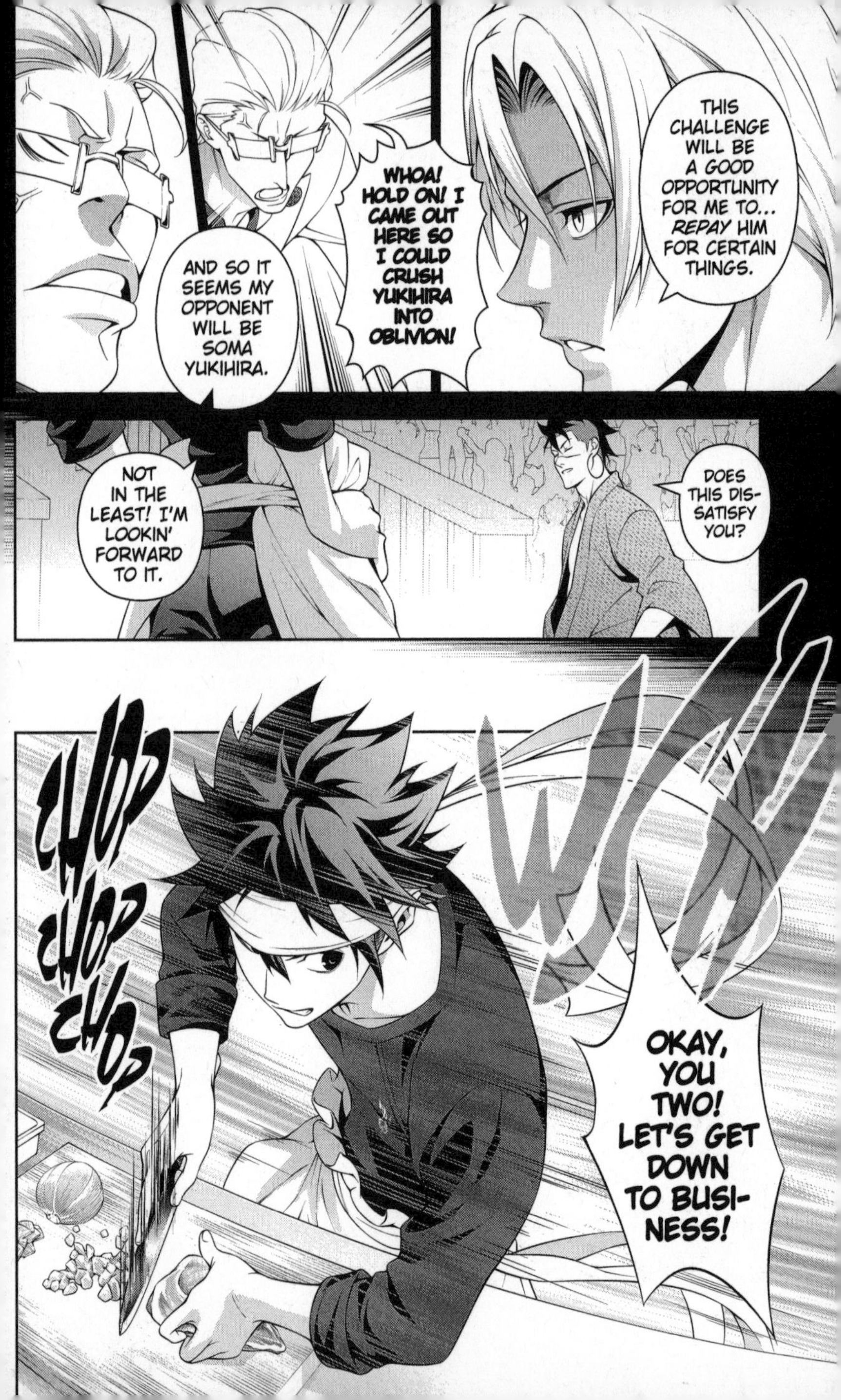
THIS CHALLENGE WILL BE A GOOD OPPORTUNITY FOR ME TO... *REPAY* HIM FOR CERTAIN THINGS.
WHOA! HOLD ON! I CAME OUT HERE SO I COULD CRUSH YUKIHIRA INTO OBLIVION!
AND SO IT SEEMS MY OPPONENT WILL BE SOMA YUKIHIRA.
DOES THIS DIS-SATISFY YOU?
NOT IN THE LEAST! I'M LOOKIN' FORWARD TO IT.
OKAY, YOU TWO! LET'S GET DOWN TO BUSI-NESS!
CHOP CHOP CHOP

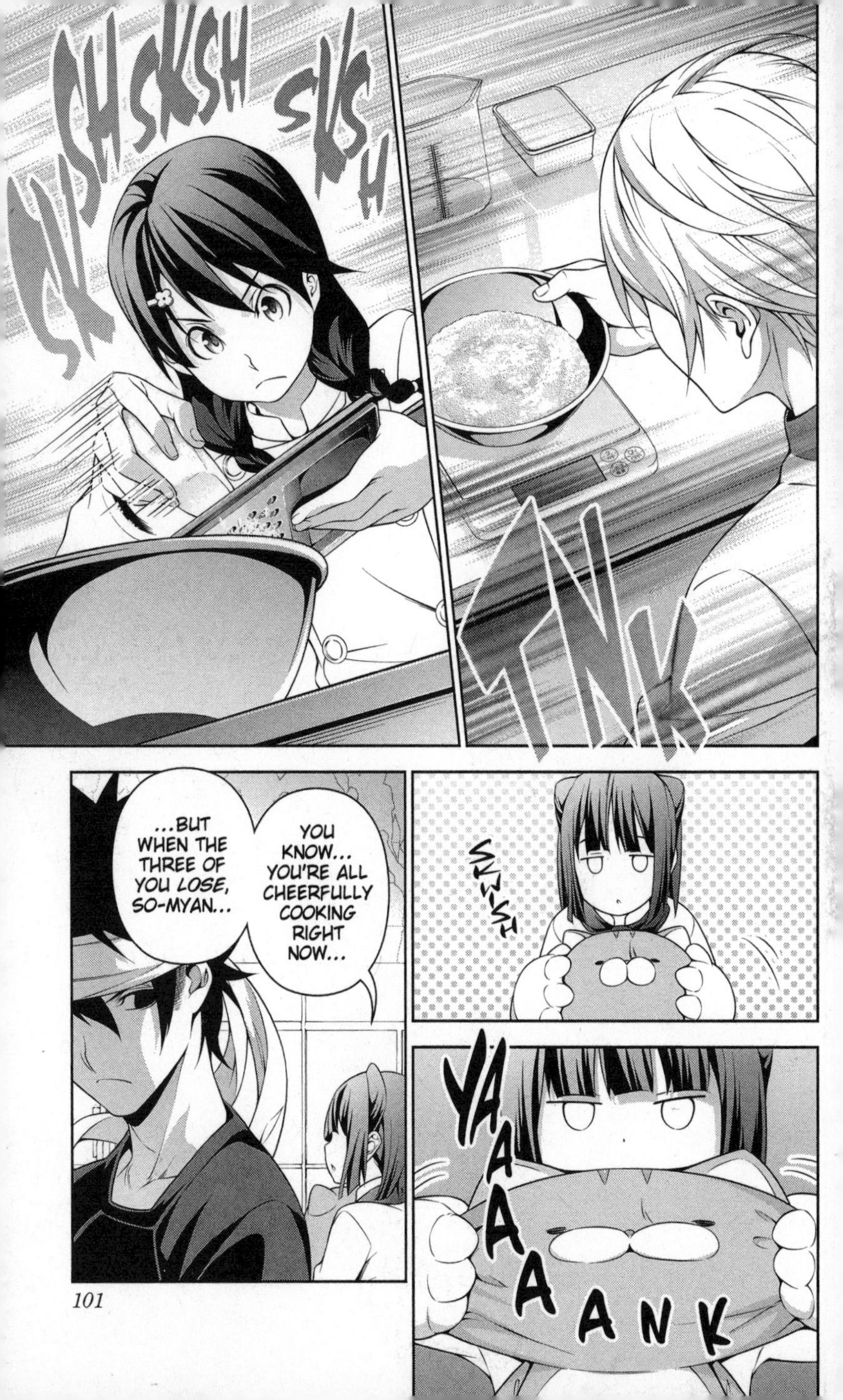
TINK
SHSHSKSH
SKSHH
SWISH
YAAAAANK
YOU KNOW... YOU'RE ALL CHEERFULLY COOKING RIGHT NOW...
...BUT WHEN THE THREE OF YOU *LOSE*, SO-MYAN...

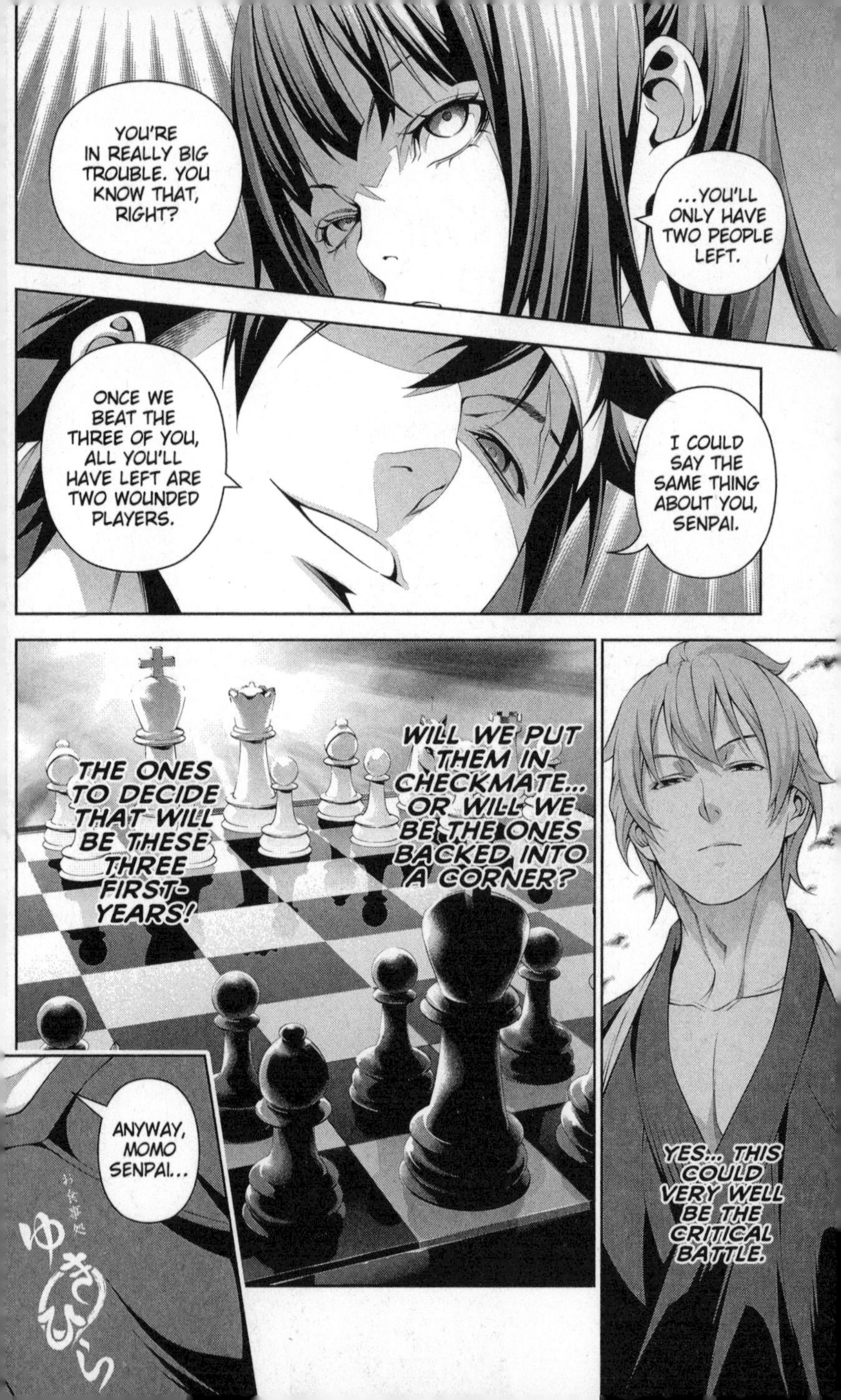
...YOU'LL ONLY HAVE TWO PEOPLE LEFT.
YOU'RE IN REALLY BIG TROUBLE. YOU KNOW THAT, RIGHT?
I COULD SAY THE SAME THING ABOUT YOU, SENPAI.
ONCE WE BEAT THE THREE OF YOU, ALL YOU'LL HAVE LEFT ARE TWO WOUNDED PLAYERS.
YES... THIS COULD VERY WELL BE THE CRITICAL BATTLE.
WILL WE PUT THEM IN CHECKMATE... OR WILL WE BE THE ONES BACKED INTO A CORNER?
THE ONES TO DECIDE THAT WILL BE THESE THREE FIRST-YEARS!
ANYWAY, MOMO SENPAI...
お食事処
ゆきひら

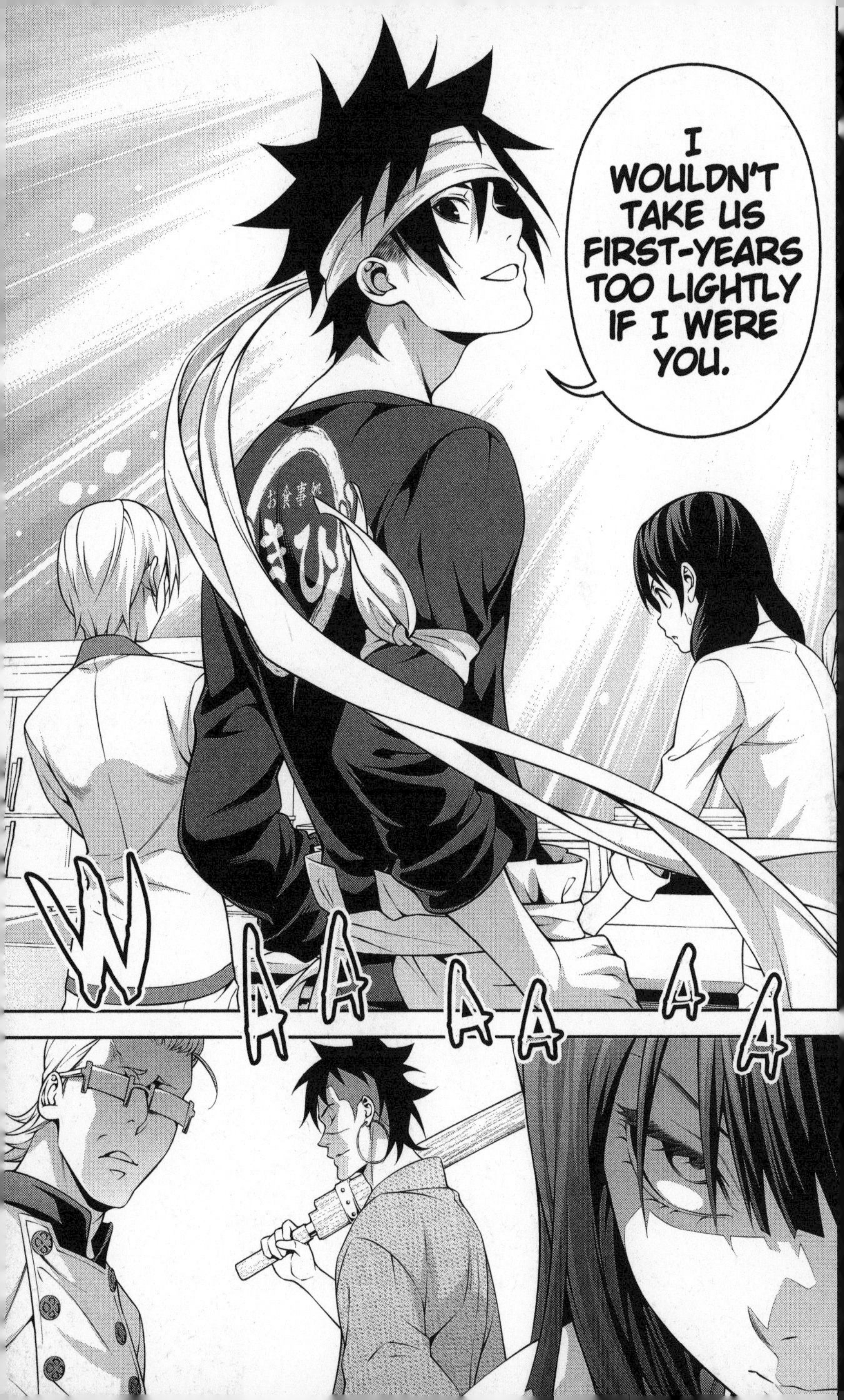
I WOULDN'T TAKE US FIRST-YEARS TOO LIGHTLY IF I WERE YOU.
WAAAAAA

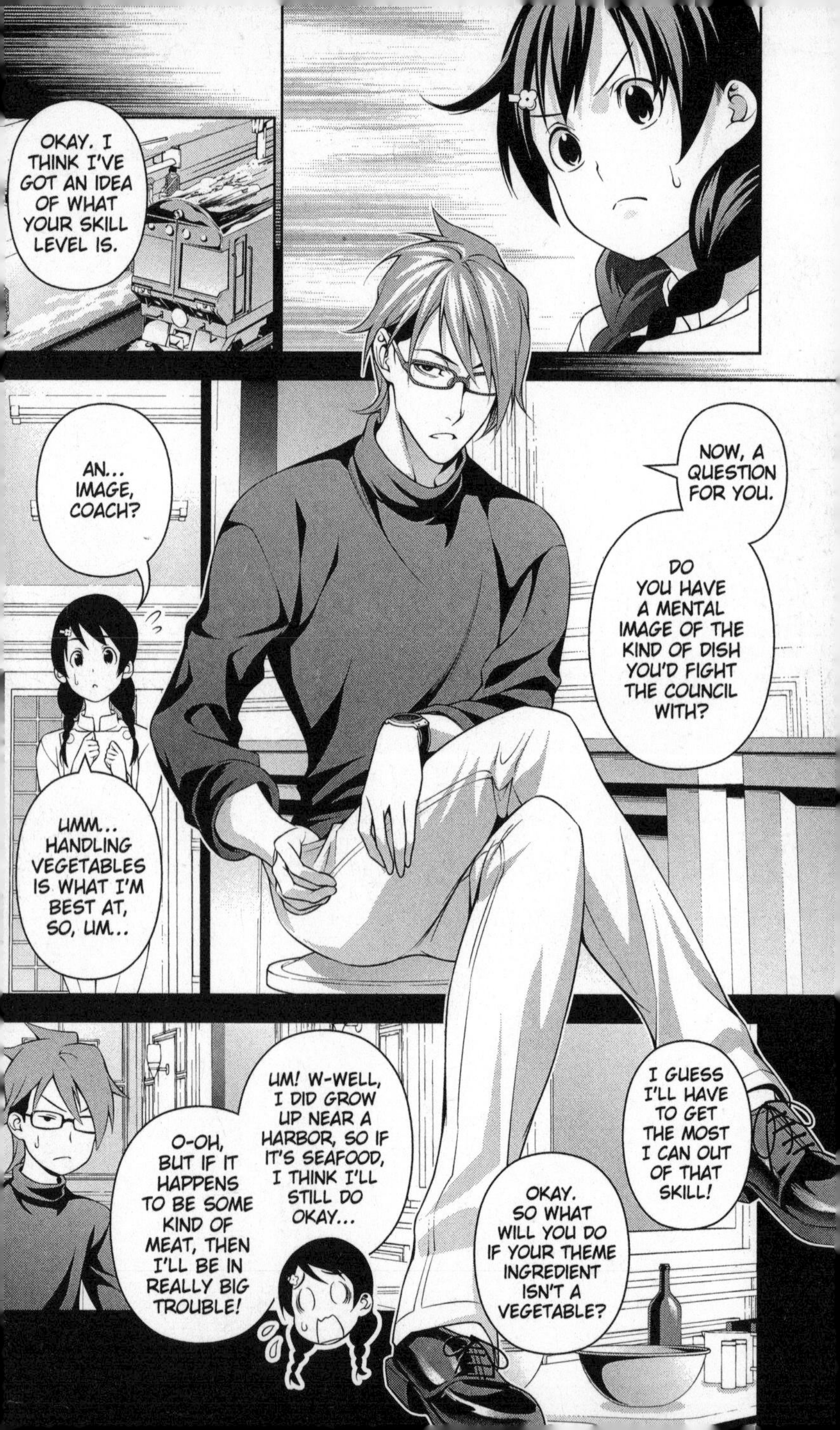
OKAY. I THINK I'VE GOT AN IDEA OF WHAT YOUR SKILL LEVEL IS.
NOW, A QUESTION FOR YOU.
DO YOU HAVE A MENTAL IMAGE OF THE KIND OF DISH YOU'D FIGHT THE COUNCIL WITH?
AN... IMAGE, COACH?
UMM... HANDLING VEGETABLES IS WHAT I'M BEST AT, SO, UM...
I GUESS I'LL HAVE TO GET THE MOST I CAN OUT OF THAT SKILL!
OKAY. SO WHAT WILL YOU DO IF YOUR THEME INGREDIENT ISN'T A VEGETABLE?
UM! W-WELL, I DID GROW UP NEAR A HARBOR, SO IF IT'S SEAFOOD, I THINK I'LL STILL DO OKAY...
O-OH, BUT IF IT HAPPENS TO BE SOME KIND OF MEAT, THEN I'LL BE IN REALLY BIG TROUBLE!

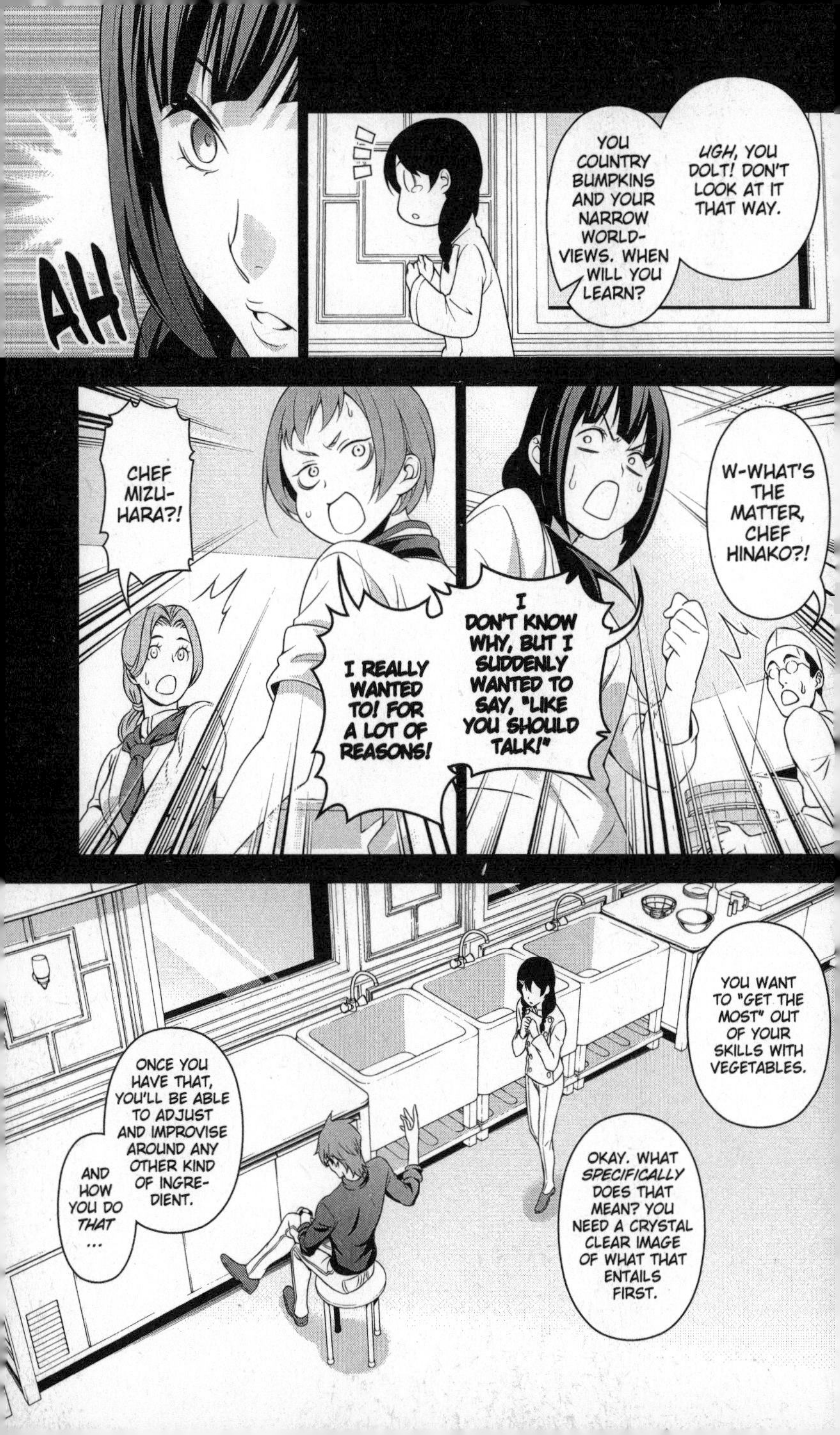
UGH, YOU DOLT! DON'T LOOK AT IT THAT WAY.
YOU COUNTRY BUMPKINS AND YOUR NARROW WORLD-VIEWS. WHEN WILL YOU LEARN?
AH
W-WHAT'S THE MATTER, CHEF HINAKO?!
I DON'T KNOW WHY, BUT I SUDDENLY WANTED TO SAY, "LIKE YOU SHOULD TALK!"
CHEF MIZU-HARA?!
I REALLY WANTED TO! FOR A LOT OF REASONS!
YOU WANT TO "GET THE MOST" OUT OF YOUR SKILLS WITH VEGETABLES.
OKAY. WHAT SPECIFICALLY DOES THAT MEAN? YOU NEED A CRYSTAL CLEAR IMAGE OF WHAT THAT ENTAILS FIRST.
ONCE YOU HAVE THAT, YOU'LL BE ABLE TO ADJUST AND IMPROVISE AROUND ANY OTHER KIND OF INGRE-DIENT.
AND HOW YOU DO THAT ...

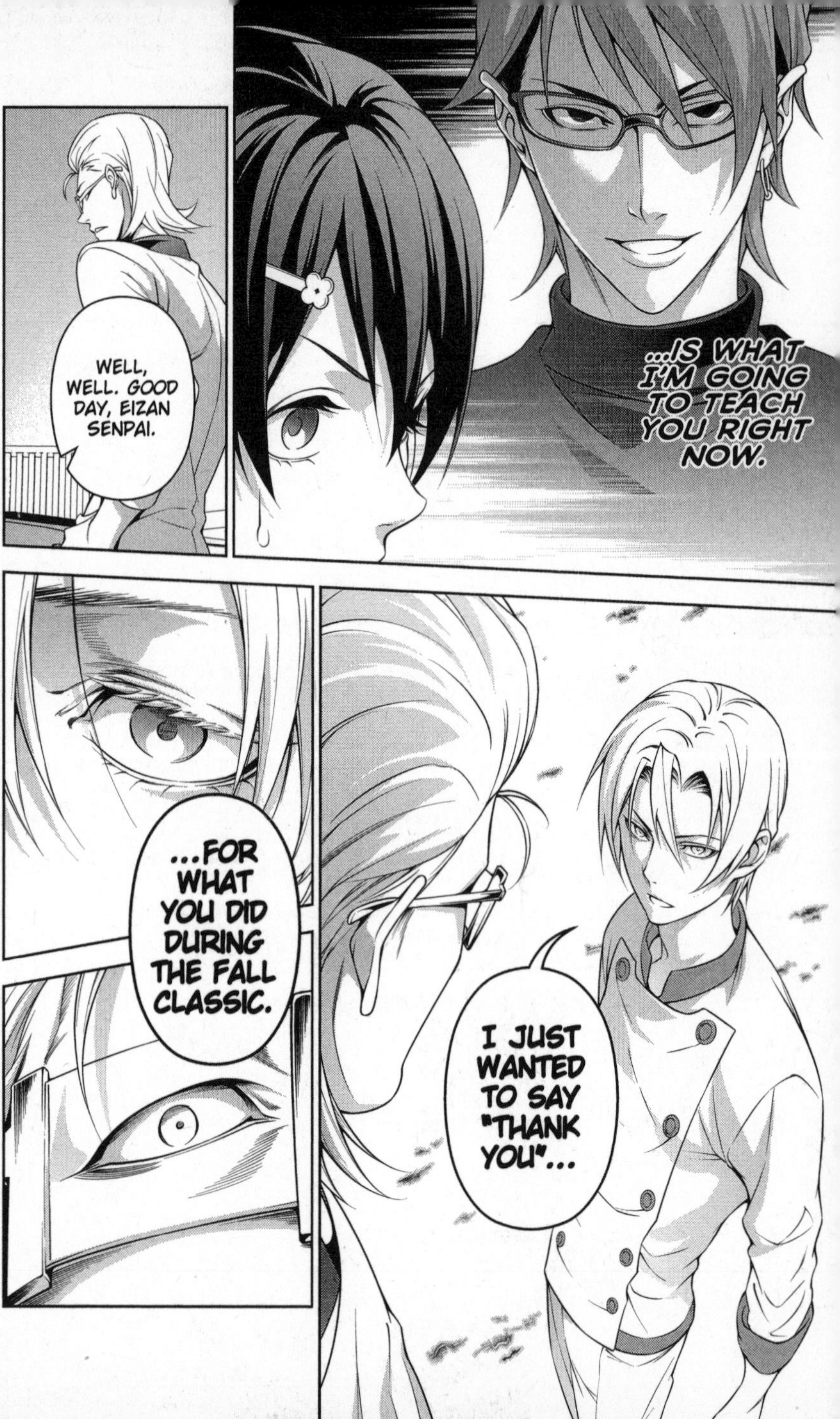
...IS WHAT I'M GOING TO TEACH YOU RIGHT NOW.
WELL, WELL. GOOD DAY, EIZAN SENPAI.
I JUST WANTED TO SAY "THANK YOU"...
...FOR WHAT YOU DID DURING THE FALL CLASSIC.

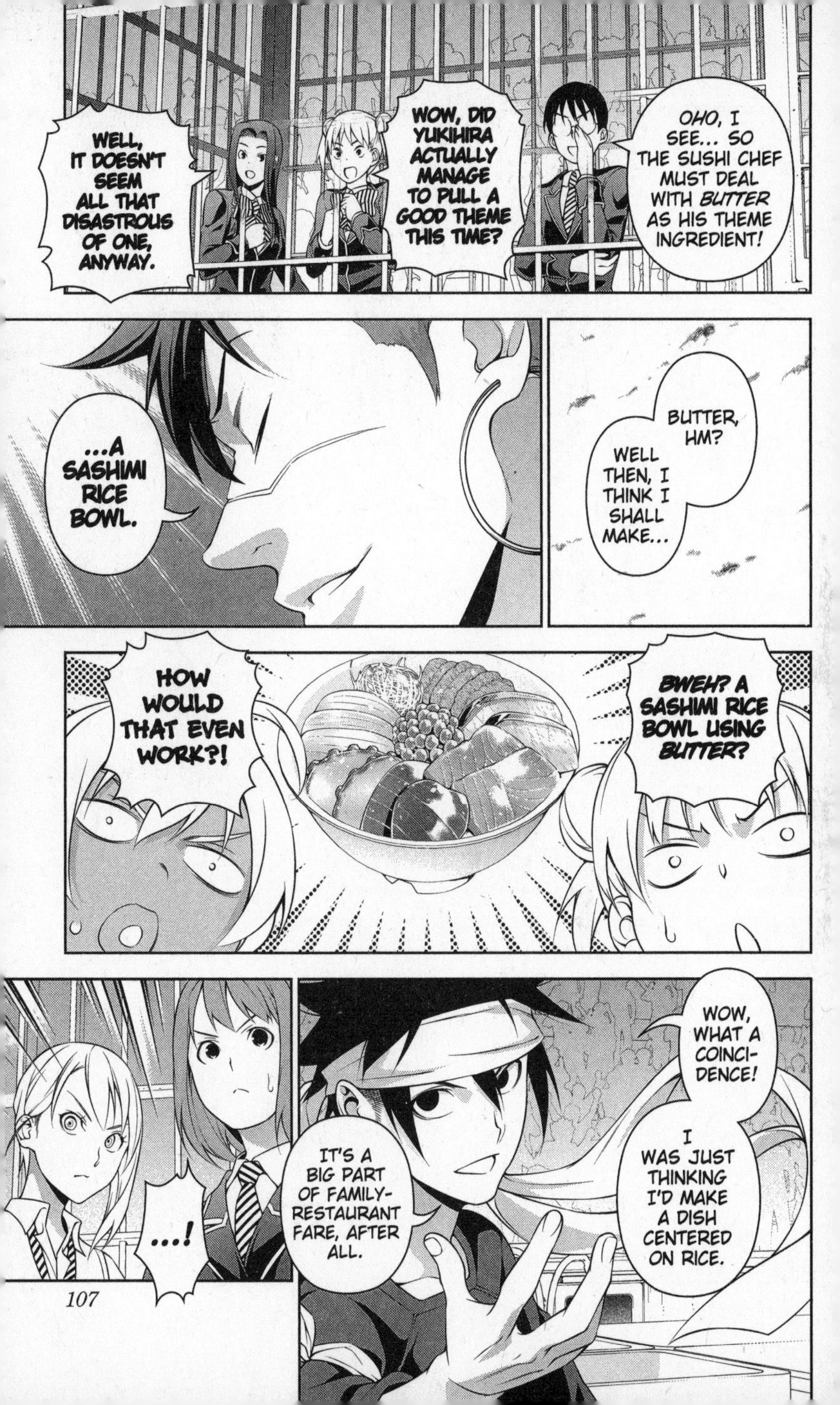
OHO, I SEE... SO THE SUSHI CHEF MUST DEAL WITH *BUTTER* AS HIS THEME INGREDIENT!
WOW, DID YUKIHIRA ACTUALLY MANAGE TO PULL A GOOD THEME THIS TIME?
WELL, IT DOESN'T SEEM ALL THAT DISASTROUS OF ONE, ANYWAY.
BUTTER, HM?
WELL THEN, I THINK I SHALL MAKE...
...A SASHIMI RICE BOWL.
BWEH? A SASHIMI RICE BOWL USING *BUTTER?*
HOW WOULD THAT EVEN WORK?!
WOW, WHAT A COINCI-DENCE!
I WAS JUST THINKING I'D MAKE A DISH CENTERED ON RICE.
IT'S A BIG PART OF FAMILY-RESTAURANT FARE, AFTER ALL.
...!

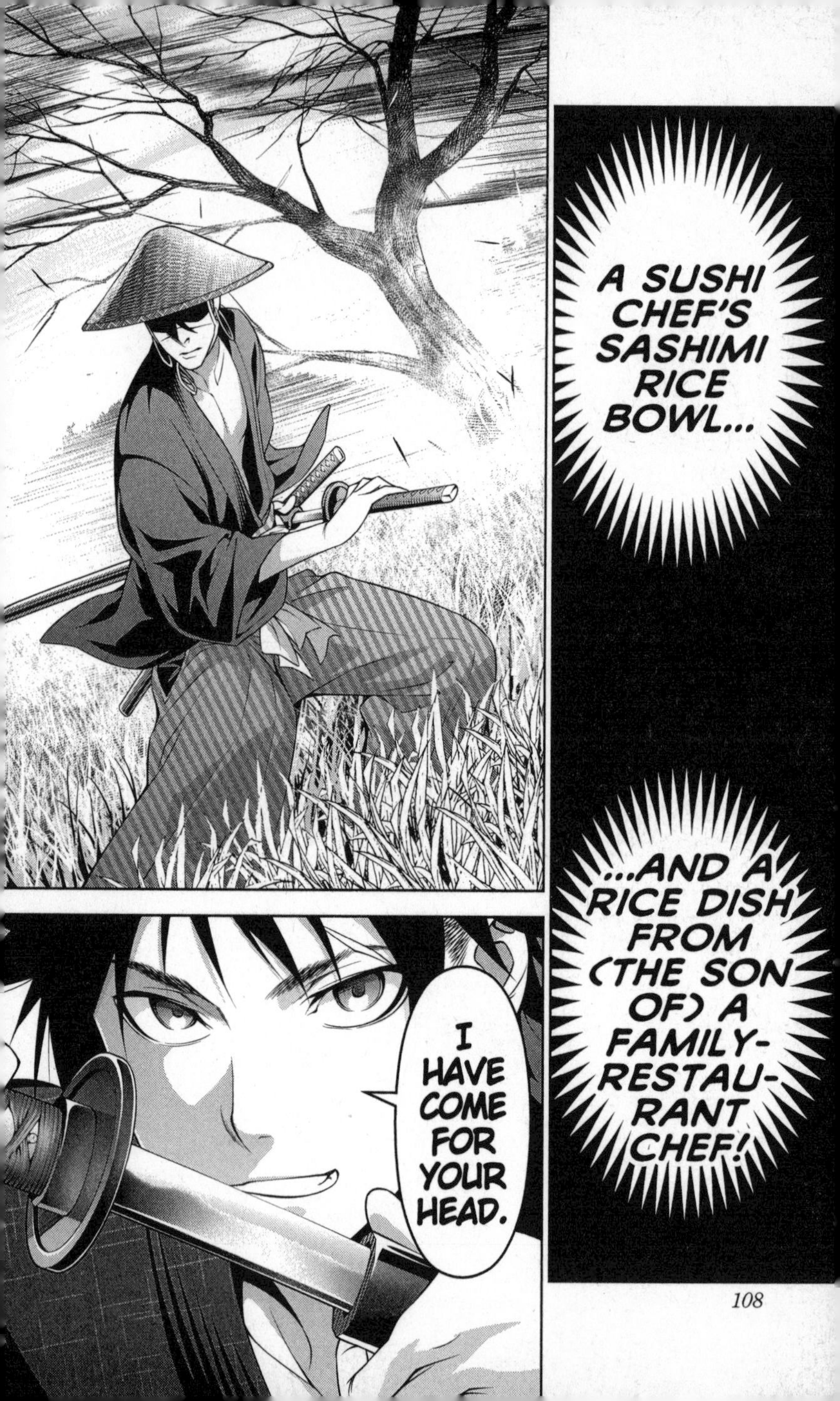
A SUSHI CHEF'S SASHIMI RICE BOWL...
...AND A RICE DISH FROM (THE SON OF) A FAMILY-RESTAURANT CHEF!
I HAVE COME FOR YOUR HEAD.

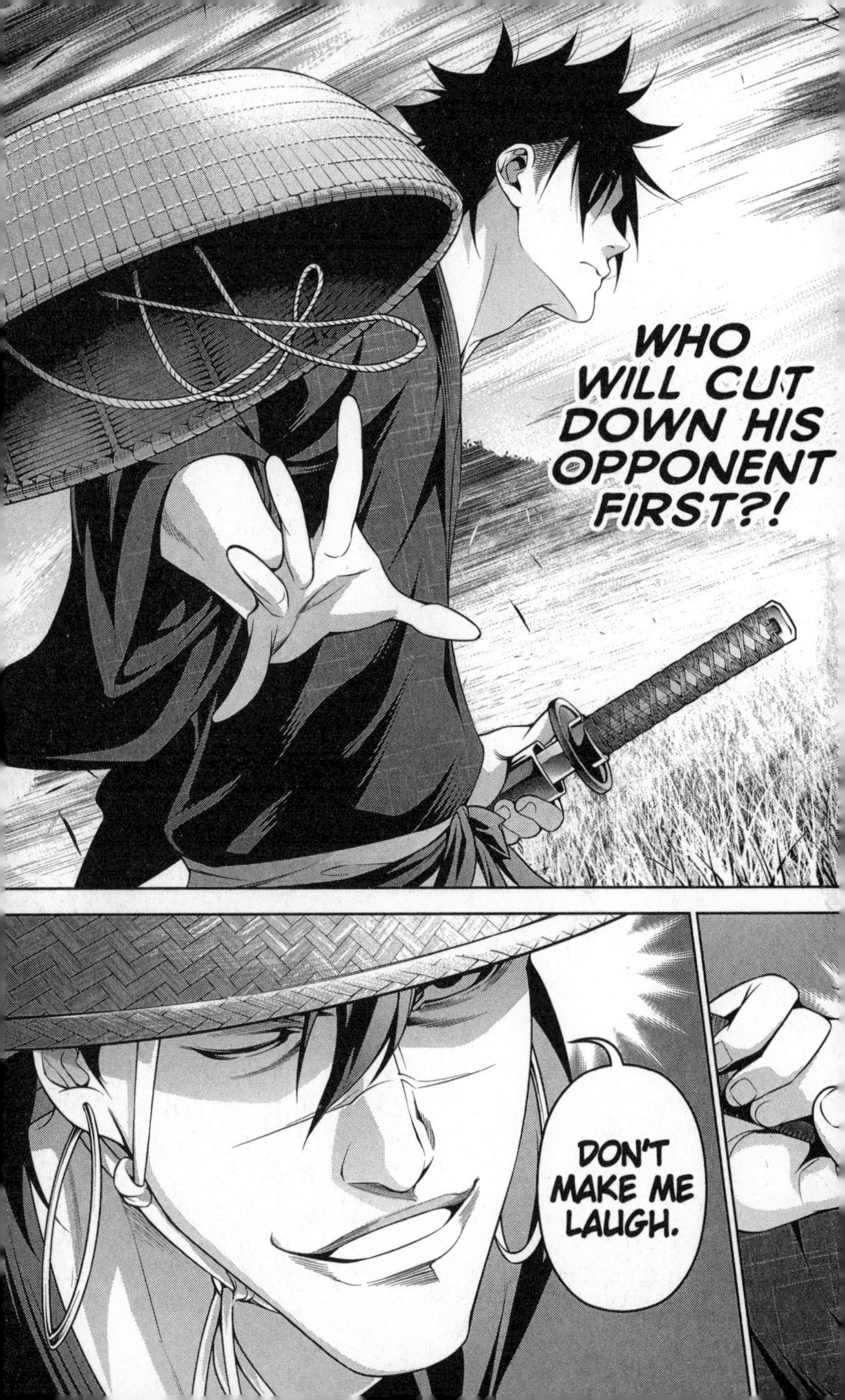
WHO WILL CUT DOWN HIS OPPONENT FIRST?!
DON'T MAKE ME LAUGH.

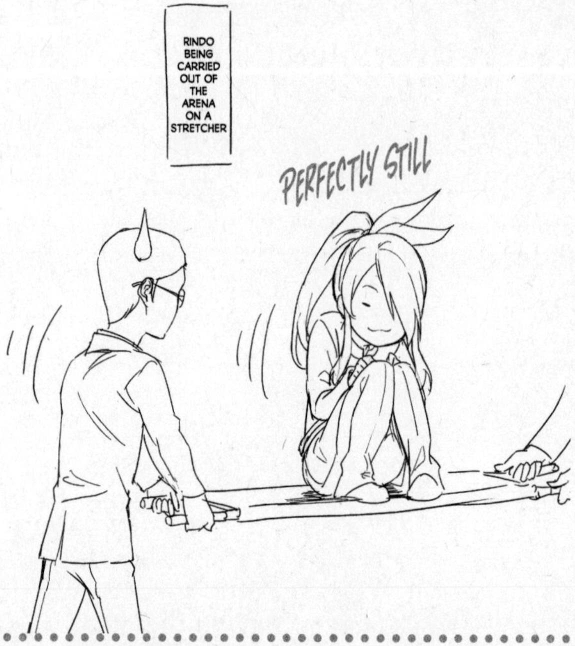
RINDO BEING CARRIED OUT OF THE ARENA ON A STRETCHER
PERFECTLY STILL

232 ALL OR NOTHING

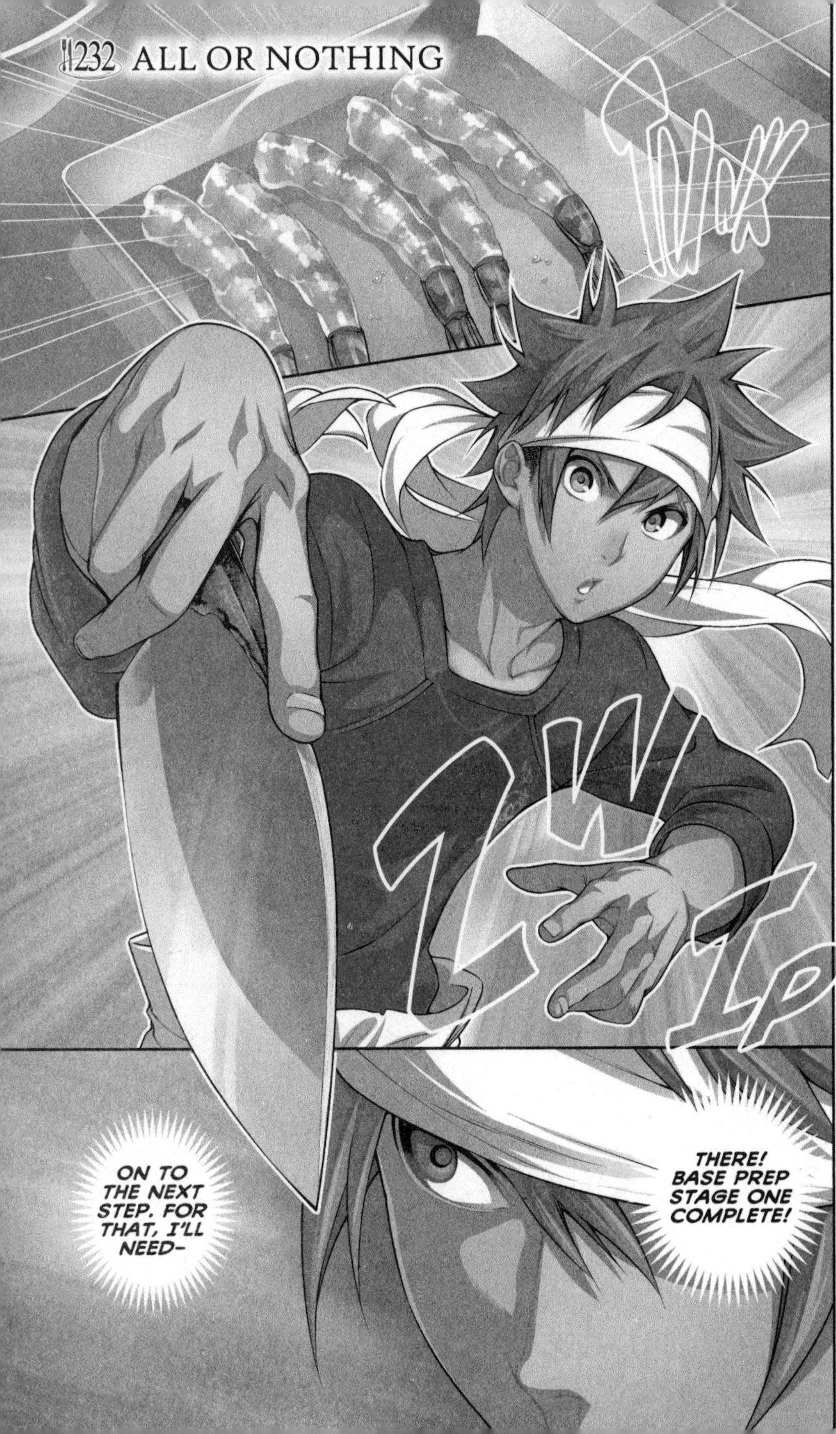
ZWIP
THERE! BASE PREP STAGE ONE COMPLETE!
ON TO THE NEXT STEP. FOR THAT, I'LL NEED-

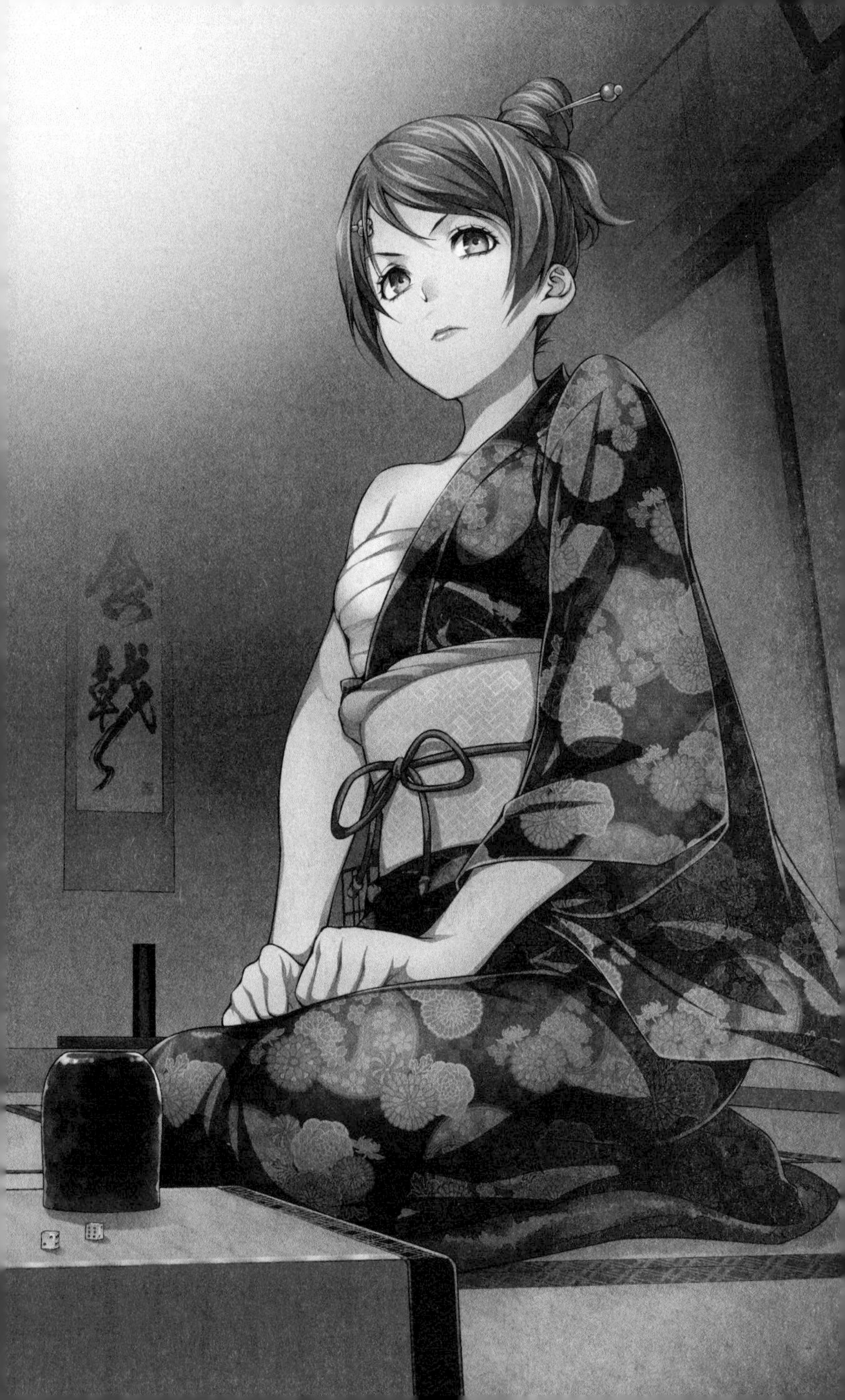

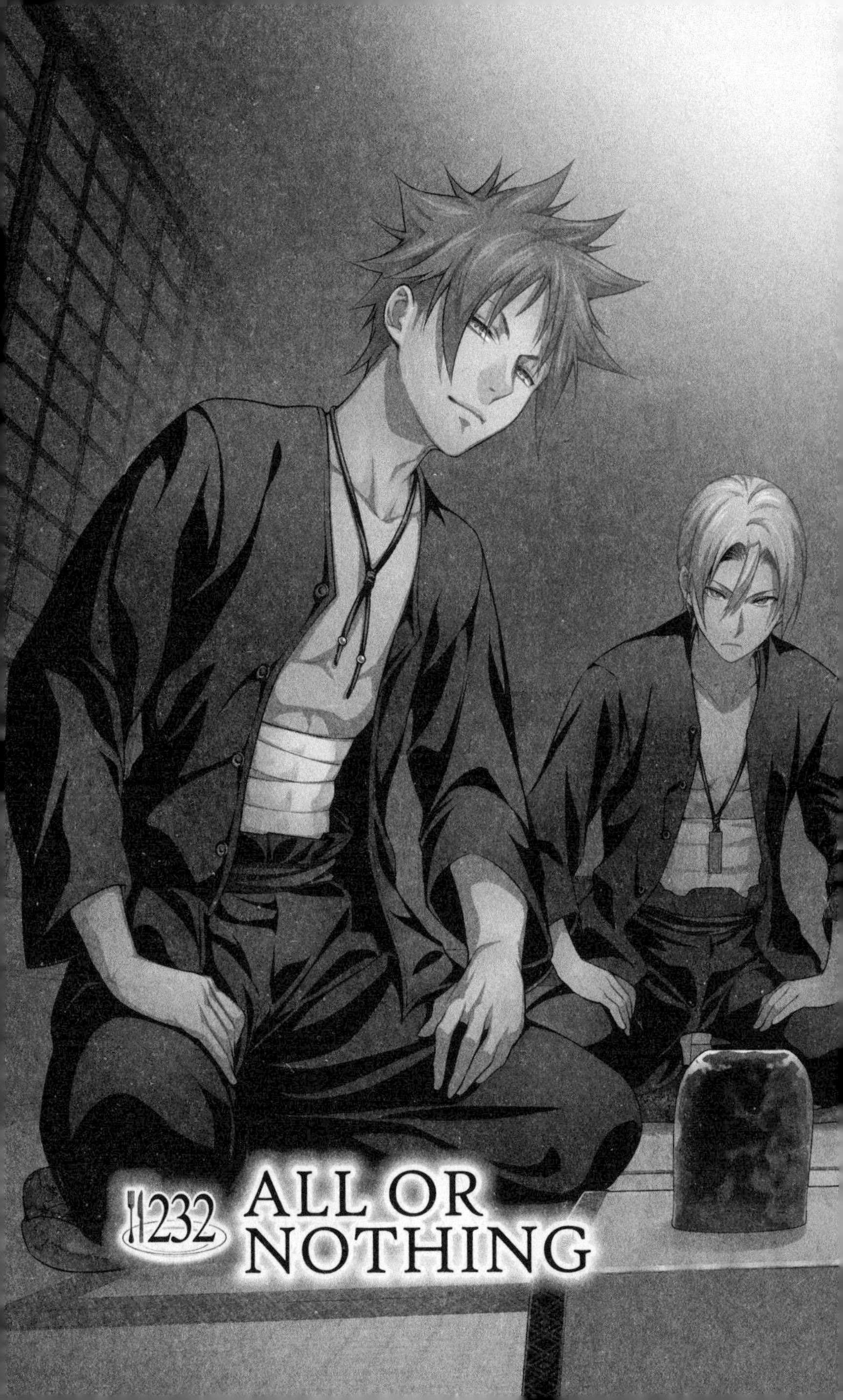
232
ALL OR NOTHING

EVENS OR ODDS?!

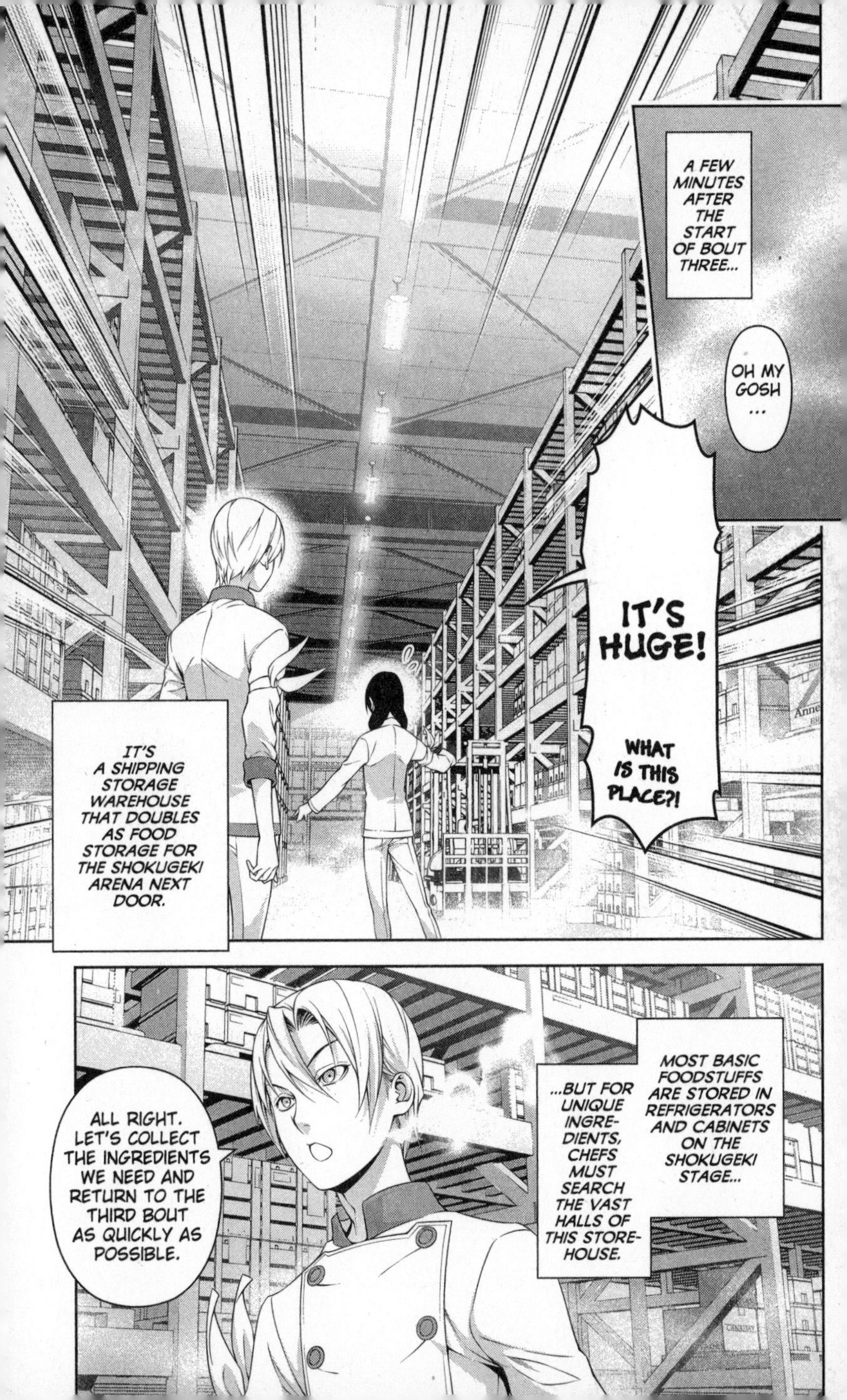
A FEW MINUTES AFTER THE START OF BOUT THREE...
OH MY GOSH ...
IT'S HUGE!
WHAT IS THIS PLACE?!
IT'S A SHIPPING STORAGE WAREHOUSE THAT DOUBLES AS FOOD STORAGE FOR THE SHOKUGEKI ARENA NEXT DOOR.
MOST BASIC FOODSTUFFS ARE STORED IN REFRIGERATORS AND CABINETS ON THE SHOKUGEKI STAGE...
...BUT FOR UNIQUE INGRE-DIENTS, CHEFS MUST SEARCH THE VAST HALLS OF THIS STORE-HOUSE.
ALL RIGHT. LET'S COLLECT THE INGREDIENTS WE NEED AND RETURN TO THE THIRD BOUT AS QUICKLY AS POSSIBLE.

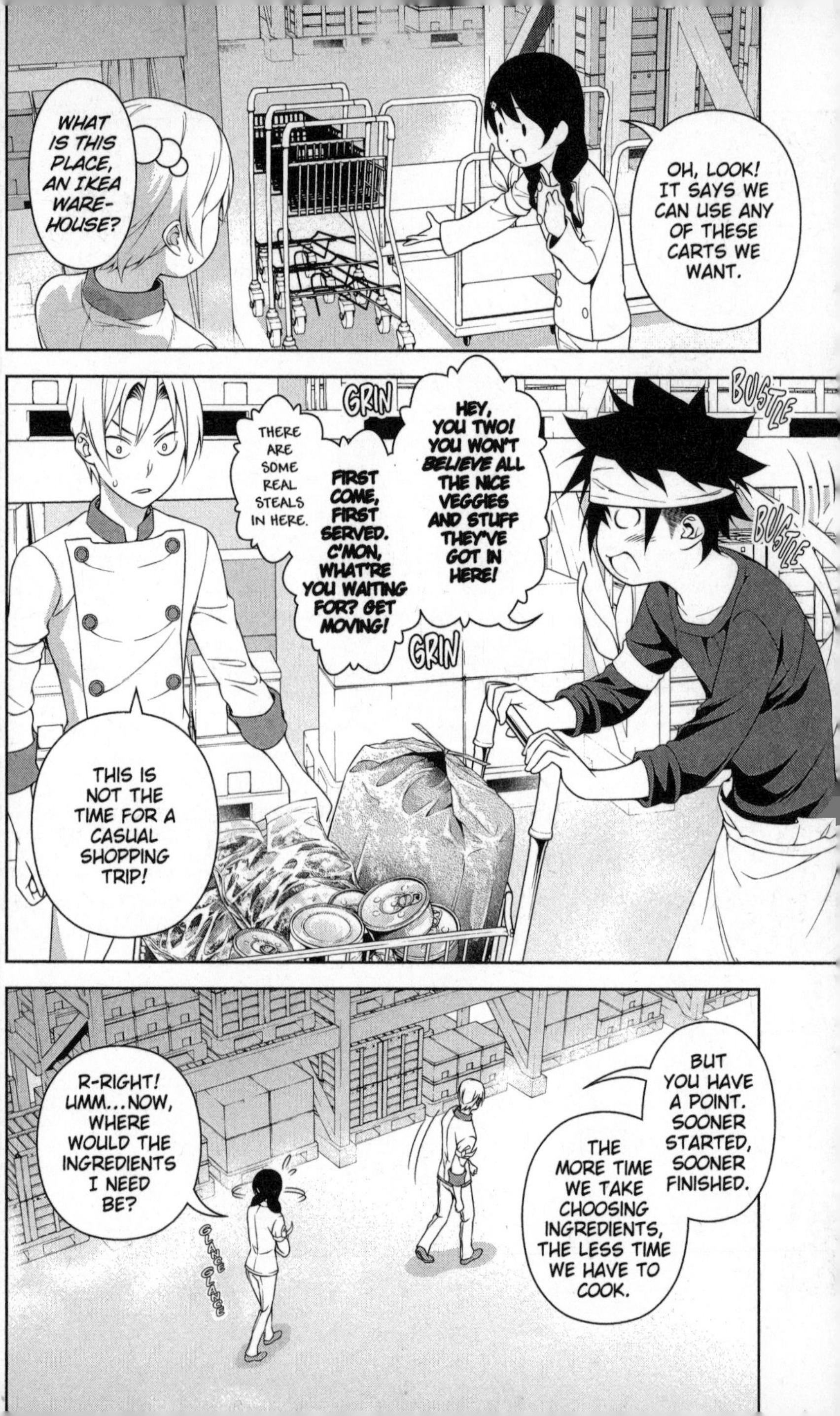
OH, LOOK! IT SAYS WE CAN USE ANY OF THESE CARTS WE WANT.
WHAT IS THIS PLACE, AN IKEA WARE-HOUSE?
BUSTLE
BUSTLE
HEY, YOU TWO! YOU WON'T BELIEVE ALL THE NICE VEGGIES AND STUFF THEY'VE GOT IN HERE!
GRIN
FIRST COME, FIRST SERVED. C'MON, WHAT'RE YOU WAITING FOR? GET MOVING!
THERE ARE SOME REAL STEALS IN HERE.
GRIN
THIS IS NOT THE TIME FOR A CASUAL SHOPPING TRIP!
BUT YOU HAVE A POINT. SOONER STARTED, SOONER FINISHED.
THE MORE TIME WE TAKE CHOOSING INGREDIENTS, THE LESS TIME WE HAVE TO COOK.
GLANCE GLANCE
R-RIGHT! UMM...NOW, WHERE WOULD THE INGREDIENTS I NEED BE?

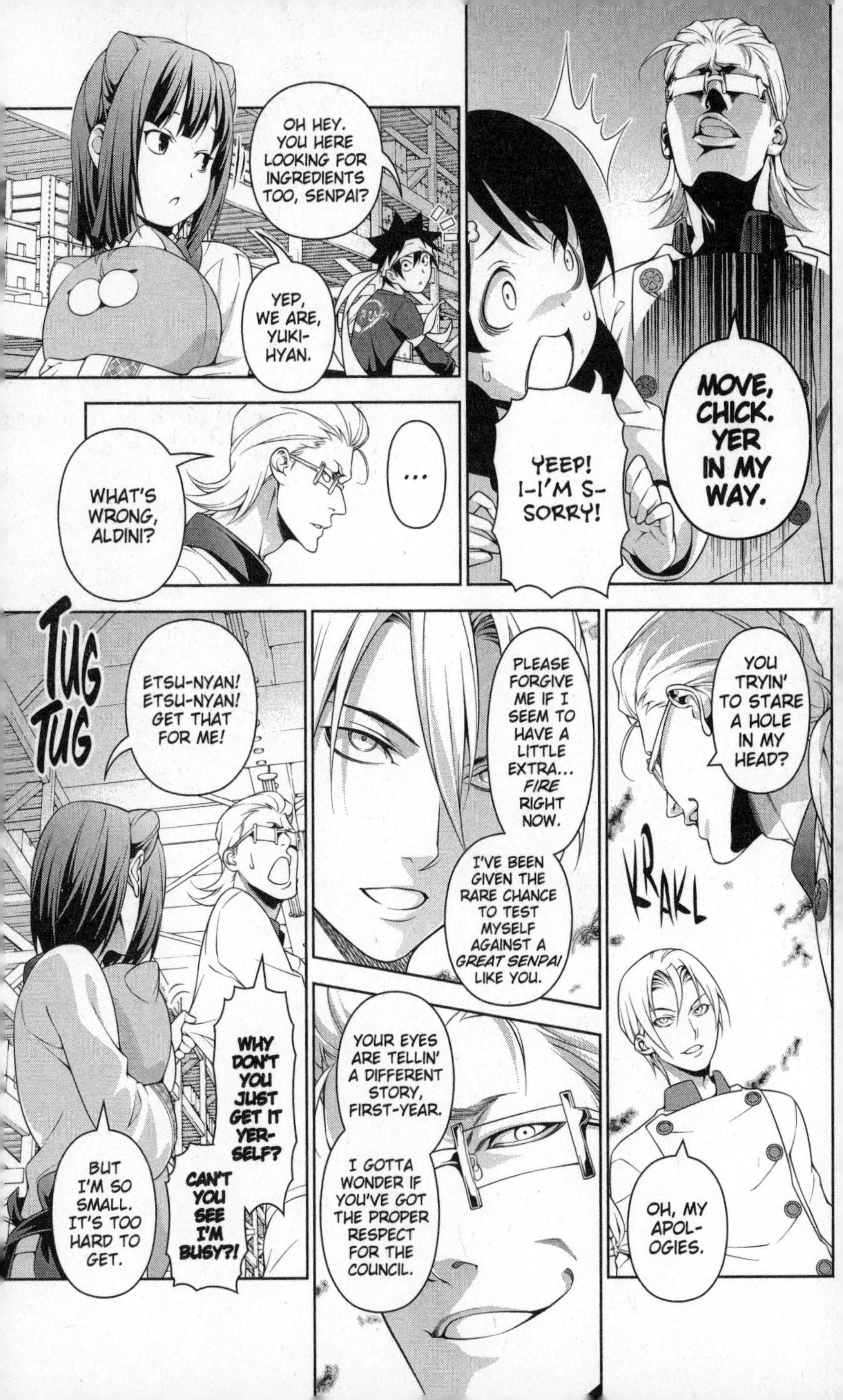
MOVE, CHICK. YER IN MY WAY.
YEEP! I-I'M S-SORRY!
OH HEY. YOU HERE LOOKING FOR INGREDIENTS TOO, SENPAI?
YEP, WE ARE, YUKI-HYAN.
...
WHAT'S WRONG, ALDINI?
YOU TRYIN' TO STARE A HOLE IN MY HEAD?
KRAKL
OH, MY APOLOGIES.
PLEASE FORGIVE ME IF I SEEM TO HAVE A LITTLE EXTRA... *FIRE* RIGHT NOW.
I'VE BEEN GIVEN THE RARE CHANCE TO TEST MYSELF AGAINST A *GREAT SENPAI* LIKE YOU.
YOUR EYES ARE TELLIN' A DIFFERENT STORY, FIRST-YEAR.
I GOTTA WONDER IF YOU'VE GOT THE PROPER RESPECT FOR THE COUNCIL.
TUG TUG
ETSU-NYAN! ETSU-NYAN! GET THAT FOR ME!
WHY DON'T YOU JUST GET IT YER-SELF?
CAN'T YOU SEE I'M BUSY?!
BUT I'M SO SMALL. IT'S TOO HARD TO GET.

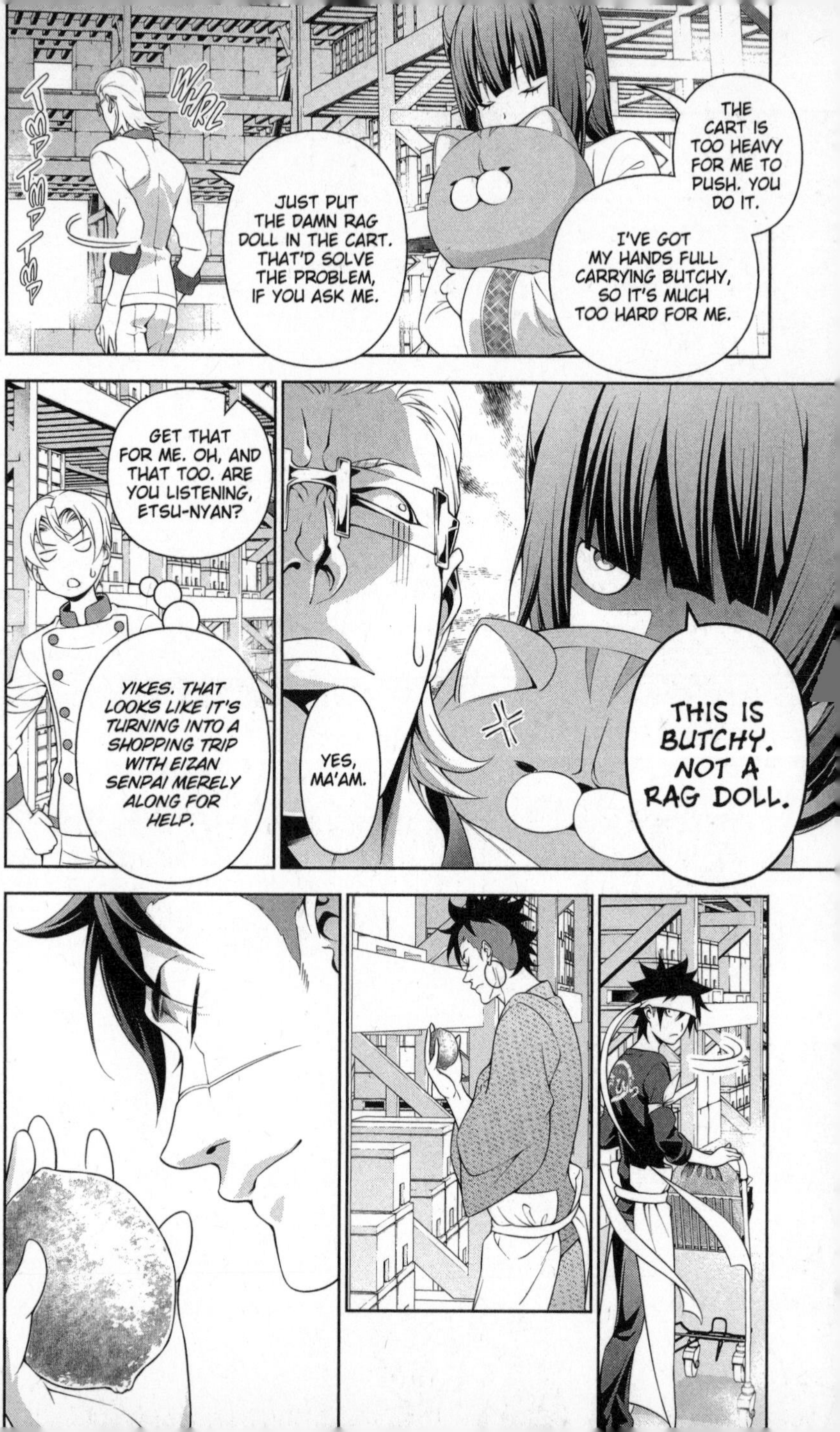
THE CART IS TOO HEAVY FOR ME TO PUSH. YOU DO IT.
I'VE GOT MY HANDS FULL CARRYING BUTCHY, SO IT'S MUCH TOO HARD FOR ME.
WHIRL
JUST PUT THE DAMN RAG DOLL IN THE CART. THAT'D SOLVE THE PROBLEM, IF YOU ASK ME.
TMP TMP TMP
THIS IS BUTCHY. NOT A RAG DOLL.
YES, MA'AM.
GET THAT FOR ME. OH, AND THAT TOO. ARE YOU LISTENING, ETSU-NYAN?
YIKES. THAT LOOKS LIKE IT'S TURNING INTO A SHOPPING TRIP WITH EIZAN SENPAI MERELY ALONG FOR HELP.

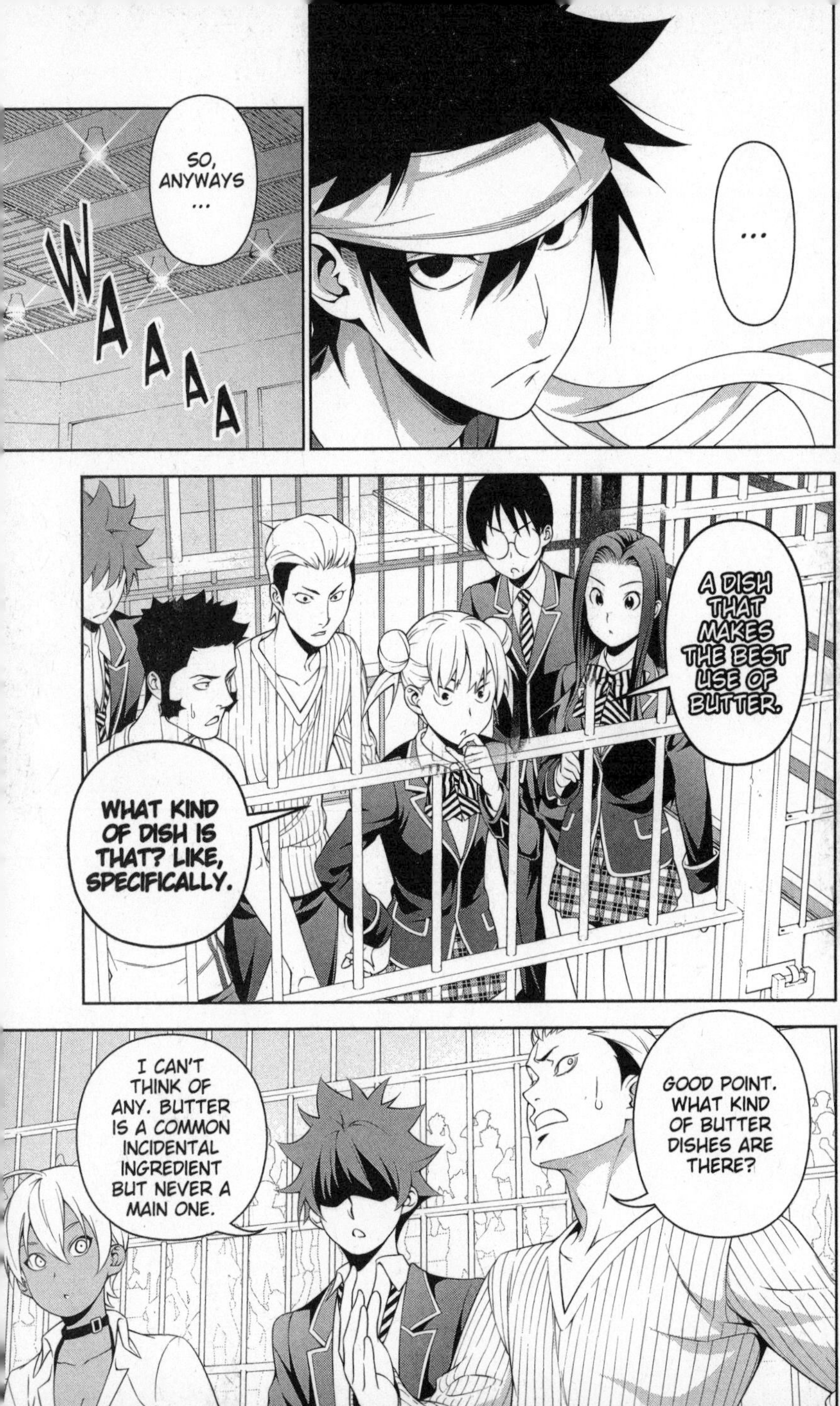
...
SO, ANYWAYS ...
WAAAA
A DISH THAT MAKES THE BEST USE OF BUTTER.
WHAT KIND OF DISH IS THAT? LIKE, SPECIFICALLY.
GOOD POINT. WHAT KIND OF BUTTER DISHES ARE THERE?
I CAN'T THINK OF ANY. BUTTER IS A COMMON INCIDENTAL INGREDIENT BUT NEVER A MAIN ONE.

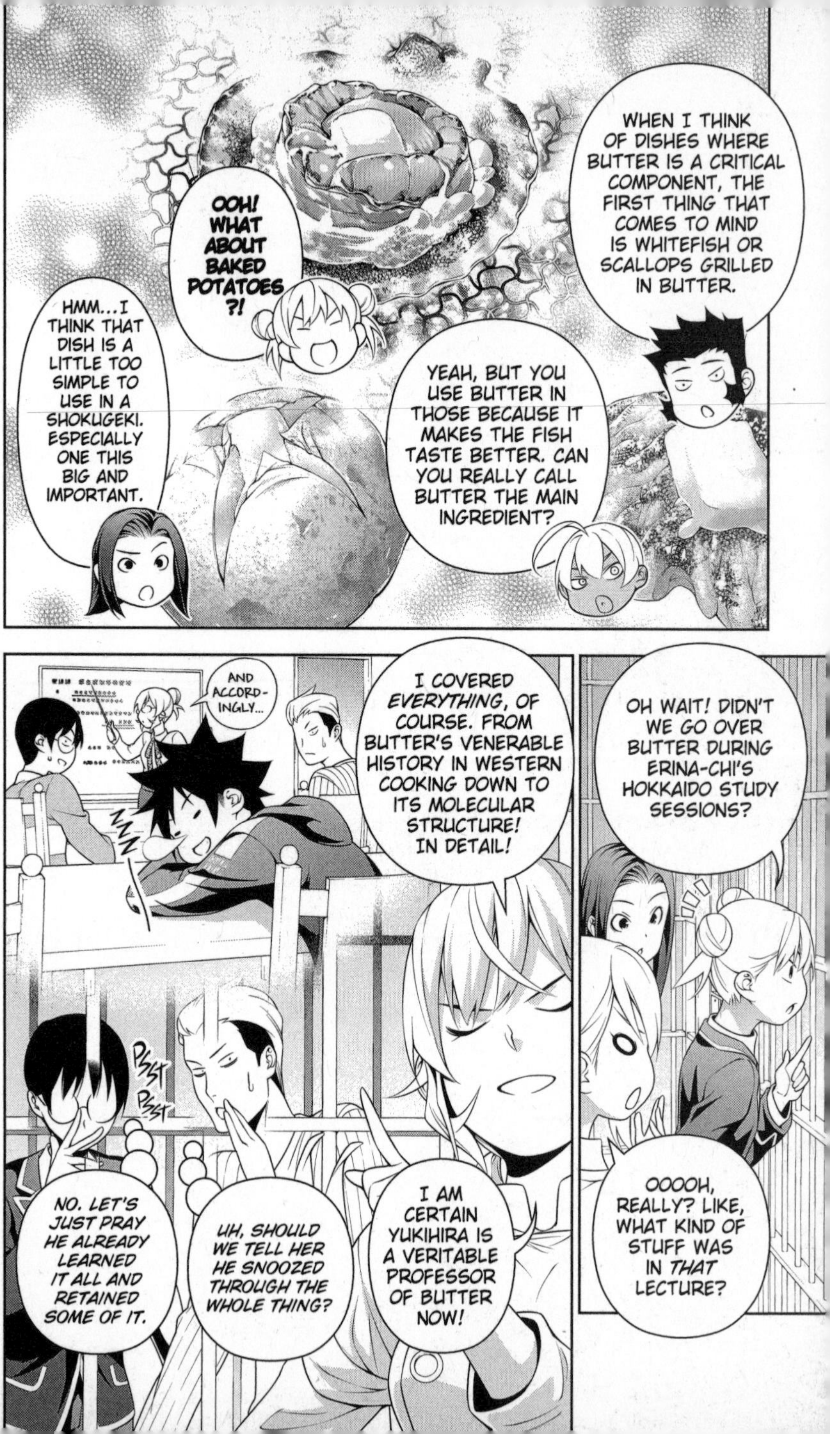
WHEN I THINK OF DISHES WHERE BUTTER IS A CRITICAL COMPONENT, THE FIRST THING THAT COMES TO MIND IS WHITEFISH OR SCALLOPS GRILLED IN BUTTER.
YEAH, BUT YOU USE BUTTER IN THOSE BECAUSE IT MAKES THE FISH TASTE BETTER. CAN YOU REALLY CALL BUTTER THE MAIN INGREDIENT?
OOH! WHAT ABOUT BAKED POTATOES?!
HMM...I THINK THAT DISH IS A LITTLE TOO SIMPLE TO USE IN A SHOKUGEKI. ESPECIALLY ONE THIS BIG AND IMPORTANT.
OH WAIT! DIDN'T WE GO OVER BUTTER DURING ERINA-CHI'S HOKKAIDO STUDY SESSIONS?
OOOOH, REALLY? LIKE, WHAT KIND OF STUFF WAS IN *THAT* LECTURE?
I COVERED *EVERYTHING*, OF COURSE. FROM BUTTER'S VENERABLE HISTORY IN WESTERN COOKING DOWN TO ITS MOLECULAR STRUCTURE! IN DETAIL!
AND ACCORDINGLY...
ZZZ
I AM CERTAIN YUKIHIRA IS A VERITABLE PROFESSOR OF BUTTER NOW!
UH, SHOULD WE TELL HER HE SNOOZED THROUGH THE WHOLE THING?
PSST PSST
NO. LET'S JUST PRAY HE ALREADY LEARNED IT ALL AND RETAINED SOME OF IT.

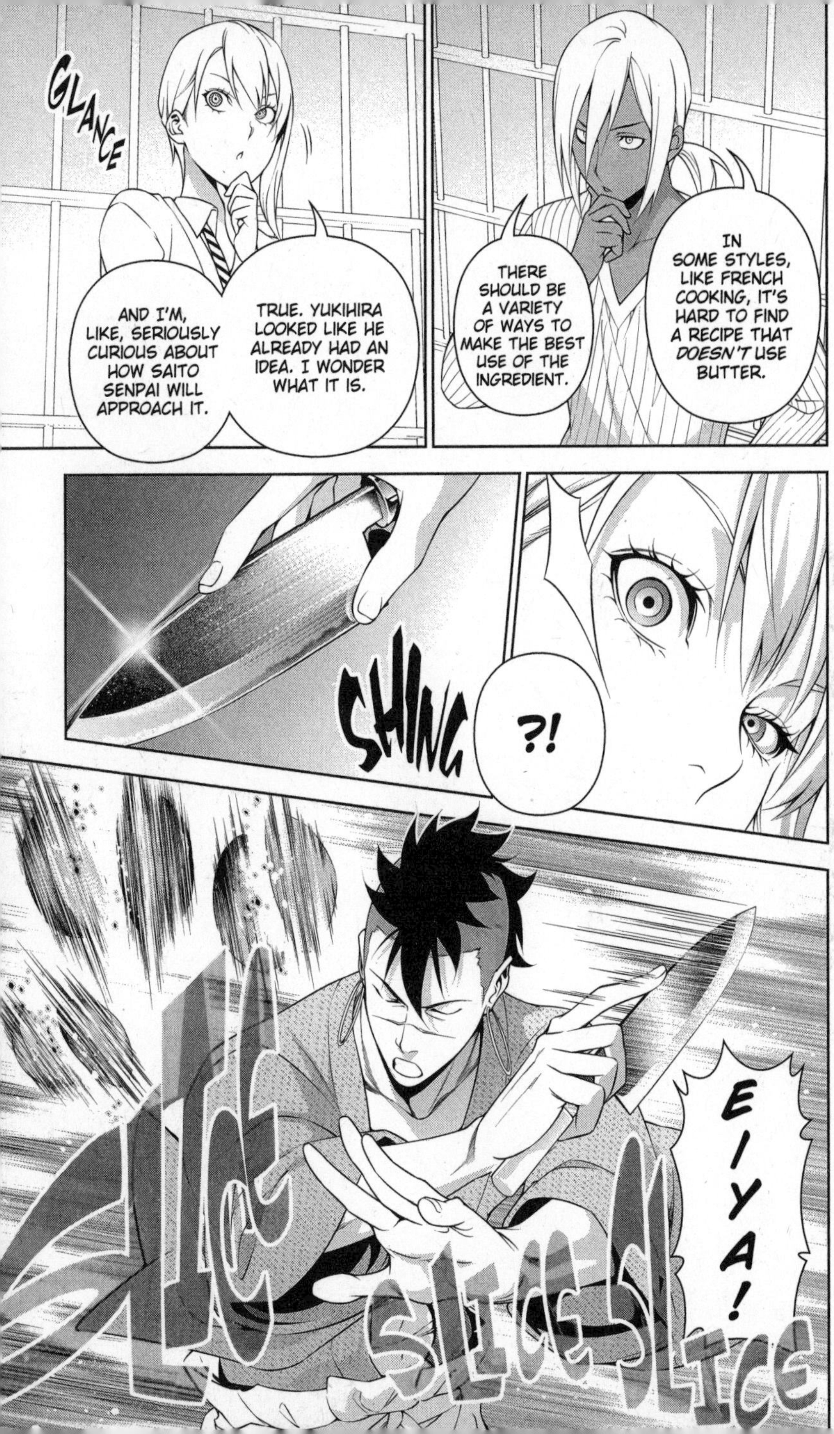
IN SOME STYLES, LIKE FRENCH COOKING, IT'S HARD TO FIND A RECIPE THAT *DOESN'T* USE BUTTER.
THERE SHOULD BE A VARIETY OF WAYS TO MAKE THE BEST USE OF THE INGREDIENT.
GLANCE
TRUE. YUKIHIRA LOOKED LIKE HE ALREADY HAD AN IDEA. I WONDER WHAT IT IS.
AND I'M, LIKE, SERIOUSLY CURIOUS ABOUT HOW SAITO SENPAI WILL APPROACH IT.
?!
SHING
EIYA!
SLICE SLICE SLICE

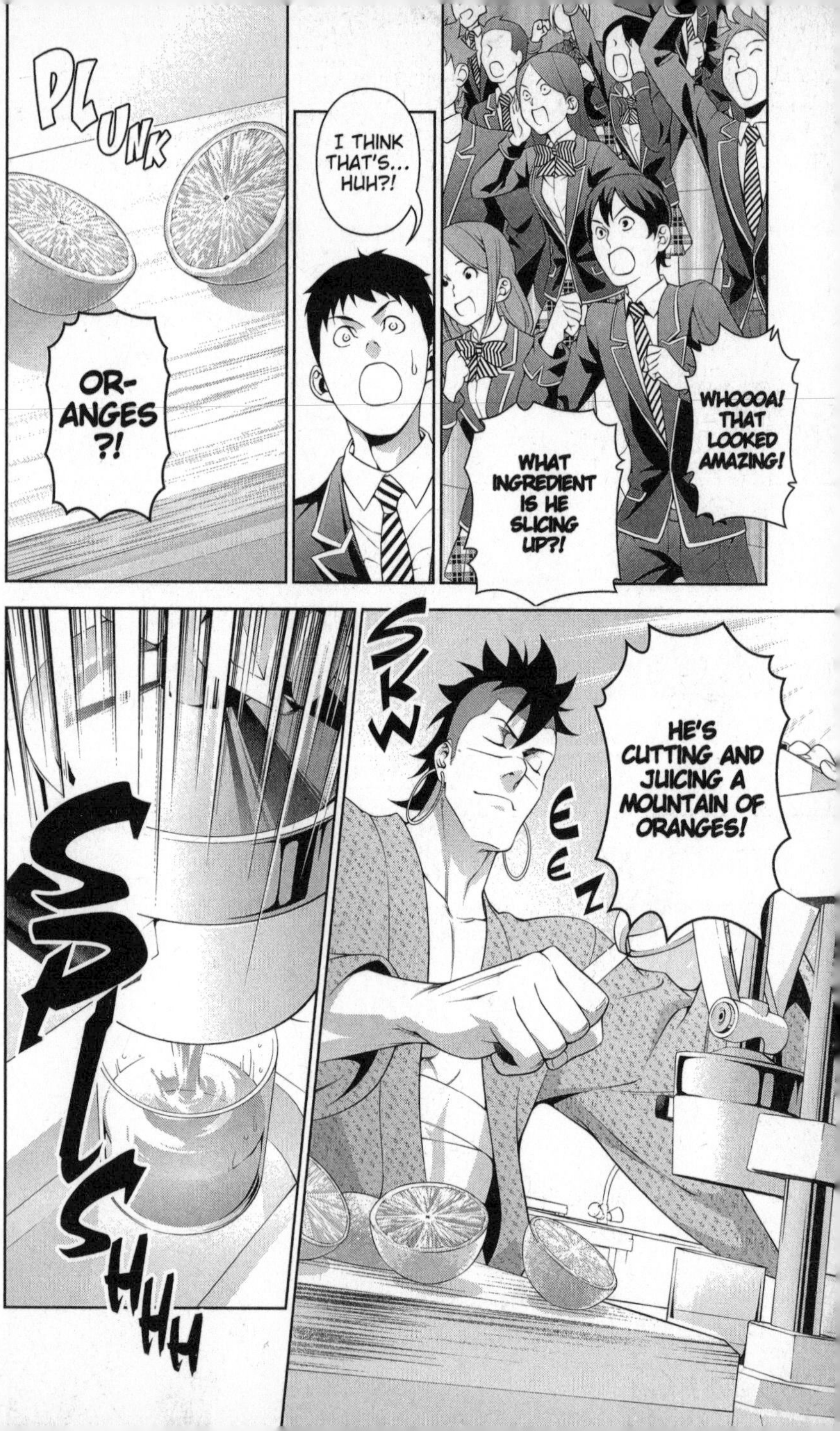
WHOOOA! THAT LOOKED AMAZING!
WHAT INGREDIENT IS HE SLICING UP?!
I THINK THAT'S... HUH?!
PLUNK
OR-ANGES?!
HE'S CUTTING AND JUICING A MOUNTAIN OF ORANGES!
SKWEEZ
SPLUSHHH

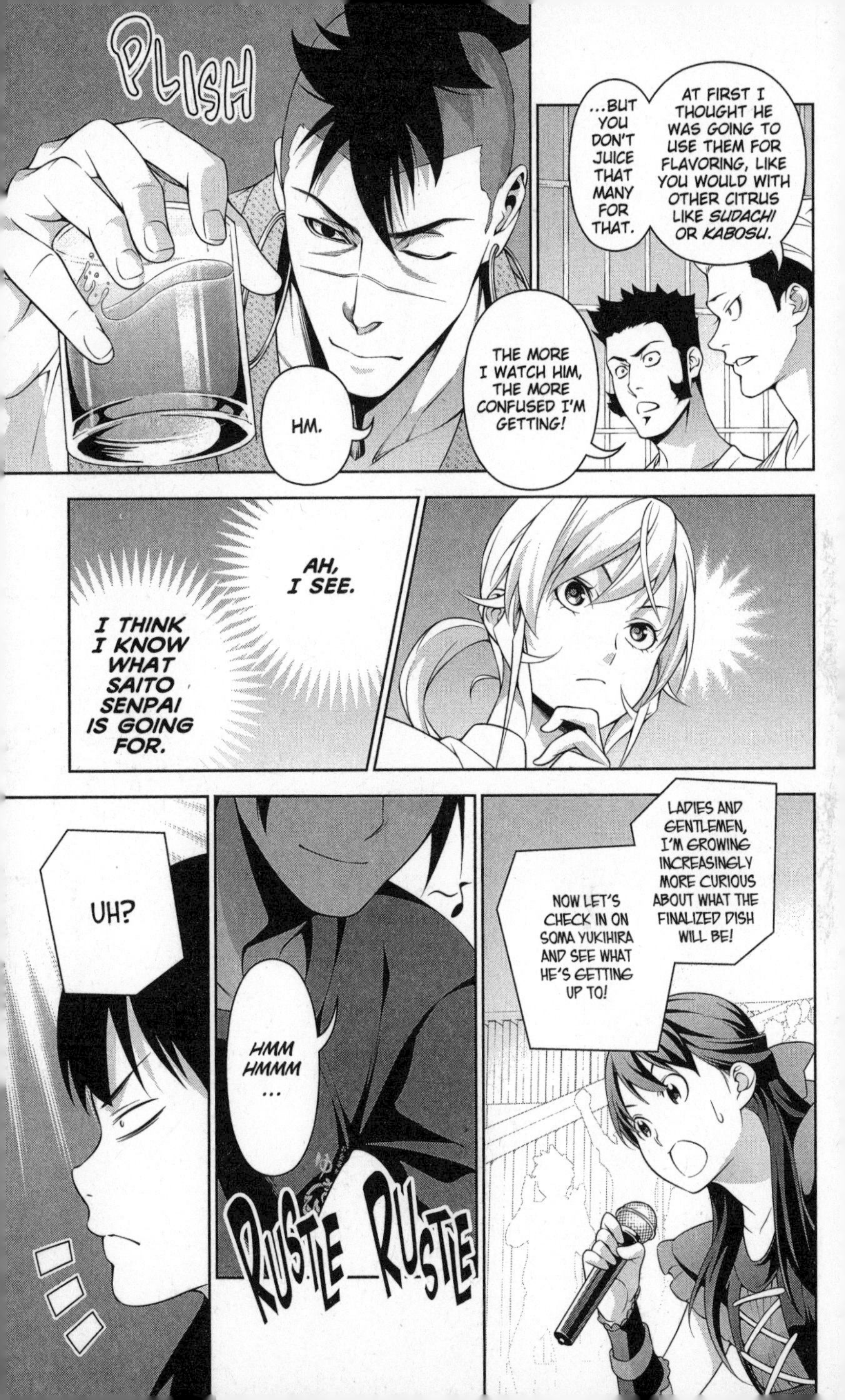
AT FIRST I THOUGHT HE WAS GOING TO USE THEM FOR FLAVORING, LIKE YOU WOULD WITH OTHER CITRUS LIKE *SUDACHI* OR *KABOSU*.
...BUT YOU DON'T JUICE THAT MANY FOR THAT.
THE MORE I WATCH HIM, THE MORE CONFUSED I'M GETTING!
PLISH
HM.
AH, I SEE.
I THINK I KNOW WHAT SAITO SENPAI IS GOING FOR.
LADIES AND GENTLEMEN, I'M GROWING INCREASINGLY MORE CURIOUS ABOUT WHAT THE FINALIZED DISH WILL BE!
NOW LET'S CHECK IN ON SOMA YUKIHIRA AND SEE WHAT HE'S GETTING UP TO!
HMM HMMM ...
RUSTLE RUSTLE
UH?

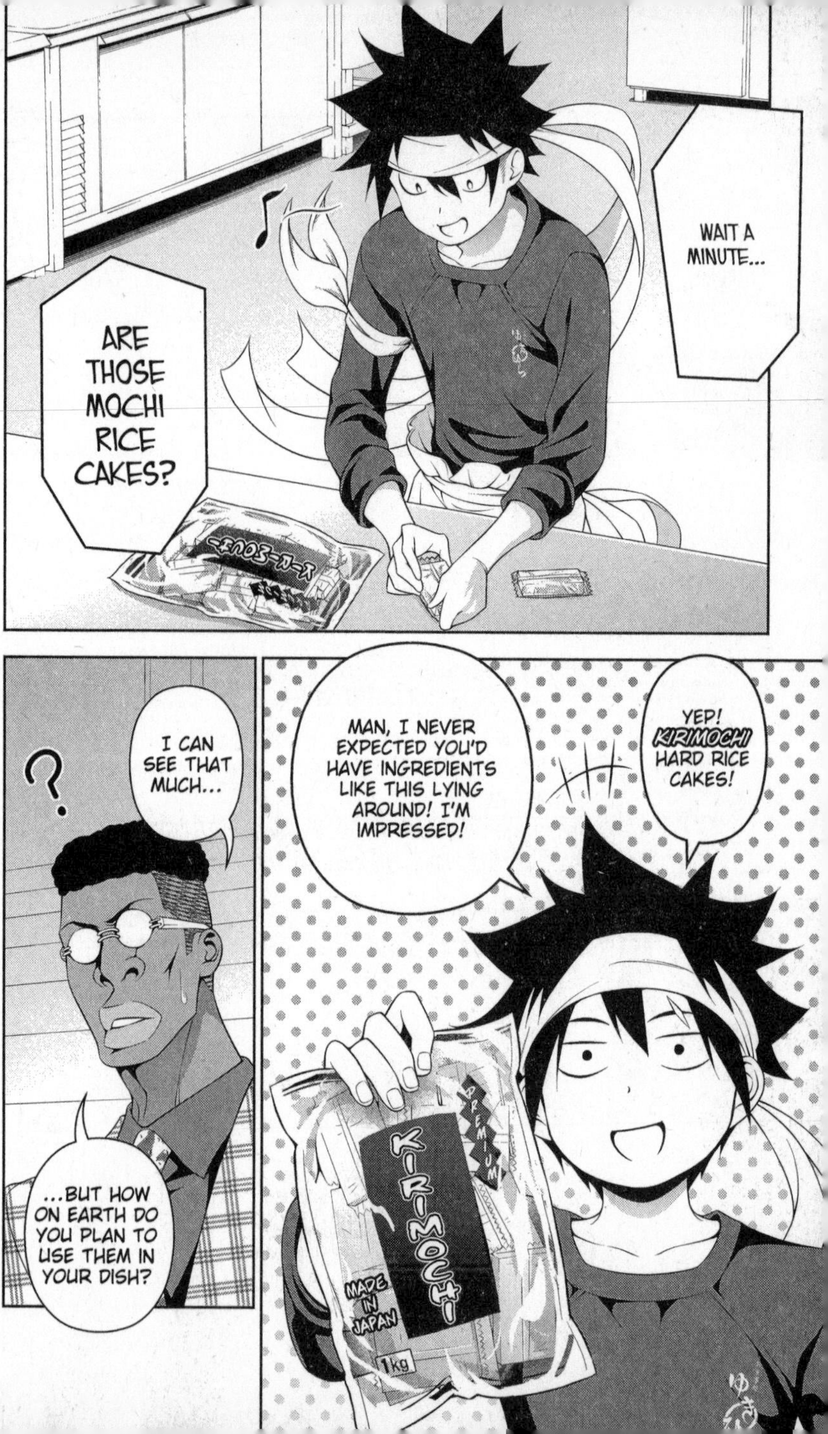
WAIT A MINUTE...
ARE THOSE MOCHI RICE CAKES?
YEP! KIRIMOCHI HARD RICE CAKES!
MAN, I NEVER EXPECTED YOU'D HAVE INGREDIENTS LIKE THIS LYING AROUND! I'M IMPRESSED!
PREMIUM
KIRIMOCHI
MADE IN JAPAN
1kg
I CAN SEE THAT MUCH...
...BUT HOW ON EARTH DO YOU PLAN TO USE THEM IN YOUR DISH?

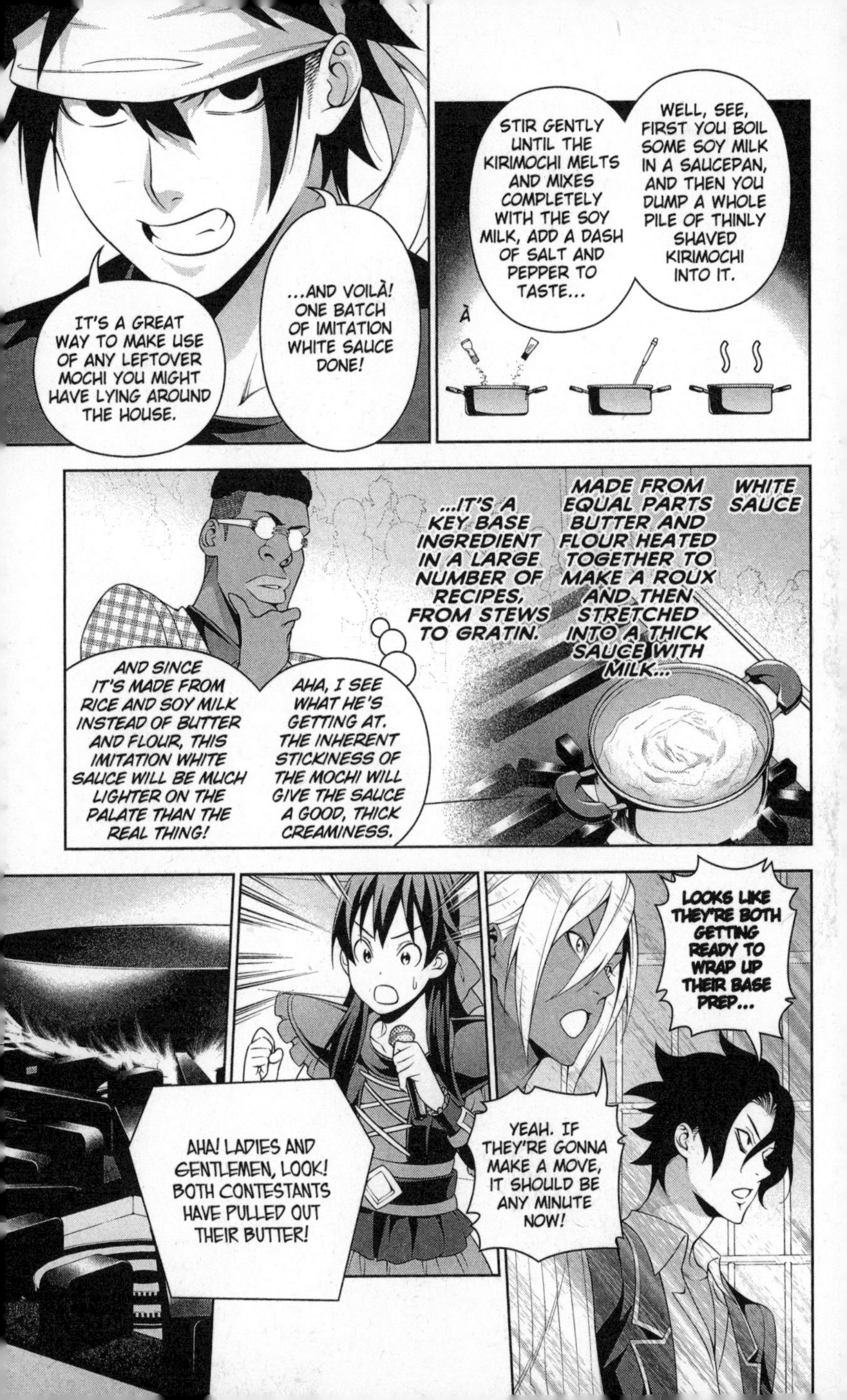
WELL, SEE, FIRST YOU BOIL SOME SOY MILK IN A SAUCEPAN, AND THEN YOU DUMP A WHOLE PILE OF THINLY SHAVED KIRIMOCHI INTO IT.
STIR GENTLY UNTIL THE KIRIMOCHI MELTS AND MIXES COMPLETELY WITH THE SOY MILK, ADD A DASH OF SALT AND PEPPER TO TASTE...
...AND VOILÀ! ONE BATCH OF IMITATION WHITE SAUCE DONE!
IT'S A GREAT WAY TO MAKE USE OF ANY LEFTOVER MOCHI YOU MIGHT HAVE LYING AROUND THE HOUSE.
WHITE SAUCE
MADE FROM EQUAL PARTS BUTTER AND FLOUR HEATED TOGETHER TO MAKE A ROUX AND THEN STRETCHED INTO A THICK SAUCE WITH MILK...
...IT'S A KEY BASE INGREDIENT IN A LARGE NUMBER OF RECIPES, FROM STEWS TO GRATIN.
AHA, I SEE WHAT HE'S GETTING AT. THE INHERENT STICKINESS OF THE MOCHI WILL GIVE THE SAUCE A GOOD, THICK CREAMINESS.
AND SINCE IT'S MADE FROM RICE AND SOY MILK INSTEAD OF BUTTER AND FLOUR, THIS IMITATION WHITE SAUCE WILL BE MUCH LIGHTER ON THE PALATE THAN THE REAL THING!
LOOKS LIKE THEY'RE BOTH GETTING READY TO WRAP UP THEIR BASE PREP...
YEAH. IF THEY'RE GONNA MAKE A MOVE, IT SHOULD BE ANY MINUTE NOW!
AHA! LADIES AND GENTLEMEN, LOOK! BOTH CONTESTANTS HAVE PULLED OUT THEIR BUTTER!

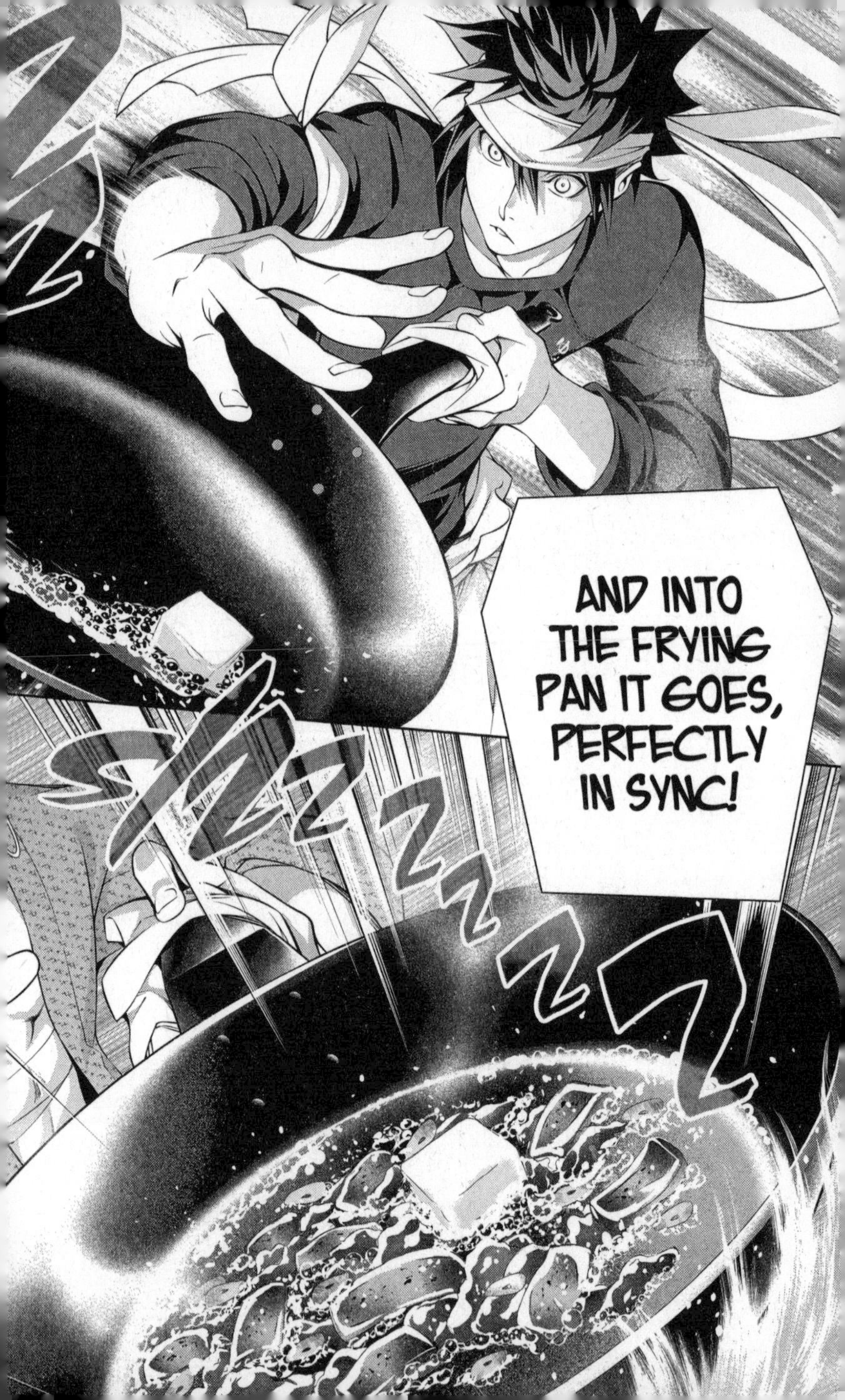
AND INTO THE FRYING PAN IT GOES, PERFECTLY IN SYNC!
SHZZZZZZ

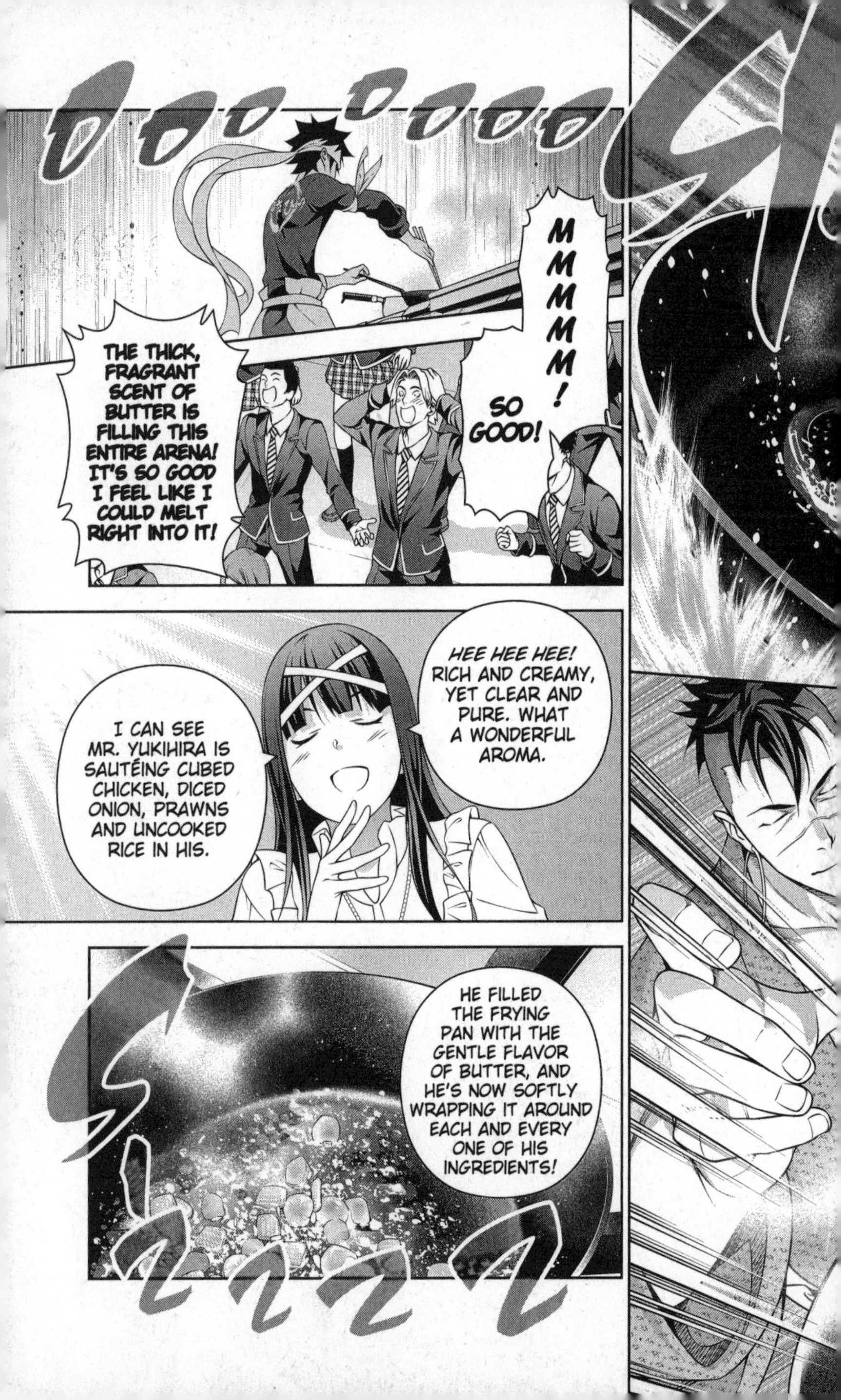
MMMMMM!
SO GOOD!
THE THICK, FRAGRANT SCENT OF BUTTER IS FILLING THIS ENTIRE ARENA! IT'S SO GOOD I FEEL LIKE I COULD MELT RIGHT INTO IT!
HEE HEE HEE! RICH AND CREAMY, YET CLEAR AND PURE. WHAT A WONDERFUL AROMA.
I CAN SEE MR. YUKIHIRA IS SAUTÉING CUBED CHICKEN, DICED ONION, PRAWNS AND UNCOOKED RICE IN HIS.
HE FILLED THE FRYING PAN WITH THE GENTLE FLAVOR OF BUTTER, AND HE'S NOW SOFTLY WRAPPING IT AROUND EACH AND EVERY ONE OF HIS INGREDIENTS!

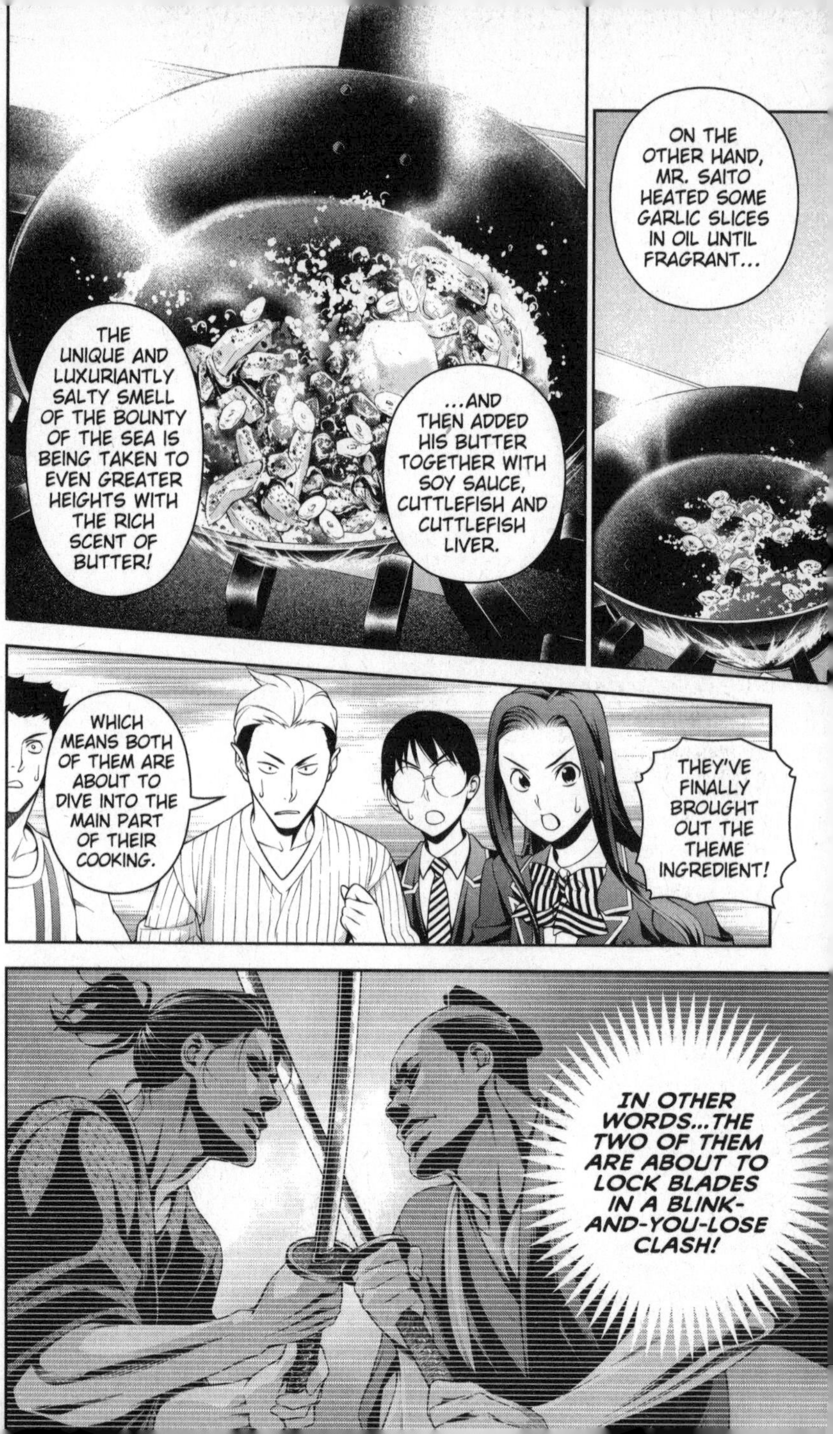
ON THE OTHER HAND, MR. SAITO HEATED SOME GARLIC SLICES IN OIL UNTIL FRAGRANT...
...AND THEN ADDED HIS BUTTER TOGETHER WITH SOY SAUCE, CUTTLEFISH AND CUTTLEFISH LIVER.
THE UNIQUE AND LUXURIANTLY SALTY SMELL OF THE BOUNTY OF THE SEA IS BEING TAKEN TO EVEN GREATER HEIGHTS WITH THE RICH SCENT OF BUTTER!
THEY'VE FINALLY BROUGHT OUT THE THEME INGREDIENT!
WHICH MEANS BOTH OF THEM ARE ABOUT TO DIVE INTO THE MAIN PART OF THEIR COOKING.
IN OTHER WORDS...THE TWO OF THEM ARE ABOUT TO LOCK BLADES IN A BLINK-AND-YOU-LOSE CLASH!

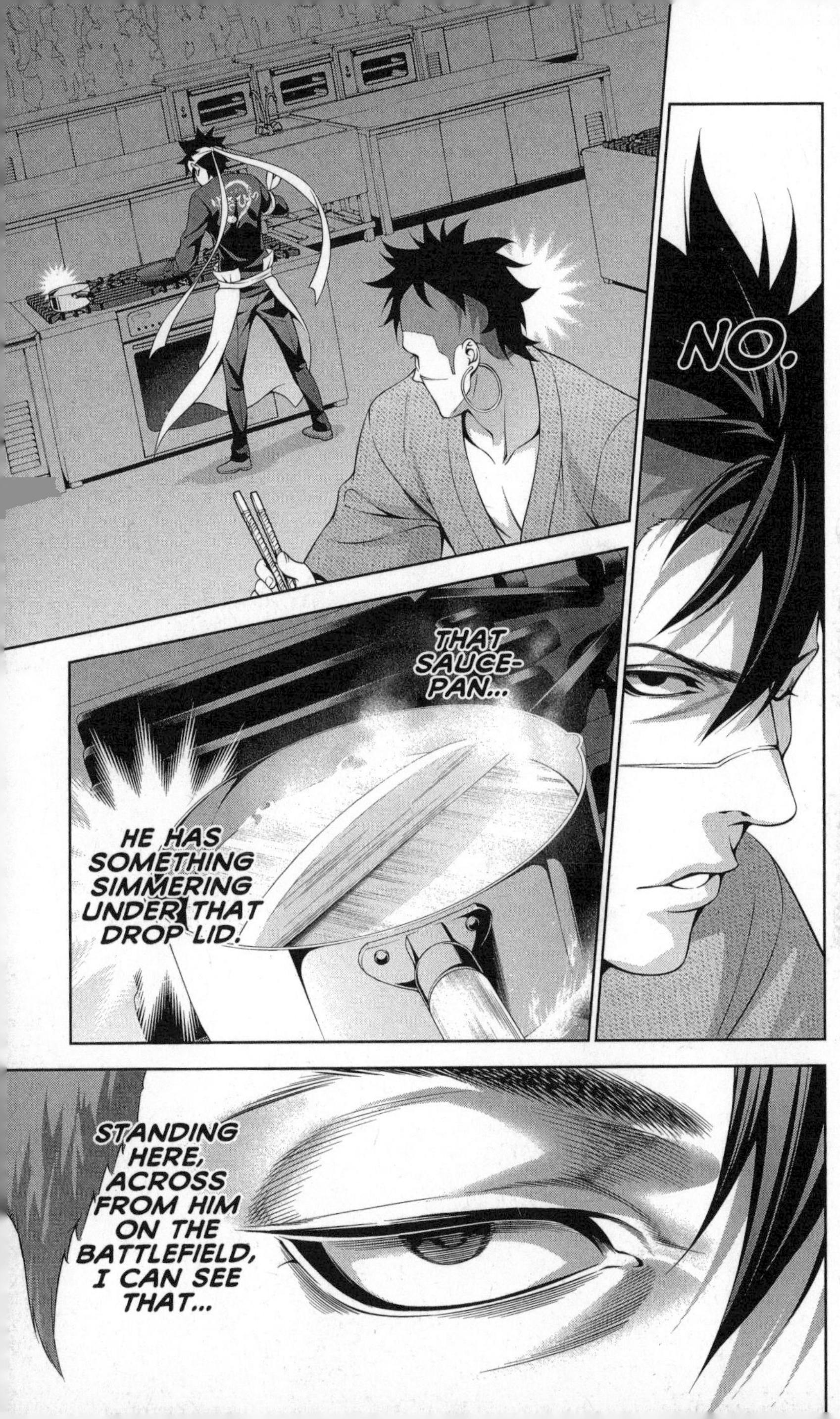
NO.
THAT SAUCE-PAN...
HE HAS SOMETHING SIMMERING UNDER THAT DROP LID.
STANDING HERE, ACROSS FROM HIM ON THE BATTLEFIELD, I CAN SEE THAT...

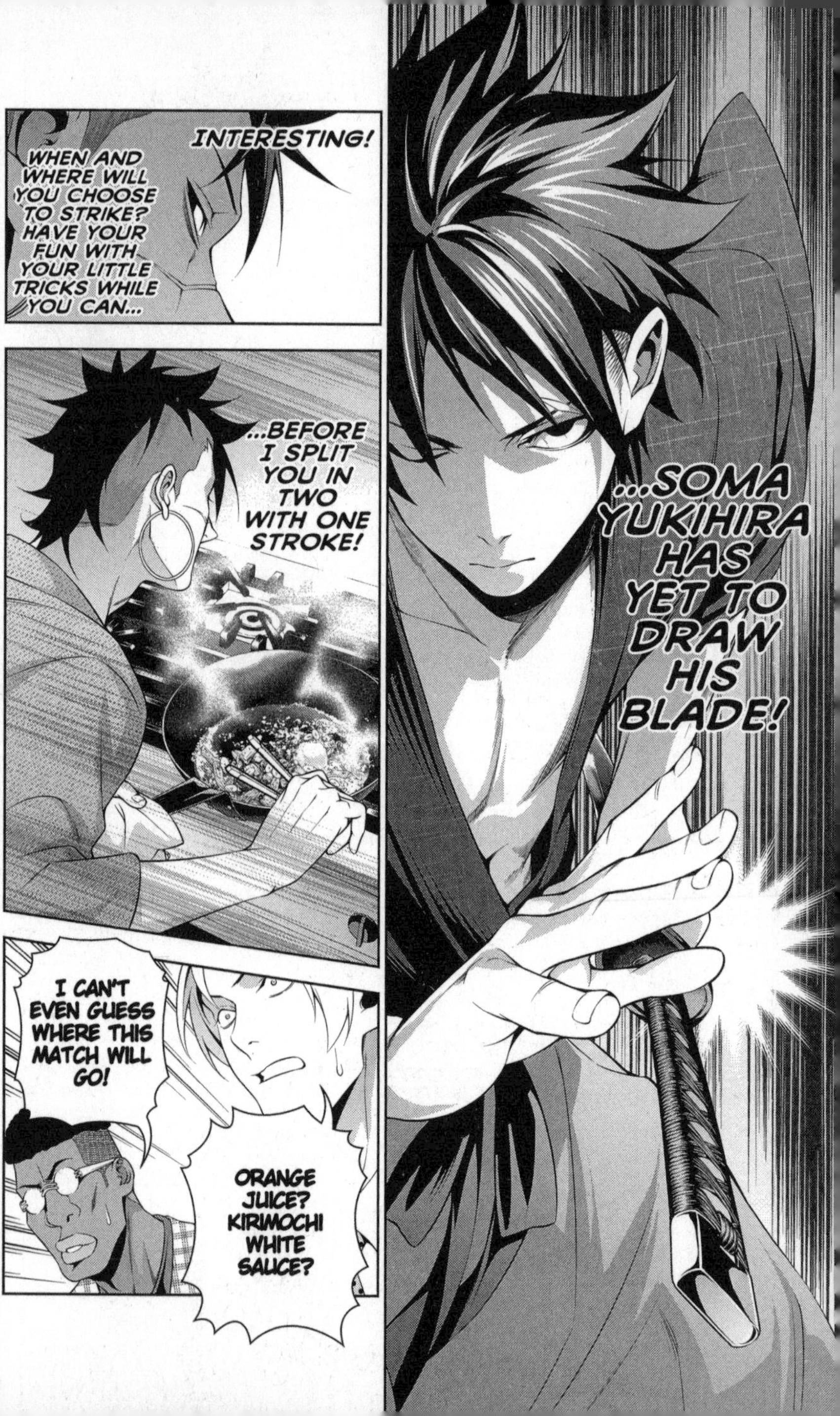
...SOMA YUKIHIRA HAS YET TO DRAW HIS BLADE!
INTERESTING!
WHEN AND WHERE WILL YOU CHOOSE TO STRIKE? HAVE YOUR FUN WITH YOUR LITTLE TRICKS WHILE YOU CAN...
...BEFORE I SPLIT YOU IN TWO WITH ONE STROKE!
I CAN'T EVEN GUESS WHERE THIS MATCH WILL GO!
ORANGE JUICE? KIRIMOCHI WHITE SAUCE?

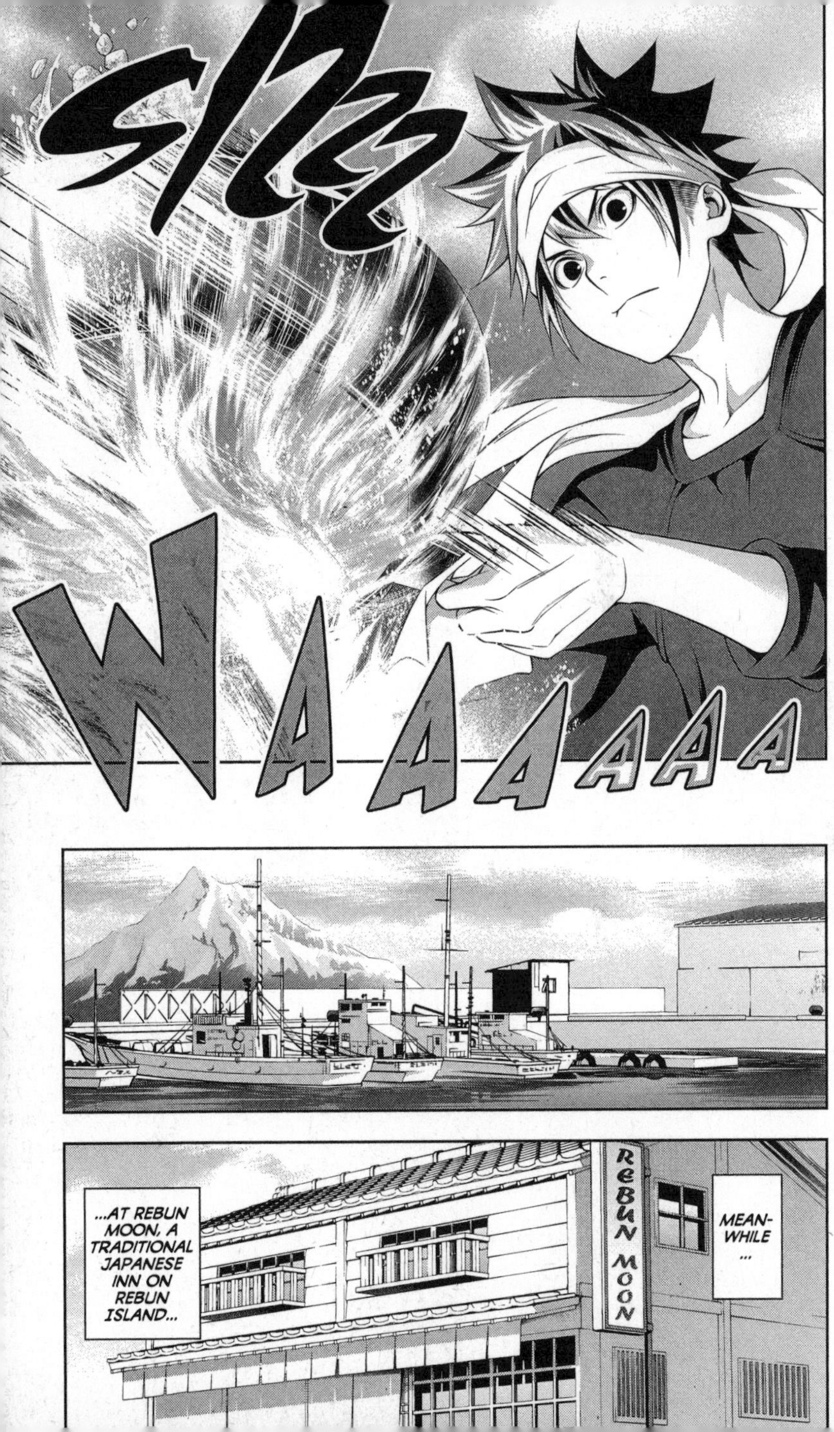
WAAAAAA
MEAN-WHILE ...
REBUN MOON
...AT REBUN MOON, A TRADITIONAL JAPANESE INN ON REBUN ISLAND...

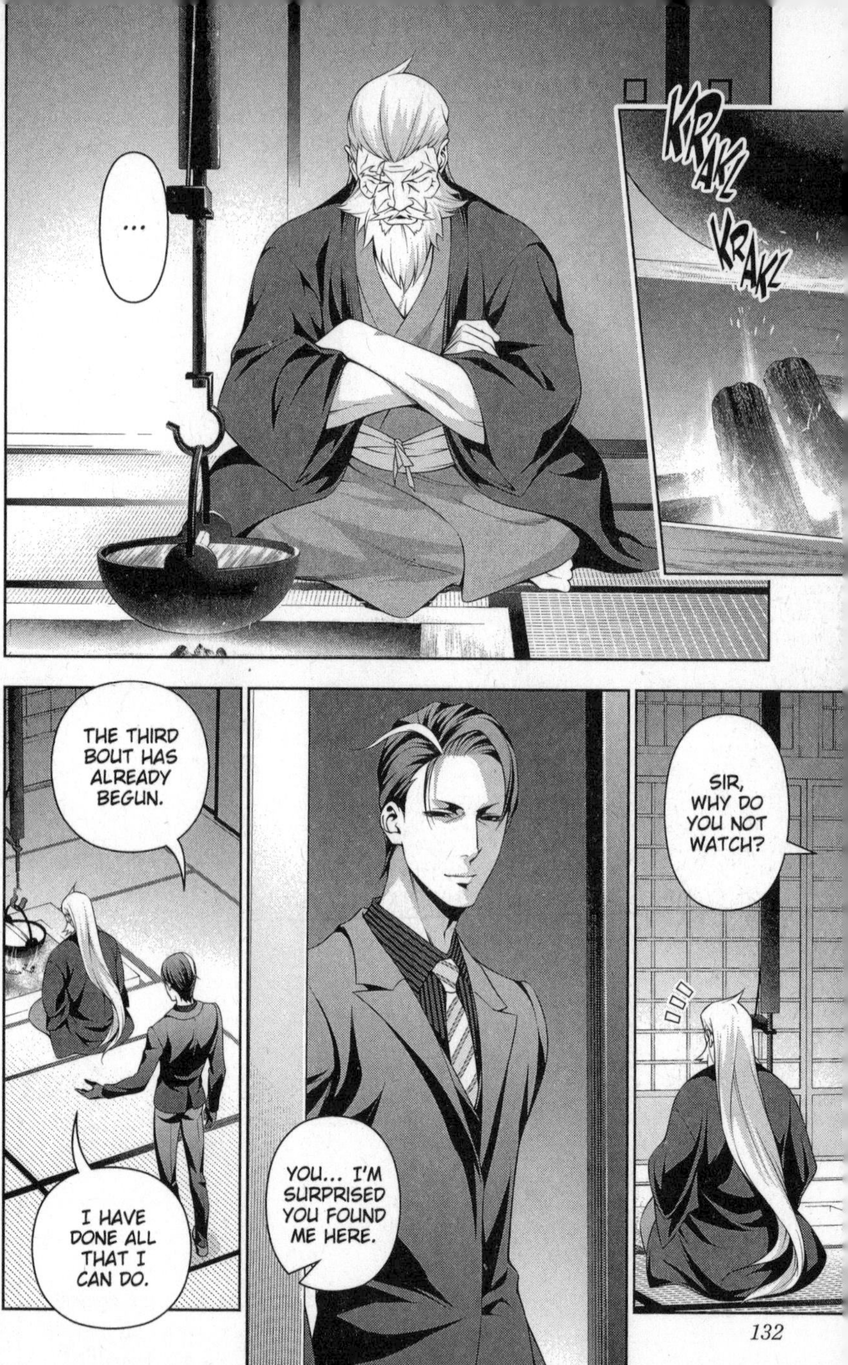
KRAKL
KRAKL
...
SIR, WHY DO YOU NOT WATCH?
...
YOU... I'M SURPRISED YOU FOUND ME HERE.
THE THIRD BOUT HAS ALREADY BEGUN.
I HAVE DONE ALL THAT I CAN DO.

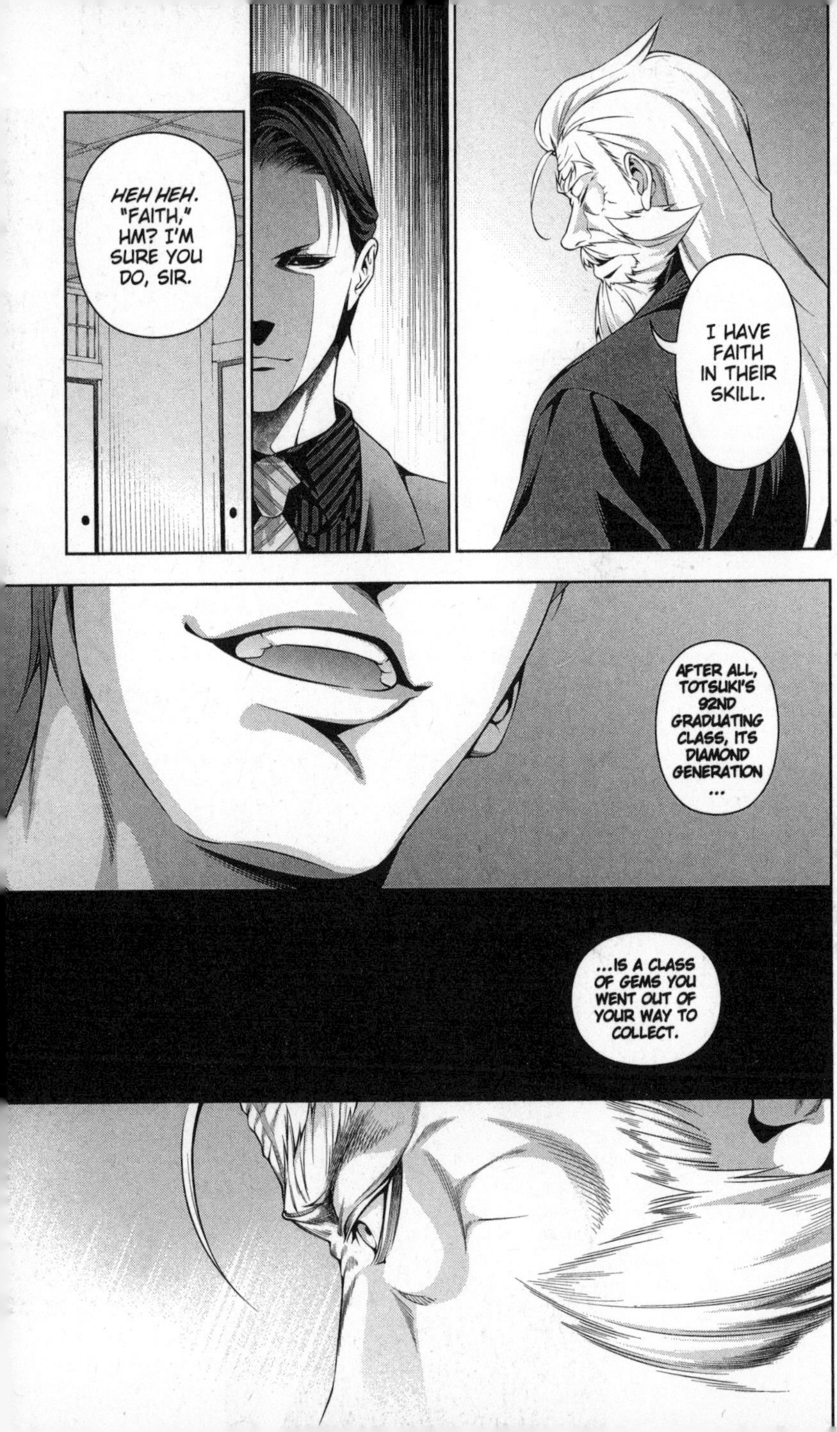
I HAVE FAITH IN THEIR SKILL.
HEH HEH. "FAITH," HM? I'M SURE YOU DO, SIR.
AFTER ALL, TOTSUKI'S 92ND GRADUATING CLASS, ITS DIAMOND GENERATION...
...IS A CLASS OF GEMS YOU WENT OUT OF YOUR WAY TO COLLECT.

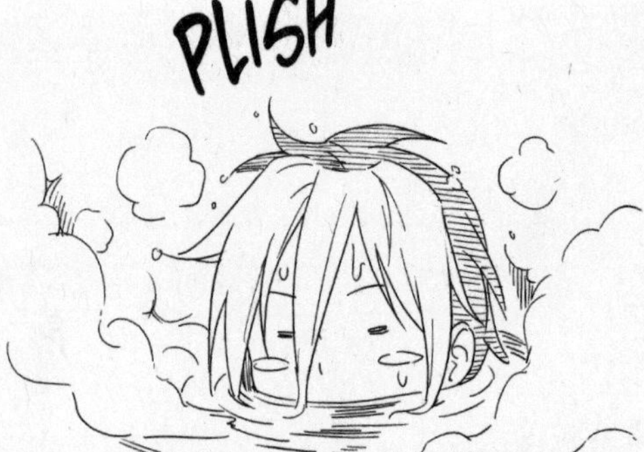
PLISH

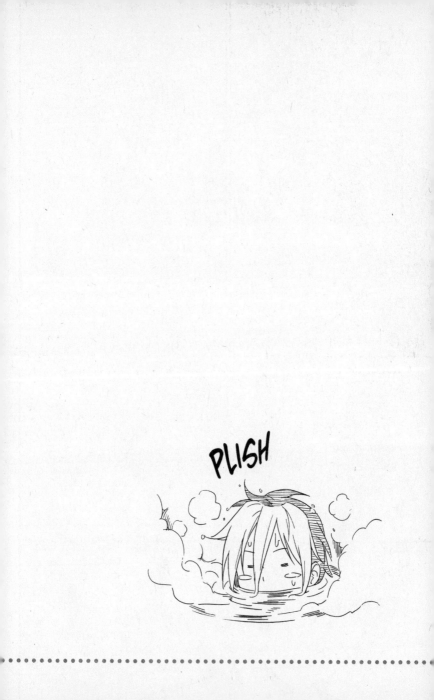

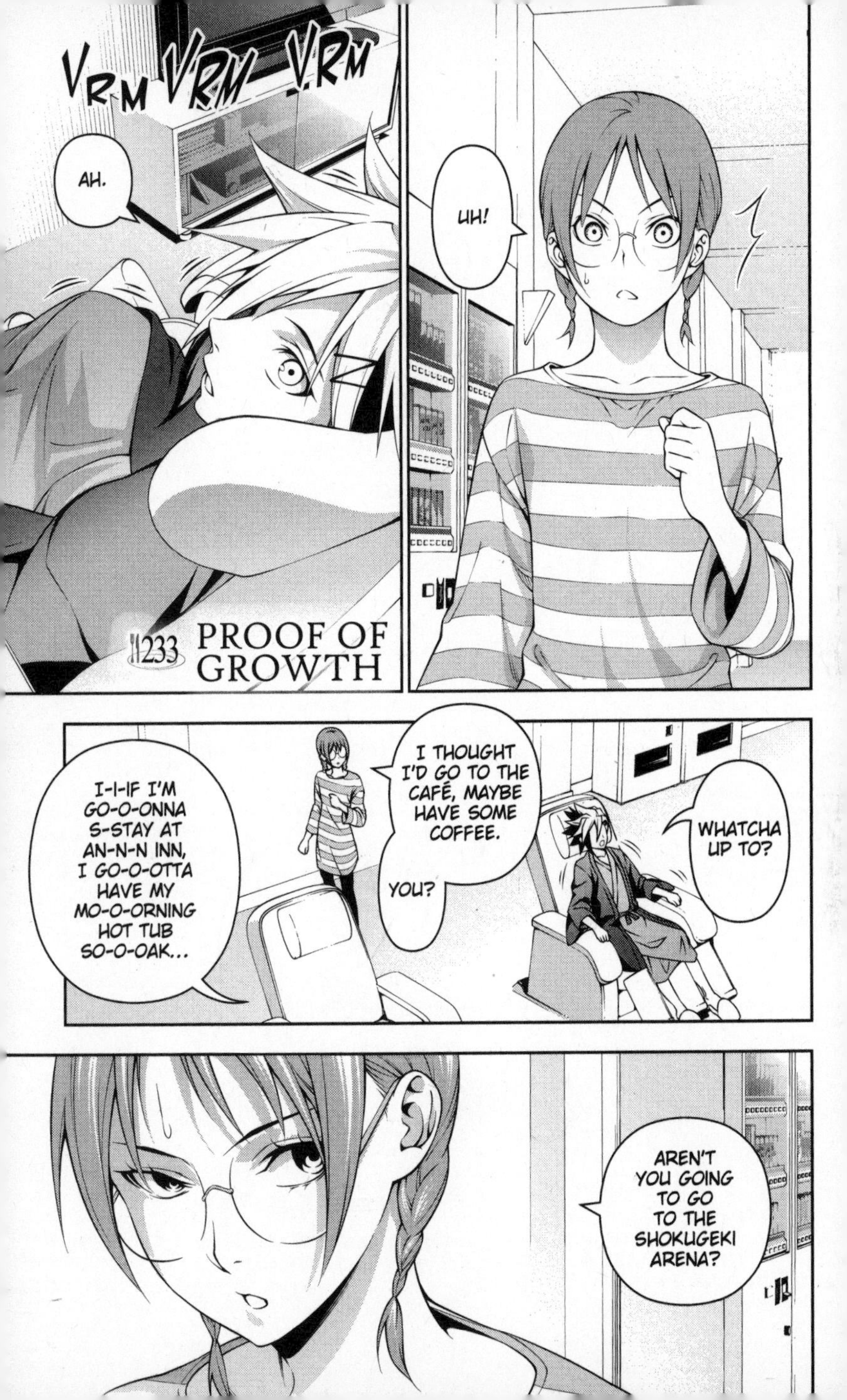
UH!
VRM VRM VRM
AH.
233 PROOF OF GROWTH
WHATCHA UP TO?
I THOUGHT I'D GO TO THE CAFÉ, MAYBE HAVE SOME COFFEE.
YOU?
I-I-IF I'M GO-O-ONNA S-STAY AT AN-N-N INN, I GO-O-OTTA HAVE MY MO-O-ORNING HOT TUB SO-O-OAK...
AREN'T YOU GOING TO GO TO THE SHOKUGEKI ARENA?

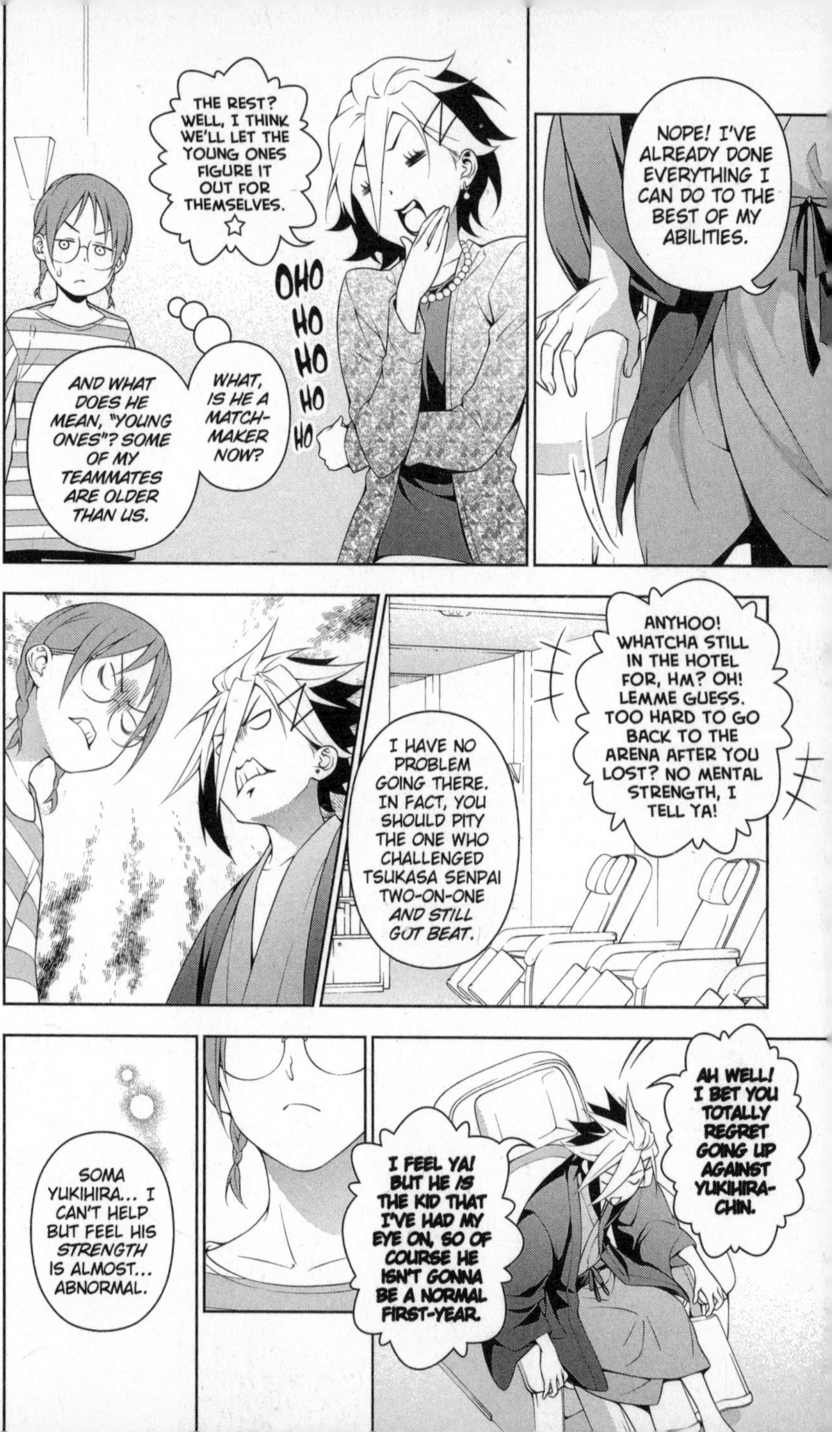
NOPE! I'VE ALREADY DONE EVERYTHING I CAN DO TO THE BEST OF MY ABILITIES.
THE REST? WELL, I THINK WE'LL LET THE YOUNG ONES FIGURE IT OUT FOR THEMSELVES. ☆
OHO HO HO HO HO
WHAT, IS HE A MATCH-MAKER NOW?
AND WHAT DOES HE MEAN, "YOUNG ONES"? SOME OF MY TEAMMATES ARE OLDER THAN US.
ANYHOO! WHATCHA STILL IN THE HOTEL FOR, HM? OH! LEMME GUESS. TOO HARD TO GO BACK TO THE ARENA AFTER YOU LOST? NO MENTAL STRENGTH, I TELL YA!
I HAVE NO PROBLEM GOING THERE. IN FACT, YOU SHOULD PITY THE ONE WHO CHALLENGED TSUKASA SENPAI TWO-ON-ONE *AND STILL* GOT BEAT.
AH WELL! I BET YOU TOTALLY REGRET GOING UP AGAINST YUKIHIRA-CHIN.
I FEEL YA! BUT HE *IS* THE KID THAT I'VE HAD MY EYE ON, SO OF COURSE HE ISN'T GONNA BE A NORMAL FIRST-YEAR.
SOMA YUKIHIRA... I CAN'T HELP BUT FEEL HIS *STRENGTH* IS ALMOST... ABNORMAL.

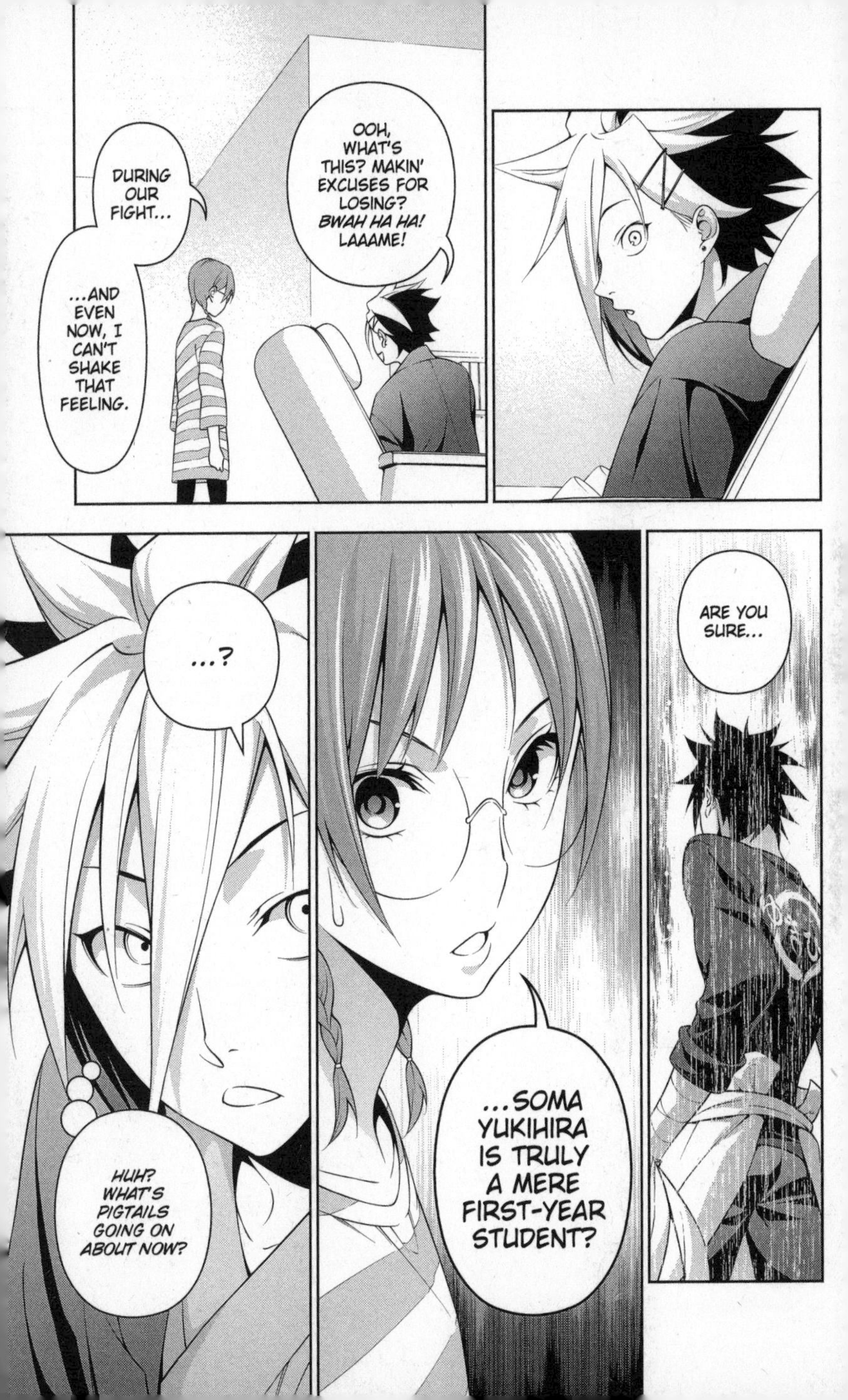
OOH, WHAT'S THIS? MAKIN' EXCUSES FOR LOSING? *BWAH HA HA!* LAAAME!
DURING OUR FIGHT...
...AND EVEN NOW, I CAN'T SHAKE THAT FEELING.
ARE YOU SURE...
...SOMA YUKIHIRA IS TRULY A MERE FIRST-YEAR STUDENT?
...?
HUH? WHAT'S PIGTAILS GOING ON ABOUT NOW?

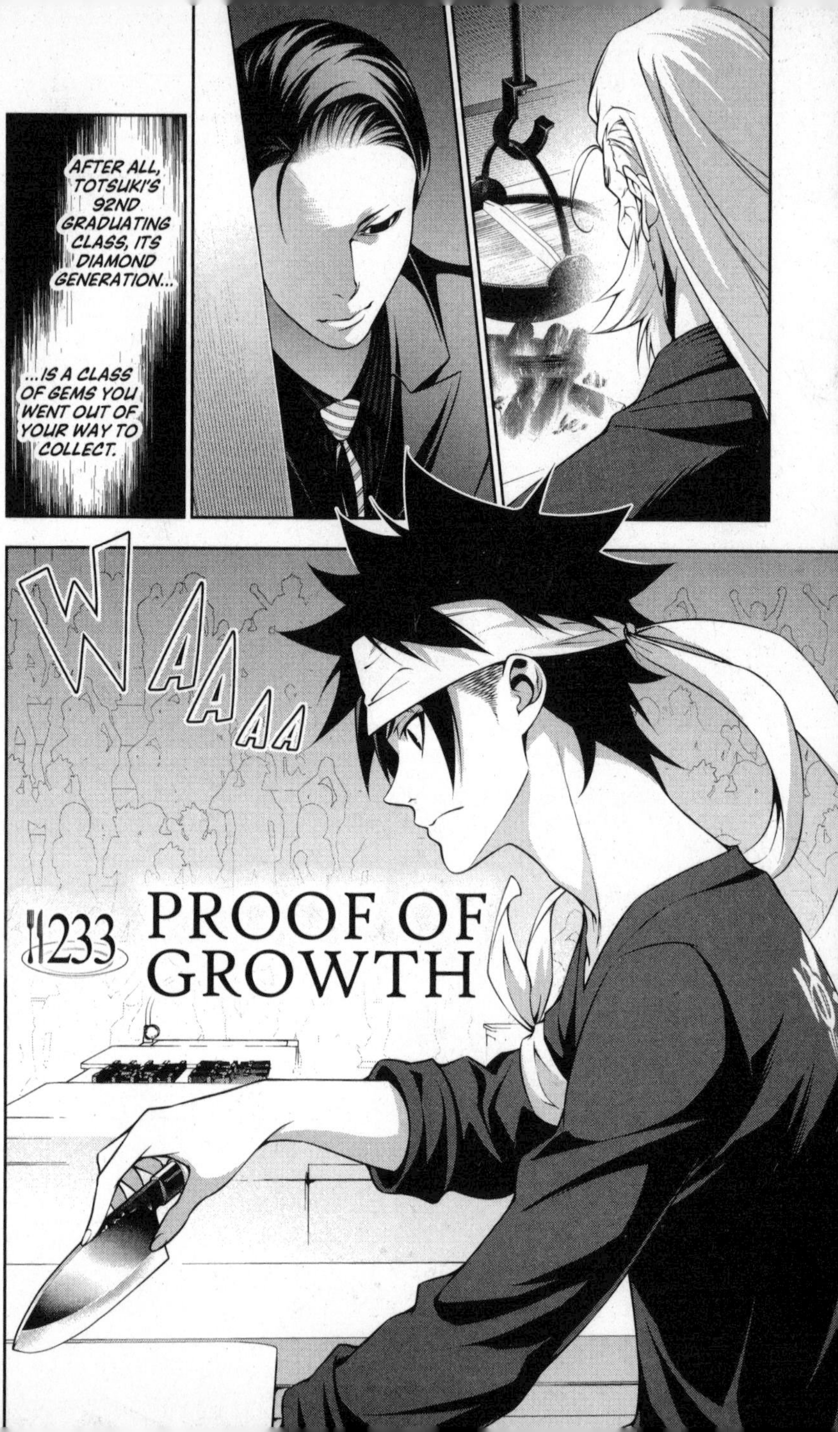
AFTER ALL, TOTSUKI'S 92ND GRADUATING CLASS, ITS DIAMOND GENERATION...
...IS A CLASS OF GEMS YOU WENT OUT OF YOUR WAY TO COLLECT.
WAAAAA
233 PROOF OF GROWTH

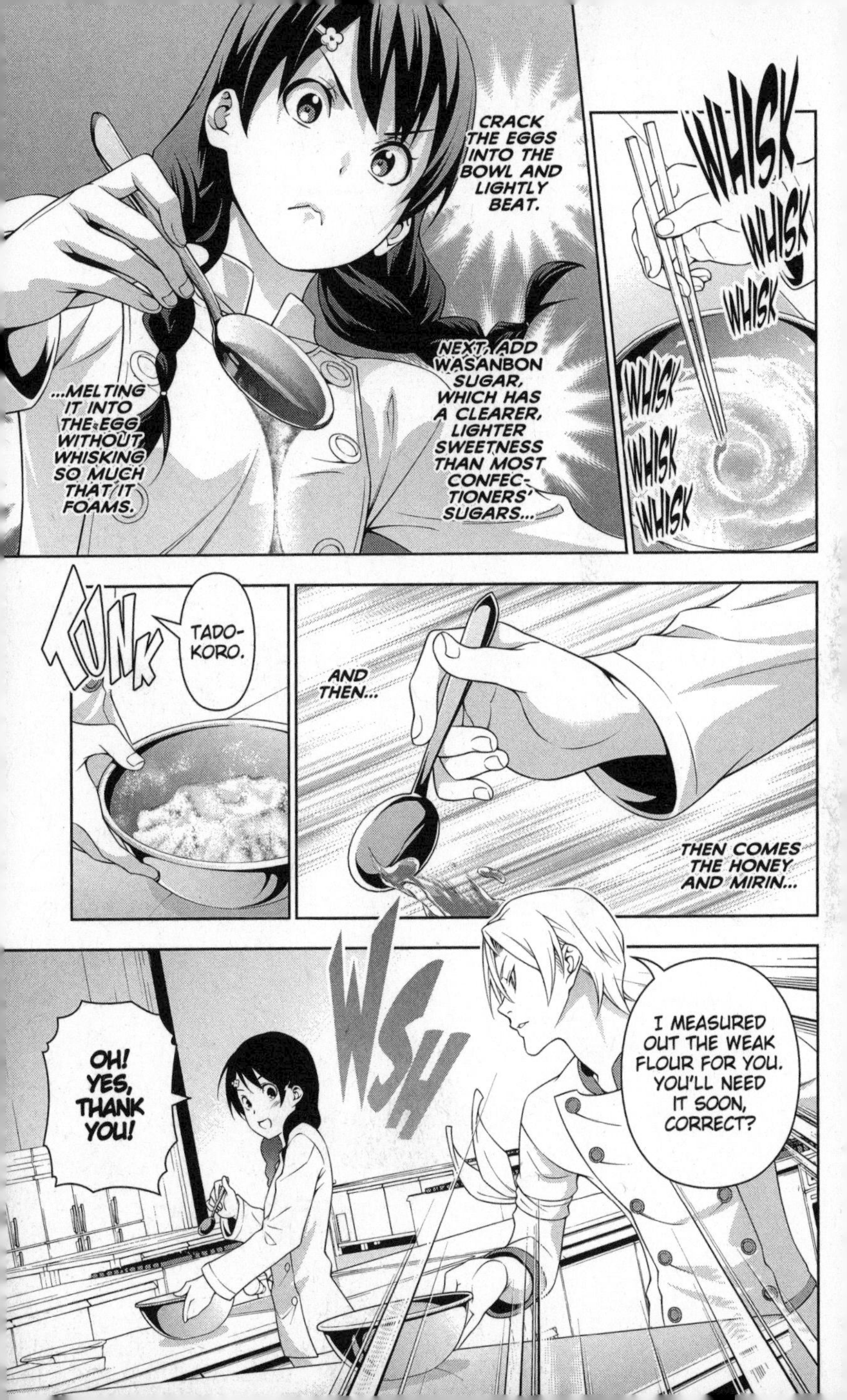
WHISK
WHISK
WHISK
WHISK
WHISK
WHISK
CRACK THE EGGS INTO THE BOWL AND LIGHTLY BEAT.
NEXT, ADD WASANBON SUGAR, WHICH HAS A CLEARER, LIGHTER SWEETNESS THAN MOST CONFEC-TIONERS' SUGARS...
...MELTING IT INTO THE EGG WITHOUT WHISKING SO MUCH THAT IT FOAMS.
AND THEN...
THEN COMES THE HONEY AND MIRIN...
TADO-KORO.
TUNK
WSH
I MEASURED OUT THE WEAK FLOUR FOR YOU. YOU'LL NEED IT SOON, CORRECT?
OH! YES, THANK YOU!

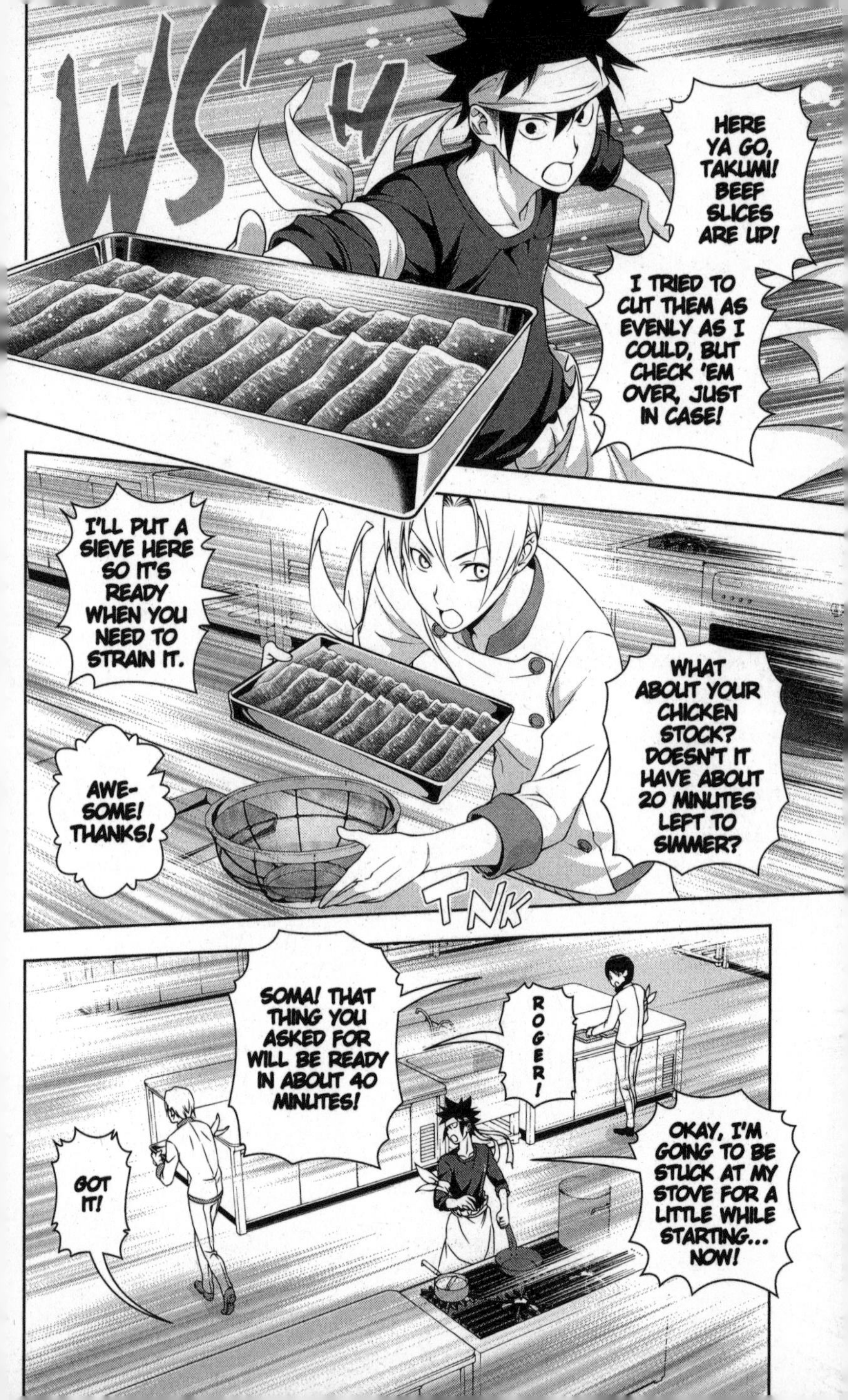
WSH
HERE YA GO, TAKUMI! BEEF SLICES ARE UP!
I TRIED TO CUT THEM AS EVENLY AS I COULD, BUT CHECK 'EM OVER, JUST IN CASE!
WHAT ABOUT YOUR CHICKEN STOCK? DOESN'T IT HAVE ABOUT 20 MINUTES LEFT TO SIMMER?
I'LL PUT A SIEVE HERE SO IT'S READY WHEN YOU NEED TO STRAIN IT.
AWE-SOME! THANKS!
TNK
SOMA! THAT THING YOU ASKED FOR WILL BE READY IN ABOUT 40 MINUTES!
ROGER!
OKAY, I'M GOING TO BE STUCK AT MY STOVE FOR A LITTLE WHILE STARTING... NOW!
GOT IT!

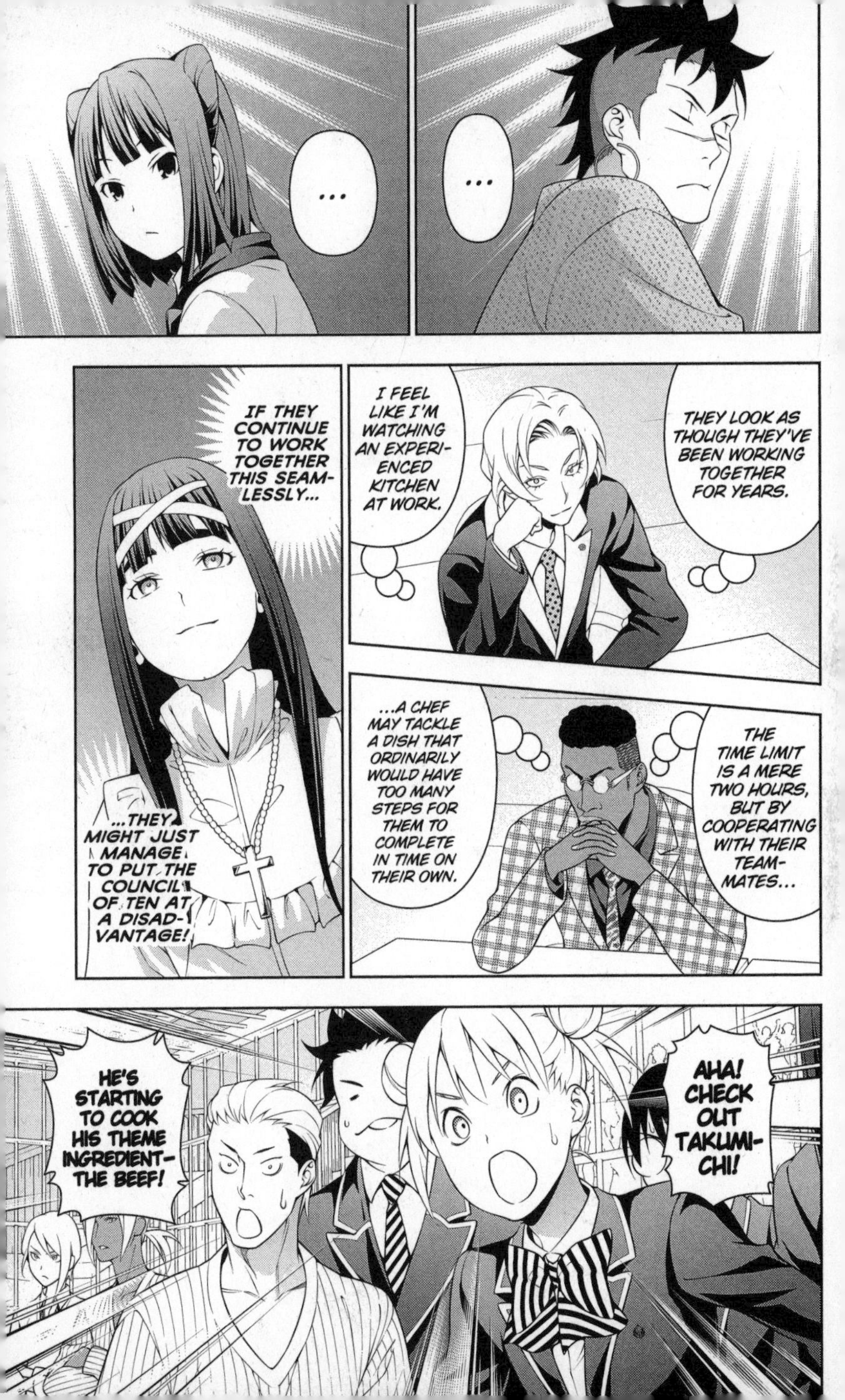
...
...
THEY LOOK AS THOUGH THEY'VE BEEN WORKING TOGETHER FOR YEARS.
I FEEL LIKE I'M WATCHING AN EXPERIENCED KITCHEN AT WORK.
THE TIME LIMIT IS A MERE TWO HOURS, BUT BY COOPERATING WITH THEIR TEAMMATES...
...A CHEF MAY TACKLE A DISH THAT ORDINARILY WOULD HAVE TOO MANY STEPS FOR THEM TO COMPLETE IN TIME ON THEIR OWN.
IF THEY CONTINUE TO WORK TOGETHER THIS SEAMLESSLY...
...THEY MIGHT JUST MANAGE TO PUT THE COUNCIL OF TEN AT A DISADVANTAGE!
AHA! CHECK OUT TAKUMI-CHI!
HE'S STARTING TO COOK HIS THEME INGREDIENT—THE BEEF!

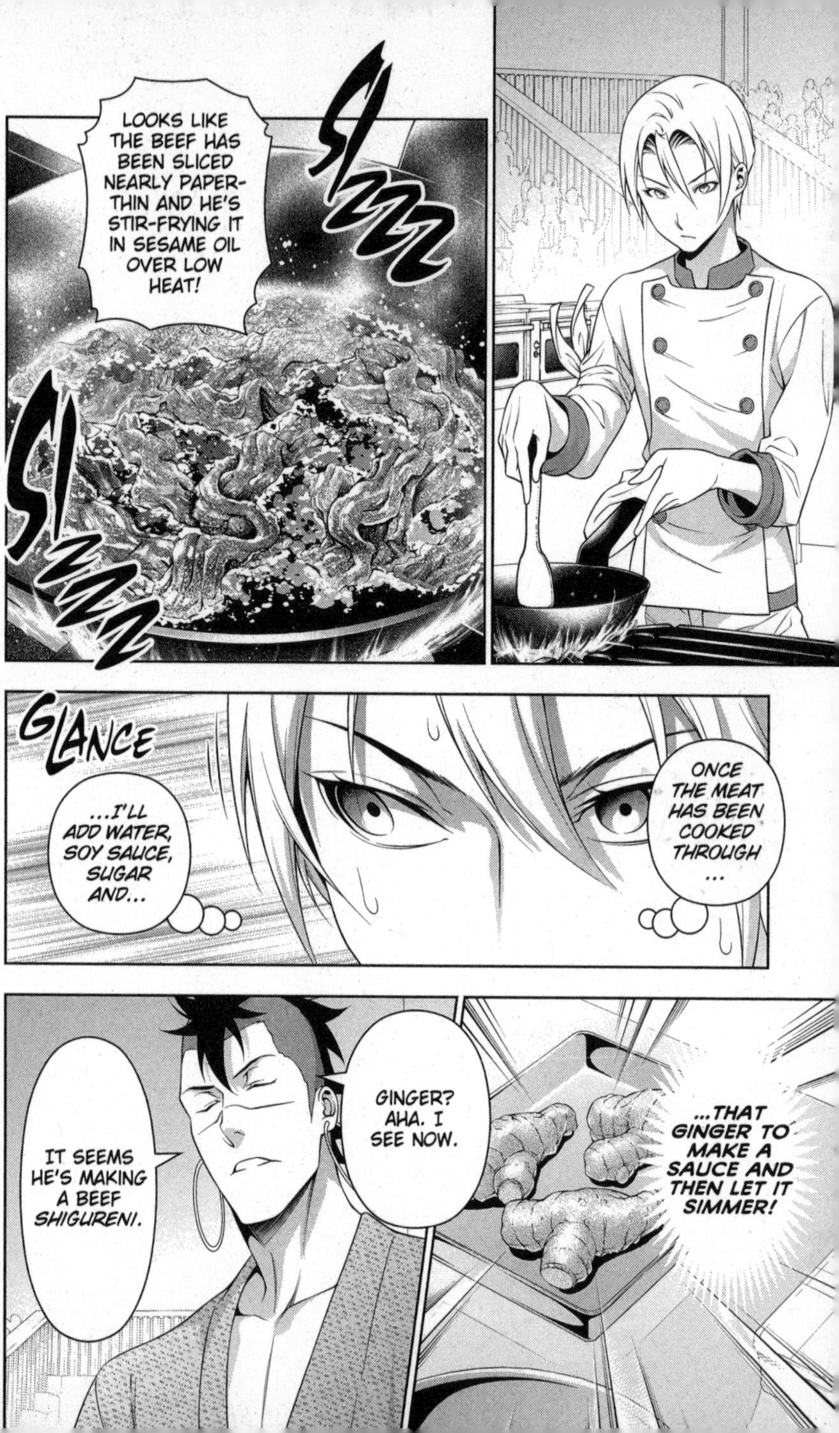
SIZZZ
LOOKS LIKE THE BEEF HAS BEEN SLICED NEARLY PAPER-THIN AND HE'S STIR-FRYING IT IN SESAME OIL OVER LOW HEAT!
SIZZZZ
ONCE THE MEAT HAS BEEN COOKED THROUGH...
GLANCE
...I'LL ADD WATER, SOY SAUCE, SUGAR AND...
...THAT GINGER TO MAKE A SAUCE AND THEN LET IT SIMMER!
GINGER? AHA. I SEE NOW.
IT SEEMS HE'S MAKING A BEEF SHIGURENI.

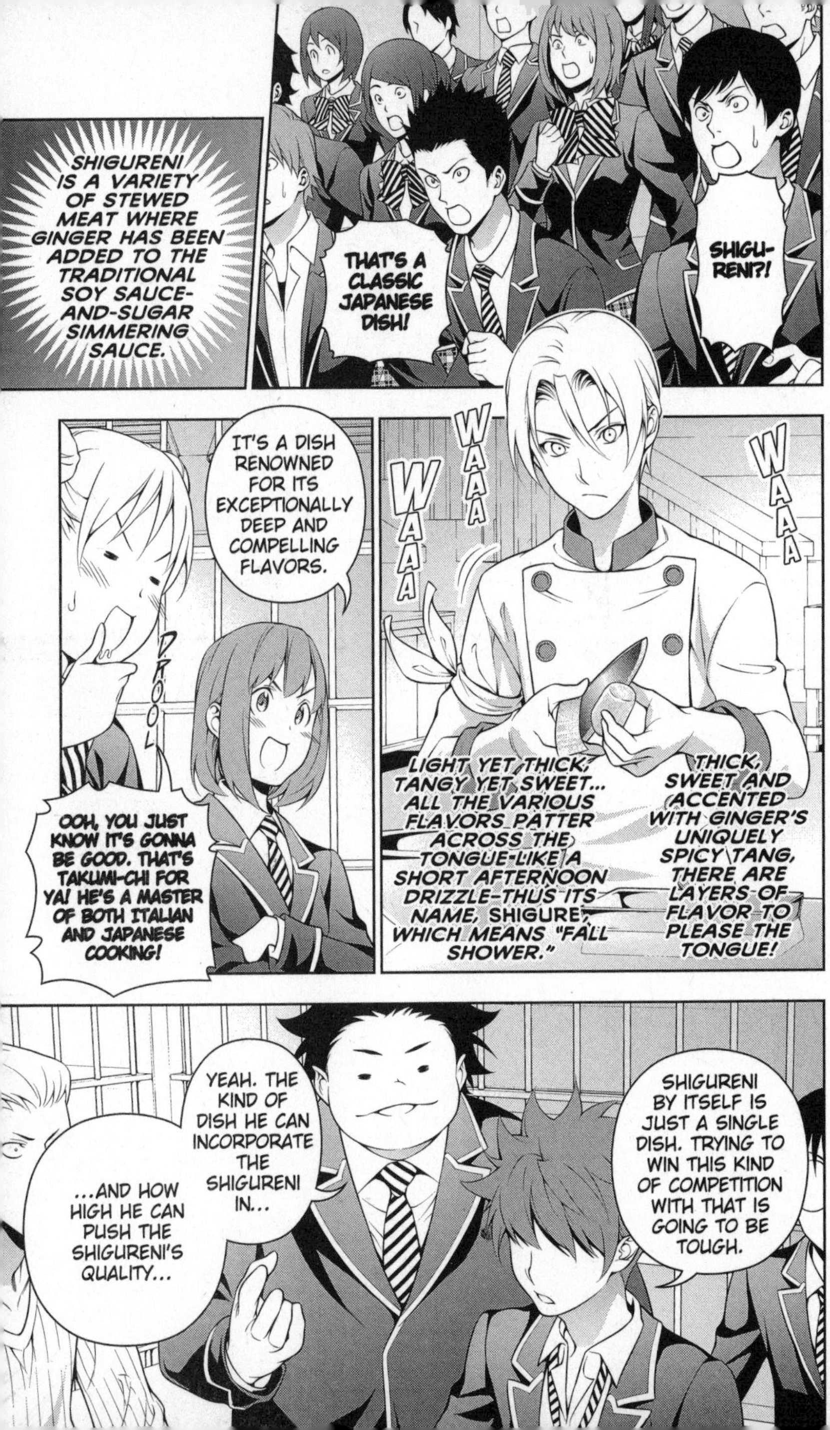
SHIGU-RENI?!
THAT'S A CLASSIC JAPANESE DISH!
SHIGURENI IS A VARIETY OF STEWED MEAT WHERE GINGER HAS BEEN ADDED TO THE TRADITIONAL SOY SAUCE-AND-SUGAR SIMMERING SAUCE.
WAAAA
WAAA
WAAAA
THICK, SWEET AND ACCENTED WITH GINGER'S UNIQUELY SPICY TANG, THERE ARE LAYERS OF FLAVOR TO PLEASE THE TONGUE!
LIGHT YET THICK, TANGY YET SWEET... ALL THE VARIOUS FLAVORS PATTER ACROSS THE TONGUE LIKE A SHORT AFTERNOON DRIZZLE—THUS ITS NAME, SHIGURE, WHICH MEANS "FALL SHOWER."
IT'S A DISH RENOWNED FOR ITS EXCEPTIONALLY DEEP AND COMPELLING FLAVORS.
DROOL
OOH, YOU JUST KNOW IT'S GONNA BE GOOD. THAT'S TAKUMI-CHI FOR YA! HE'S A MASTER OF BOTH ITALIAN AND JAPANESE COOKING!
SHIGURENI BY ITSELF IS JUST A SINGLE DISH. TRYING TO WIN THIS KIND OF COMPETITION WITH THAT IS GOING TO BE TOUGH.
YEAH. THE KIND OF DISH HE CAN INCORPORATE THE SHIGURENI IN...
...AND HOW HIGH HE CAN PUSH THE SHIGURENI'S QUALITY...

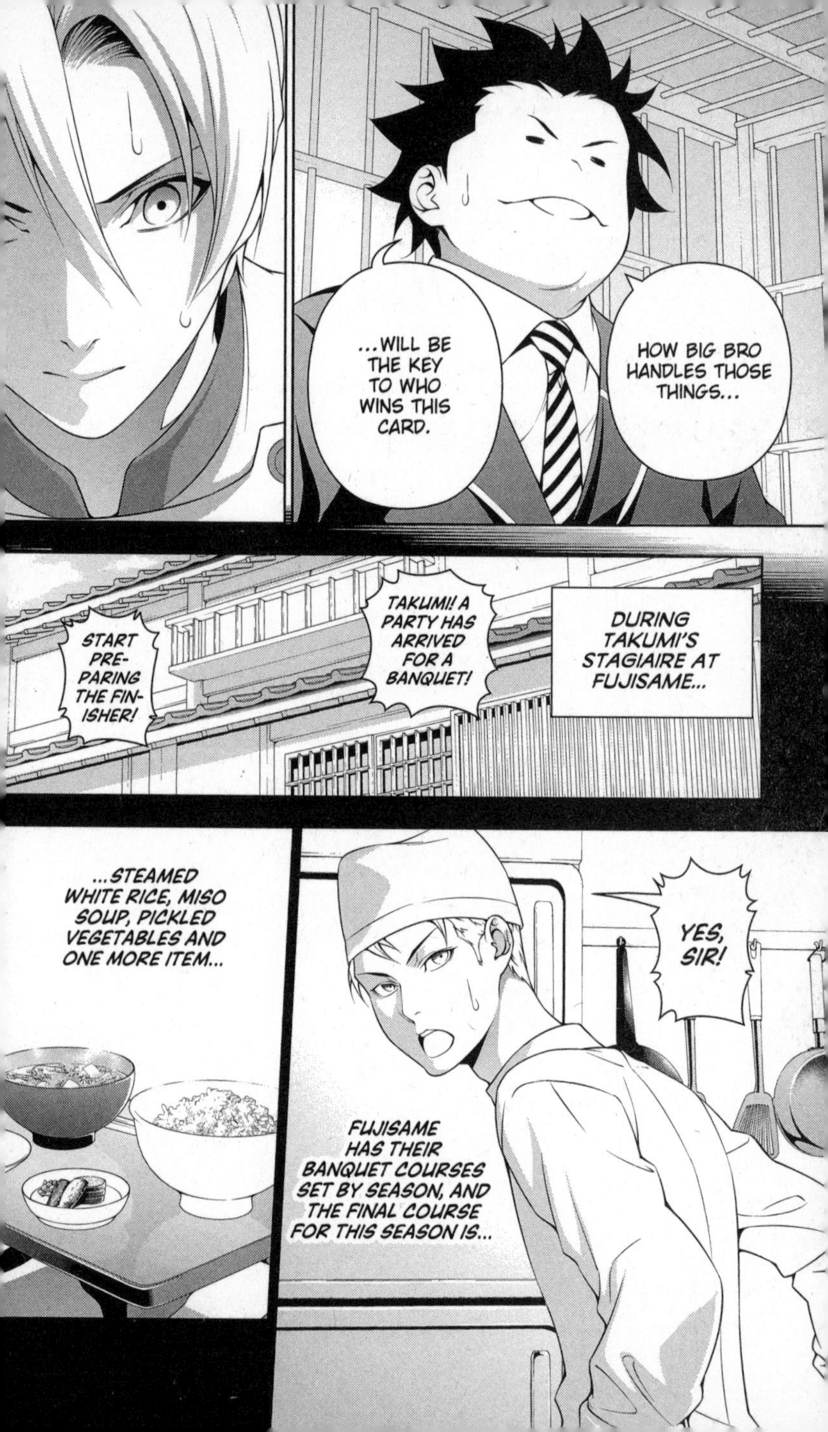
HOW BIG BRO HANDLES THOSE THINGS...
...WILL BE THE KEY TO WHO WINS THIS CARD.
DURING TAKUMI'S STAGIAIRE AT FUJISAME...
TAKUMI! A PARTY HAS ARRIVED FOR A BANQUET!
START PRE-PARING THE FIN-ISHER!
YES, SIR!
FUJISAME HAS THEIR BANQUET COURSES SET BY SEASON, AND THE FINAL COURSE FOR THIS SEASON IS...
...STEAMED WHITE RICE, MISO SOUP, PICKLED VEGETABLES AND ONE MORE ITEM...

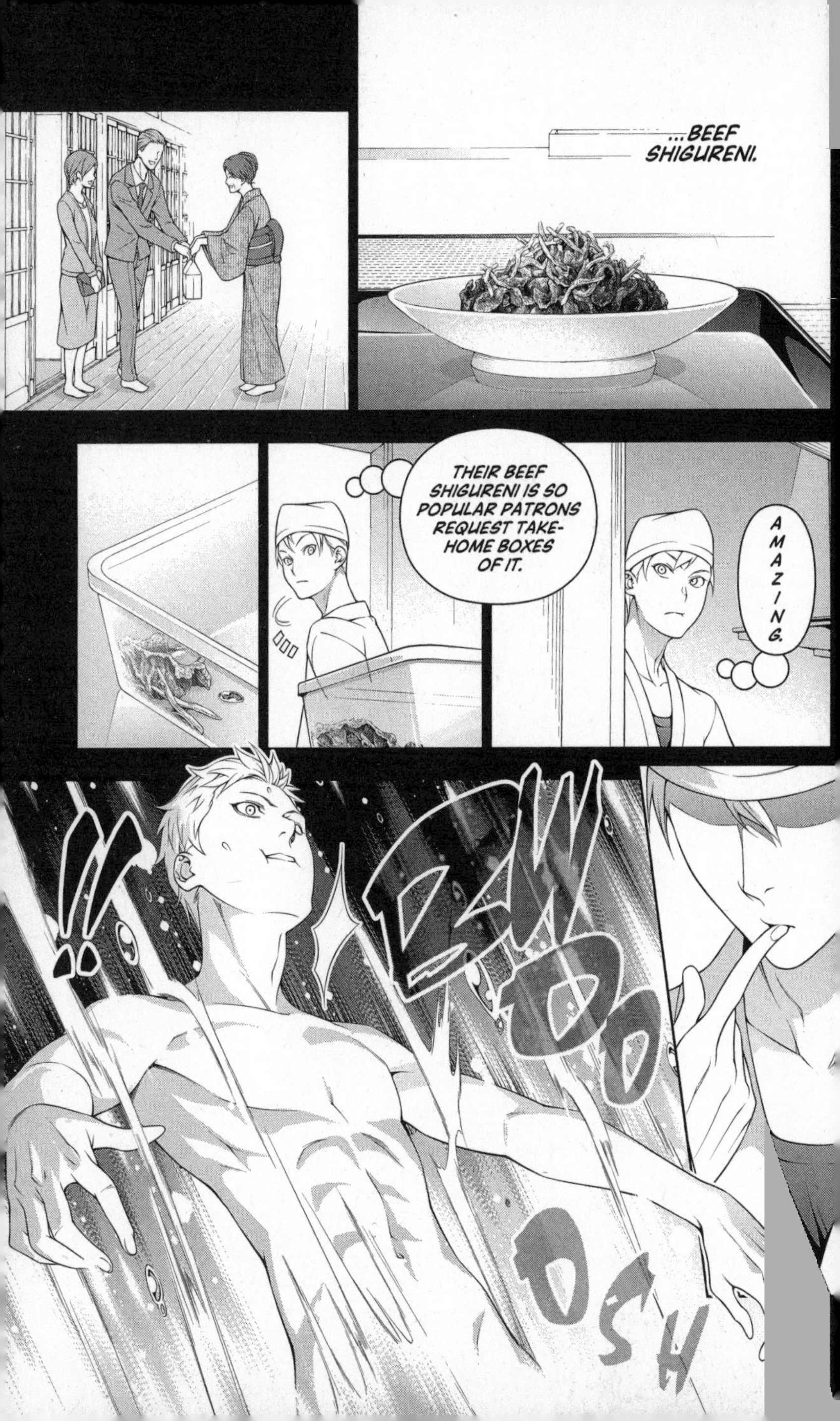
...BEEF SHIGURENI.
AMAZING.
THEIR BEEF SHIGURENI IS SO POPULAR PATRONS REQUEST TAKE-HOME BOXES OF IT.
!!

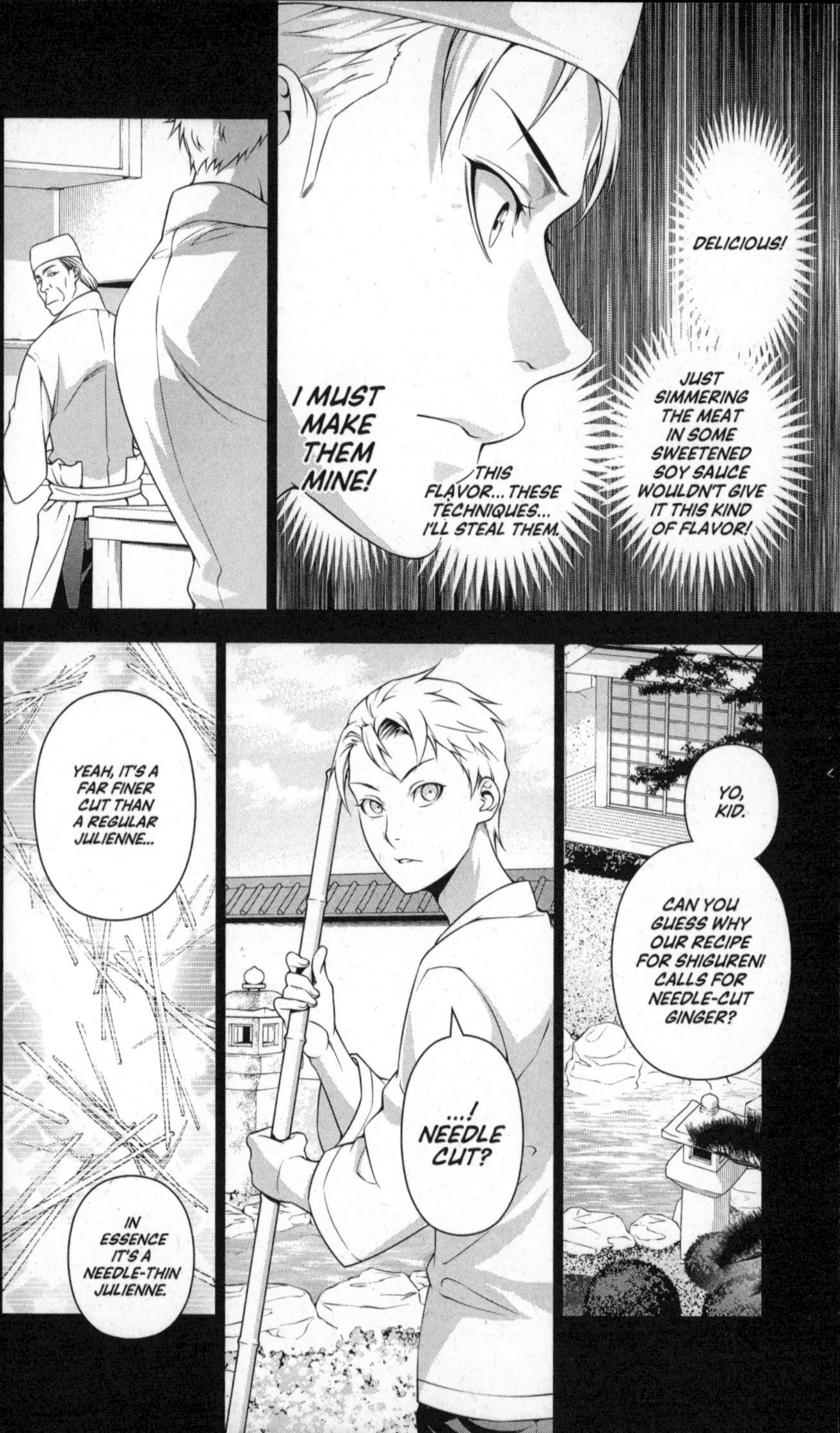
DELICIOUS!
JUST SIMMERING THE MEAT IN SOME SWEETENED SOY SAUCE WOULDN'T GIVE IT THIS KIND OF FLAVOR!
THIS FLAVOR... THESE TECHNIQUES... I'LL STEAL THEM.
I MUST MAKE THEM MINE!
YO, KID.
CAN YOU GUESS WHY OUR RECIPE FOR SHIGURENI CALLS FOR NEEDLE-CUT GINGER?
...! NEEDLE CUT?
YEAH, IT'S A FAR FINER CUT THAN A REGULAR JULIENNE...
IN ESSENCE IT'S A NEEDLE-THIN JULIENNE.

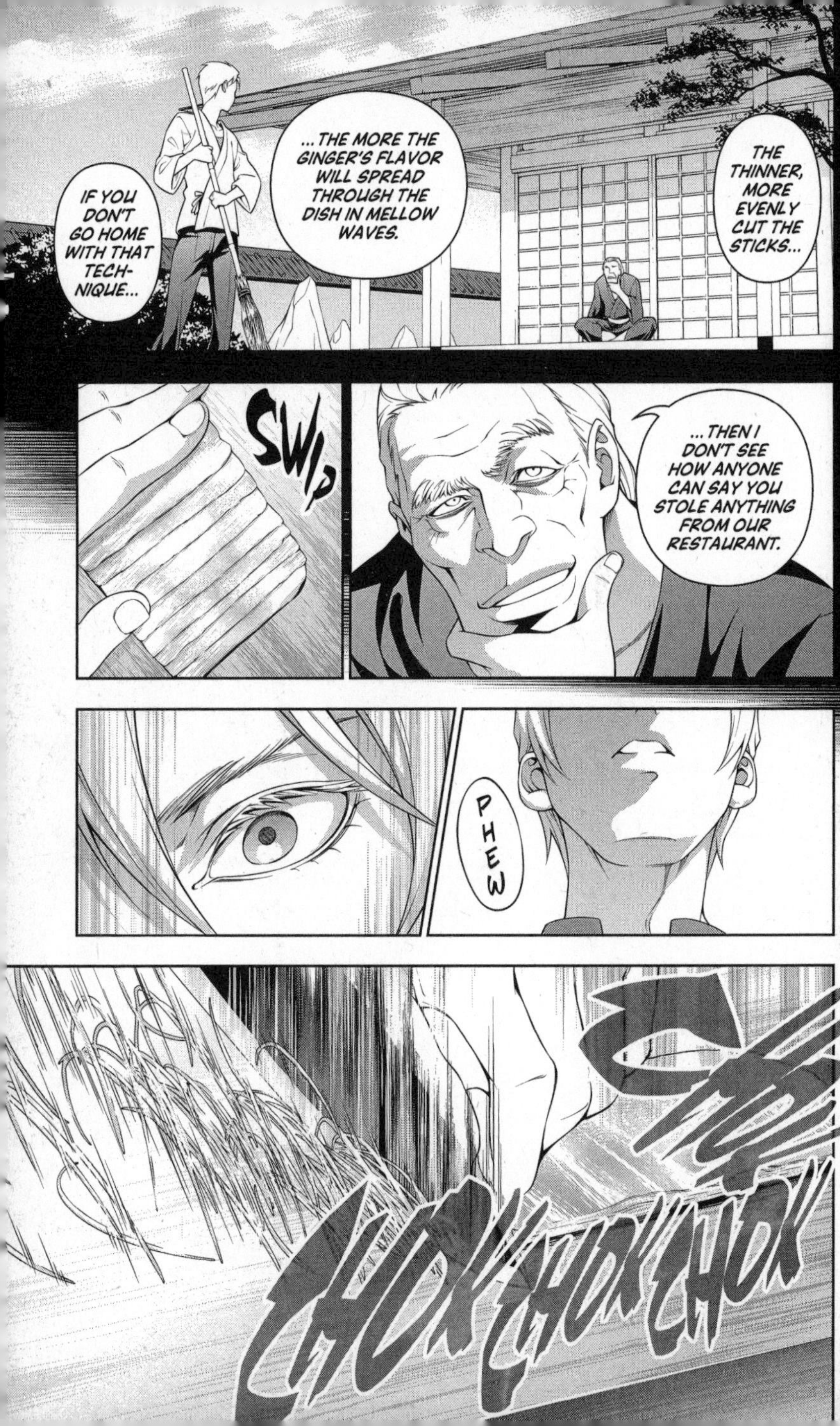
THE THINNER, MORE EVENLY CUT THE STICKS...
...THE MORE THE GINGER'S FLAVOR WILL SPREAD THROUGH THE DISH IN MELLOW WAVES.
IF YOU DON'T GO HOME WITH THAT TECH-NIQUE...
...THEN I DON'T SEE HOW ANYONE CAN SAY YOU STOLE ANYTHING FROM OUR RESTAURANT.
SWIP
PHEW
CHOK CHOK CHOK CHOK

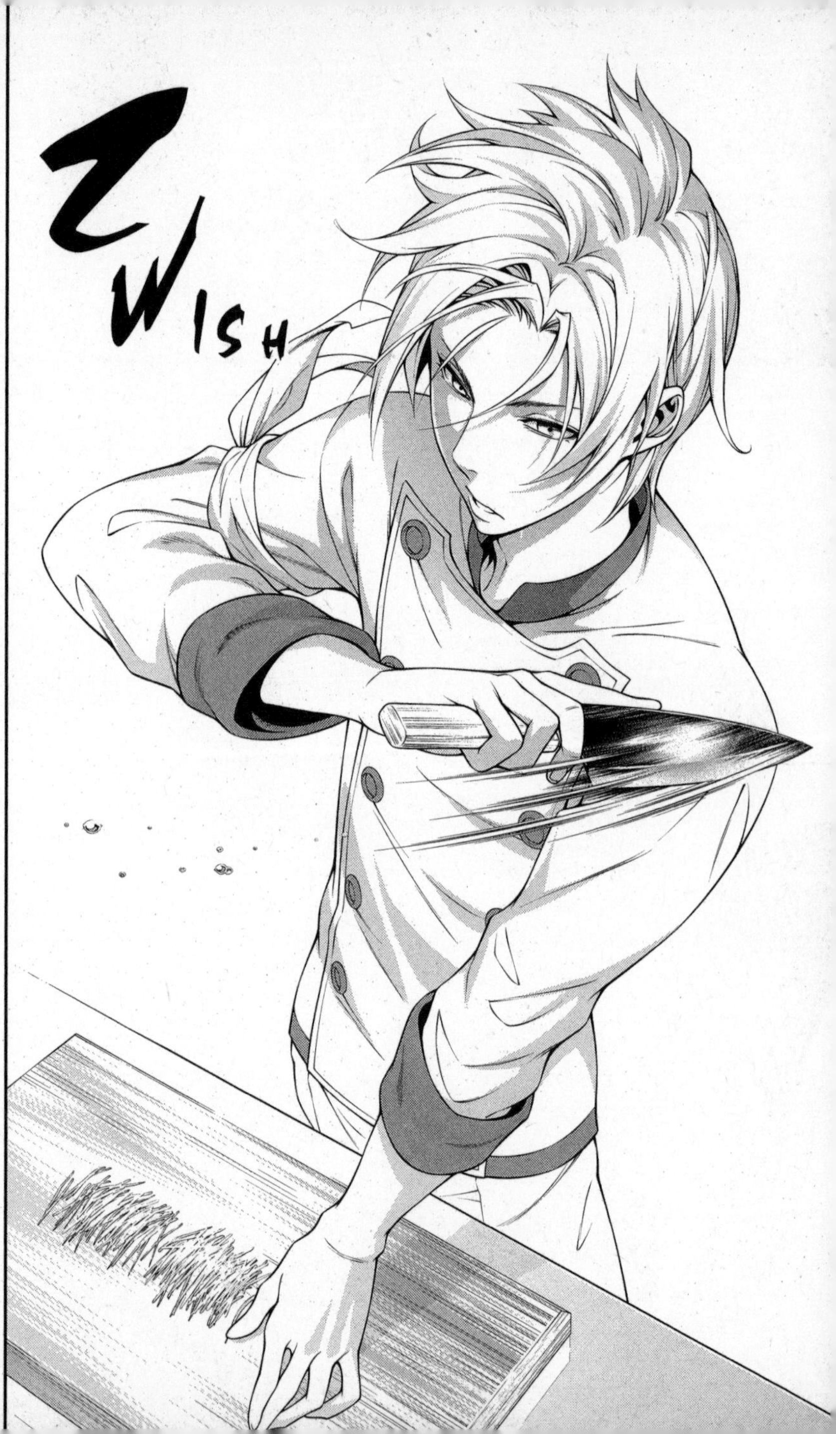
ZWISH

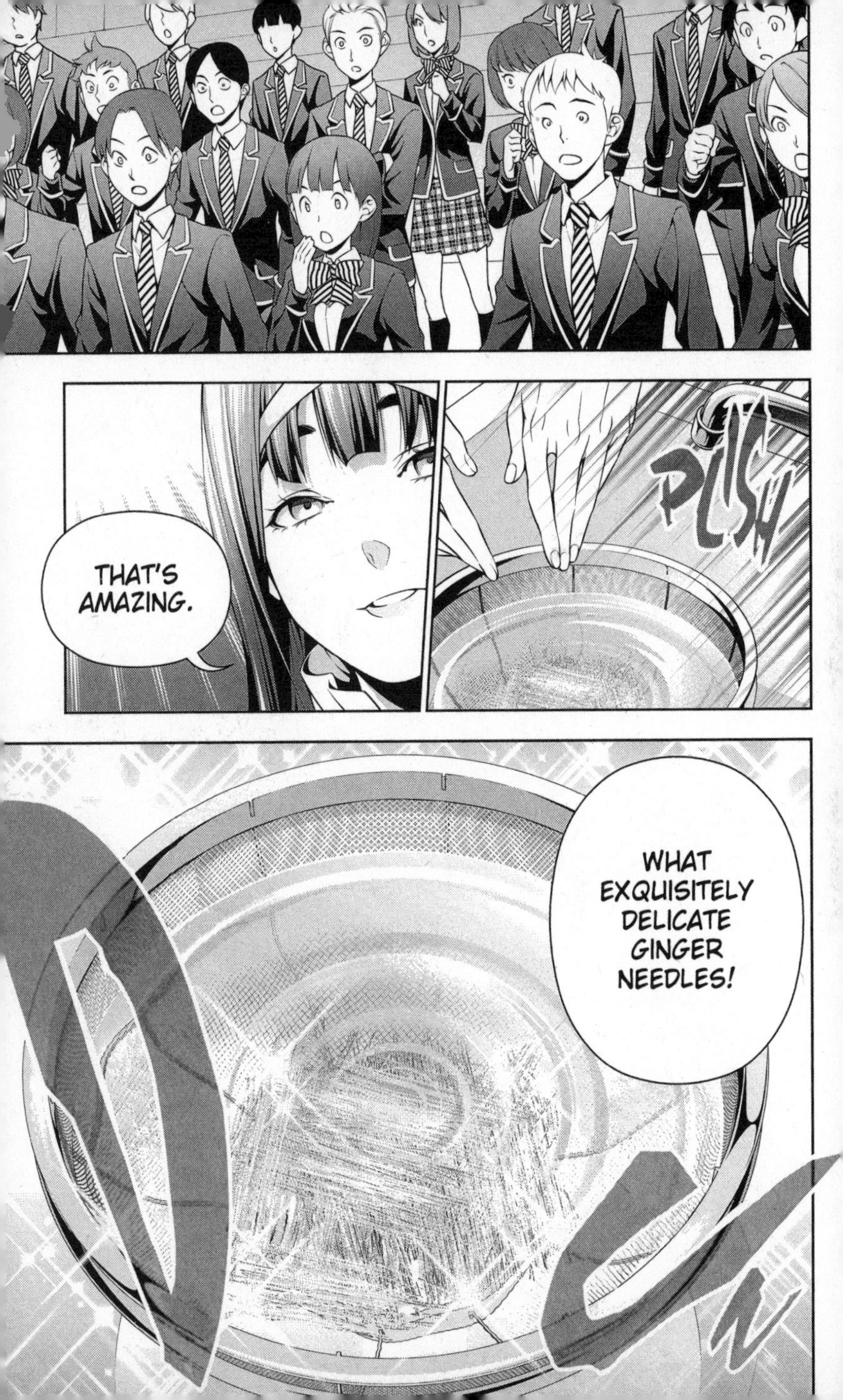
PUSH
THAT'S AMAZING.
WHAT EXQUISITELY DELICATE GINGER NEEDLES!

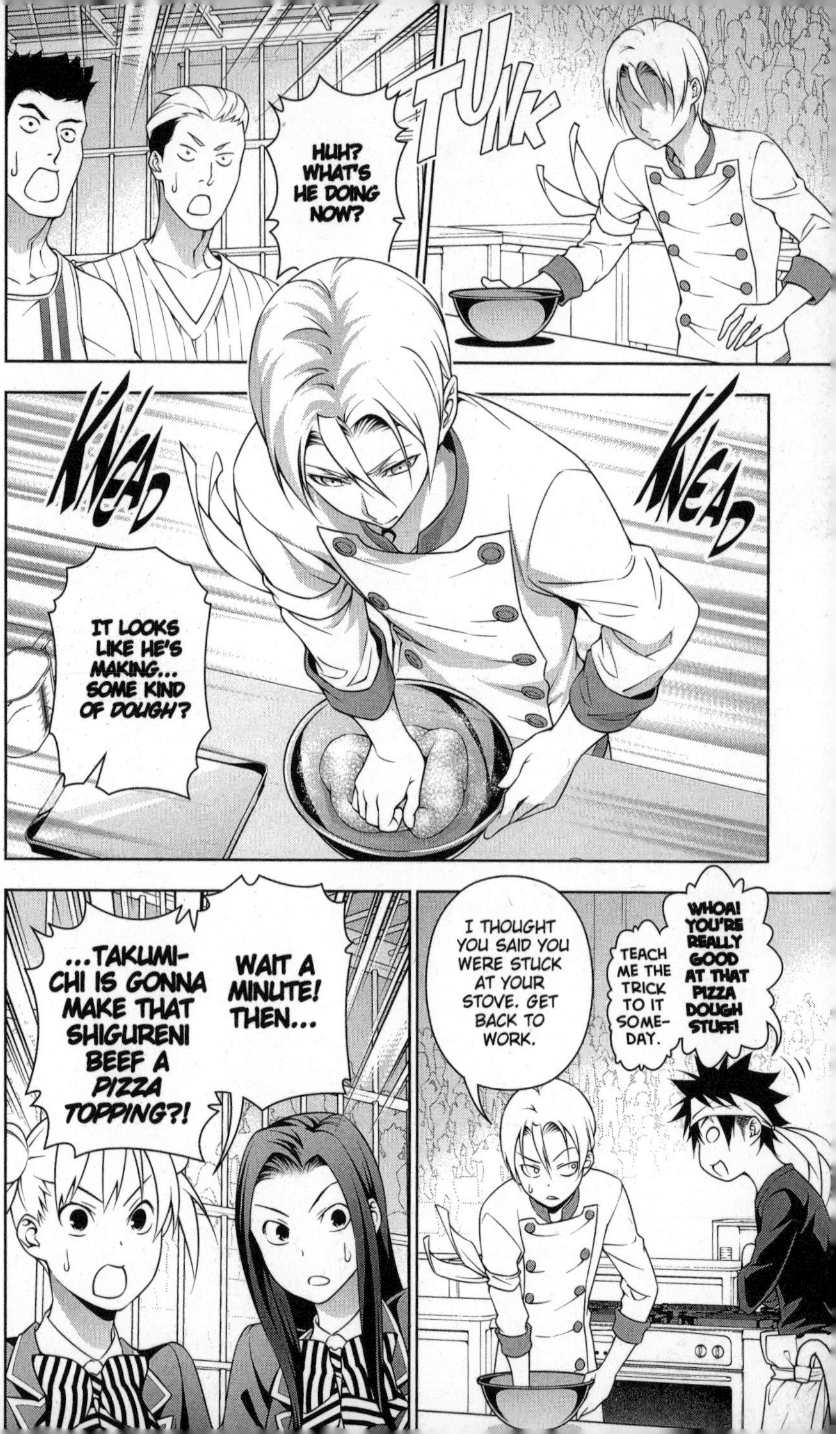
TUNK
HUH? WHAT'S HE DOING NOW?
KNEAD
KNEAD
IT LOOKS LIKE HE'S MAKING... SOME KIND OF DOUGH?
WHOA! YOU'RE REALLY GOOD AT THAT PIZZA DOUGH STUFF!
TEACH ME THE TRICK TO IT SOME-DAY.
I THOUGHT YOU SAID YOU WERE STUCK AT YOUR STOVE. GET BACK TO WORK.
WAIT A MINUTE! THEN...
...TAKUMI-CHI IS GONNA MAKE THAT SHIGURENI BEEF A PIZZA TOPPING?!

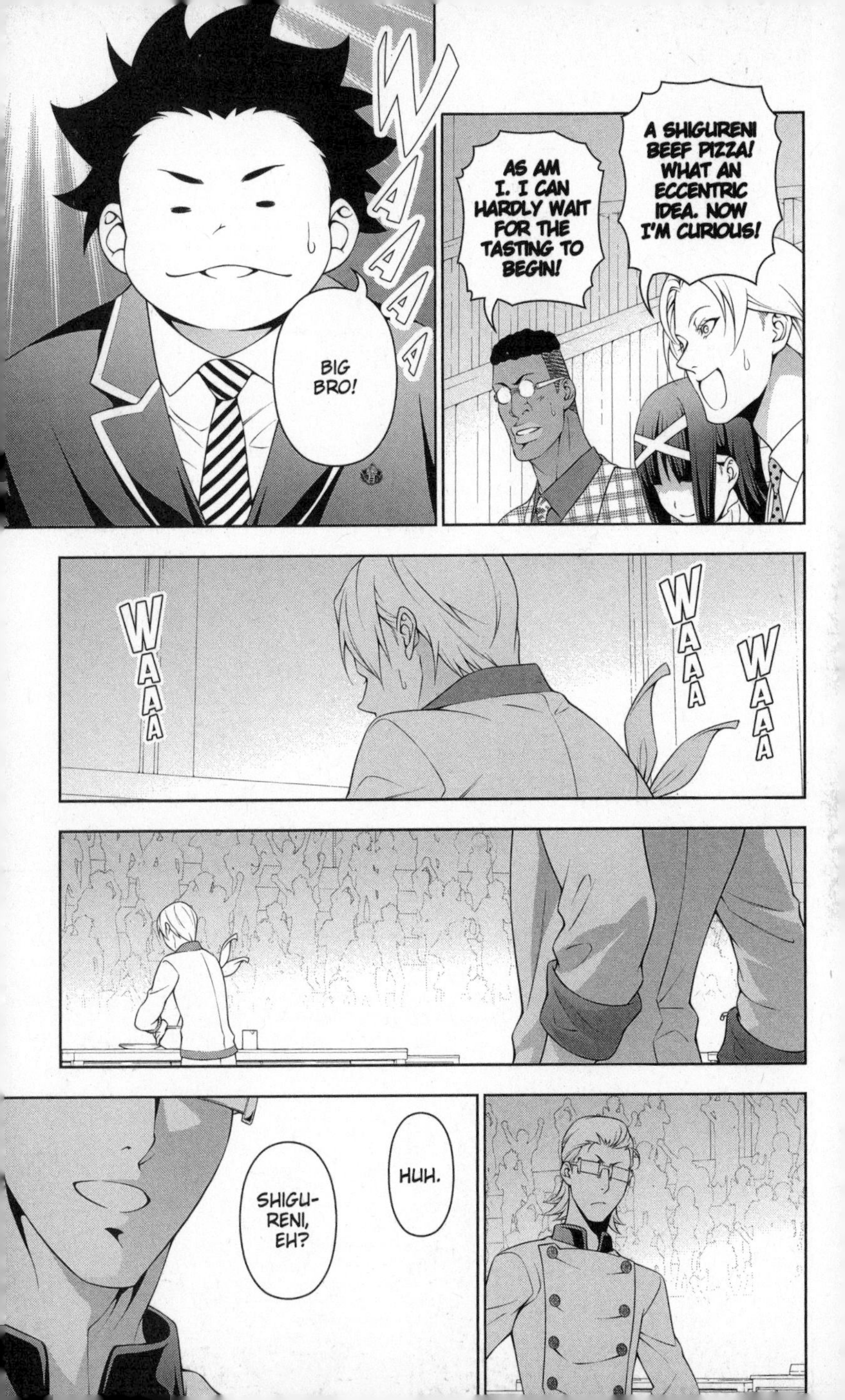
A SHIGURENI BEEF PIZZA! WHAT AN ECCENTRIC IDEA. NOW I'M CURIOUS!
AS AM I. I CAN HARDLY WAIT FOR THE TASTING TO BEGIN!
WAAAAAA
BIG BRO!
WAAA
WAAA
WAAA
HUH.
SHIGU-RENI, EH?

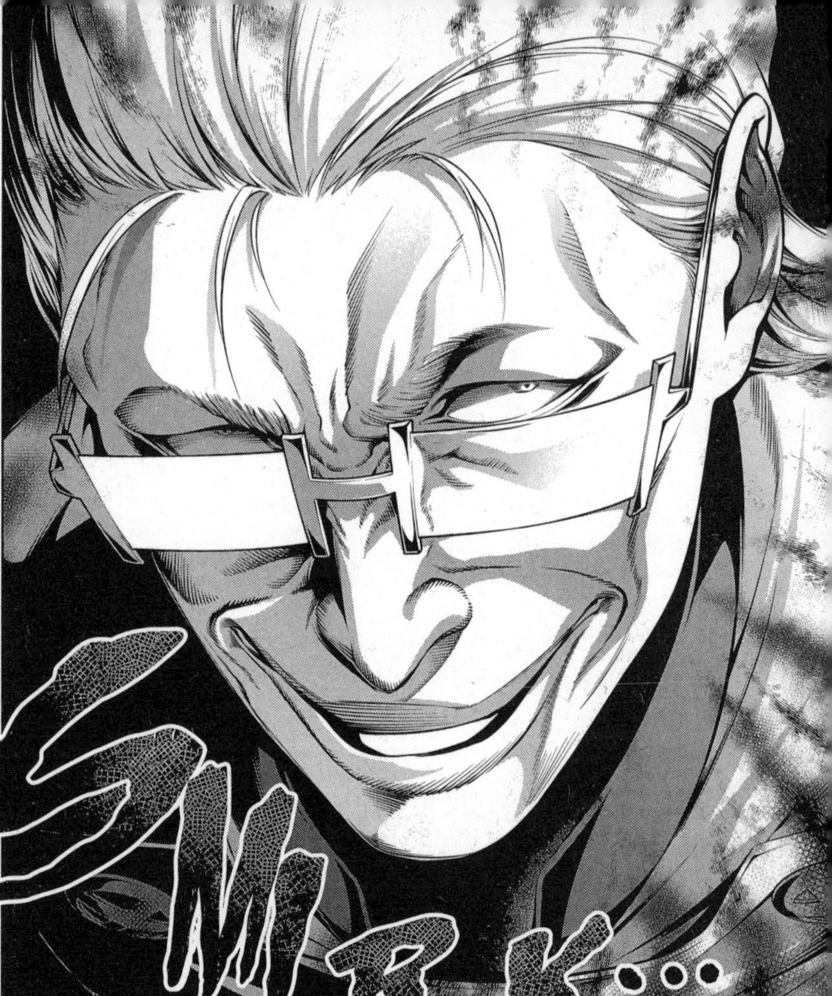
SMIRK...
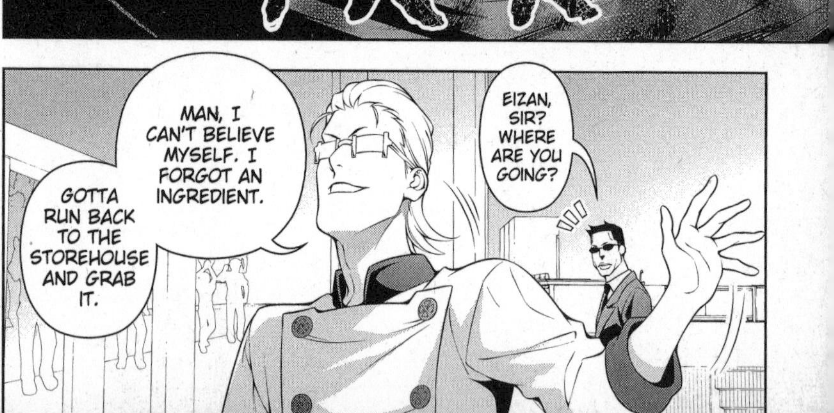
EIZAN, SIR? WHERE ARE YOU GOING?
MAN, I CAN'T BELIEVE MYSELF. I FORGOT AN INGREDIENT.
GOTTA RUN BACK TO THE STOREHOUSE AND GRAB IT.

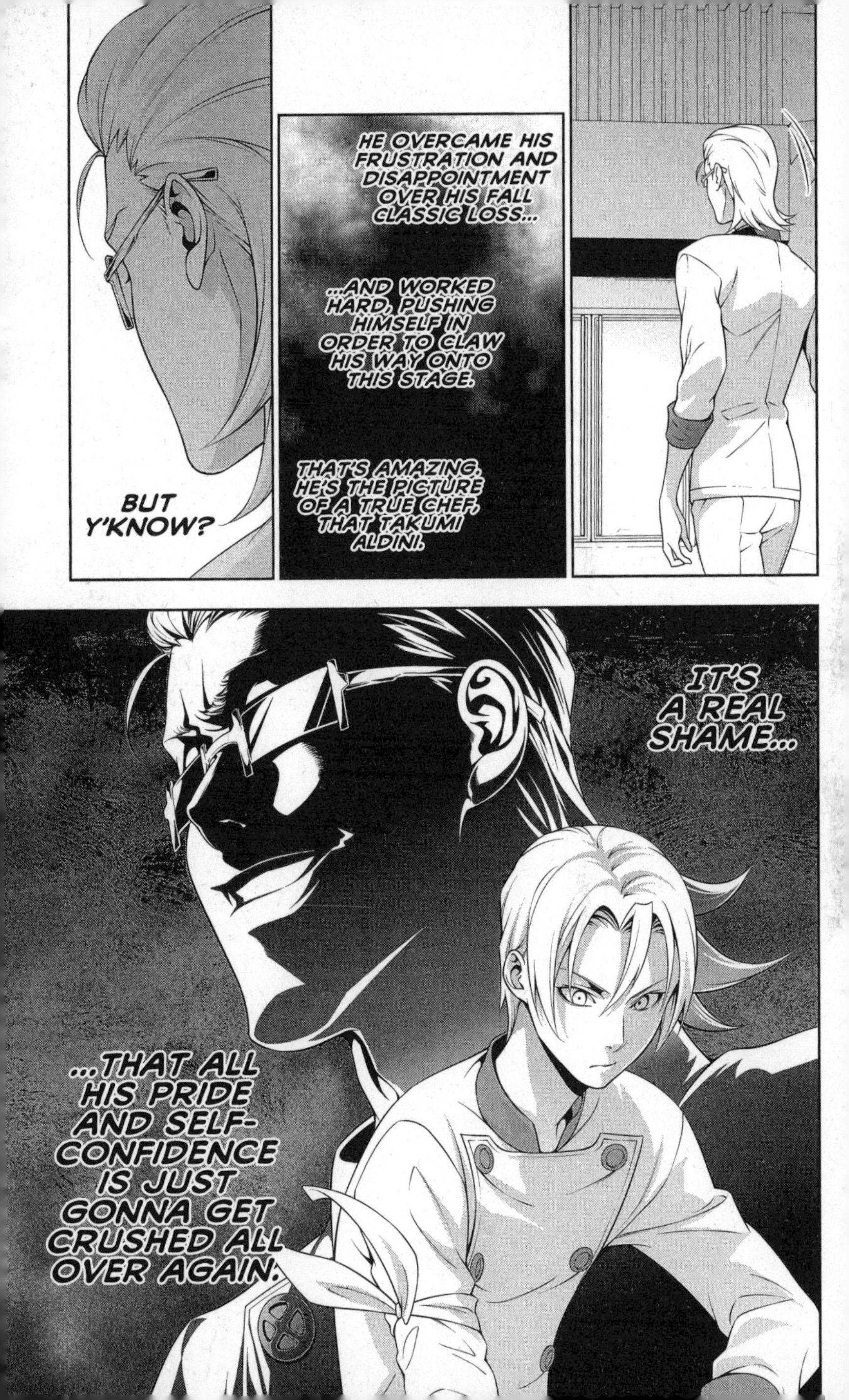
HE OVERCAME HIS FRUSTRATION AND DISAPPOINTMENT OVER HIS FALL CLASSIC LOSS...
...AND WORKED HARD, PUSHING HIMSELF IN ORDER TO CLAW HIS WAY ONTO THIS STAGE.
THAT'S AMAZING. HE'S THE PICTURE OF A TRUE CHEF, THAT TAKUMI ALDINI.
BUT Y'KNOW?
IT'S A REAL SHAME...
...THAT ALL HIS PRIDE AND SELF-CONFIDENCE IS JUST GONNA GET CRUSHED ALL OVER AGAIN.

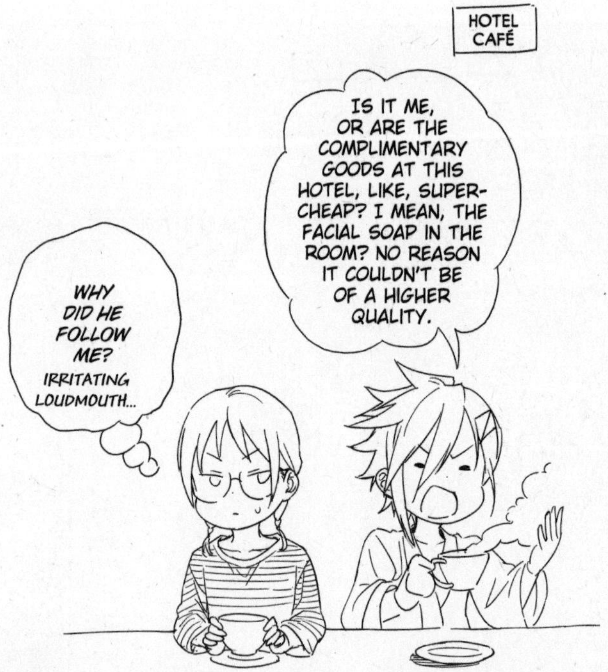
HOTEL CAFÉ
IS IT ME, OR ARE THE COMPLIMENTARY GOODS AT THIS HOTEL, LIKE, SUPER-CHEAP? I MEAN, THE FACIAL SOAP IN THE ROOM? NO REASON IT COULDN'T BE OF A HIGHER QUALITY.
WHY DID HE FOLLOW ME? IRRITATING LOUDMOUTH...

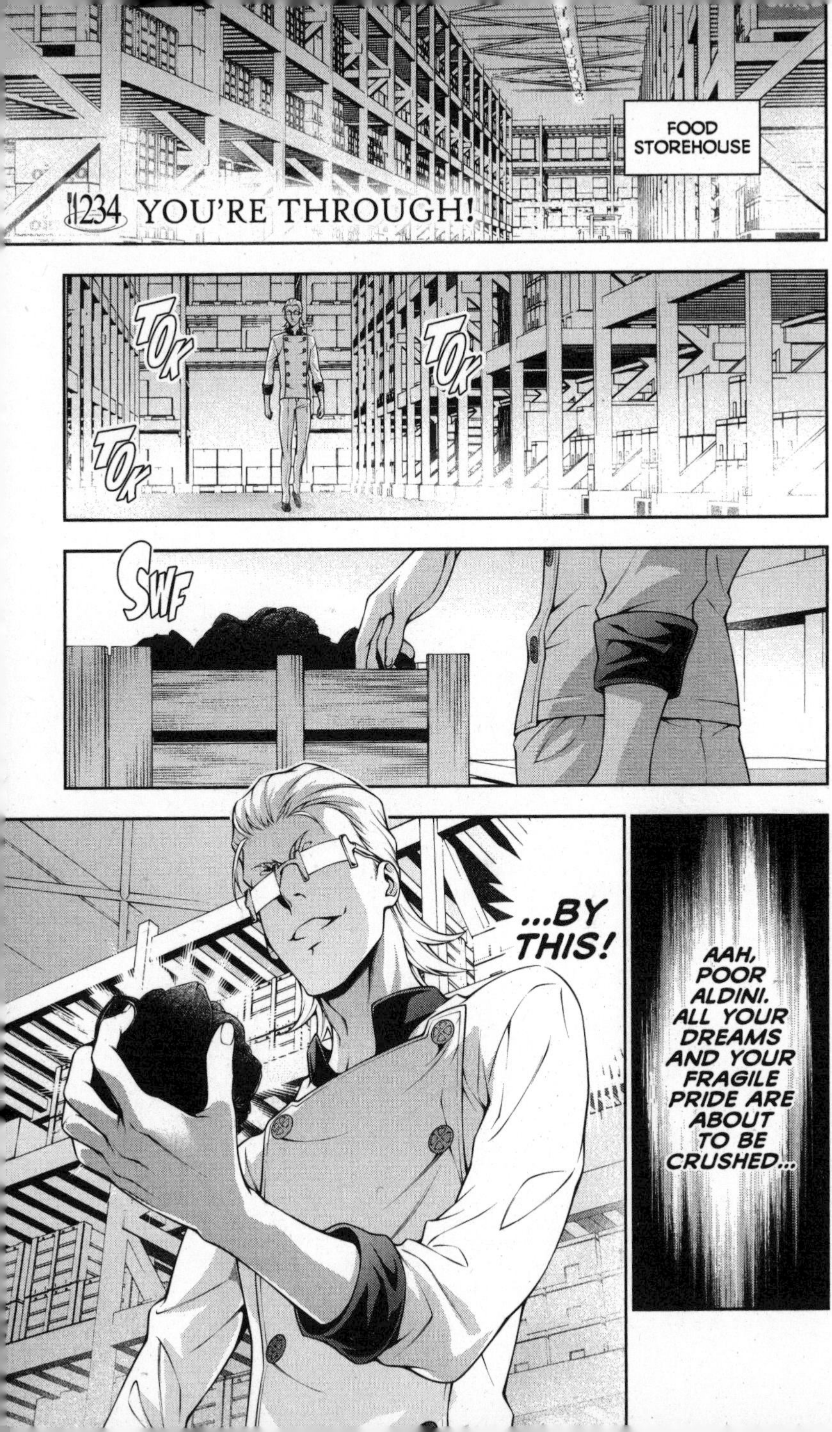
FOOD STOREHOUSE
234 YOU'RE THROUGH!
TOK
TOK
TOK
SWF
AAH, POOR ALDINI. ALL YOUR DREAMS AND YOUR FRAGILE PRIDE ARE ABOUT TO BE CRUSHED...
...BY THIS!

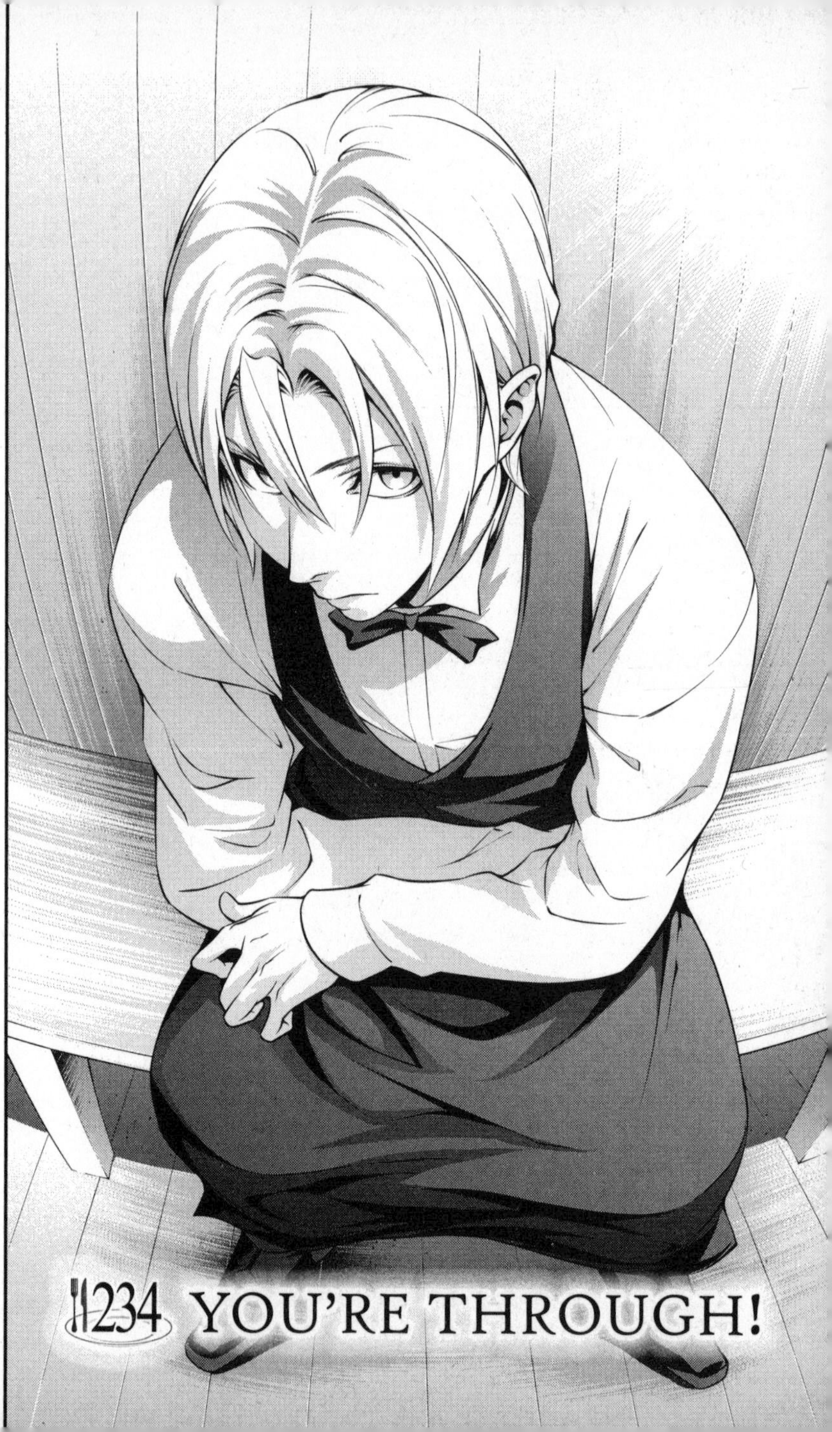
234 YOU'RE THROUGH!

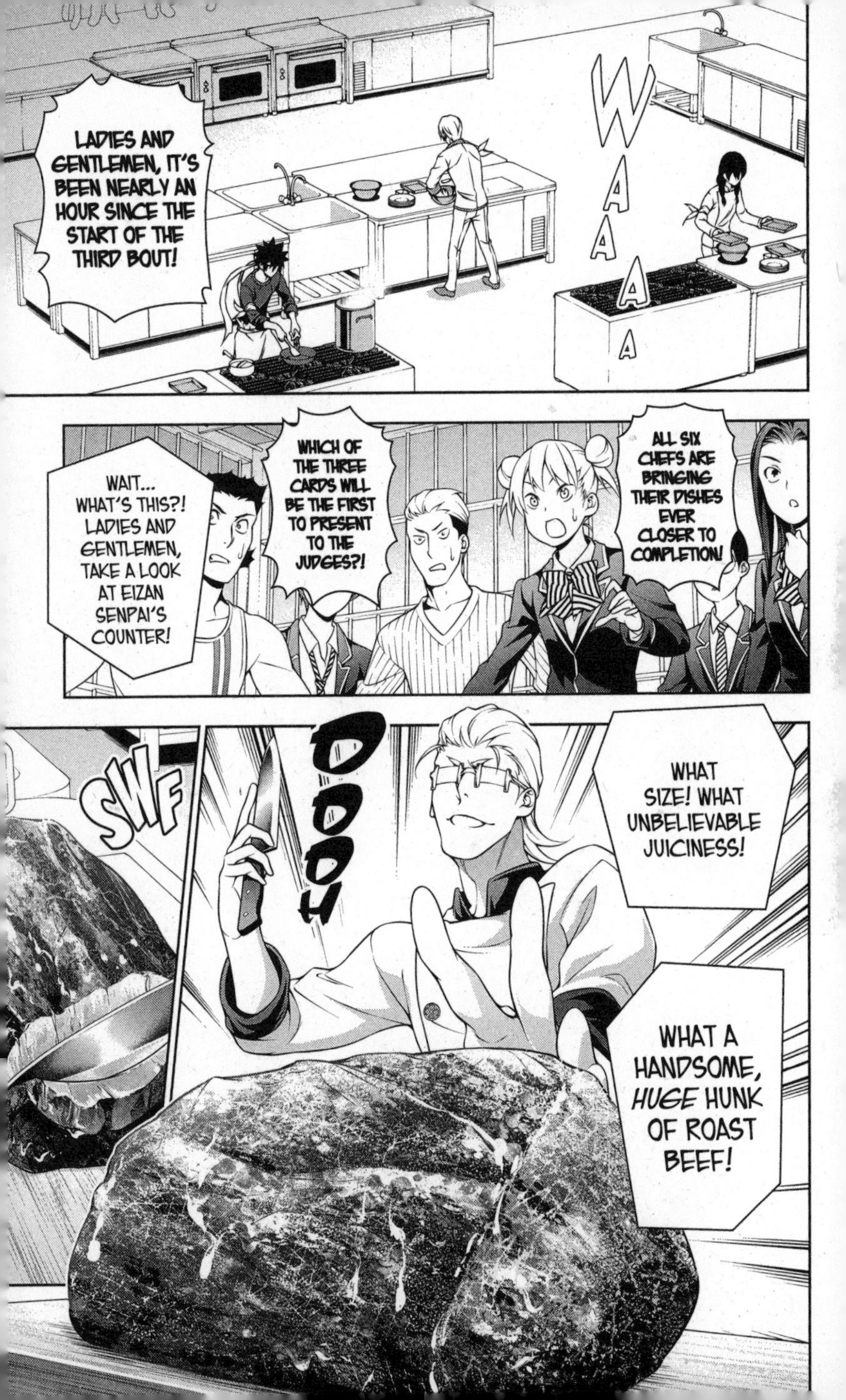
WAAAAA
LADIES AND GENTLEMEN, IT'S BEEN NEARLY AN HOUR SINCE THE START OF THE THIRD BOUT!
ALL SIX CHEFS ARE BRINGING THEIR DISHES EVER CLOSER TO COMPLETION!
WHICH OF THE THREE CARDS WILL BE THE FIRST TO PRESENT TO THE JUDGES?!
WAIT... WHAT'S THIS?! LADIES AND GENTLEMEN, TAKE A LOOK AT EIZAN SENPAI'S COUNTER!
WHAT SIZE! WHAT UNBELIEVABLE JUICINESS!
WHAT A HANDSOME, *HUGE* HUNK OF ROAST BEEF!
OOOOH
SWF

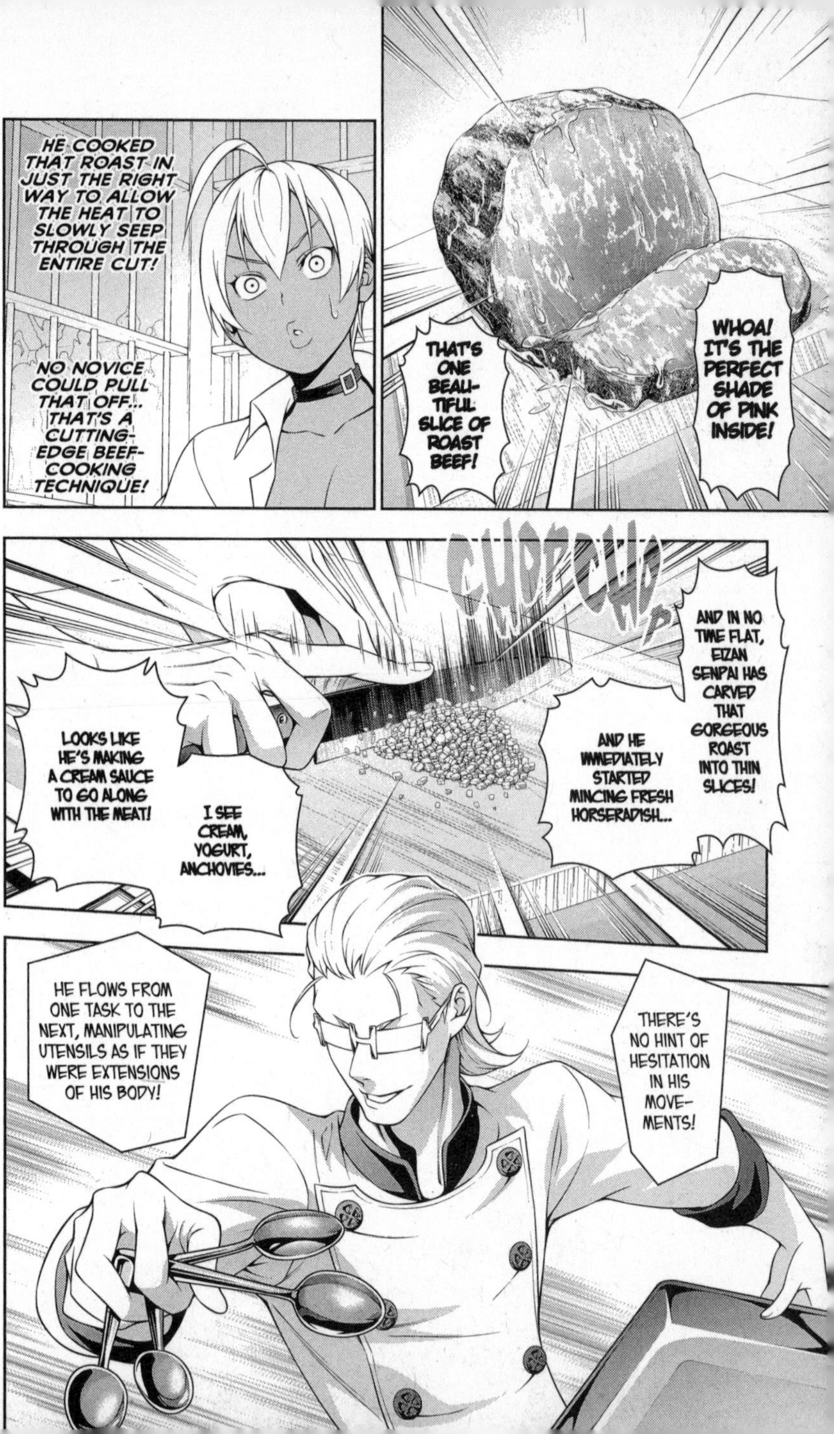
WHOA! IT'S THE PERFECT SHADE OF PINK INSIDE!
THAT'S ONE BEAUTIFUL SLICE OF ROAST BEEF!
HE COOKED THAT ROAST IN JUST THE RIGHT WAY TO ALLOW THE HEAT TO SLOWLY SEEP THROUGH THE ENTIRE CUT!
NO NOVICE COULD PULL THAT OFF... THAT'S A CUTTING-EDGE BEEF-COOKING TECHNIQUE!
CHOP CHOP
AND IN NO TIME FLAT, EIZAN SENPAI HAS CARVED THAT GORGEOUS ROAST INTO THIN SLICES!
AND HE IMMEDIATELY STARTED MINCING FRESH HORSERADISH...
I SEE CREAM, YOGURT, ANCHOVIES...
LOOKS LIKE HE'S MAKING A CREAM SAUCE TO GO ALONG WITH THE MEAT!
THERE'S NO HINT OF HESITATION IN HIS MOVEMENTS!
HE FLOWS FROM ONE TASK TO THE NEXT, MANIPULATING UTENSILS AS IF THEY WERE EXTENSIONS OF HIS BODY!

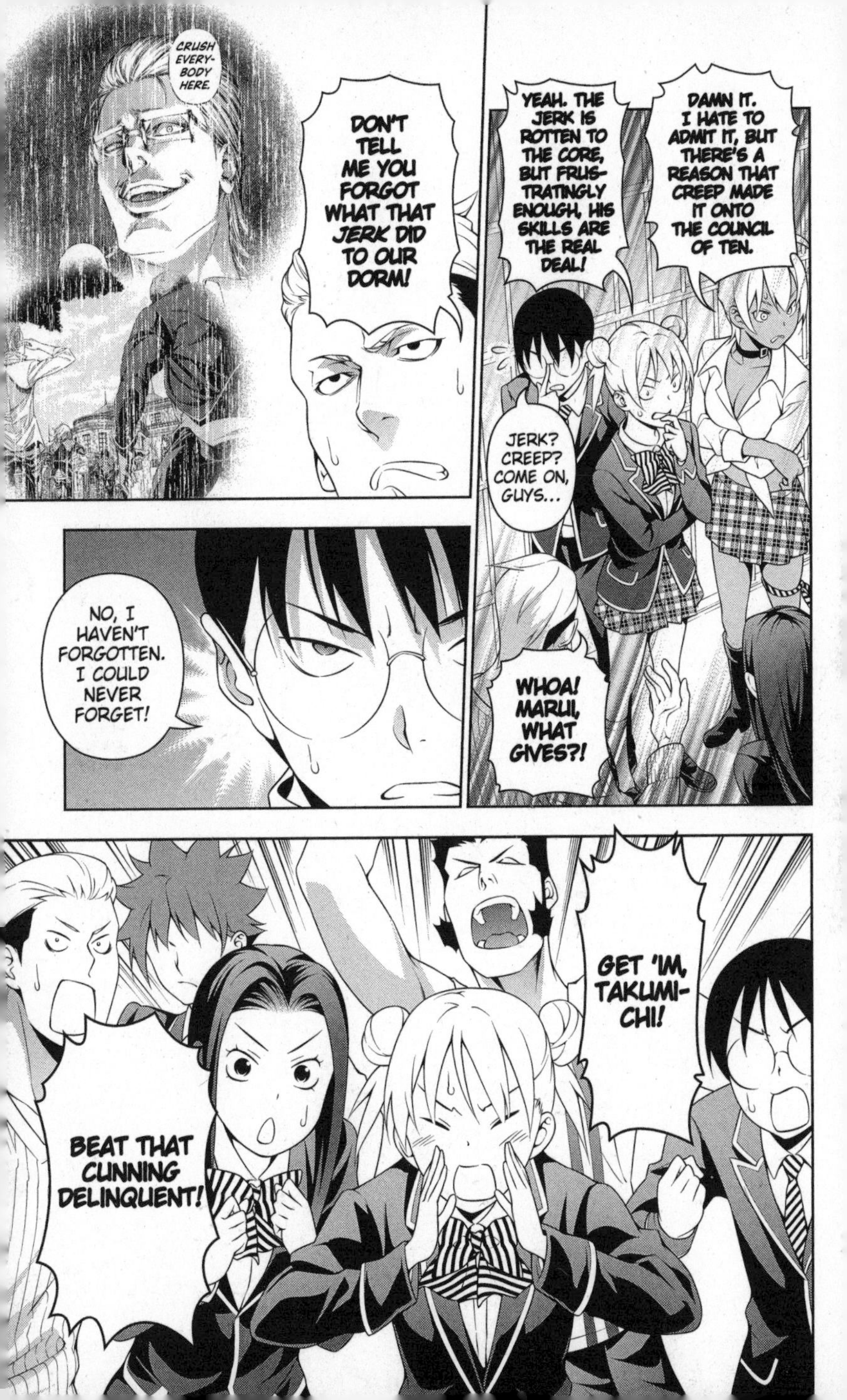
DAMN IT. I HATE TO ADMIT IT, BUT THERE'S A REASON THAT CREEP MADE IT ONTO THE COUNCIL OF TEN.
YEAH. THE JERK IS ROTTEN TO THE CORE, BUT FRUS-TRATINGLY ENOUGH, HIS SKILLS ARE THE REAL DEAL!
JERK? CREEP? COME ON, GUYS...
WHOA! MARUI, WHAT GIVES?!
CRUSH EVERY-BODY HERE.
DON'T TELL ME YOU FORGOT WHAT THAT JERK DID TO OUR DORM!
NO, I HAVEN'T FORGOTTEN. I COULD NEVER FORGET!
GET 'IM, TAKUMI-CHI!
BEAT THAT CUNNING DELINQUENT!

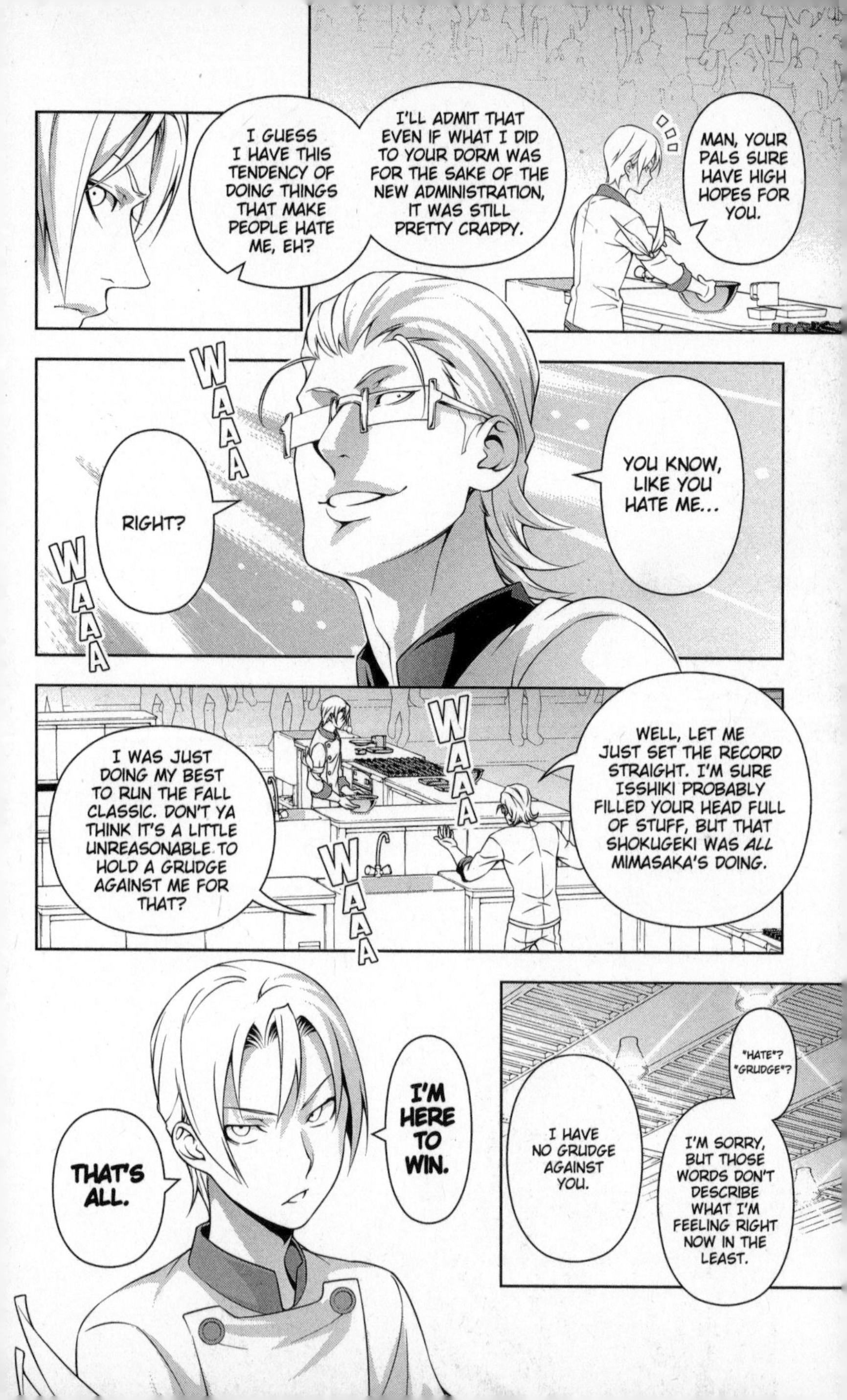
MAN, YOUR PALS SURE HAVE HIGH HOPES FOR YOU.
I'LL ADMIT THAT EVEN IF WHAT I DID TO YOUR DORM WAS FOR THE SAKE OF THE NEW ADMINISTRATION, IT WAS STILL PRETTY CRAPPY.
I GUESS I HAVE THIS TENDENCY OF DOING THINGS THAT MAKE PEOPLE HATE ME, EH?
YOU KNOW, LIKE YOU HATE ME...
WAAAA
RIGHT?
WAAAA
WELL, LET ME JUST SET THE RECORD STRAIGHT. I'M SURE ISSHIKI PROBABLY FILLED YOUR HEAD FULL OF STUFF, BUT THAT SHOKUGEKI WAS *ALL* MIMASAKA'S DOING.
WAAAA
I WAS JUST DOING MY BEST TO RUN THE FALL CLASSIC. DON'T YA THINK IT'S A LITTLE UNREASONABLE TO HOLD A GRUDGE AGAINST ME FOR THAT?
WAAAA
"HATE"? "GRUDGE"?
I'M SORRY, BUT THOSE WORDS DON'T DESCRIBE WHAT I'M FEELING RIGHT NOW IN THE LEAST.
I HAVE NO GRUDGE AGAINST YOU.
I'M HERE TO WIN.
THAT'S ALL.

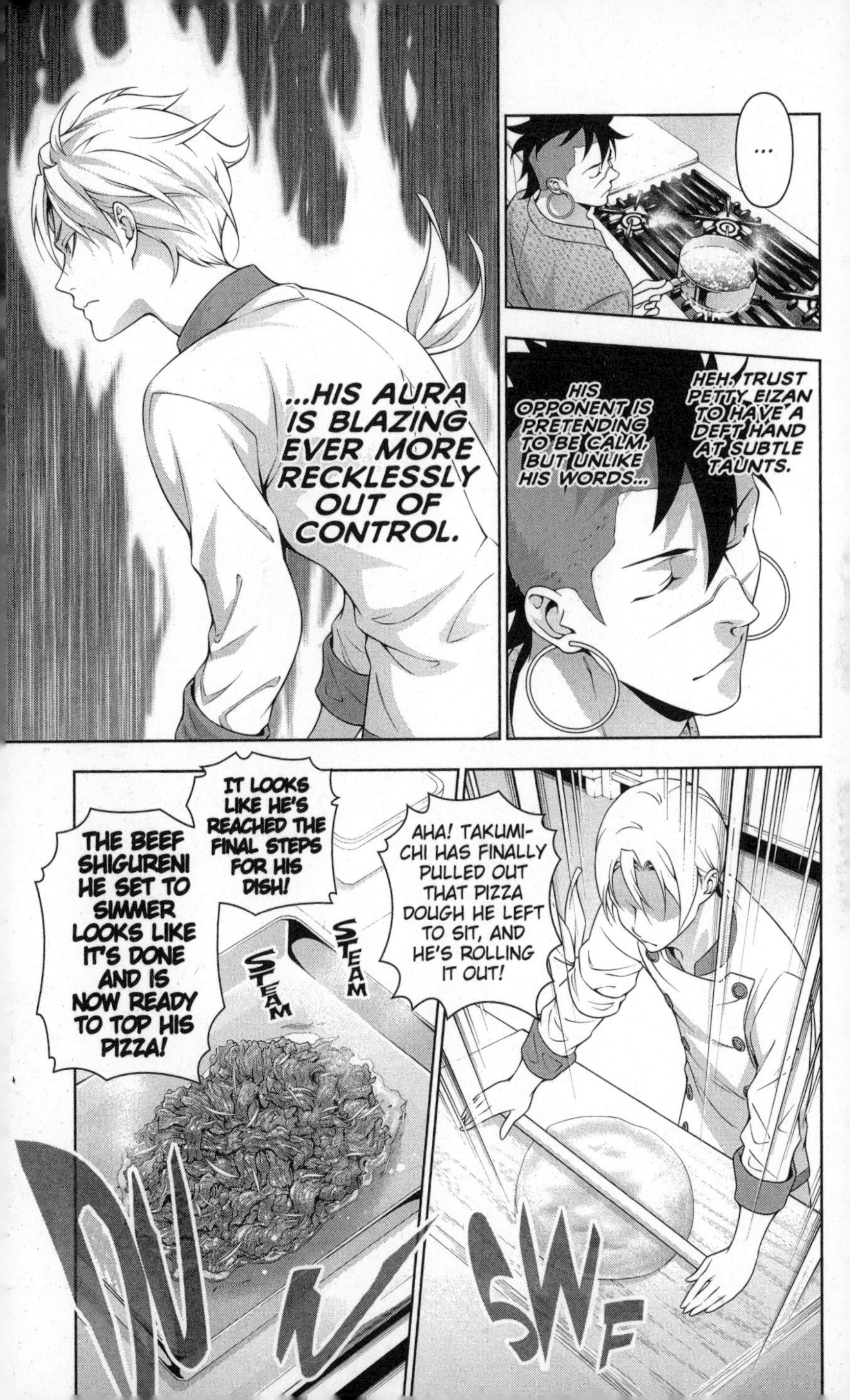
...
HEH. TRUST PETTY EIZAN TO HAVE A DEFT HAND AT SUBTLE TAUNTS.
HIS OPPONENT IS PRETENDING TO BE CALM, BUT UNLIKE HIS WORDS...
...HIS AURA IS BLAZING EVER MORE RECKLESSLY OUT OF CONTROL.
AHA! TAKUMI-CHI HAS FINALLY PULLED OUT THAT PIZZA DOUGH HE LEFT TO SIT, AND HE'S ROLLING IT OUT!
SWF
IT LOOKS LIKE HE'S REACHED THE FINAL STEPS FOR HIS DISH!
THE BEEF SHIGURENI HE SET TO SIMMER LOOKS LIKE IT'S DONE AND IS NOW READY TO TOP HIS PIZZA!
STEAM
STEAM

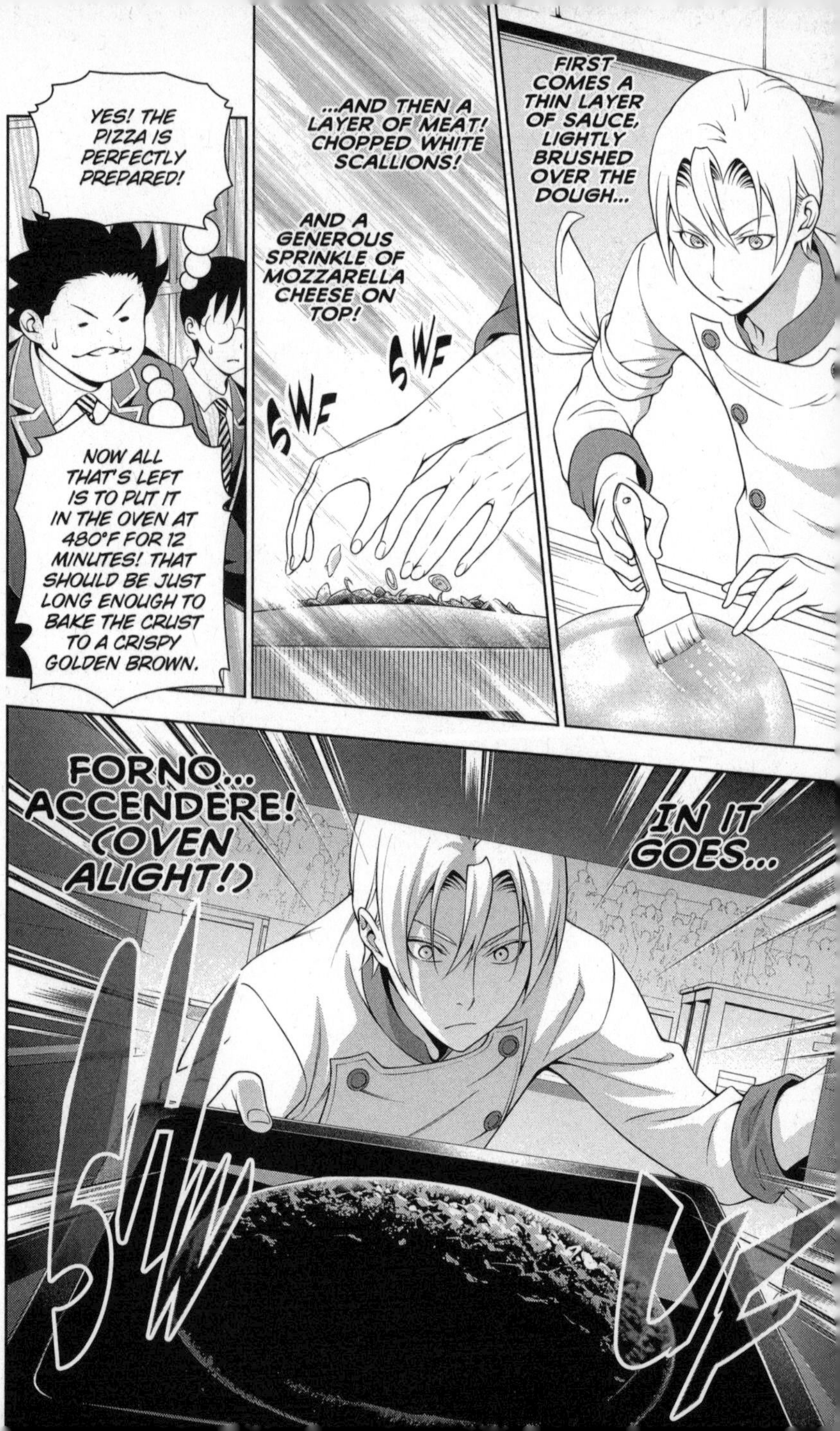
FIRST COMES A THIN LAYER OF SAUCE, LIGHTLY BRUSHED OVER THE DOUGH...
...AND THEN A LAYER OF MEAT! CHOPPED WHITE SCALLIONS!
AND A GENEROUS SPRINKLE OF MOZZARELLA CHEESE ON TOP!
SWF
SWF
YES! THE PIZZA IS PERFECTLY PREPARED!
NOW ALL THAT'S LEFT IS TO PUT IT IN THE OVEN AT 480°F FOR 12 MINUTES! THAT SHOULD BE JUST LONG ENOUGH TO BAKE THE CRUST TO A CRISPY GOLDEN BROWN.
IN IT GOES...
FORNO... ACCENDERE! (OVEN ALIGHT!)

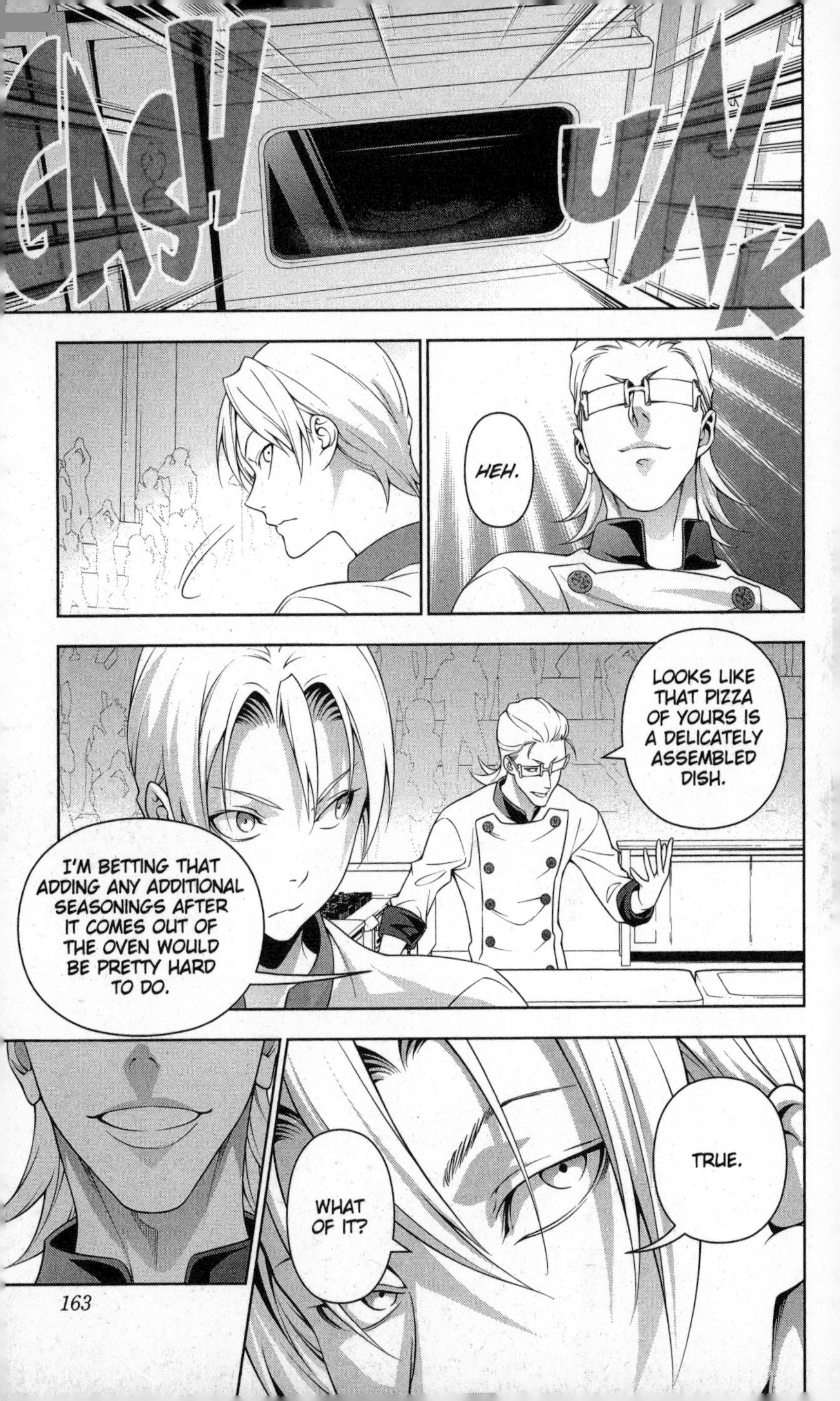
HEH.
LOOKS LIKE THAT PIZZA OF YOURS IS A DELICATELY ASSEMBLED DISH.
I'M BETTING THAT ADDING ANY ADDITIONAL SEASONINGS AFTER IT COMES OUT OF THE OVEN WOULD BE PRETTY HARD TO DO.
TRUE.
WHAT OF IT?

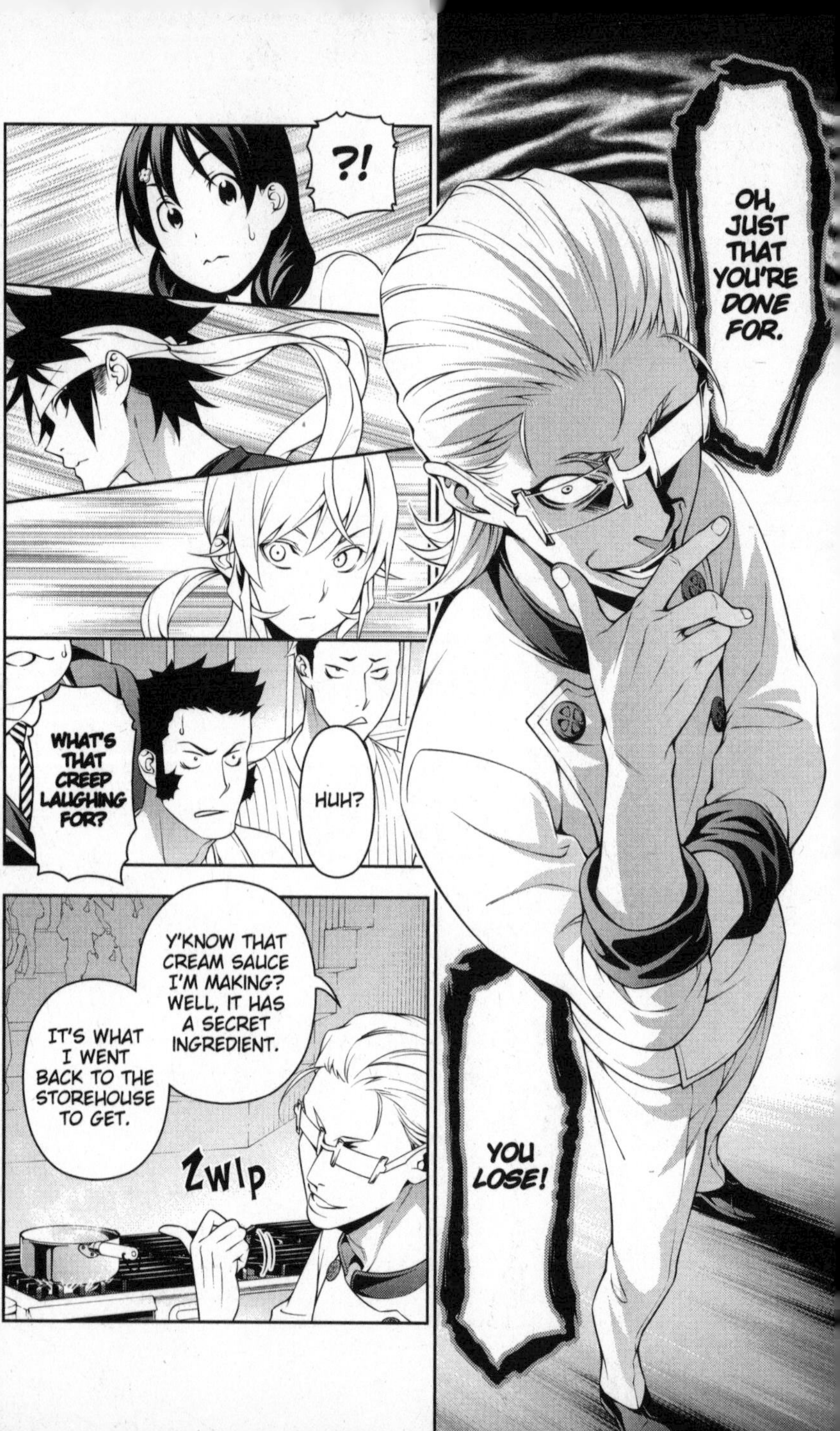
OH, JUST THAT YOU'RE DONE FOR.
YOU LOSE!
?!
HUH?
WHAT'S THAT CREEP LAUGHING FOR?
Y'KNOW THAT CREAM SAUCE I'M MAKING? WELL, IT HAS A SECRET INGREDIENT.
IT'S WHAT I WENT BACK TO THE STOREHOUSE TO GET.
ZWIP

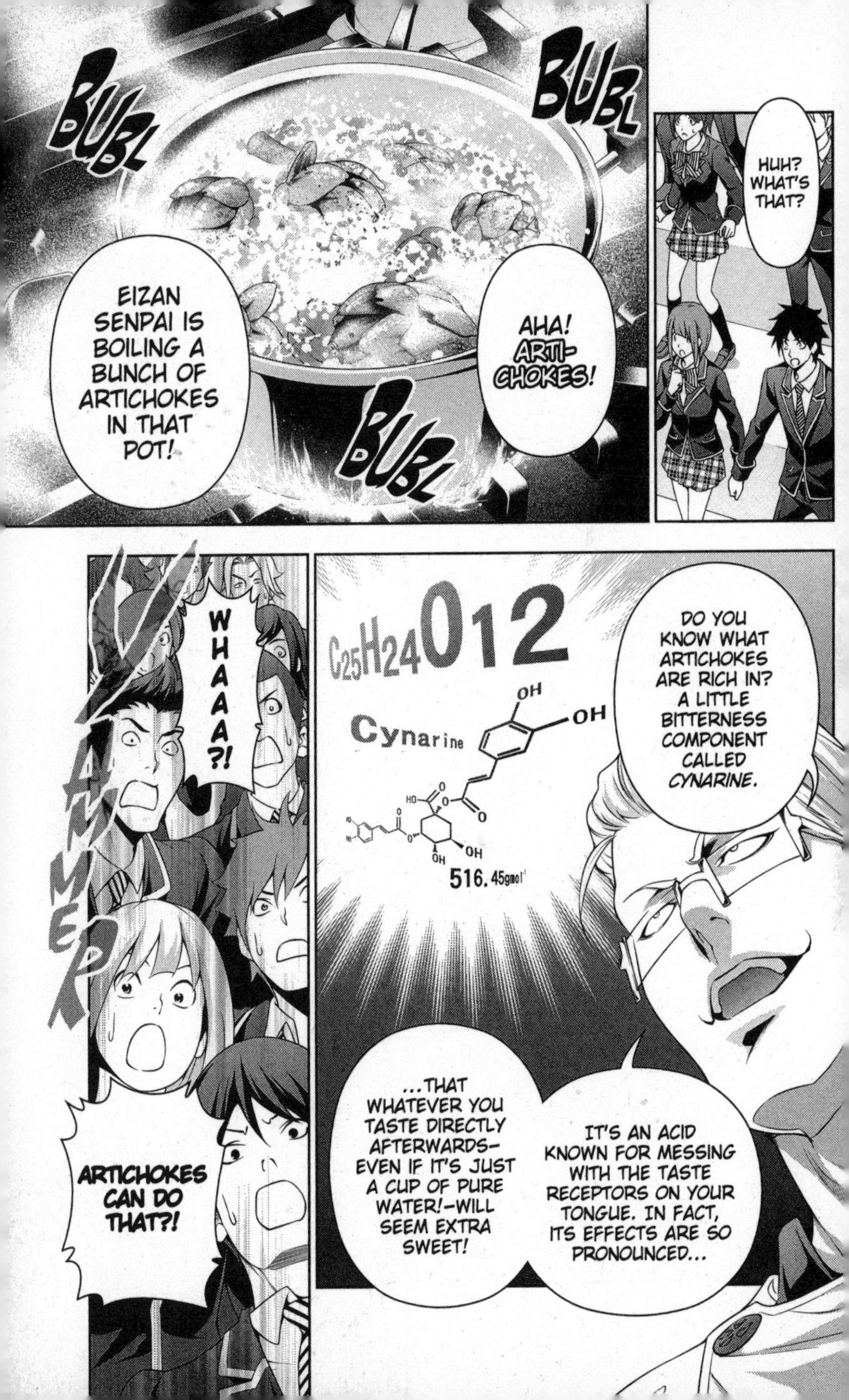
HUH? WHAT'S THAT?
BUBL
AHA! ARTI-CHOKES!
BUBL
EIZAN SENPAI IS BOILING A BUNCH OF ARTICHOKES IN THAT POT!
BUBL
C25H24O12
Cynarine
OH
OH
516.45gmol-1
DO YOU KNOW WHAT ARTICHOKES ARE RICH IN? A LITTLE BITTERNESS COMPONENT CALLED CYNARINE.
IT'S AN ACID KNOWN FOR MESSING WITH THE TASTE RECEPTORS ON YOUR TONGUE. IN FACT, ITS EFFECTS ARE SO PRONOUNCED...
...THAT WHATEVER YOU TASTE DIRECTLY AFTERWARDS—EVEN IF IT'S JUST A CUP OF PURE WATER!—WILL SEEM EXTRA SWEET!
WHAAAA?!
ARTICHOKES CAN DO THAT?!

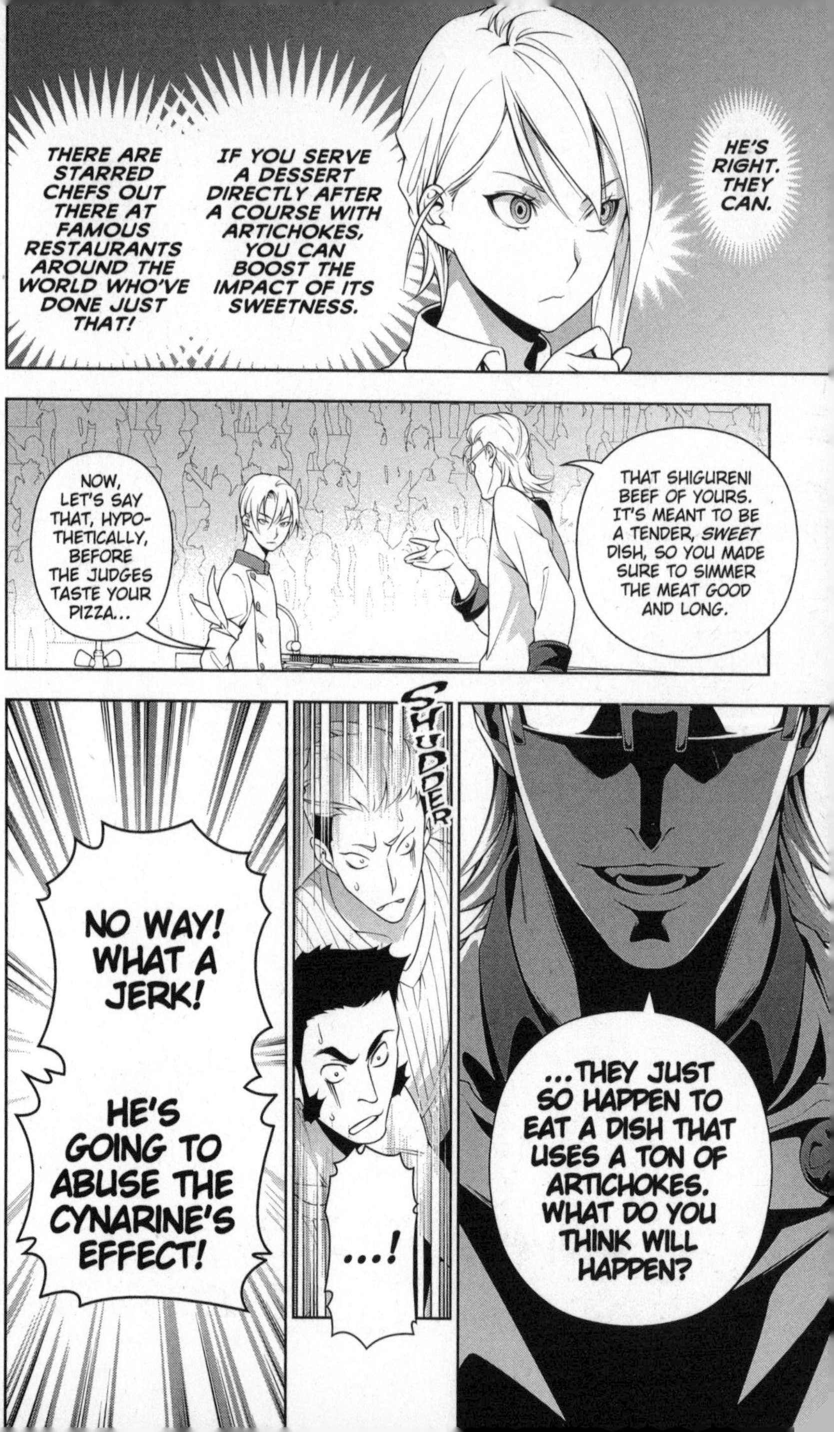
IF YOU SERVE A DESSERT DIRECTLY AFTER A COURSE WITH ARTICHOKES, YOU CAN BOOST THE IMPACT OF ITS SWEETNESS.
THERE ARE STARRED CHEFS OUT THERE AT FAMOUS RESTAURANTS AROUND THE WORLD WHO'VE DONE JUST THAT!
HE'S RIGHT. THEY CAN.
THAT SHIGURENI BEEF OF YOURS. IT'S MEANT TO BE A TENDER, SWEET DISH, SO YOU MADE SURE TO SIMMER THE MEAT GOOD AND LONG.
NOW, LET'S SAY THAT, HYPOTHETICALLY, BEFORE THE JUDGES TASTE YOUR PIZZA...
...THEY JUST SO HAPPEN TO EAT A DISH THAT USES A TON OF ARTICHOKES. WHAT DO YOU THINK WILL HAPPEN?
SHUDDER
...!
NO WAY! WHAT A JERK!
HE'S GOING TO ABUSE THE CYNARINE'S EFFECT!

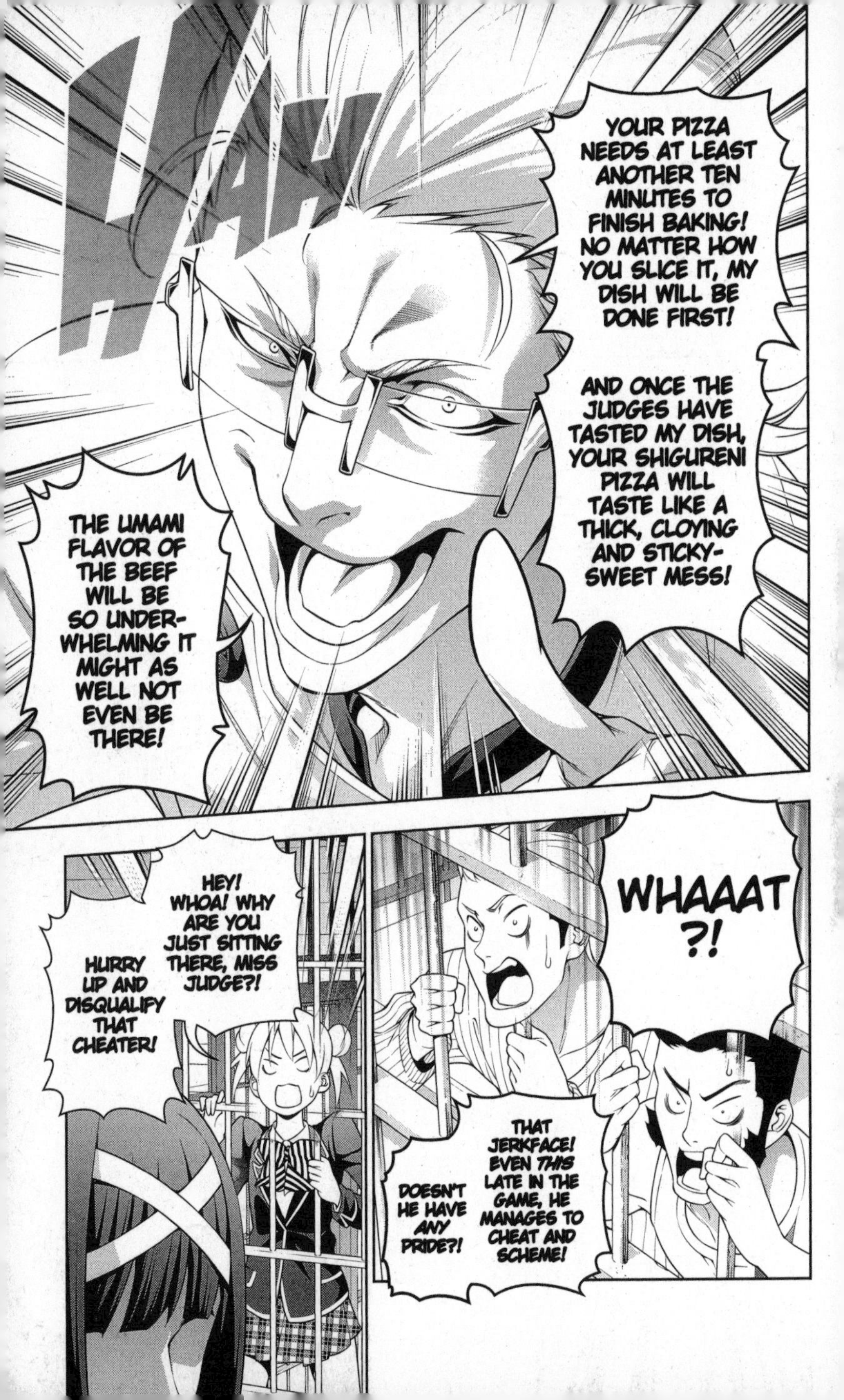
YOUR PIZZA NEEDS AT LEAST ANOTHER TEN MINUTES TO FINISH BAKING! NO MATTER HOW YOU SLICE IT, MY DISH WILL BE DONE FIRST!
AND ONCE THE JUDGES HAVE TASTED MY DISH, YOUR SHIGURENI PIZZA WILL TASTE LIKE A THICK, CLOYING AND STICKY-SWEET MESS!
THE UMAMI FLAVOR OF THE BEEF WILL BE SO UNDER-WHELMING IT MIGHT AS WELL NOT EVEN BE THERE!
WHAAAT ?!
THAT JERKFACE! EVEN *THIS* LATE IN THE GAME, HE MANAGES TO CHEAT AND SCHEME!
DOESN'T HE HAVE *ANY* PRIDE?!
HEY! WHOA! WHY ARE YOU JUST SITTING THERE, MISS JUDGE?!
HURRY UP AND DISQUALIFY THAT CHEATER!

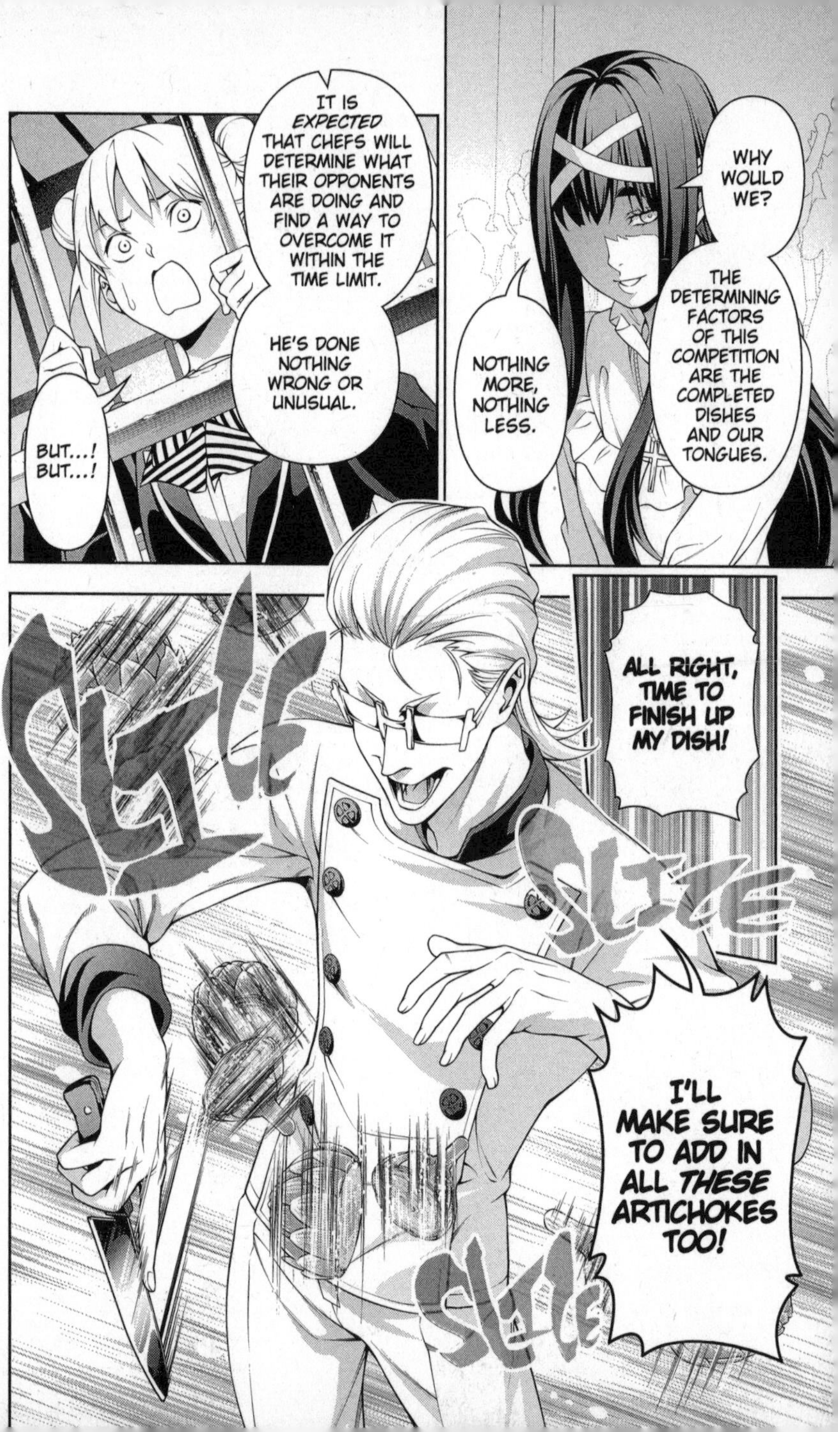
WHY WOULD WE?
THE DETERMINING FACTORS OF THIS COMPETITION ARE THE COMPLETED DISHES AND OUR TONGUES.
NOTHING MORE, NOTHING LESS.
IT IS *EXPECTED* THAT CHEFS WILL DETERMINE WHAT THEIR OPPONENTS ARE DOING AND FIND A WAY TO OVERCOME IT WITHIN THE TIME LIMIT.
HE'S DONE NOTHING WRONG OR UNUSUAL.
BUT...! BUT...!
ALL RIGHT, TIME TO FINISH UP MY DISH!
SLICE
SLICE
I'LL MAKE SURE TO ADD IN ALL *THESE* ARTICHOKES TOO!
SLICE

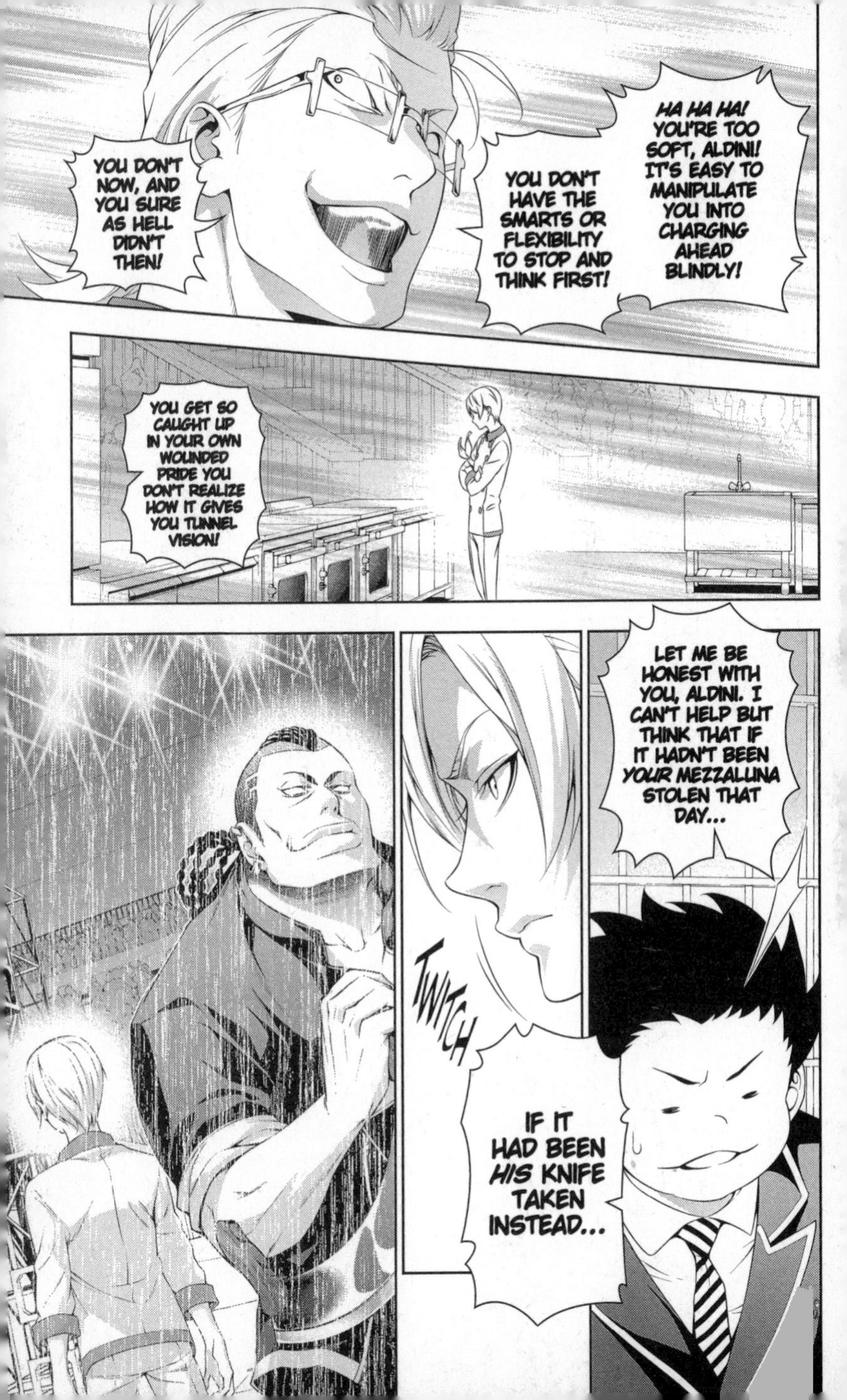
HA HA HA! YOU'RE TOO SOFT, ALDINI! IT'S EASY TO MANIPULATE YOU INTO CHARGING AHEAD BLINDLY!
YOU DON'T HAVE THE SMARTS OR FLEXIBILITY TO STOP AND THINK FIRST!
YOU DON'T NOW, AND YOU SURE AS HELL DIDN'T THEN!
YOU GET SO CAUGHT UP IN YOUR OWN WOUNDED PRIDE YOU DON'T REALIZE HOW IT GIVES YOU TUNNEL VISION!
LET ME BE HONEST WITH YOU, ALDINI. I CAN'T HELP BUT THINK THAT IF IT HADN'T BEEN *YOUR* MEZZALUNA STOLEN THAT DAY...
TWITCH
IF IT HAD BEEN *HIS* KNIFE TAKEN INSTEAD...

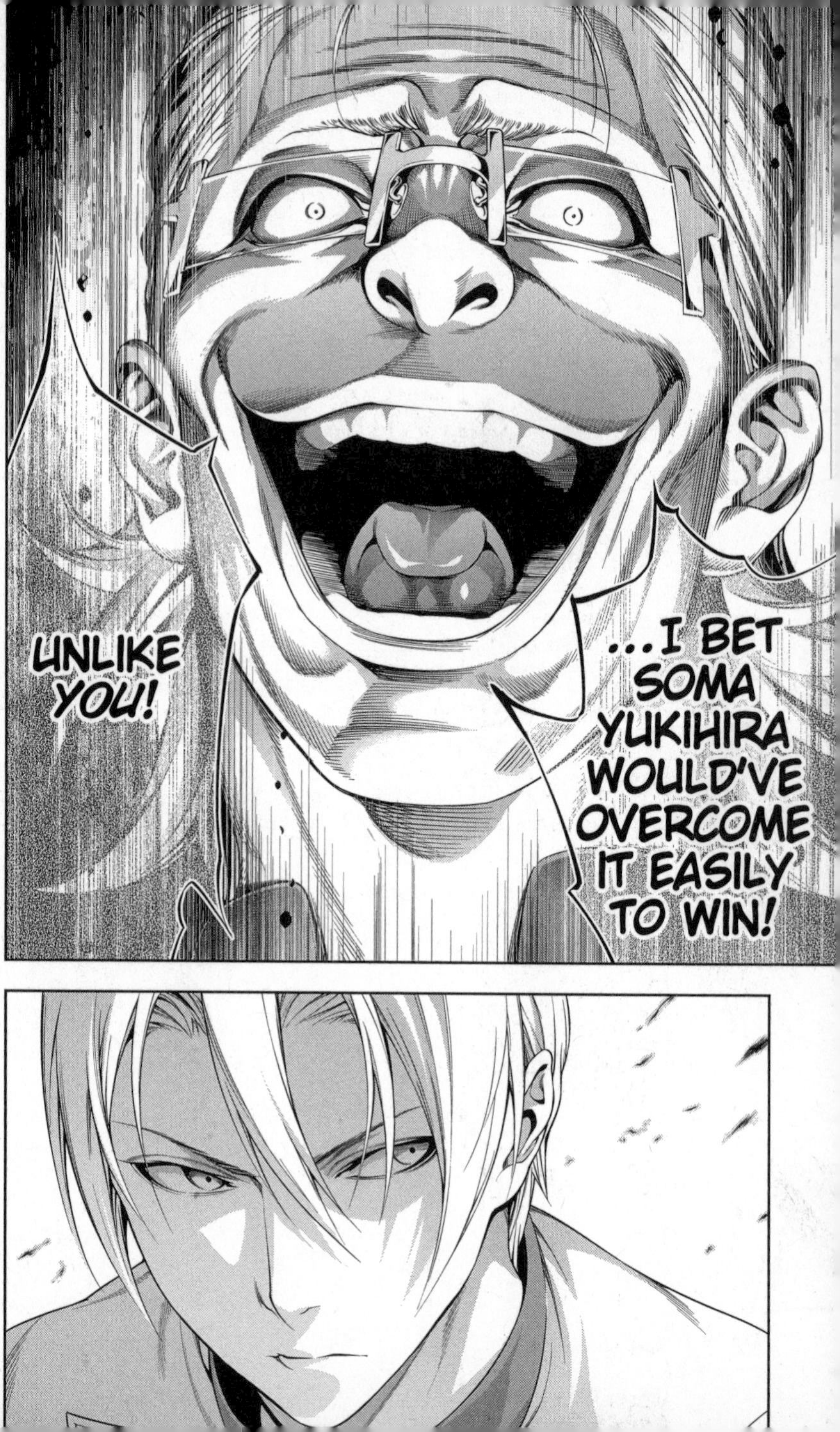
...I BET SOMA YUKIHIRA WOULD'VE OVERCOME IT EASILY TO WIN!
UNLIKE YOU!

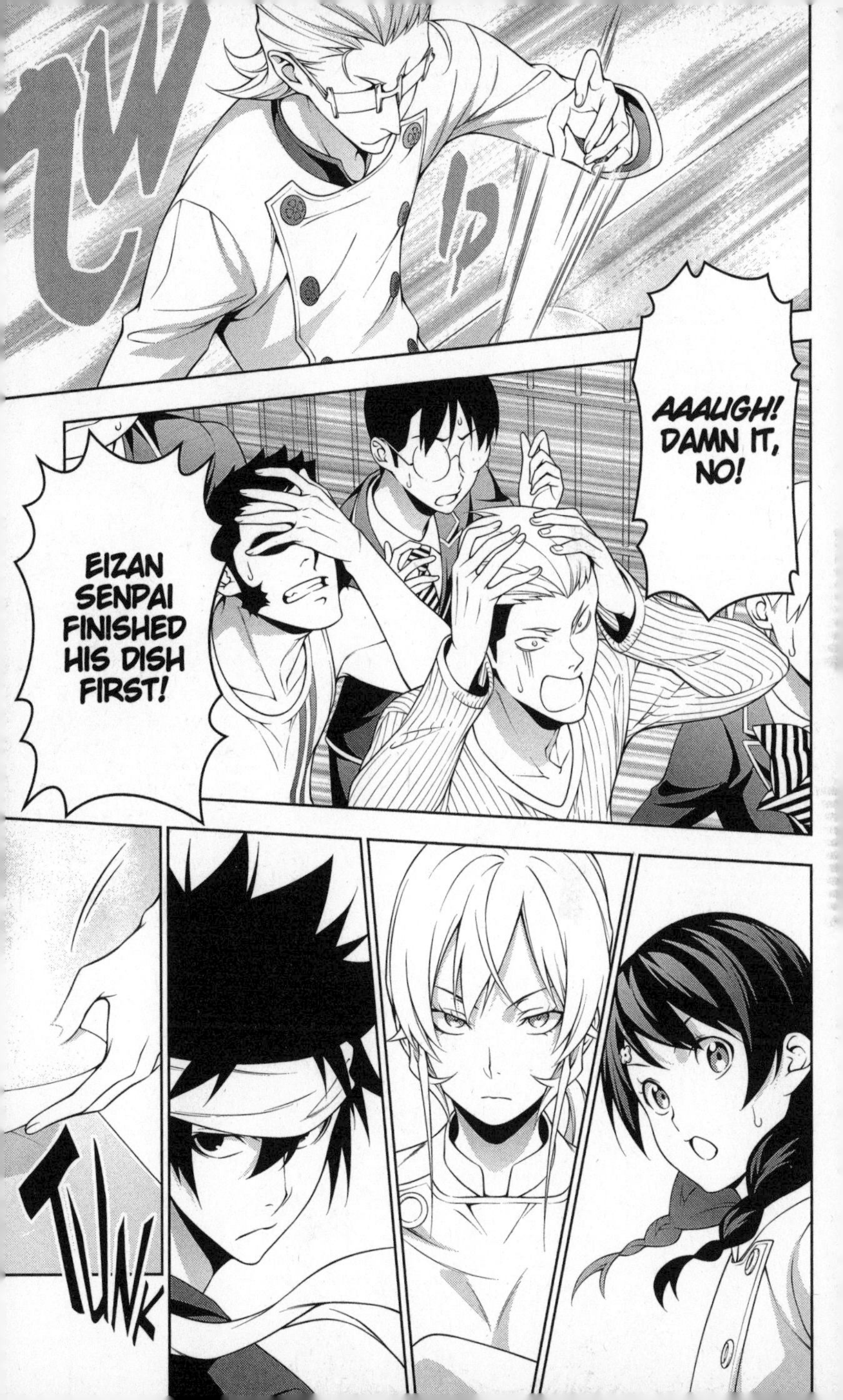
AAAUGH! DAMN IT, NO!
EIZAN SENPAI FINISHED HIS DISH FIRST!
TUNK

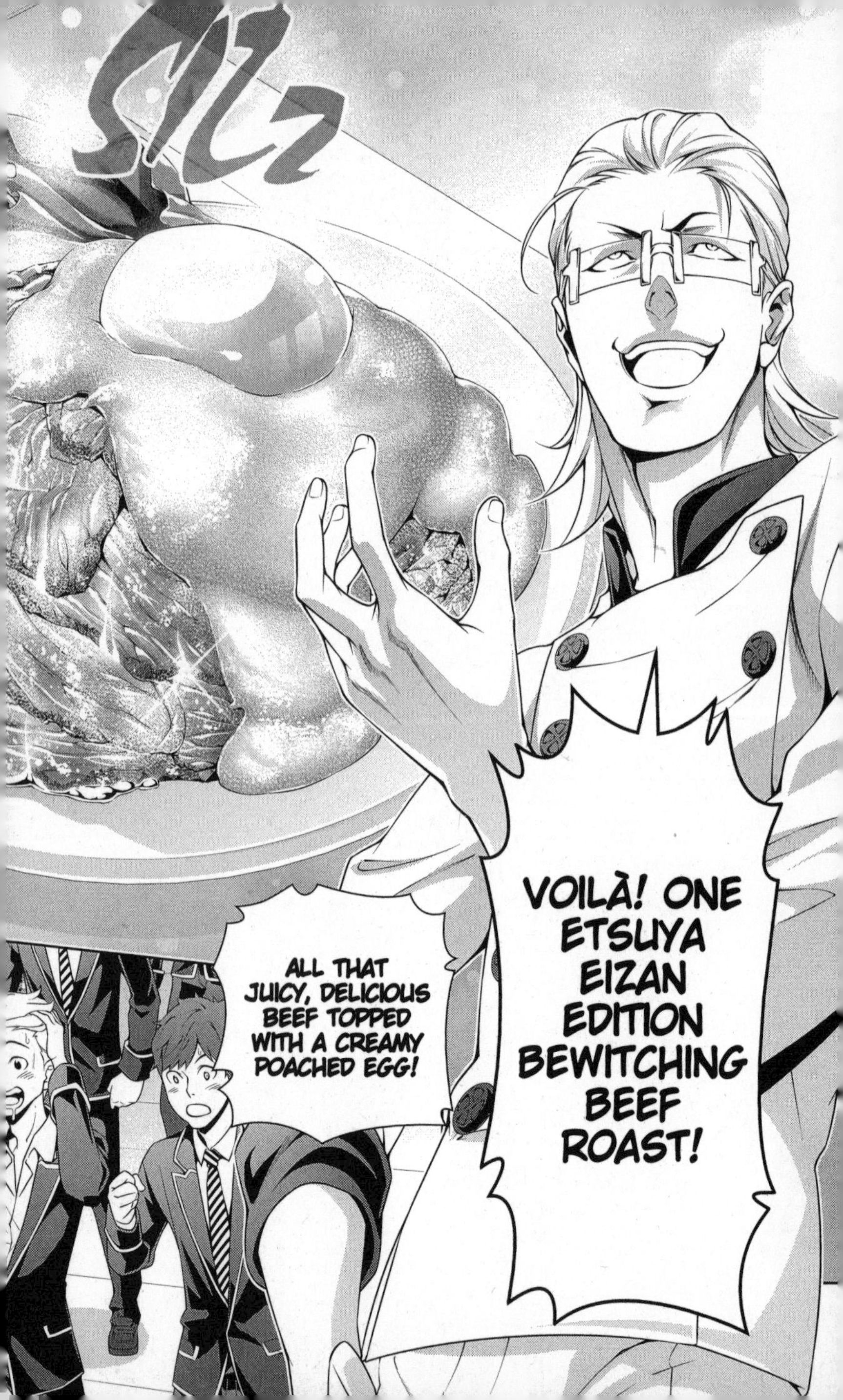
VOILÀ! ONE ETSUYA EIZAN EDITION BEWITCHING BEEF ROAST!
ALL THAT JUICY, DELICIOUS BEEF TOPPED WITH A CREAMY POACHED EGG!

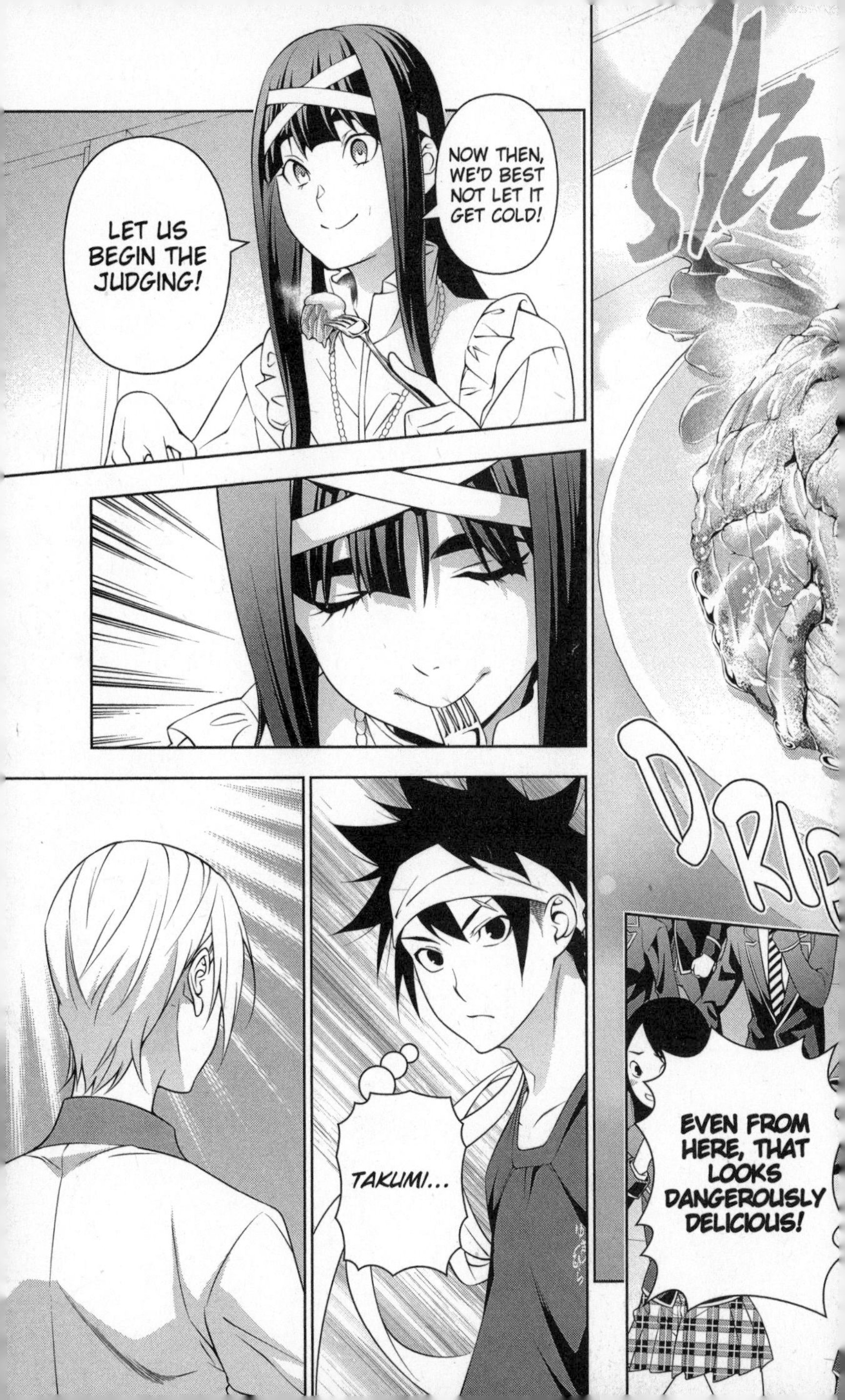
EVEN FROM HERE, THAT LOOKS DANGEROUSLY DELICIOUS!
NOW THEN, WE'D BEST NOT LET IT GET COLD!
LET US BEGIN THE JUDGING!
TAKUMI...

NEW TOP SPOT IN THE EIZAN
FUNNY-FACE RANKING!

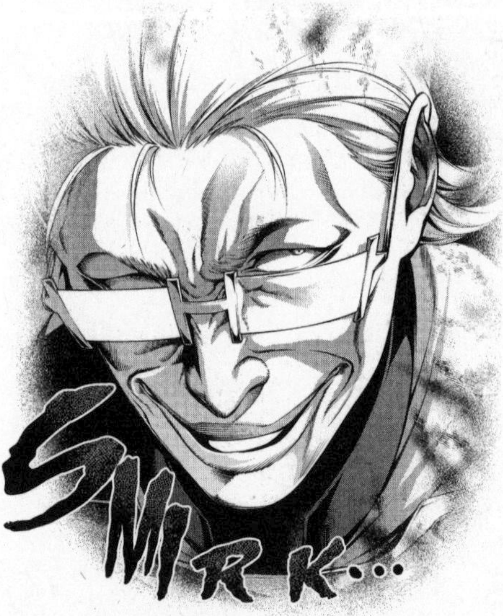
SMIRK...

235 THE ALCHEMIST OF GOURMET

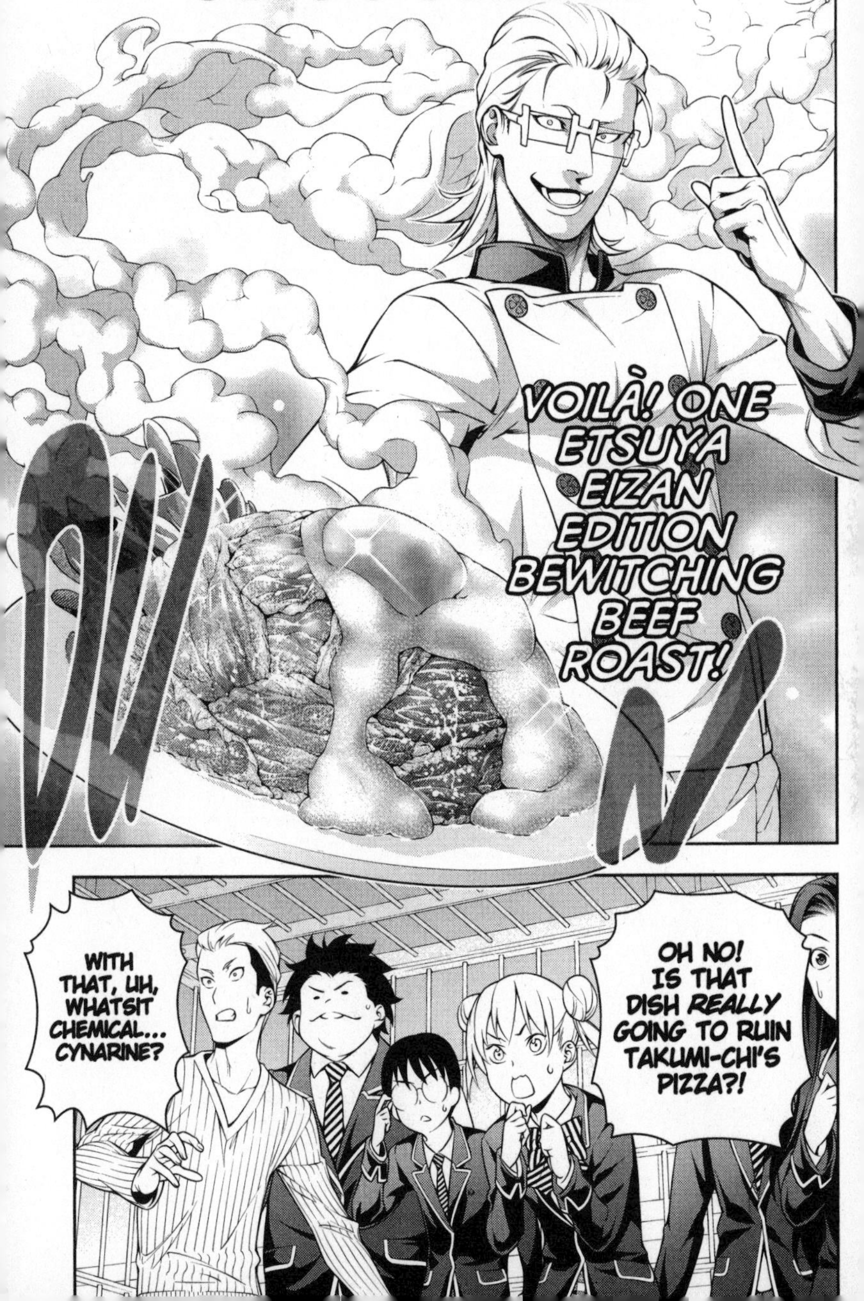
VOILÀ! ONE ETSUYA EIZAN EDITION BEWITCHING BEEF ROAST!
OH NO! IS THAT DISH *REALLY* GOING TO RUIN TAKUMI-CHI'S PIZZA?!
WITH THAT, UH, WHATSIT CHEMICAL... CYNARINE?

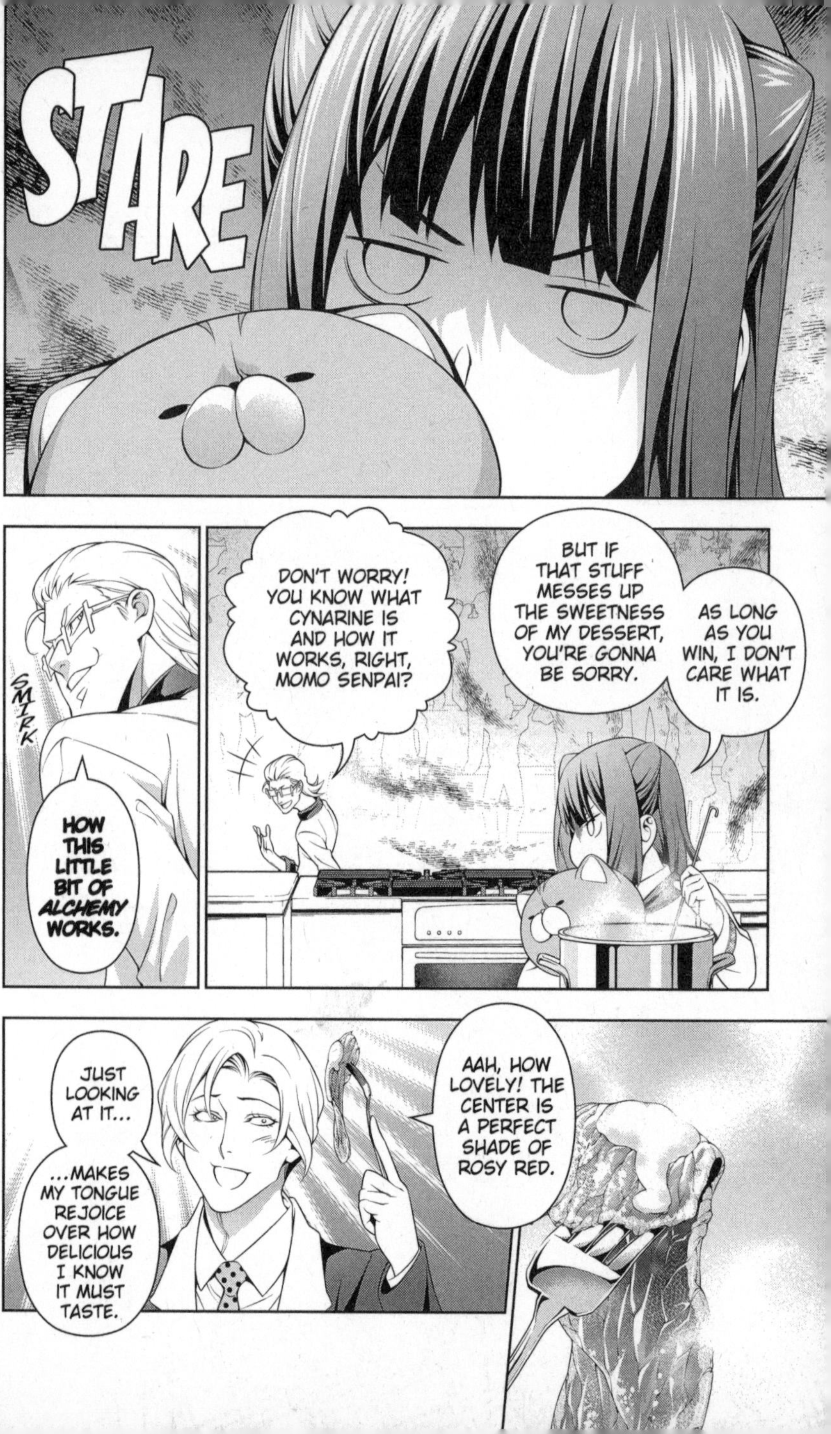
STARE
AS LONG AS YOU WIN, I DON'T CARE WHAT IT IS.
BUT IF THAT STUFF MESSES UP THE SWEETNESS OF MY DESSERT, YOU'RE GONNA BE SORRY.
DON'T WORRY! YOU KNOW WHAT CYNARINE IS AND HOW IT WORKS, RIGHT, MOMO SENPAI?
SMIRK
HOW THIS LITTLE BIT OF *ALCHEMY* WORKS.
AAH, HOW LOVELY! THE CENTER IS A PERFECT SHADE OF ROSY RED.
JUST LOOKING AT IT...
...MAKES MY TONGUE REJOICE OVER HOW DELICIOUS I KNOW IT MUST TASTE.

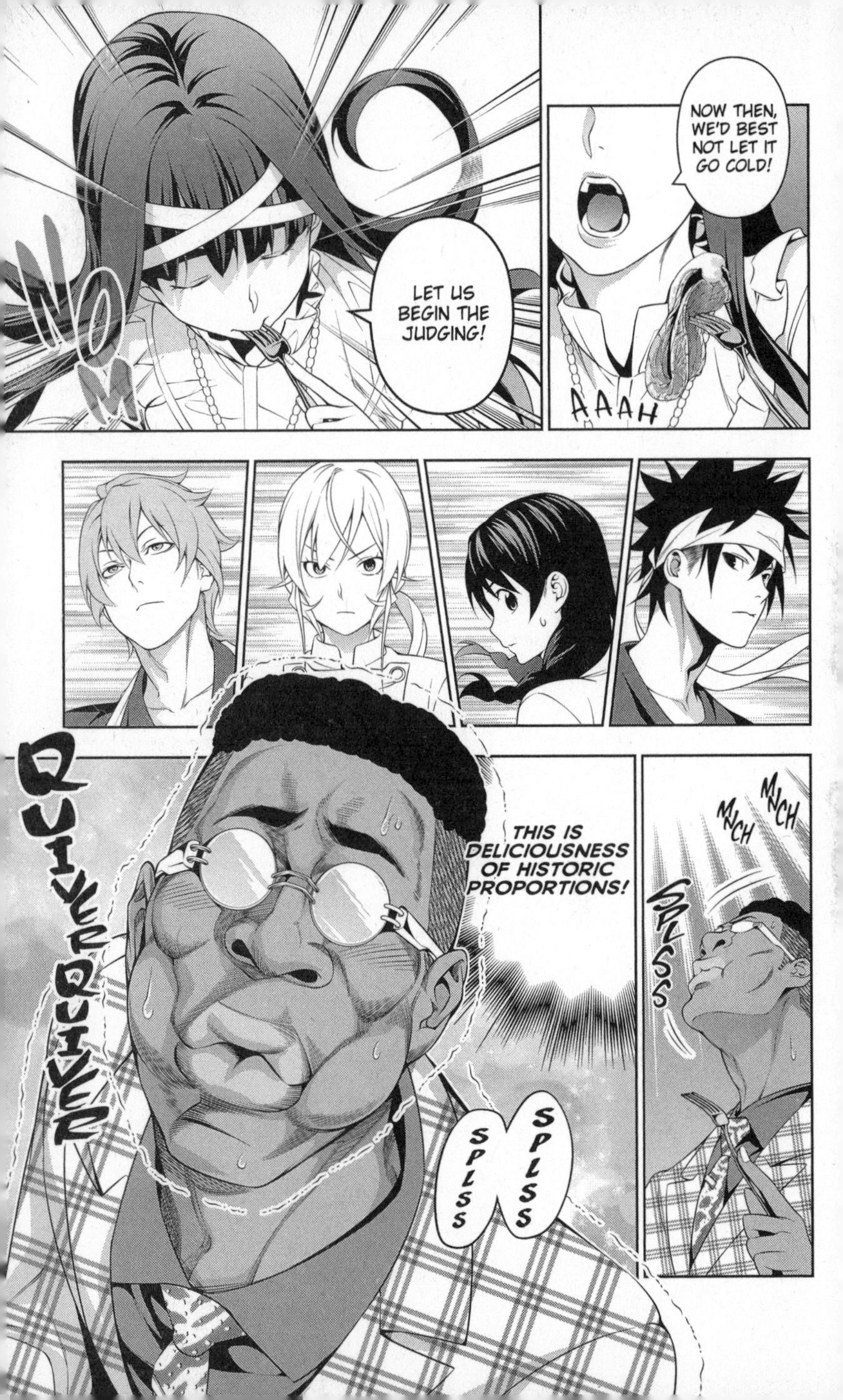
NOW THEN, WE'D BEST NOT LET IT GO COLD!
AAAH
LET US BEGIN THE JUDGING!
NOM
MNCH
MNCH
SPLSS
THIS IS DELICIOUSNESS OF HISTORIC PROPORTIONS!
SPLSS
SPLSS
QUIVER QUIVER

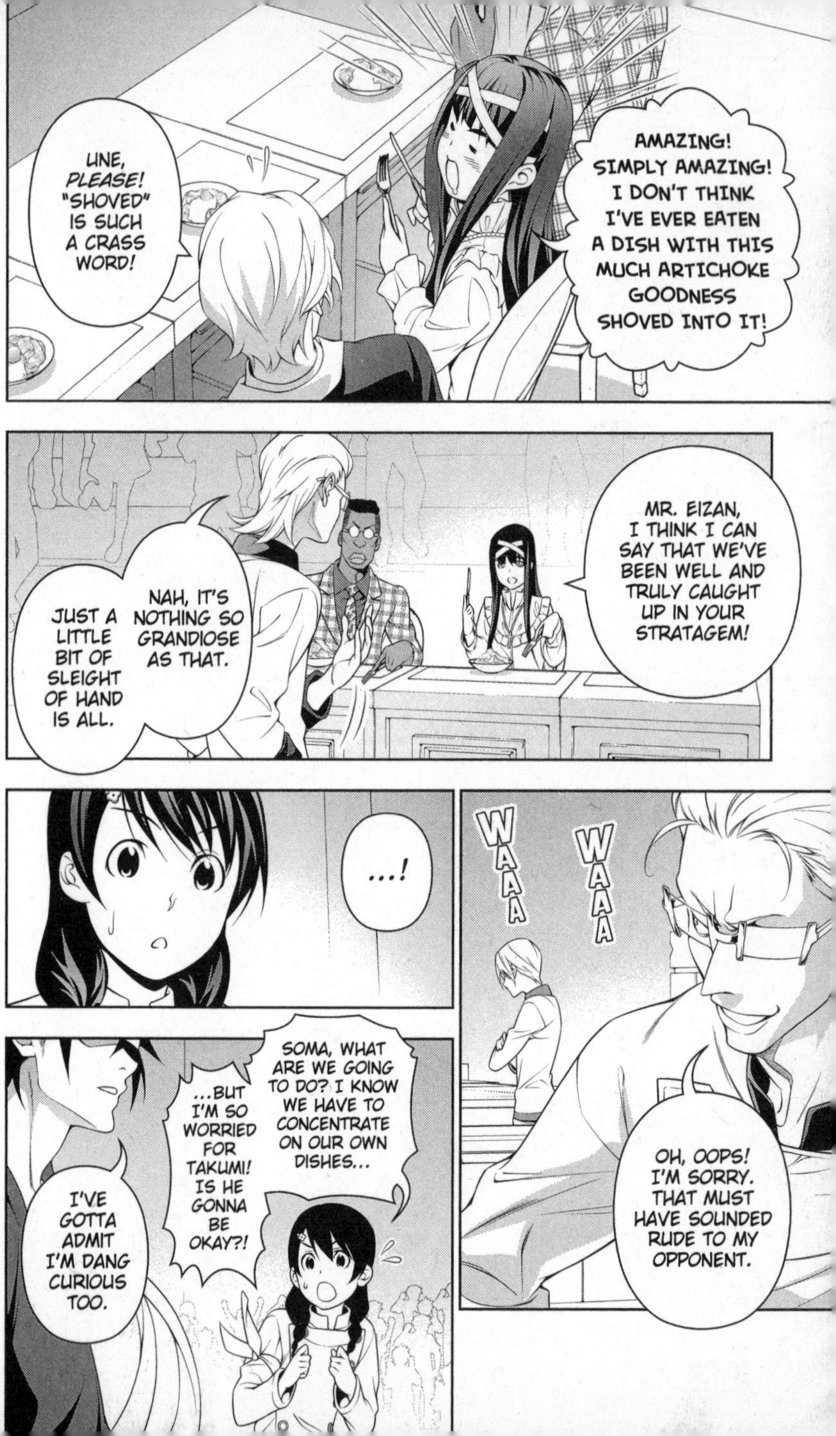
AMAZING! SIMPLY AMAZING! I DON'T THINK I'VE EVER EATEN A DISH WITH THIS MUCH ARTICHOKE GOODNESS SHOVED INTO IT!
UNE, *PLEASE!* "SHOVED" IS SUCH A CRASS WORD!
MR. EIZAN, I THINK I CAN SAY THAT WE'VE BEEN WELL AND TRULY CAUGHT UP IN YOUR STRATAGEM!
NAH, IT'S NOTHING SO GRANDIOSE AS THAT.
JUST A LITTLE BIT OF SLEIGHT OF HAND IS ALL.
WAAA
WAAA
OH, OOPS! I'M SORRY. THAT MUST HAVE SOUNDED RUDE TO MY OPPONENT.
...!
SOMA, WHAT ARE WE GOING TO DO? I KNOW WE HAVE TO CONCENTRATE ON OUR OWN DISHES...
...BUT I'M SO WORRIED FOR TAKUMI! IS HE GONNA BE OKAY?!
I'VE GOTTA ADMIT I'M DANG CURIOUS TOO.

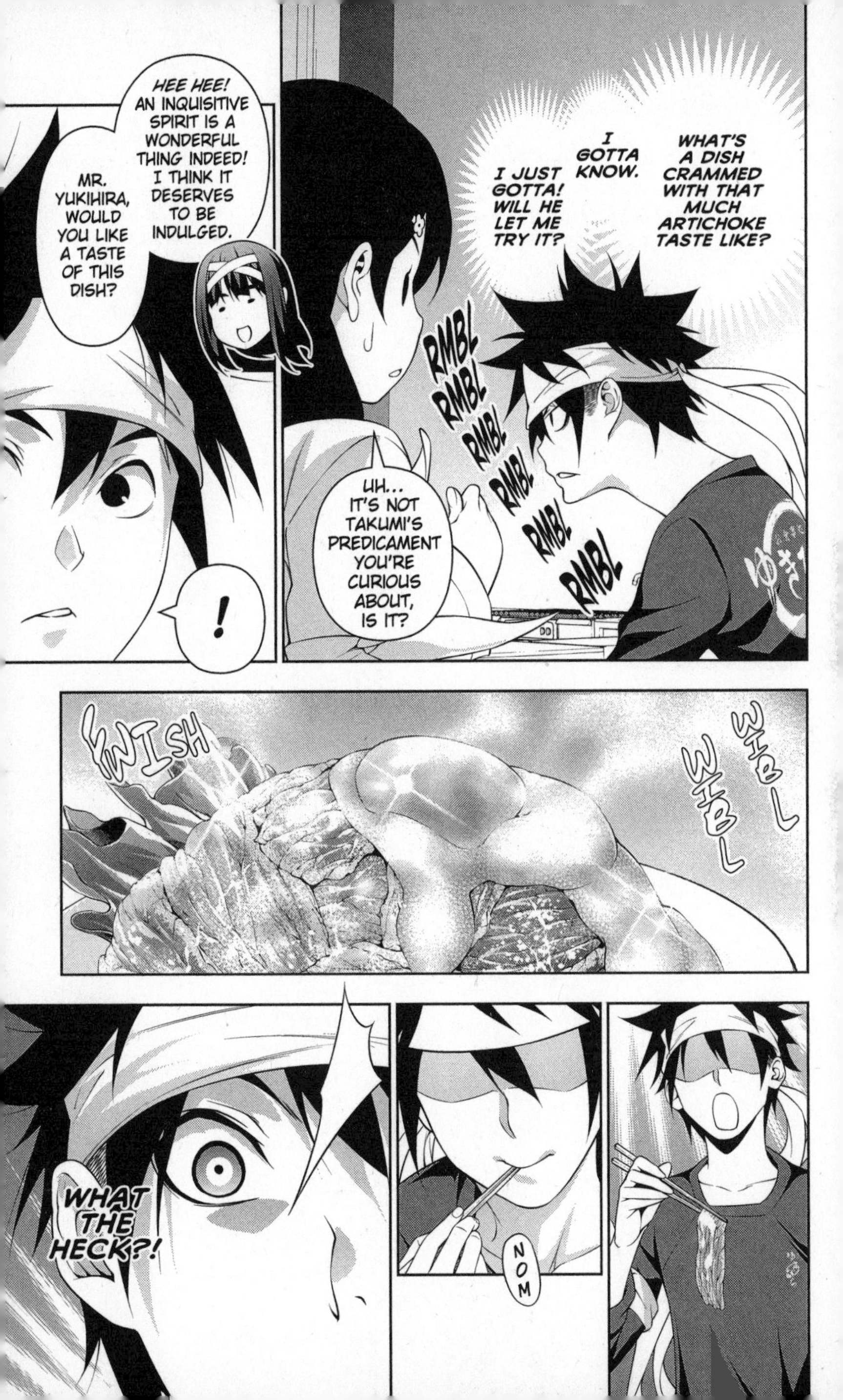
WHAT'S A DISH CRAMMED WITH THAT MUCH ARTICHOKE TASTE LIKE?
I GOTTA KNOW.
I JUST GOTTA! WILL HE LET ME TRY IT?
RMBL RMBL RMBL RMBL RMBL RMBL
UH... IT'S NOT TAKUMI'S PREDICAMENT YOU'RE CURIOUS ABOUT, IS IT?
HEE HEE! AN INQUISITIVE SPIRIT IS A WONDERFUL THING INDEED! I THINK IT DESERVES TO BE INDULGED.
MR. YUKIHIRA, WOULD YOU LIKE A TASTE OF THIS DISH?
!
SHIBL SHIBL
SWISH
NOM
WHAT THE HECK?!

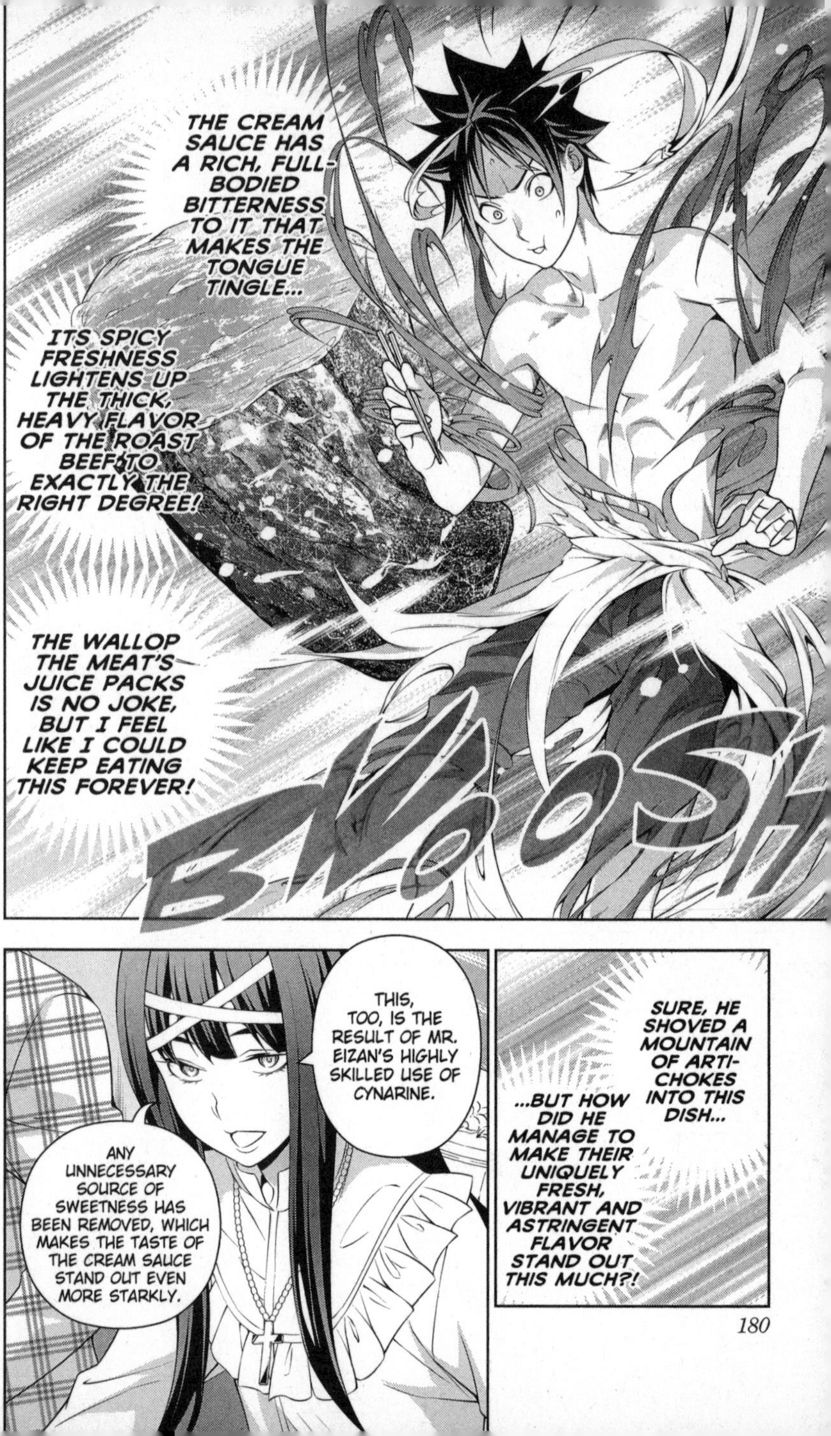
THE CREAM SAUCE HAS A RICH, FULL-BODIED BITTERNESS TO IT THAT MAKES THE TONGUE TINGLE...
ITS SPICY FRESHNESS LIGHTENS UP THE THICK, HEAVY FLAVOR OF THE ROAST BEEF TO EXACTLY THE RIGHT DEGREE!
THE WALLOP THE MEAT'S JUICE PACKS IS NO JOKE, BUT I FEEL LIKE I COULD KEEP EATING THIS FOREVER!
BWOOSH!!
SURE, HE SHOVED A MOUNTAIN OF ARTI-CHOKES INTO THIS DISH...
...BUT HOW DID HE MANAGE TO MAKE THEIR UNIQUELY FRESH, VIBRANT AND ASTRINGENT FLAVOR STAND OUT THIS MUCH?!
THIS, TOO, IS THE RESULT OF MR. EIZAN'S HIGHLY SKILLED USE OF CYNARINE.
ANY UNNECESSARY SOURCE OF SWEETNESS HAS BEEN REMOVED, WHICH MAKES THE TASTE OF THE CREAM SAUCE STAND OUT EVEN MORE STARKLY.

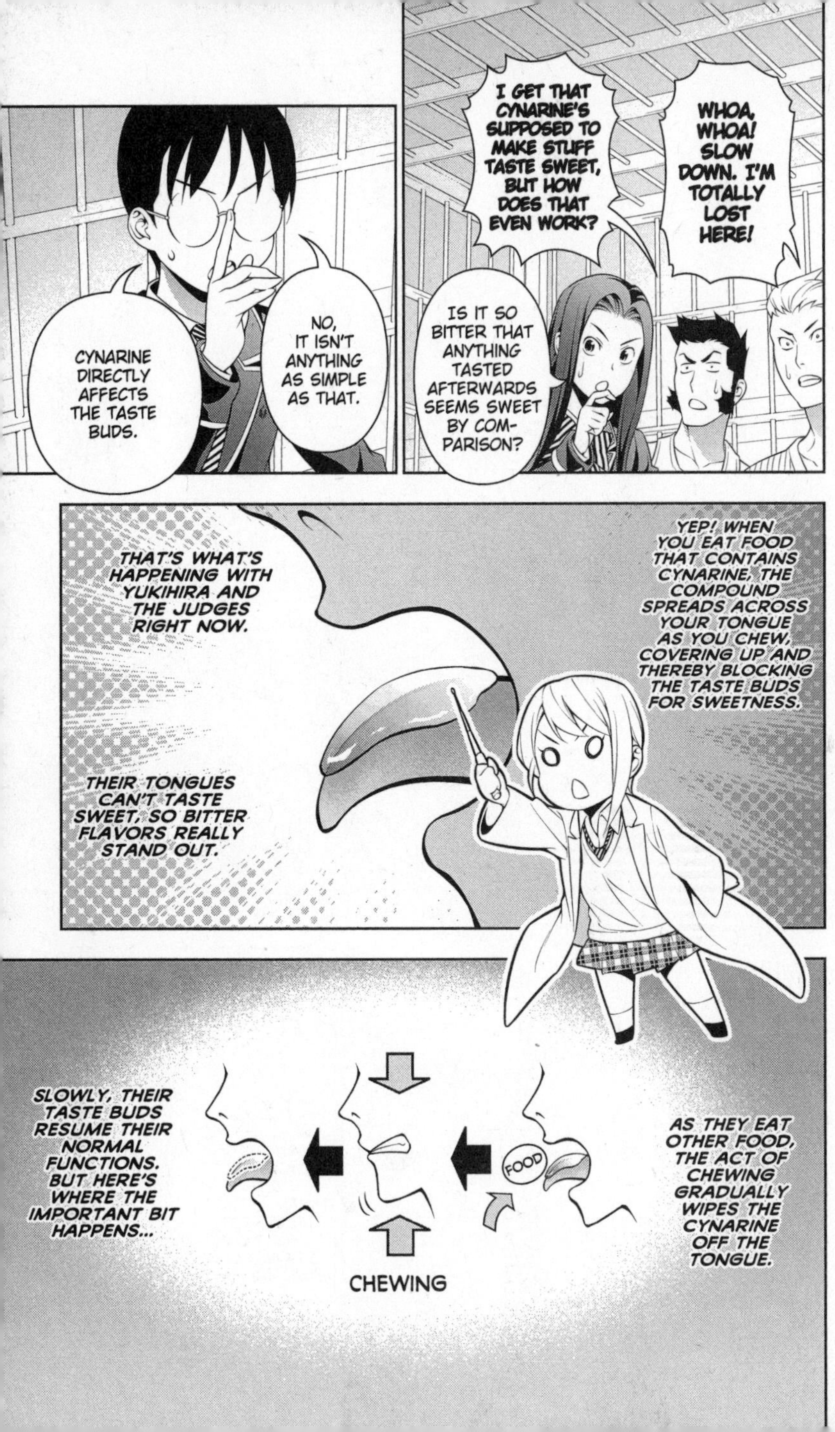
WHOA, WHOA! SLOW DOWN. I'M TOTALLY LOST HERE!
I GET THAT CYNARINE'S SUPPOSED TO MAKE STUFF TASTE SWEET, BUT HOW DOES THAT EVEN WORK?
IS IT SO BITTER THAT ANYTHING TASTED AFTERWARDS SEEMS SWEET BY COMPARISON?
NO, IT ISN'T ANYTHING AS SIMPLE AS THAT.
CYNARINE DIRECTLY AFFECTS THE TASTE BUDS.
YEP! WHEN YOU EAT FOOD THAT CONTAINS CYNARINE, THE COMPOUND SPREADS ACROSS YOUR TONGUE AS YOU CHEW, COVERING UP AND THEREBY BLOCKING THE TASTE BUDS FOR SWEETNESS.
THAT'S WHAT'S HAPPENING WITH YUKIHIRA AND THE JUDGES RIGHT NOW.
THEIR TONGUES CAN'T TASTE SWEET, SO BITTER FLAVORS REALLY STAND OUT.
AS THEY EAT OTHER FOOD, THE ACT OF CHEWING GRADUALLY WIPES THE CYNARINE OFF THE TONGUE.
FOOD
CHEWING
SLOWLY, THEIR TASTE BUDS RESUME THEIR NORMAL FUNCTIONS. BUT HERE'S WHERE THE IMPORTANT BIT HAPPENS...

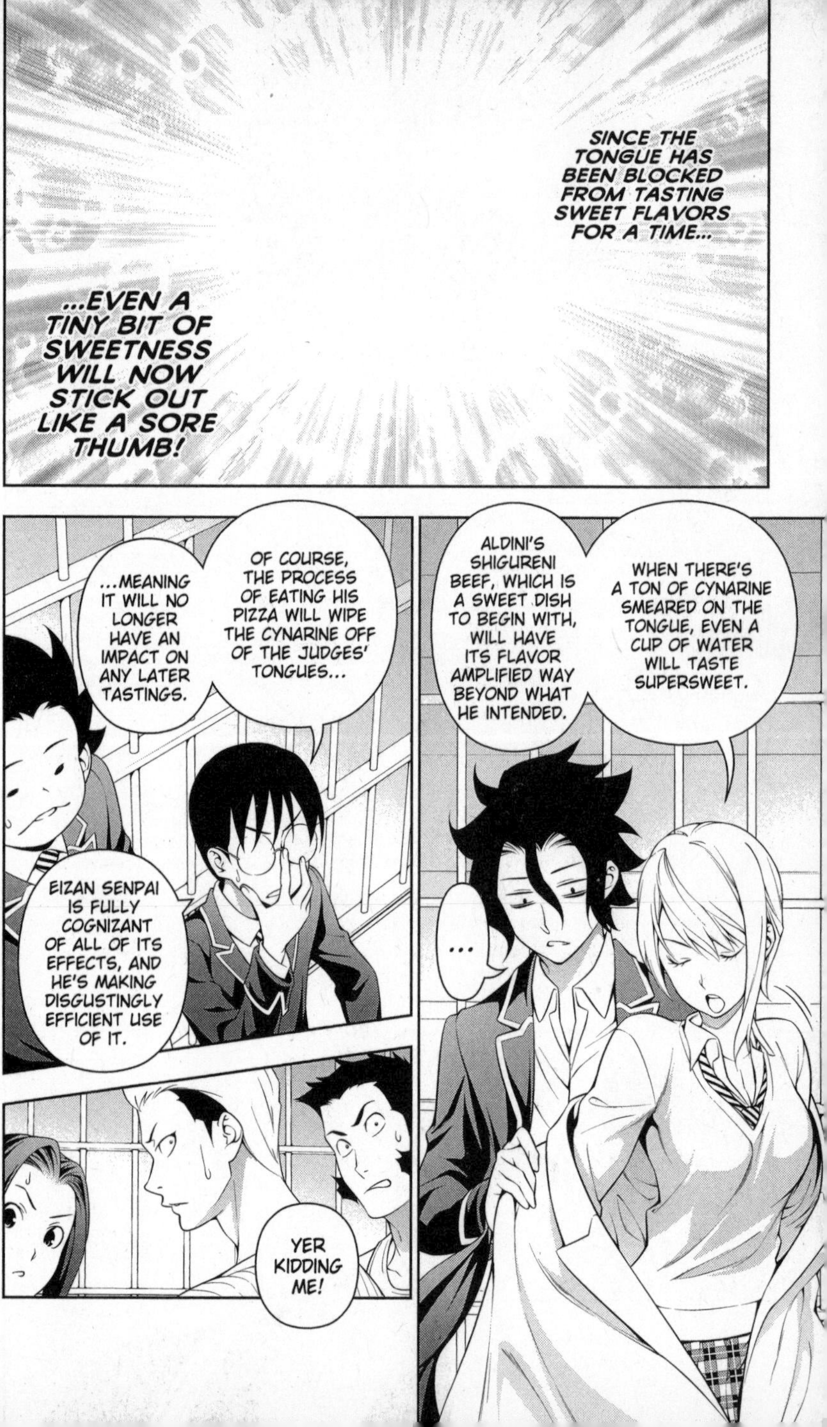
SINCE THE TONGUE HAS BEEN BLOCKED FROM TASTING SWEET FLAVORS FOR A TIME...
...EVEN A TINY BIT OF SWEETNESS WILL NOW STICK OUT LIKE A SORE THUMB!
WHEN THERE'S A TON OF CYNARINE SMEARED ON THE TONGUE, EVEN A CUP OF WATER WILL TASTE SUPERSWEET.
ALDINI'S SHIGURENI BEEF, WHICH IS A SWEET DISH TO BEGIN WITH, WILL HAVE ITS FLAVOR AMPLIFIED WAY BEYOND WHAT HE INTENDED.
...
OF COURSE, THE PROCESS OF EATING HIS PIZZA WILL WIPE THE CYNARINE OFF OF THE JUDGES' TONGUES...
...MEANING IT WILL NO LONGER HAVE AN IMPACT ON ANY LATER TASTINGS.
EIZAN SENPAI IS FULLY COGNIZANT OF ALL OF ITS EFFECTS, AND HE'S MAKING DISGUSTINGLY EFFICIENT USE OF IT.
YER KIDDING ME!

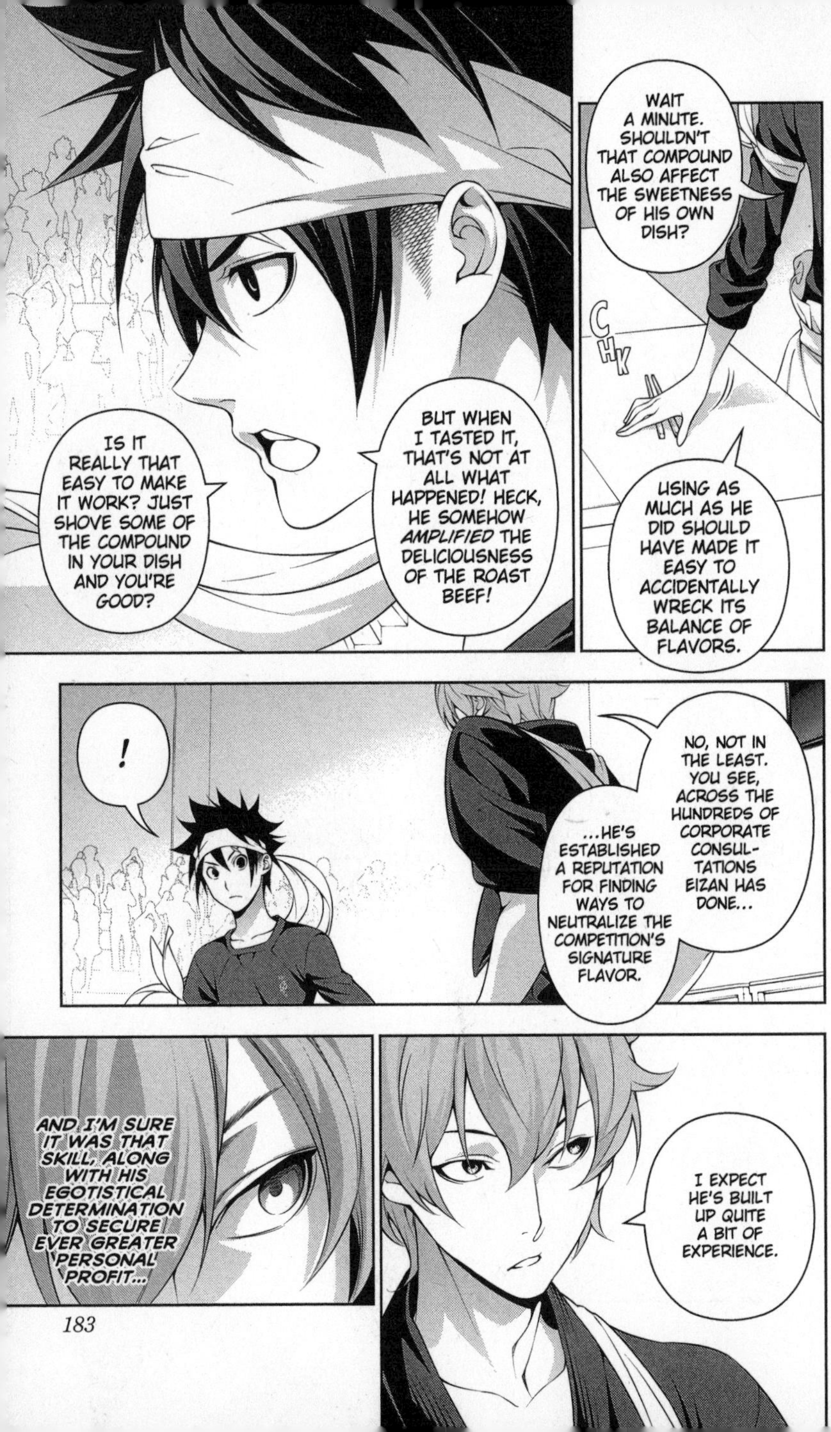
WAIT A MINUTE. SHOULDN'T THAT COMPOUND ALSO AFFECT THE SWEETNESS OF HIS OWN DISH?
CHK
USING AS MUCH AS HE DID SHOULD HAVE MADE IT EASY TO ACCIDENTALLY WRECK ITS BALANCE OF FLAVORS.
BUT WHEN I TASTED IT, THAT'S NOT AT ALL WHAT HAPPENED! HECK, HE SOMEHOW *AMPLIFIED* THE DELICIOUSNESS OF THE ROAST BEEF!
IS IT REALLY THAT EASY TO MAKE IT WORK? JUST SHOVE SOME OF THE COMPOUND IN YOUR DISH AND YOU'RE GOOD?
NO, NOT IN THE LEAST. YOU SEE, ACROSS THE HUNDREDS OF CORPORATE CONSUL-TATIONS EIZAN HAS DONE...
...HE'S ESTABLISHED A REPUTATION FOR FINDING WAYS TO NEUTRALIZE THE COMPETITION'S SIGNATURE FLAVOR.
!
I EXPECT HE'S BUILT UP QUITE A BIT OF EXPERIENCE.
AND I'M SURE IT WAS THAT SKILL, ALONG WITH HIS EGOTISTICAL DETERMINATION TO SECURE EVER GREATER PERSONAL PROFIT...

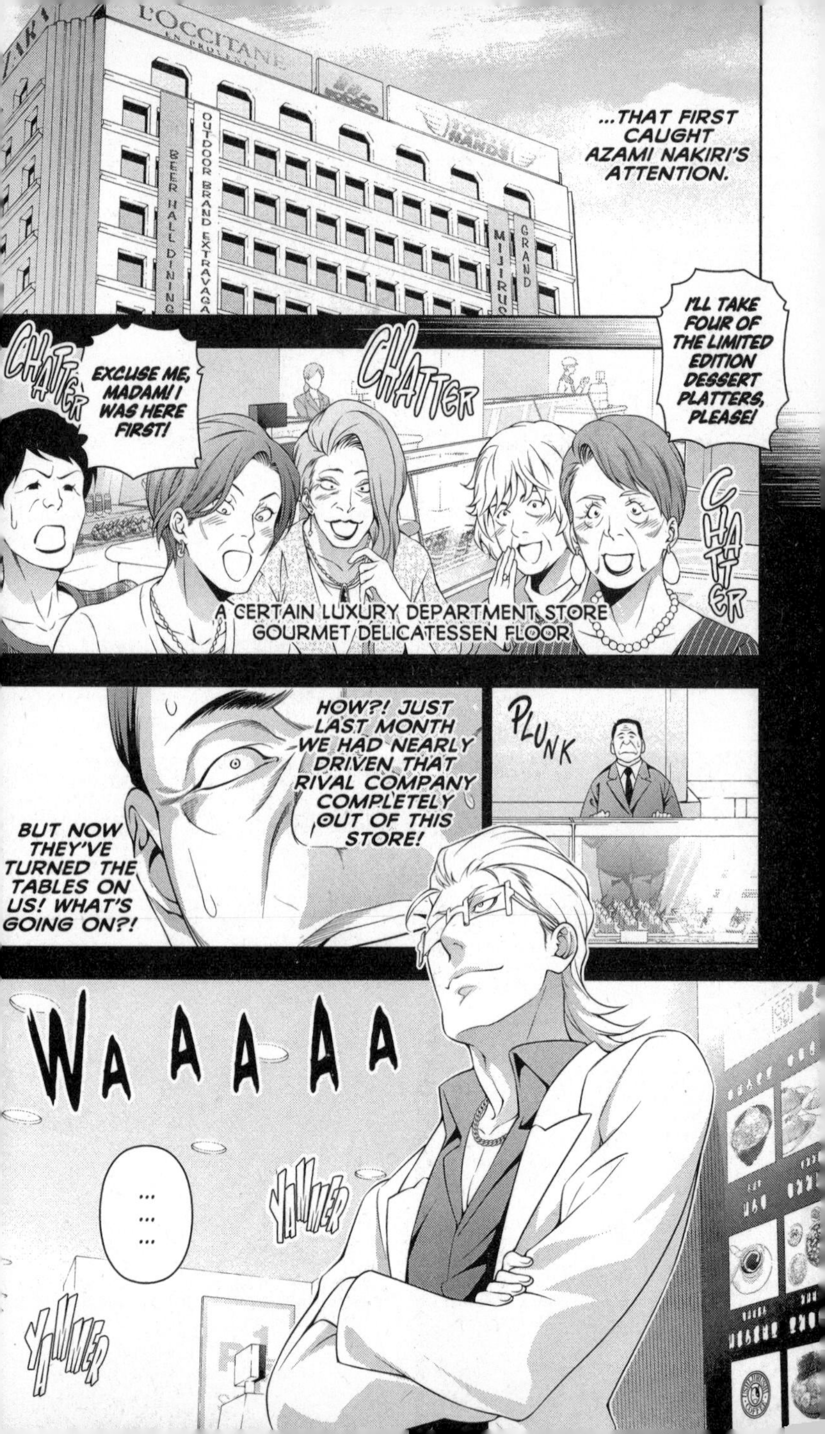
L'OCCITANE
OUTDOOR BRAND EXTRAVAGA
BEER HALL DINING
GRAND
MIJIRUS
...THAT FIRST CAUGHT AZAMI NAKIRI'S ATTENTION.
I'LL TAKE FOUR OF THE LIMITED EDITION DESSERT PLATTERS, PLEASE!
CHATTER
CHATTER
EXCUSE ME, MADAM! I WAS HERE FIRST!
CHATTER
A CERTAIN LUXURY DEPARTMENT STORE GOURMET DELICATESSEN FLOOR
PLUNK
HOW?! JUST LAST MONTH WE HAD NEARLY DRIVEN THAT RIVAL COMPANY COMPLETELY OUT OF THIS STORE!
BUT NOW THEY'VE TURNED THE TABLES ON US! WHAT'S GOING ON?!
WAAAAA
YAMMER
...
...
...
YAMMER

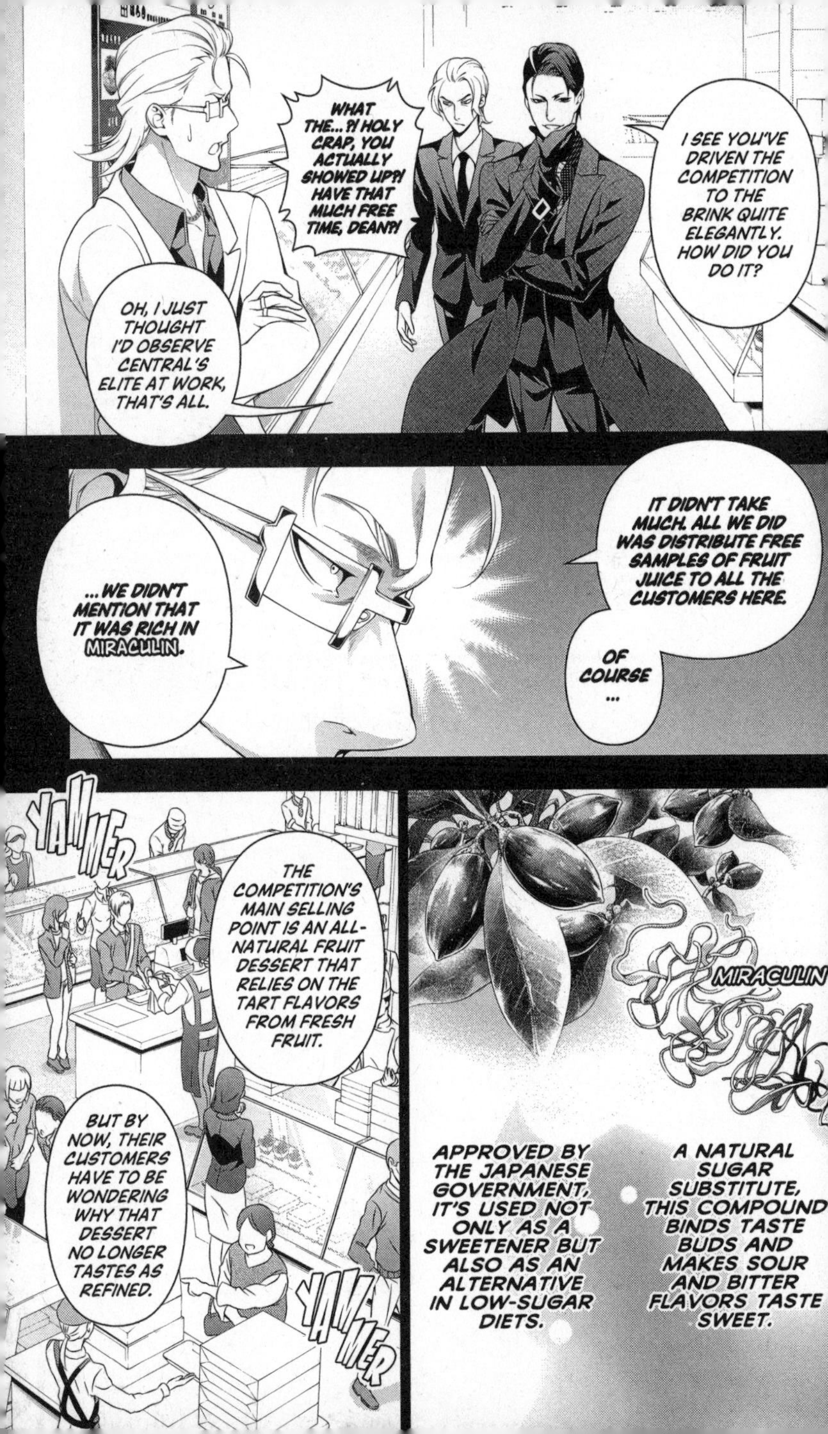
WHAT THE...?! HOLY CRAP, YOU ACTUALLY SHOWED UP?! HAVE THAT MUCH FREE TIME, DEAN?!
OH, I JUST THOUGHT I'D OBSERVE CENTRAL'S ELITE AT WORK, THAT'S ALL.
I SEE YOU'VE DRIVEN THE COMPETITION TO THE BRINK QUITE ELEGANTLY. HOW DID YOU DO IT?
IT DIDN'T TAKE MUCH. ALL WE DID WAS DISTRIBUTE FREE SAMPLES OF FRUIT JUICE TO ALL THE CUSTOMERS HERE.
OF COURSE...
...WE DIDN'T MENTION THAT IT WAS RICH IN MIRACULIN.
MIRACULIN
A NATURAL SUGAR SUBSTITUTE, THIS COMPOUND BINDS TASTE BUDS AND MAKES SOUR AND BITTER FLAVORS TASTE SWEET.
APPROVED BY THE JAPANESE GOVERNMENT, IT'S USED NOT ONLY AS A SWEETENER BUT ALSO AS AN ALTERNATIVE IN LOW-SUGAR DIETS.
YAMMER
THE COMPETITION'S MAIN SELLING POINT IS AN ALL-NATURAL FRUIT DESSERT THAT RELIES ON THE TART FLAVORS FROM FRESH FRUIT.
BUT BY NOW, THEIR CUSTOMERS HAVE TO BE WONDERING WHY THAT DESSERT NO LONGER TASTES AS REFINED.
YAMMER

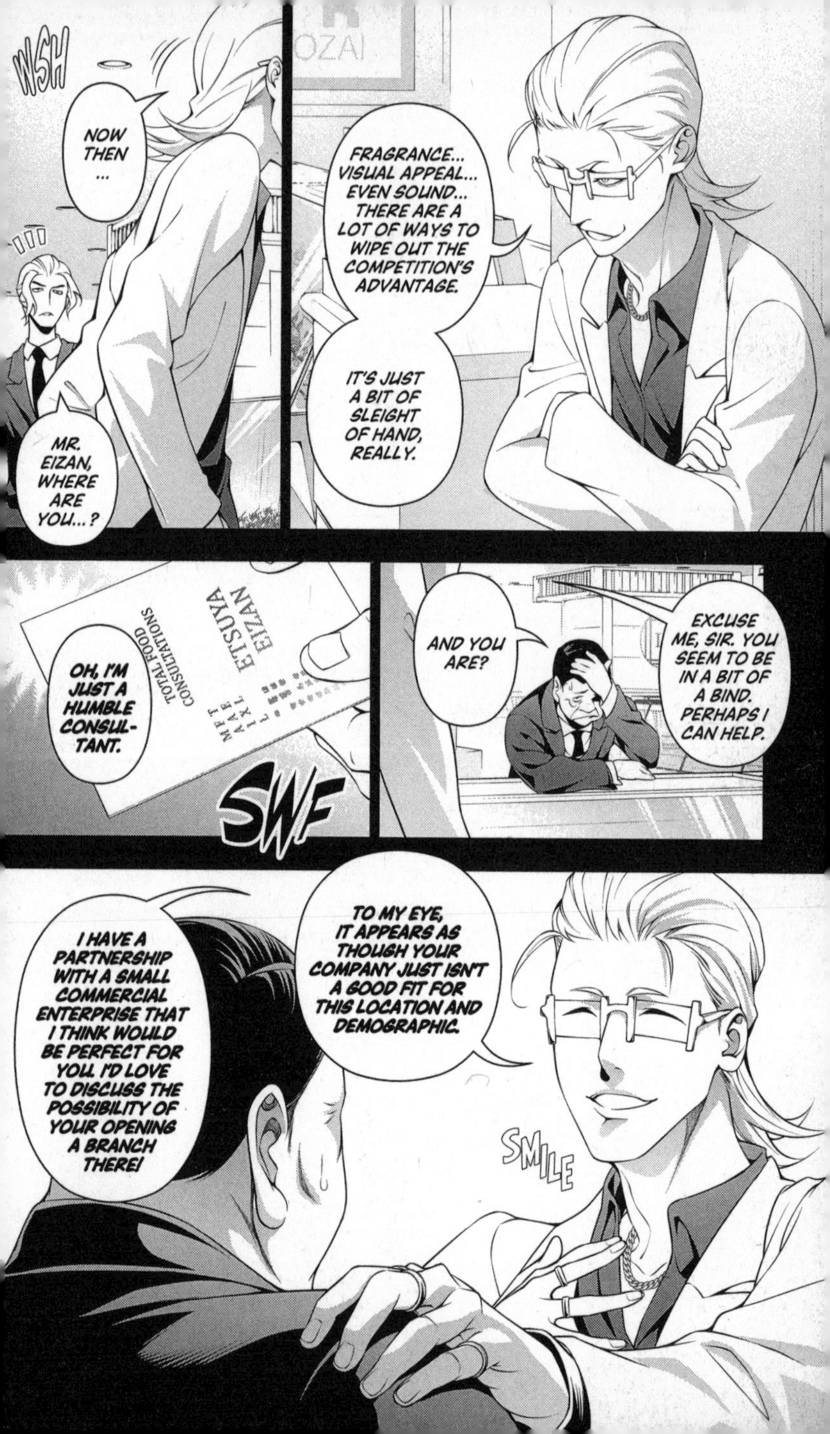
FRAGRANCE... VISUAL APPEAL... EVEN SOUND... THERE ARE A LOT OF WAYS TO WIPE OUT THE COMPETITION'S ADVANTAGE.
IT'S JUST A BIT OF SLEIGHT OF HAND, REALLY.
WSH
NOW THEN ...
MR. EIZAN, WHERE ARE YOU...?
EXCUSE ME, SIR. YOU SEEM TO BE IN A BIT OF A BIND. PERHAPS I CAN HELP.
AND YOU ARE?
ETSUYA EIZAN
TOTAL FOOD CONSULTATIONS
OH, I'M JUST A HUMBLE CONSUL-TANT.
SWF
TO MY EYE, IT APPEARS AS THOUGH YOUR COMPANY JUST ISN'T A GOOD FIT FOR THIS LOCATION AND DEMOGRAPHIC.
I HAVE A PARTNERSHIP WITH A SMALL COMMERCIAL ENTERPRISE THAT I THINK WOULD BE PERFECT FOR YOU. I'D LOVE TO DISCUSS THE POSSIBILITY OF YOUR OPENING A BRANCH THERE!
SMILE

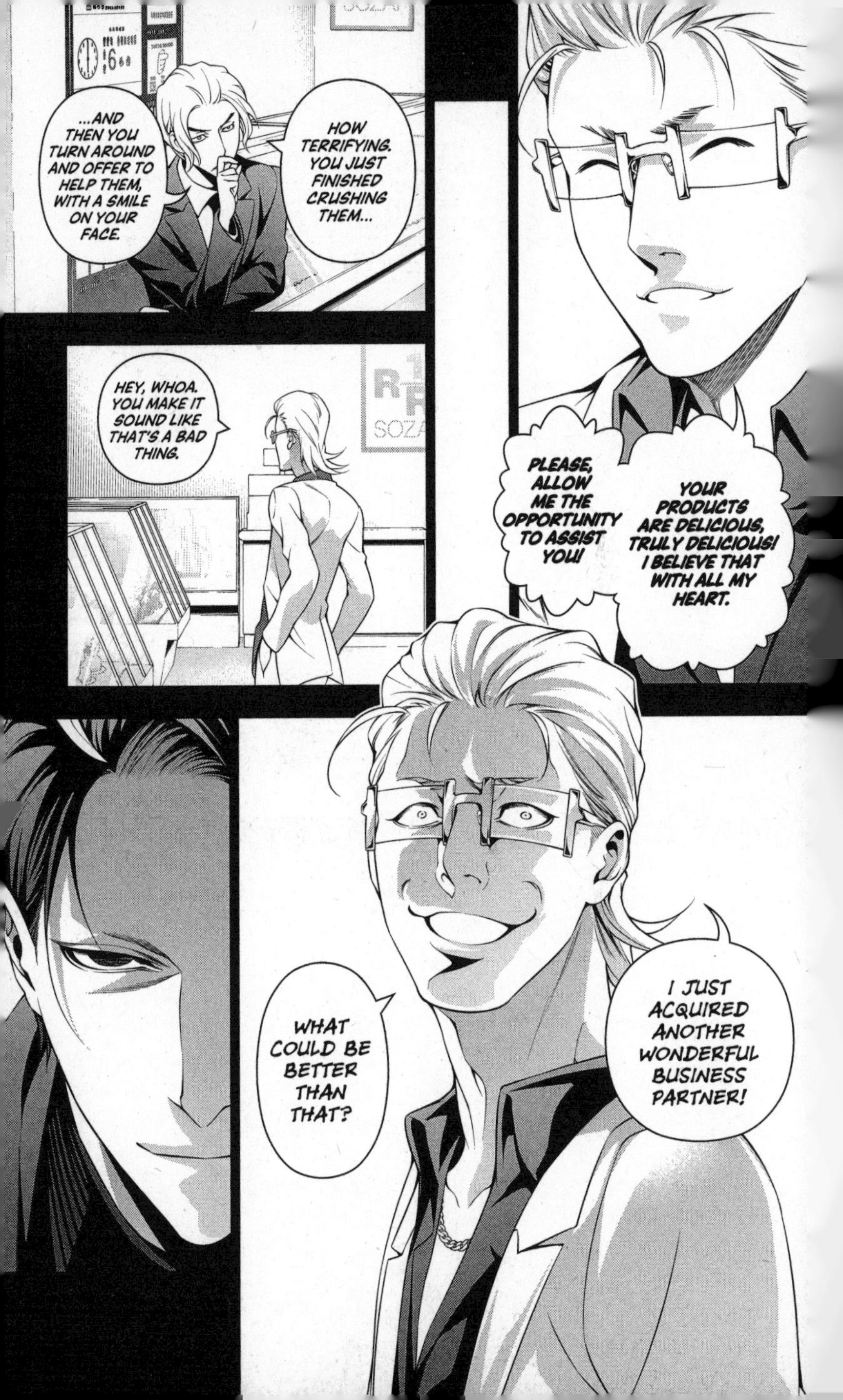
YOUR PRODUCTS ARE DELICIOUS, TRULY DELICIOUS! I BELIEVE THAT WITH ALL MY HEART.
PLEASE, ALLOW ME THE OPPORTUNITY TO ASSIST YOU!
HOW TERRIFYING. YOU JUST FINISHED CRUSHING THEM...
...AND THEN YOU TURN AROUND AND OFFER TO HELP THEM, WITH A SMILE ON YOUR FACE.
HEY, WHOA. YOU MAKE IT SOUND LIKE THAT'S A BAD THING.
I JUST ACQUIRED ANOTHER WONDERFUL BUSINESS PARTNER!
WHAT COULD BE BETTER THAN THAT?

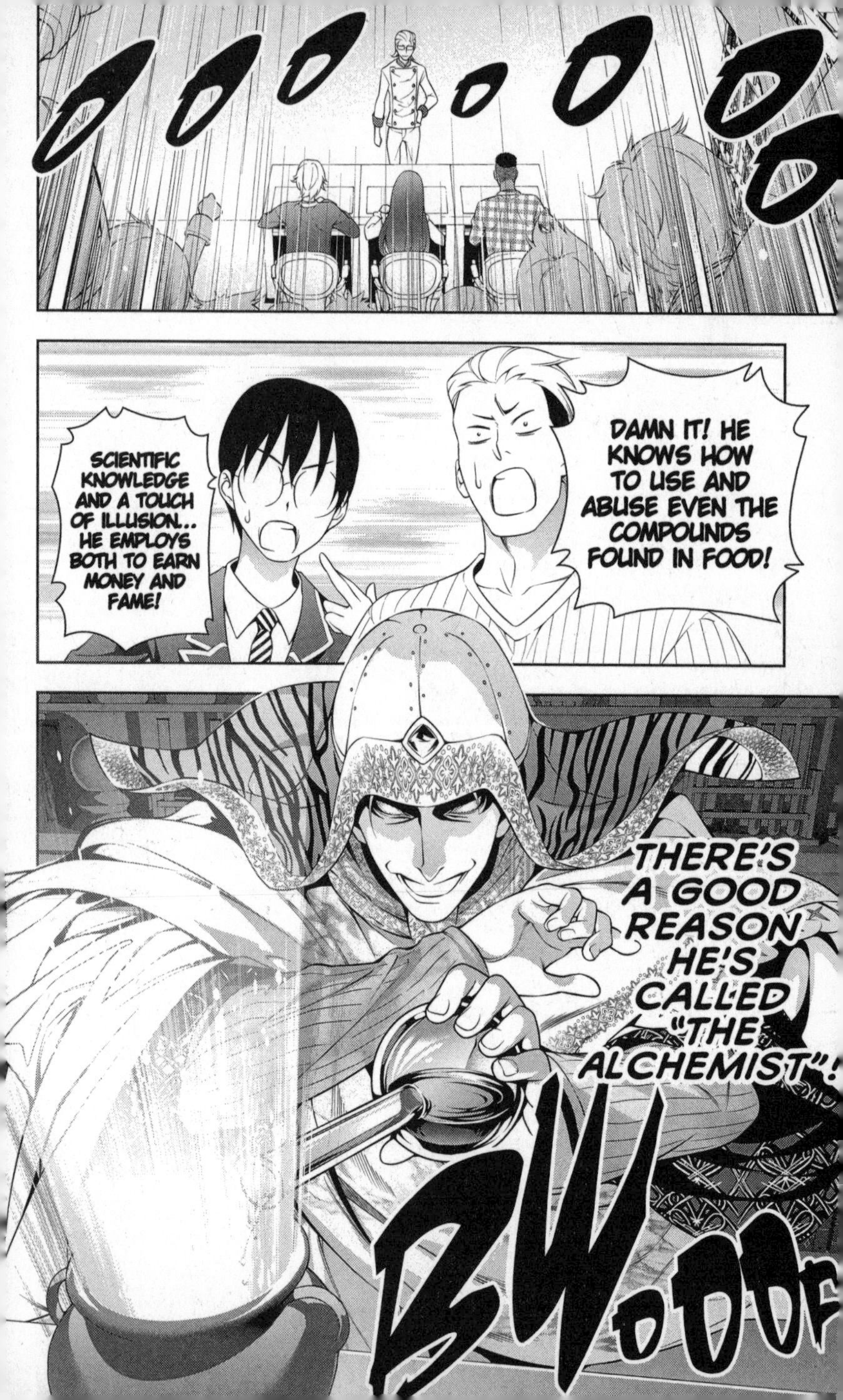
DAMN IT! HE KNOWS HOW TO USE AND ABUSE EVEN THE COMPOUNDS FOUND IN FOOD!
SCIENTIFIC KNOWLEDGE AND A TOUCH OF ILLUSION... HE EMPLOYS BOTH TO EARN MONEY AND FAME!
THERE'S A GOOD REASON HE'S CALLED "THE ALCHEMIST"!
BWOOOF

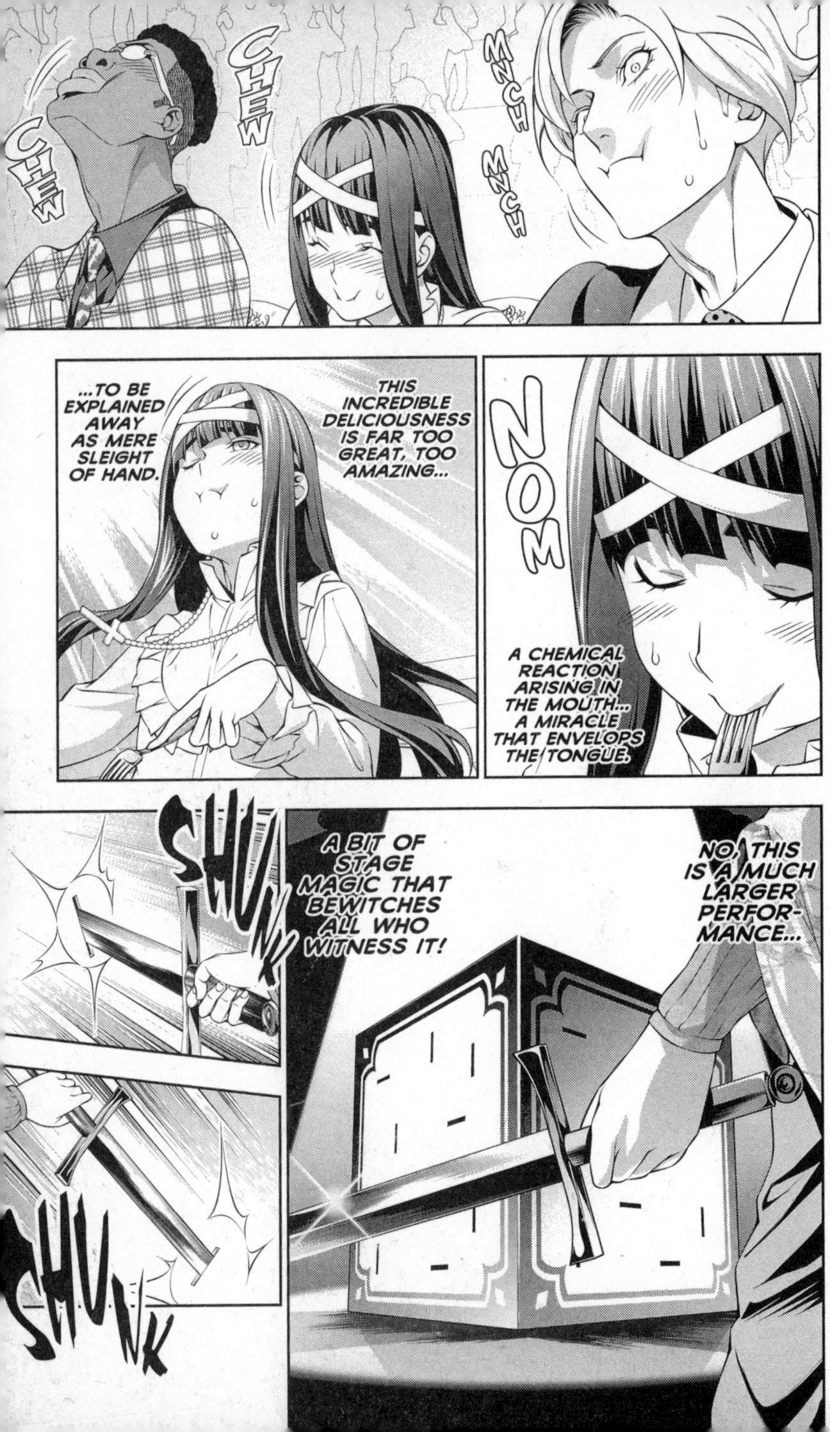
MNCH MNCH
CHEW
CHEW
NOM
A CHEMICAL REACTION ARISING IN THE MOUTH... A MIRACLE THAT ENVELOPS THE TONGUE.
THIS INCREDIBLE DELICIOUSNESS IS FAR TOO GREAT, TOO AMAZING...
...TO BE EXPLAINED AWAY AS MERE SLEIGHT OF HAND.
NO, THIS IS A MUCH LARGER PERFORMANCE...
A BIT OF STAGE MAGIC THAT BEWITCHES ALL WHO WITNESS IT!
SHUNK
SHUNK

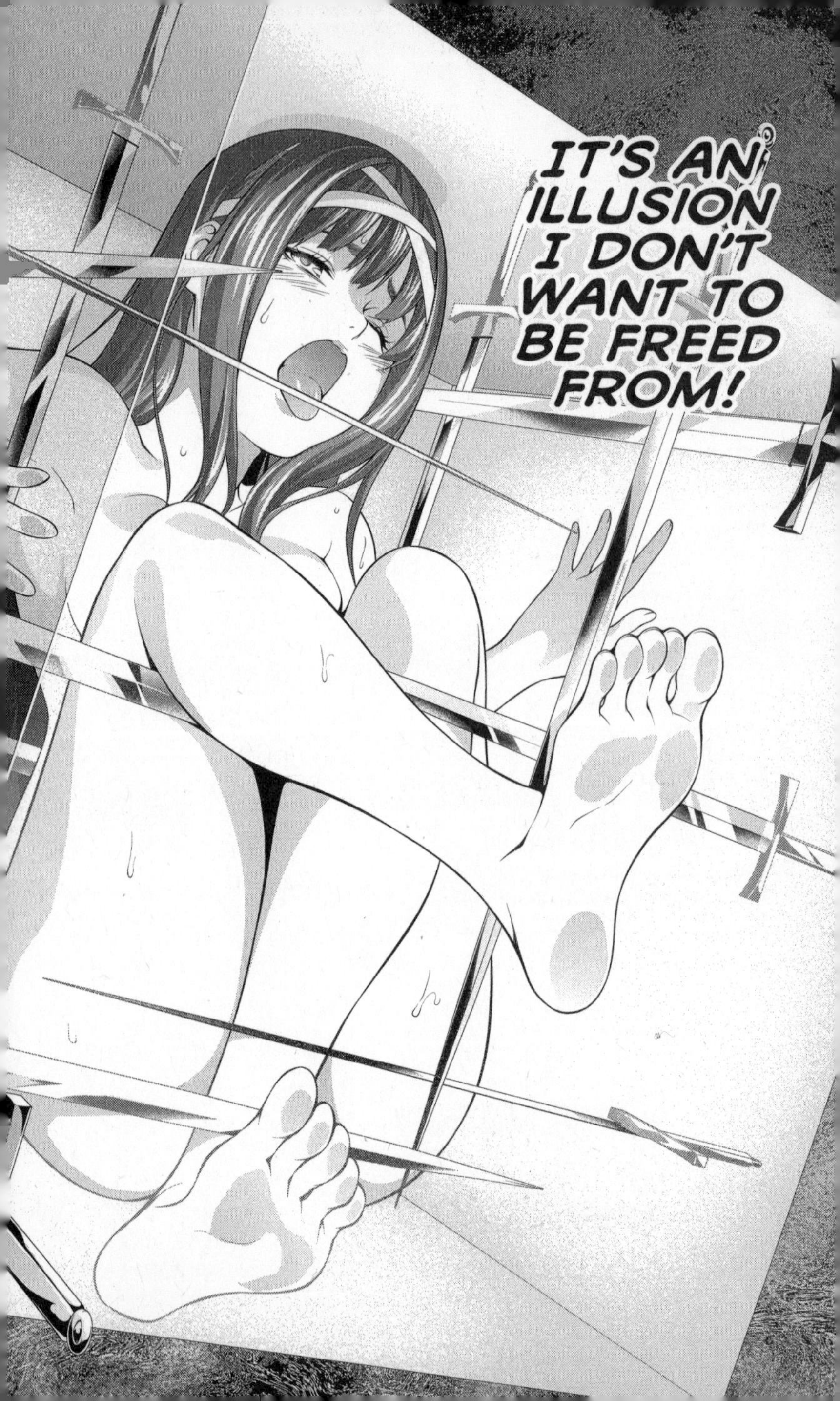
IT'S AN ILLUSION I DON'T WANT TO BE FREED FROM!

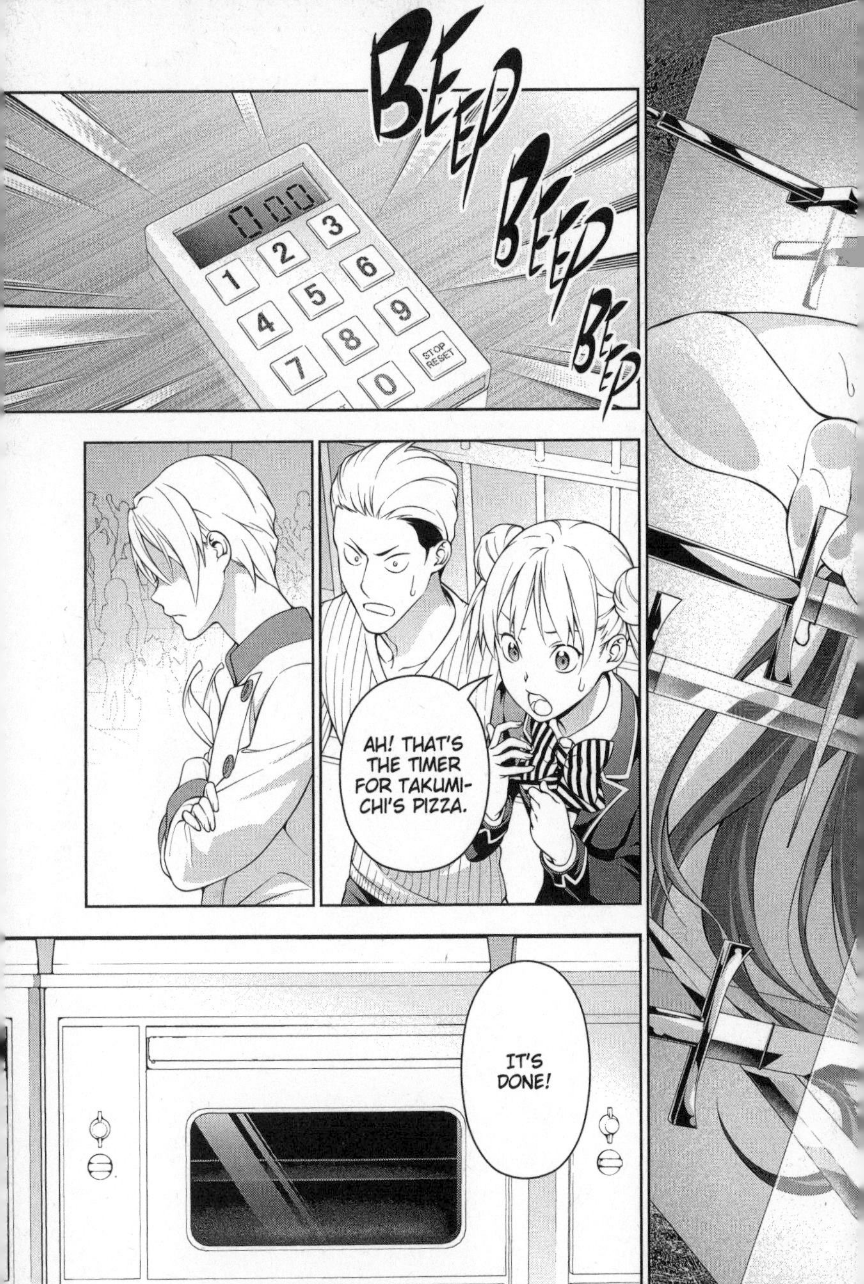
BEEP
BEEP
BEEP
0:00
1 2 3 4 5 6 7 8 9 0
STOP RESET
AH! THAT'S THE TIMER FOR TAKUMI-CHI'S PIZZA.
IT'S DONE!

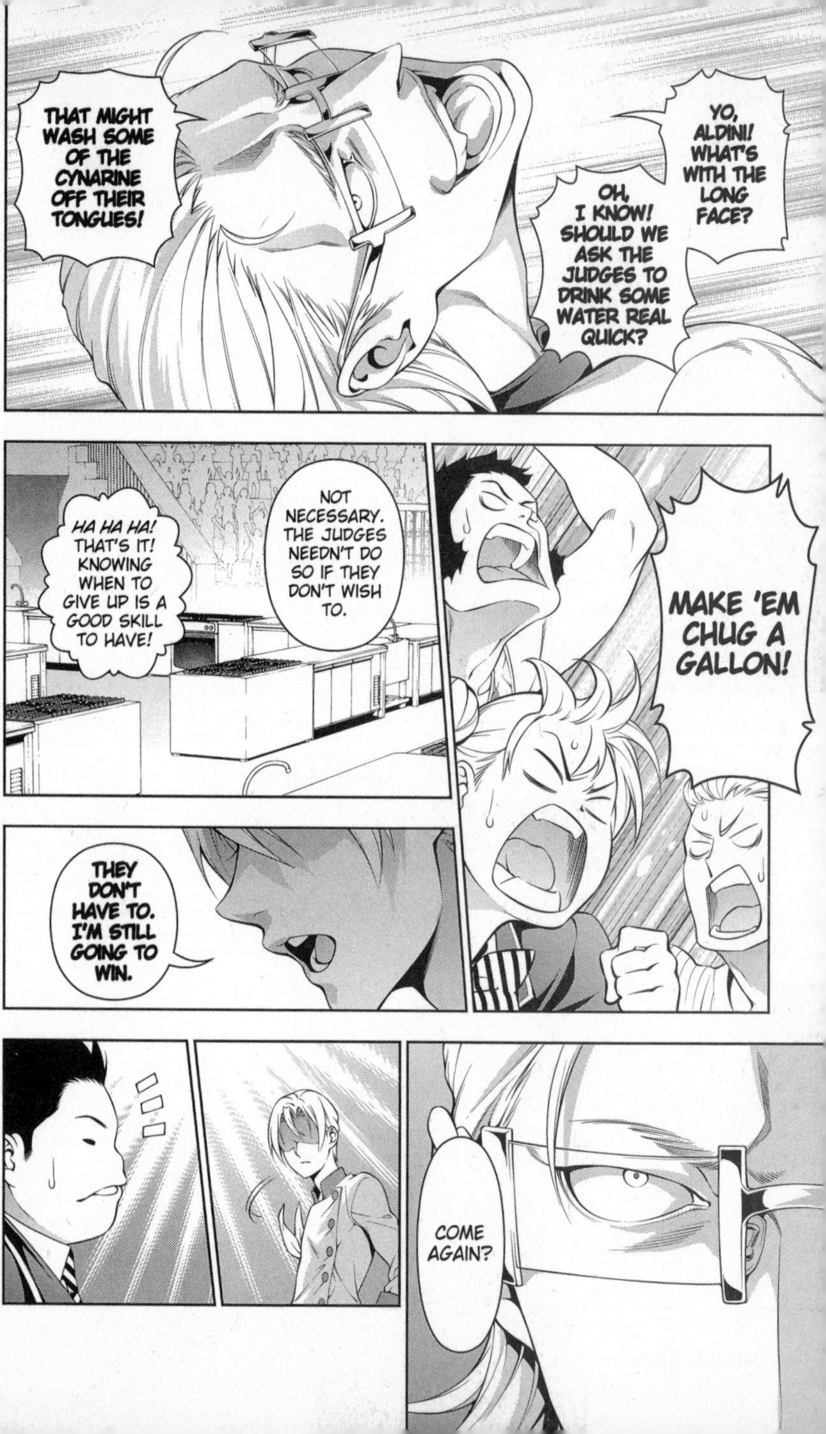
YO, ALDINI! WHAT'S WITH THE LONG FACE?
OH, I KNOW! SHOULD WE ASK THE JUDGES TO DRINK SOME WATER REAL QUICK?
THAT MIGHT WASH SOME OF THE CYNARINE OFF THEIR TONGUES!
MAKE 'EM CHUG A GALLON!
NOT NECESSARY. THE JUDGES NEEDN'T DO SO IF THEY DON'T WISH TO.
HA HA HA! THAT'S IT! KNOWING WHEN TO GIVE UP IS A GOOD SKILL TO HAVE!
THEY DON'T HAVE TO. I'M STILL GOING TO WIN.
COME AGAIN?

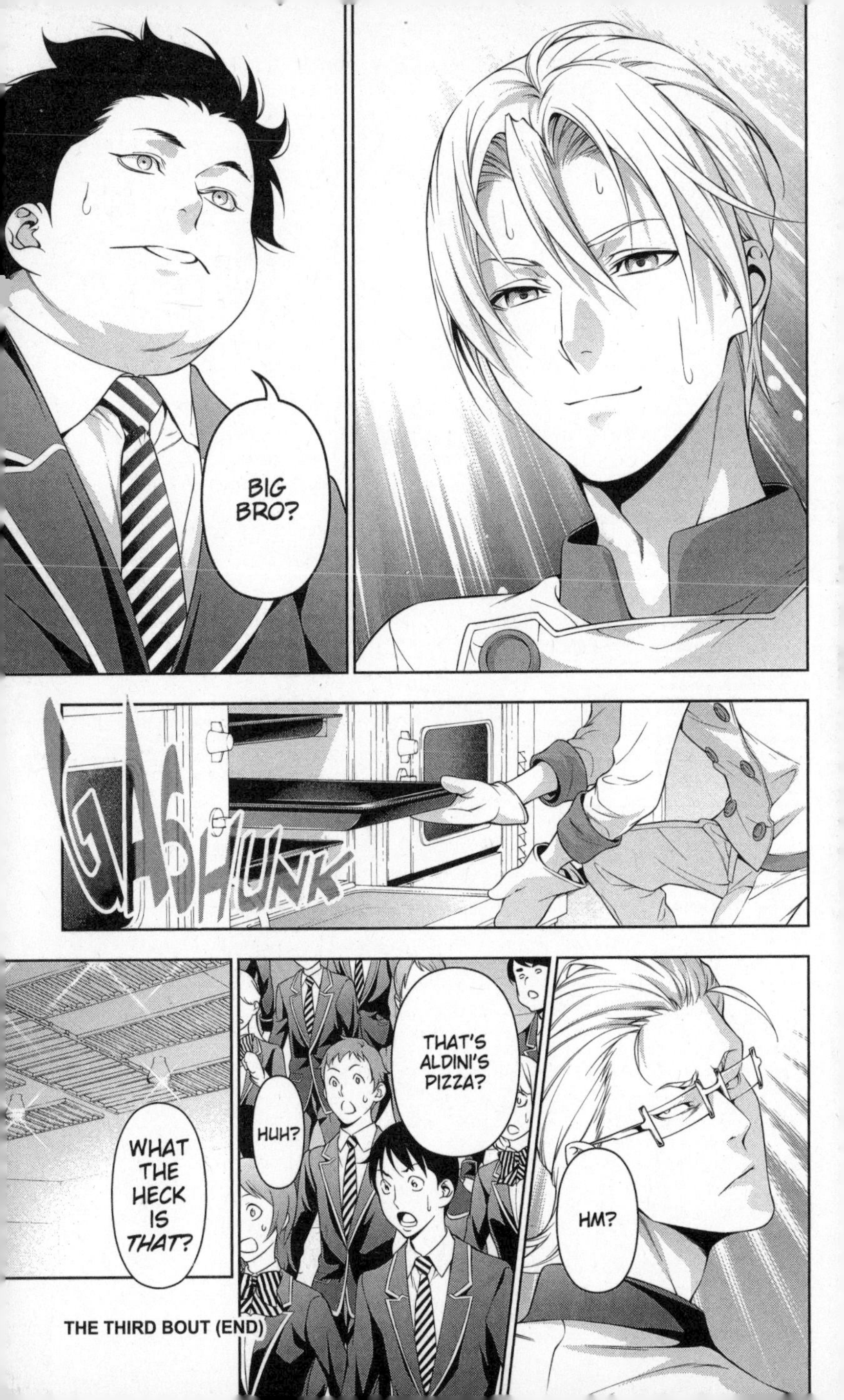
BIG BRO?
GASHUNK
HM?
THAT'S ALDINI'S PIZZA?
HUH?
WHAT THE HECK IS THAT?
THE THIRD BOUT (END)

ARTIST: YUTO TSUKUDA RECIPE BY: YUKI MORISAKI

PRACTICAL RECIPE #6

VOLUME 27 SPECIAL SUPPLEMENT!

"CYNARINE"... THE "RIN" AT THE END SOUNDS KINDA CUTE...
AH
WHO CARES?

SIMPLIFIED HOME VERSION

EIZAN'S ROAST BEEF

~WITH ARTICHOKE CREAM SAUCE~

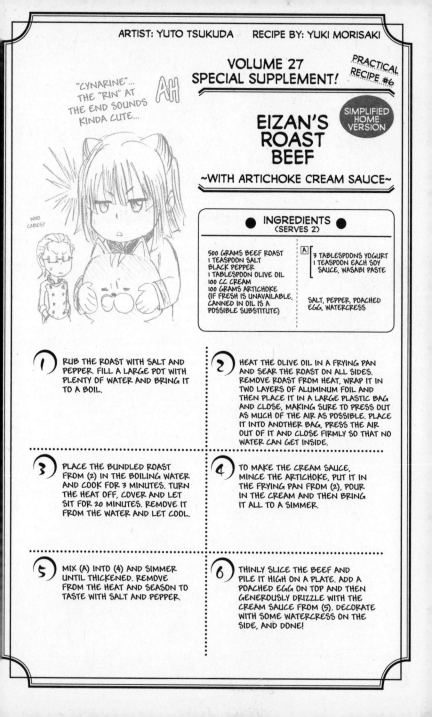

INGREDIENTS
(SERVES 2)

500 GRAMS BEEF ROAST 1 TEASPOON SALT BLACK PEPPER 1 TABLESPOON OLIVE OIL 100 CC CREAM 100 GRAMS ARTICHOKE (IF FRESH IS UNAVAILABLE, CANNED IN OIL IS A POSSIBLE SUBSTITUTE)	A [3 TABLESPOONS YOGURT 1 TEASPOON EACH SOY SAUCE, WASABI PASTE SALT, PEPPER, POACHED EGG, WATERCRESS

1. RUB THE ROAST WITH SALT AND PEPPER. FILL A LARGE POT WITH PLENTY OF WATER AND BRING IT TO A BOIL.
2. HEAT THE OLIVE OIL IN A FRYING PAN AND SEAR THE ROAST ON ALL SIDES. REMOVE ROAST FROM HEAT, WRAP IT IN TWO LAYERS OF ALUMINUM FOIL AND THEN PLACE IT IN A LARGE PLASTIC BAG AND CLOSE, MAKING SURE TO PRESS OUT AS MUCH OF THE AIR AS POSSIBLE. PLACE IT INTO ANOTHER BAG, PRESS THE AIR OUT OF IT AND CLOSE FIRMLY SO THAT NO WATER CAN GET INSIDE.
3. PLACE THE BUNDLED ROAST FROM (2) IN THE BOILING WATER AND COOK FOR 3 MINUTES. TURN THE HEAT OFF, COVER AND LET SIT FOR 20 MINUTES. REMOVE IT FROM THE WATER AND LET COOL.
4. TO MAKE THE CREAM SAUCE, MINCE THE ARTICHOKE, PUT IT IN THE FRYING PAN FROM (2), POUR IN THE CREAM AND THEN BRING IT ALL TO A SIMMER.
5. MIX (A) INTO (4) AND SIMMER UNTIL THICKENED. REMOVE FROM THE HEAT AND SEASON TO TASTE WITH SALT AND PEPPER.
6. THINLY SLICE THE BEEF AND PILE IT HIGH ON A PLATE. ADD A POACHED EGG ON TOP AND THEN GENEROUSLY DRIZZLE WITH THE CREAM SAUCE FROM (5). DECORATE WITH SOME WATERCRESS ON THE SIDE, AND DONE!

Food Wars! SHOKUGEKI NO SOMA

SECOND

VOLUME 27 SUPERSPECIAL SUPPLEMENT
CHARACTER PROFILES

RINDO KOBAYASHI

BIRTHDAY: OCTOBER 15

BLOOD TYPE: O

HEIGHT: 5'7"

FAVORITE SEASON: SUMMER

FAVORITE COUNTRY: SHE LIKES LOTS OF
THEM, BUT SPAIN IN PARTICULAR.

EISHI TSUKASA

BIRTHDAY: APRIL 2

BLOOD TYPE: A

HEIGHT: 5'9"

FAVORITE COLOR: WHITE

FAVORITE DRINK: COFFEE (BLACK)

MOMO AKANEGAKUBO

BIRTHDAY: AUGUST 21

BLOOD TYPE: B

HEIGHT: 4'7"

FAVORITE AROMA: VANILLA ESSENCE

FAVORITE PET BODY PART: TOE BEANS

TOSUKE MEGISHIMA

BIRTHDAY: JULY 4

BLOOD TYPE: O

HEIGHT: 6'4"

FAVORITE TYPE OF CHOPSTICK: *WARIBASHI*

FAVORITE ACTRESS: MEIKO KAJI

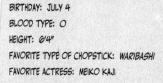

NENE KINOKUNI

BIRTHDAY: JANUARY 6

BLOOD TYPE: A

HEIGHT: 5'5"

FAVORITE PLACE: SHRINES AND TEMPLES

FAVORITE AUTHOR: HARUKI MURAKAMI

SOMEI SAITO

BIRTHDAY: FEBRUARY 11

BLOOD TYPE: B

HEIGHT: 6'1"

FAVORITE KENDO STANCE: *HASSO NO KAMAE*

FAVORITE MOVIE: *UZUMASA LIMELIGHT*

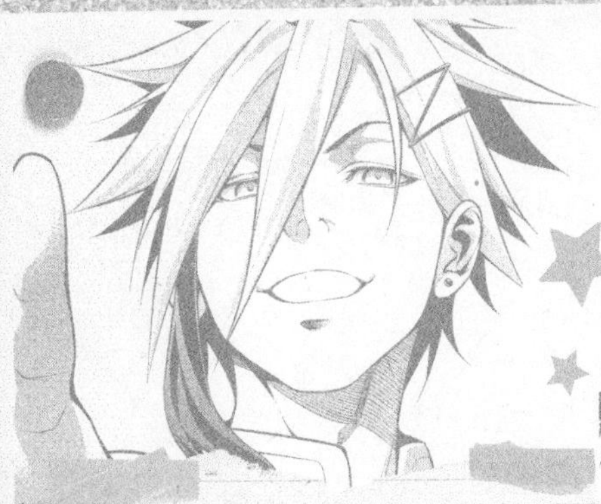

TERUNORI KUGA

BIRTHDAY: MAY 27
BLOOD TYPE: O
HEIGHT: 5'1"
FAVORITE DRINK: PIPING HOT CHAI
FAVORITE MOVIE DIRECTOR: JAMES CAMERON

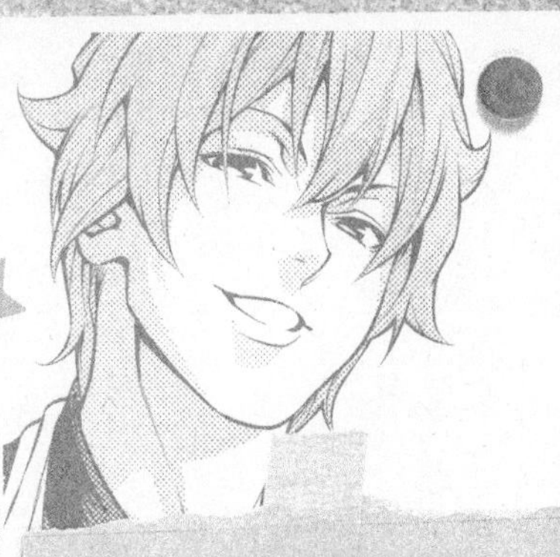

SATOSHI ISSHIKI

BIRTHDAY: MAY 2
BLOOD TYPE: AB
HEIGHT: 5'11"
FAVORITE DAILY ACTIVITY: GARDEN CHORES
FAVORITE SONG: "TABIDACHI NO HI NI"

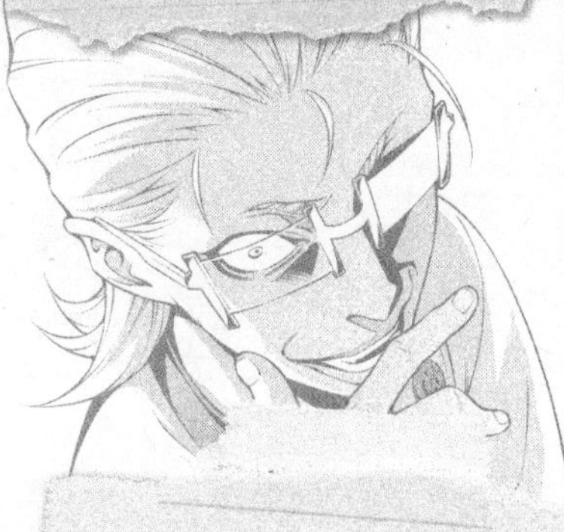

ETSUYA EIZAN

BIRTHDAY: SEPTEMBER 26
BLOOD TYPE: B
HEIGHT: 5'10"
FAVORITE THING: MONEY
FAVORITE DOG BREED: SHIBA INU

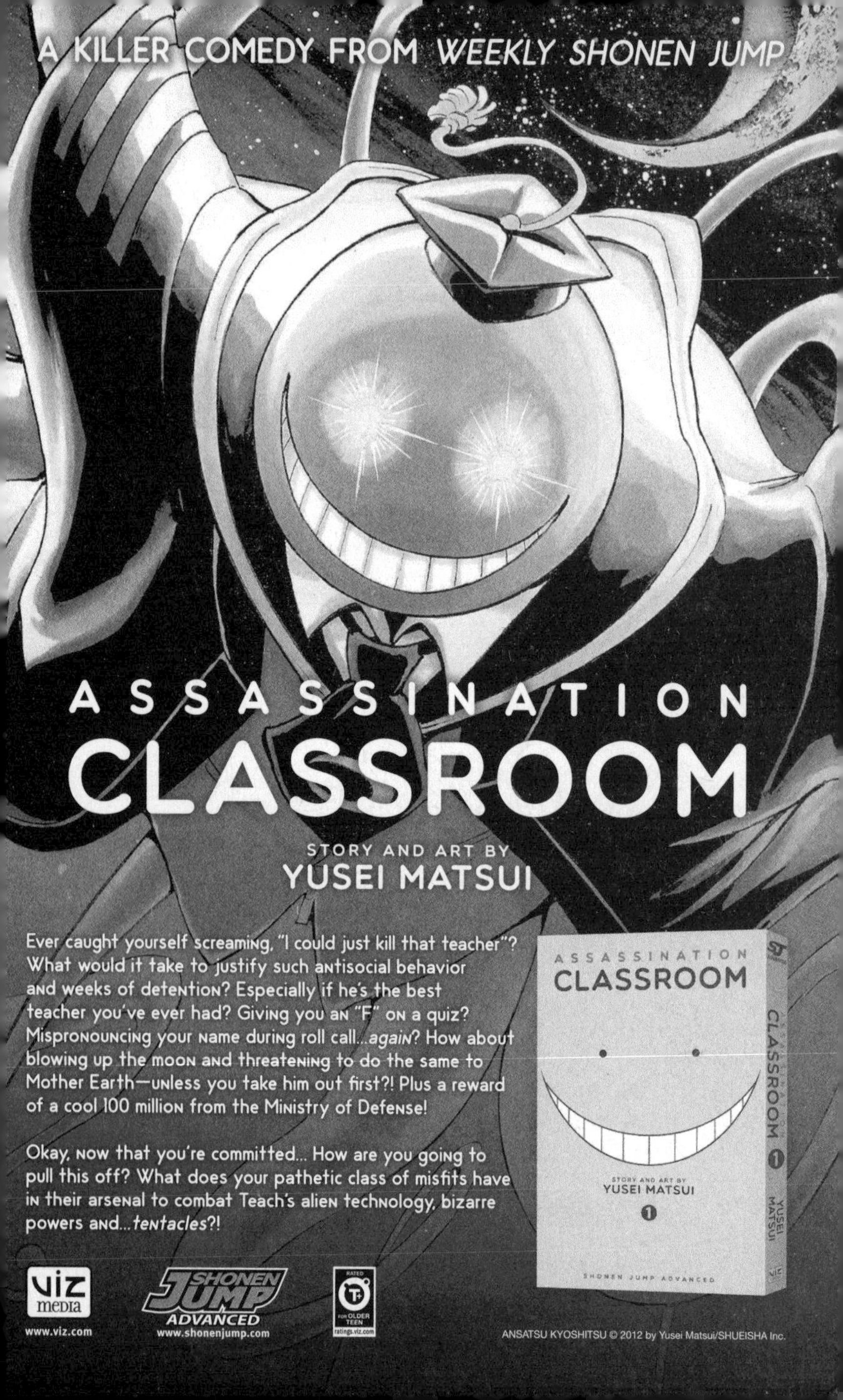
A KILLER COMEDY FROM *WEEKLY SHONEN JUMP*
ASSASSINATION
CLASSROOM
STORY AND ART BY
YUSEI MATSUI
Ever caught yourself screaming, "I could just kill that teacher"? What would it take to justify such antisocial behavior and weeks of detention? Especially if he's the best teacher you've ever had? Giving you an "F" on a quiz? Mispronouncing your name during roll call...*again*? How about blowing up the moon and threatening to do the same to Mother Earth—unless you take him out first?! Plus a reward of a cool 100 million from the Ministry of Defense!
Okay, now that you're committed... How are you going to pull this off? What does your pathetic class of misfits have in their arsenal to combat Teach's alien technology, bizarre powers and...*tentacles*?!
ASSASSINATION
CLASSROOM
STORY AND ART BY
YUSEI MATSUI
1
SHONEN JUMP ADVANCED
viz media
www.viz.com
SHONEN JUMP ADVANCED
www.shonenjump.com
RATED T+ FOR OLDER TEEN
ratings.viz.com
ANSATSU KYOSHITSU © 2012 by Yusei Matsui/SHUEISHA Inc.

THE PROMISED NEVERLAND

STORY BY **KAIU SHIRAI**

ART BY **POSUKA DEMIZU**

Emma, Norman and Ray are the brightest kids at the Grace Field House orphanage. And under the care of the woman they refer to as "Mom," all the kids have enjoyed a comfortable life. Good food, clean clothes and the perfect environment to learn—what more could an orphan ask for? One day, though, Emma and Norman uncover the dark truth of the outside world they are forbidden from seeing.

VIZ
viz.com

RATED
OLDER TEEN
T+

You're Reading in the Wrong Direction!!

1
2
3
1
2
3
4
5
6

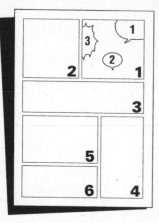

Whoops! Guess what? You're starting at the wrong end of the comic!

...It's true! In keeping with the original Japanese format, **Food Wars!** is meant to be read from right to left, starting in the upper-right corner.

Unlike English, which is read from left to right, Japanese is read from right to left, meaning that action, sound effects and word-balloon order are completely reversed... something which can make readers unfamiliar with Japanese feel pretty backwards themselves. For this reason, manga or Japanese comics published in the U.S. in English have sometimes been published "flopped"—that is, printed in exact reverse order, as though seen from the other side of a mirror.

By flopping pages, U.S. publishers can avoid confusing readers, but the compromise is not without its downside. For one thing, a character in a flopped manga series who once wore in the original Japanese version a T-shirt emblazoned with "M A Y" (as in "the merry month of") now wears one which reads "Y A M"! Additionally, many manga creators in Japan are themselves unhappy with the process, as some feel the mirror-imaging of their art skews their original intentions.

We are proud to bring you Yuto Tsukuda and Shun Saeki's **Food Wars!** in the original unflopped format.

For now, though, turn to the other side of the book and let the adventure begin...!

—Editor

Have fuuun!
IT'S NOT LIKE I'M GOING TO HOKKAIDO TO GO SIGHT-SEEING.